THE SOUNDS OF SOCIAL CHANGE

Rand McNally & Company/Chicago

edited by

R. Serge Denisoff
Bowling Green State University

and

Richard A. Peterson
Vanderbilt University

**THE
SOUNDS
OF SOCIAL
CHANGE**

studies in popular culture

RAND McNALLY SOCIOLOGY SERIES
Edgar F. Borgatta, *Advisory Editor*

To Allegra and Ruth Hill

Teen Queens of 1984

ACKNOWLEDGMENTS

Creating this anthology has been a labor of love, and our task has been greatly simplified by a number of people. To Edgar F. Borgatta and Lawrence J. Malley for their faith and encouragement, the Departments of Sociology at Bowling Green State University and Vanderbilt University for providing such excellent secretarial services, the Vanderbilt Urban and Regional Development Center and Ford Foundation for providing the second editor with released time while the project was being completed, and especially Charlotte Iglarsh for tenacity and editorial skill in rendering the manuscript into publishable form, we would like to acknowledge our debt. The first editor also particularly wishes to thank Mrs. Dorothy Darr, Dawn McCaghy, and Lauretta Lahman for their assistance in the preparation of this book.

R. SERGE DENISOFF
RICHARD A. PETERSON

January, 1972

CONTENTS

Introduction

THEORIES OF CULTURE, MUSIC, AND SOCIETY

Since the dawn of history, music has accompanied man in his work, play, and love-making. Songs have been composed to teach, convert, seduce, pacify, and arouse. Diverse persecuted groups have galvanized around music; and both political and church authorities, fearing its powers, have tried to repress the joyful noise. Ironically, though men of affairs have long considered music a potent sociopolitical tool, academic researchers have paid it scant attention.

This anthology has been put together in the hopes of focusing more scholarly attention on the uses of music as an opiate, weapon, and/or harbinger of social change. It has three related purposes: (1) to gather the best of the scattered work which has been written; (2) to organize the material into topical chapters so that coherent research problems can be articulated; (3) to thereby suggest fruitful avenues for further research. We will consider this effort successful if new research makes the anthology outdated in half a dozen years.

The articles that follow emphasize description, research findings, and opinion. Most do not self-consciously expose either their own theoretical bases or methodological assumptions. It is these underpinnings with which we will deal briefly in this introductory section and in the chapter introductions where appropriate.

A wide range of writers have been concerned with one or another of the issues bearing on the general topic at hand. But no single formulation brings them together in coherent form. To date, the closest approximation of this goal is to be found in the anthologies by Rosenberg and White (1957, 1971), Jacobs (1959), and Albrecht, *et al.*, (1970).

While we will propose no grand theory, we will examine five distinct theoretical questions that deserve special attention for those seeking to understand the diverse uses of music as a means of social protest. Each of these can be stated as a contest between two opposing positions: (1) words versus feelings, (2) high versus low or mass art, (3) massification versus pluralism, (4) "culture leads" versus "culture follows" society and (5) absolute versus contextual meaning.

Words Versus Feelings

Pitirim A. Sorokin (1937), taking entire societies as his unit of analysis, distinguishes between two opposing tendencies in all cultural fields. One he calls "ideational," the other "sensate." The former relies on clearly articulated principles in establishing truth, beauty, and goodness while the latter relies on a direct appeal to the senses. Arnold S. Toynbee (in history), A. L. Kroeber (in anthropology), F. S. C. Northrop (in philosophy), and Marshall McLuhan (in mass communication) have all drawn somewhat parallel distinctions and have applied them to whole societies or eras.

For a generation, academic researchers have collected exceptions and noted contradictions in this dichotomized view of culture. But the distinctions remain fruitful in differentiating specific types of music. For example, Lutheran hymns, country-western music, radical, Communist party, and labor songs all simplify and regularize melody and rhythm in order to accentuate the lyrical text. In contrast, Catholic masses, rhythm and blues, and songs of the New Left put the message in few words and convey them in complex rhythm and sensual sounds. As shown in several of the articles reprinted in Chapter III there has been a lively debate over the uses of rock music as propaganda, dividing along sensate versus ideational lines. Writers of the Old Left (ideational) argue that rock cannot be important because its lyrics—when not entirely swallowed by the music—do not clearly enunciate a "line." New Left defenders of rock (sensate), like media advertising men, assert that the music has great ideological impact because the message is put across in strong symbols carried by the energy of the music itself.

In Sorokin's formulation, the midpoint between sensate and ideational is a rarely achieved synthesis which he calls "idealistic." It marks a brief period of explosive creativity and innovation. Other scholars have not seen much merit in his theories of cycles involving whole societies, but it is interesting to note that the two revolutionary periods of popular music in this century have come from a fusion of ideational and sensate modes. These are the jazz age (a fusion of march music and the blues) and the rock age (a fusion of country and soul music), as noted by Gillett (1970) and Peterson (1971).

Sorokin, like Parsons (1937) after him, viewed culture—including music—as an integrated system following its own internal laws of development and little influenced by, though sometimes influencing, other aspects of society. Those empirical researchers who have looked at the place of music in total societies (Kavolis, 1968; Lomax, 1968) have not found this view fruitful. However, following Marxian theory (Harap, 1949; Finkelstein, 1970) they have shown that fine and folk music styles do reflect the economic, family, and political structure of the society or specific classes within it.

A related debate focuses particularly on popular culture, which in this century has become a multi-million dollar industry. On the one hand, the contention is made that since cultural products disseminated by movies, TV, and radio are sold on an open and competitive market, the audience gets exactly what it wants (Stanton, 1959). On the other hand, some argue that the media are pervasive enough to inhibit or develop specific public tastes (Merton and Lazarsfeld, 1968). McPhee (1966) has developed an ingenious mathematical model to show that the joint operation of these two forces does not, as it might appear, lead to a uniform and unchanging media-disseminated popular culture. The articles offered in Chapters IV and V shed light on the relative influence of audience and industry. Together, they suggest that the influence is not in one direction only and that the degree of influence changes over time.

High Culture Versus Low

At least since the sixteenth century, there has been a continuing debate over the function of the arts for society (Lowenthal, 1961: 15–25). While the battleground has shifted over time, the general view among art critics and other spokesmen for the "art establishment" came to be that the *high* art of the intelligentsia instructed, ennobled, entertained, and civilized while the commercial, or *low* art of the common people dulled and corrupted. This view, championed by critics McDonald (1965) and

Read (1966), is reflected in most of the essays in Rosenberg and White (1957, 1971) as well as in Jacobs (1959). Their view has been criticized as a form of elitist ideology by Shils (1957), Lowenthal (1961), Mendelsohn (1966), and Gans (1966).

The latter summarizes the elitist criticism of mass culture in four assertions (Gans, 1966: 552).

1. "Popular culture is undesirable because, unlike high culture, it is mass-produced by profit-minded entrepreneurs solely for the gratification of a paying audience," and since the audience has no taste, it will choose unwisely.

2. "The consumption of popular-culture content at best produces spurious gratifications, and at worst is emotionally harmful to the audience," because it merchandises violence, sentimentality, and escapist dreaming.

3. "Popular culture borrows from high culture, thus debasing it, and also lures away many potential creators of high culture, thus depleting its reservoir of talent."

4. "The wide distribution of popular culture not only reduces the level of cultural quality—or civilization—of the society, but also encourages totalitarianism by creating a passive audience peculiarly responsive to the techniques of mass persuasion used by demagogues bent on dictatorship."

While the debate raises a number of important research issues, it has been widely accepted, until recently, as a kind of dogma rather than as an hypothesis and thus has not been a topic for empirical research. Unfortunately, this dogmatic view has diverted the attention of several generations of social scientists from the concerted study of popular and folk cultures.[1]

Massification versus Pluralism

The first issue to break out of the high art ethos was the question of the impact of the mass media on politics. Concerned by the Nazi and Stalinist use of the radio and movies for state propaganda in the 1930's, a number of scholars turned to look at the impact of the mass media on

---

[1] It is interesting to note in this regard that the University of Chicago, the center of research in sociology during the 1920's did not produce a single study of the jazz age which flourished in that city (Faris, 1970). The major centers of sociology research training today have done little better in furthering the study of the rock age.

society. Krenek (1938), Blumer (1939), Adorno (1941), and Lasswell (1941) were soon joined at Columbia University by Merton and Lazarsfeld who founded the Office of Radio Research which became the Bureau of Applied Social Research. They, with their students, did a whole set of studies on the media industries, their program content, and effects on their audiences (Lazarsfeld and Stanton, 1944; Lazarsfeld and Merton, 1948; Lazarsfeld, 1961; and Merton and Lazarsfeld, 1968).[2]

As a group, these scholars assumed that democracy is sustained by a continuous political struggle between a number of overlapping interest groups. This view is called "pluralism." They found, to their horror, that the mass media breaks down diversity and generates a standardized mass (Adorno, 1941), narcotizing (Lazarsfeld and Merton, 1948) and atomizing (Riesman, 1950) the individual so that he becomes one element of "mass man," unable to participate in the affairs of civic society (Blumer, 1939).

This "massification" theory has been attacked from almost every possible position as the following partial listing suggests. Wirth (1948) asserted that the media made for integration, not massification. Friedson (1953) and Bramson (1961) have sharply criticized the research methods and conceptualization of "mass." Lipset (1961) argues that massification is not a product of the mass media but is a longstanding trait of American society. Parsons and White (1960) assert that the mass media increased both the diversity and quality of popular culture. Wilensky (1964) has shown the persistence of a pluralistic society in the presence of mass culture. Gans (1966) in a general review of the effects of the media entitled "Social Problems in a Mass Society or Social Assets in a Pluralistic Society?," also opts for the latter position.

The theoretical and methodological questions raised by the mass versus pluralist debate over the past three decades have still not been resolved, as can be seen from the articles reprinted in Chapters III and IV of this anthology. Data from the area of music, however, lend much credence to the view expressed by Wilensky (1964), Gans (1966), Glenn (1967), and Denisoff and Levine (1971) among others, that taste-cultures continue to exist in the face of two generations of presumed massification by the mass media.

---

[2] Ironically, what began in the 1930's as a concern with totalitarian political propaganda became, by the 1950's, the intellectual fountainhead of "motivation research"—the prime tool of Madison Avenue advertisers (Bauer and Greyser, 1968).

"Culture Leads" versus "Culture Follows" Society

While Sorokin (1937) has argued that changes in culture presage changes in society, most of the authors cited so far, as well as those appearing in Chapters I and II, hold that, in the realm of popular culture, culture follows society. Gans, for one (1966: 562) concludes that "the prime function of the media is to reinforce already existing behavior and attitudes, rather than to create them."[3] Greenberg (1957) and Barzun (1958) assert that popular music is simply *kitsch* background noise. The latter articles were written before the Beatles' generation of rock music transformed popular music, but most of the empirical studies conducted since that time seem to substantiate their assertion. The articles in Chapter IV, by Denisoff and Levine, and by Hirsch, report that young people cannot identify the message in such widely popular protest songs as "Eve of Destruction" and "Mr. Business Man."

There is, however, another intellectual tradition that questions the relevance of such detailed content analysis and focuses rather on the way popular culture helps to build or manipulate the master-symbols through which the world is viewed and in terms of which people act. Representative of this tradition are Burke (1954), Boorstin (1964), Duncan (1968) and Klapp (1969). These authors have not made detailed empirical studies, but a suggestive study by Williams (1961) shows how the development of "standard" English language in the last century helped to shape contemporary Britisʰ values and culture. None of these authors have studied popular music as such but several students working under the direction of the second editor of this volume have shown that style preferences operate as a strong symbol of subgroup formation and identification among college fraternity members, reform-school girls, and high-school students. More research in this area is needed but, clearly, the conclusion that popular music *reflects* but does not *shape* values and behavior may be premature.

---

[3] The revolutionary potential of culture has been ignored, perhaps, because most sociological research and theorizing is still fueled by the debate between Marxist and academic sociologists. The former have downgraded culture as an epiphenomenal super-structure. They see it as interesting only insofar as it reflects the realities of political economy. The latter tend to elevate culture to such a high level of changelessness that, in practice, it is taken as "given" and is largely ignored. The debates between these two polar views have focused the attention of social scientists on the industrial, political and urban revolutions. And it has been left to men who are at the periphery of the research community to suggest the importance of a contemporary *cultural* revolution. These writers have returned to Durkheim, Weber, and Mead in positing both the *potency* and the *frailty* of culture.

Absolute versus Contextual Meanings

The final question is as much epistemological as it is theoretical in that it deals with how the researcher justifies the assertions he makes. There is a tendency in sociology to define variables abstractly and choose simple empirical indicators to stand for the variables. This natural science strategy presumes that the relationship between an abstract concept and its indicator is unchanging, but this is seldom the case in the musical realm under investigation. To illustrate, the same piece of music may mean something quite different when played for different people (Aron, 1958: 144) or heard in dissimilar contexts (Denzin, 1970; Denisoff and Levine, 1971). It is useful, therefore, to specify five sorts of contexts which are commonly important in defining the social significance of music. Each is evidenced by describing a potential error of interpretation.

The context of creation. In one of his songs, "Soul Power," James Brown puts together a number of images. These include a call for "soul power," an invitation to love-making, a call for help from "Fred" who is asked to "get down," and a suggestion to go to the "bridge" (*Rock and Soul,* 1971:4). A naive content analyst might wrongly code this lyric as a homosexual invitation. Seen in the context of its creation, however, the lyric takes on quite another meaning for, in recent years, Brown often talks to his band members as a means of conducting. "Fred" is his lead guitarist and the "bridge" is, of course, a structural segment of the song.

The musical package. In the mid-1960's the theme song from the movie *Born Free* (which showed the psychological travail of a couple who were releasing their pet lioness into the jungle) was a minor hit in the "easy-listening" field of popular music. In metaphorical terms it contrasted freedom with captivity. Re-released several years later in a rhythm and blues rendition by a black group backed by a gospel chorus singing "Born free, Hallelujah," however, it became an anthem of black pride.

The context of time. Abstracted from the era in which it becomes popular, it is easy to misjudge the social significance of a lyric. For example, Dinah Shore's 1948 question "All of me, why not take all of me?" or Theresa Brewer's 1950 "I'd do anything for you," sound quite tame in an era of freer sexual expression and nudity in popular film. But they were quite controversial when recorded. Remember, the film censorship code then specified that a couple, even when married, had to be depicted in twin beds (Randall, 1968).

The context of performance. Numerous authors have noted that black performers of blues have two repertoires, one for black and one for white audiences (Ferris, 1970). Beyond that, frequently the same piece of material may have different meaning to different audiences. Merle Haggard singing his "Okie from Muskogee" to a country music audience in Norman, Oklahoma has a quite different meaning from the same song sung by Phil Ochs at a New York folk-rock concert or Arlo Guthrie at a rock festival. These issues are treated with particular reference to the problems of content analysis in the introduction to Chapter IV.

The context of consumption. What do people learn from music? Mick Jagger and the Rolling Stones have made the music industry and themselves rich by singing provocative songs such as "Let's spend the night together." But what meaning does this suggestion have for the millions around the world who have heard it? Is it a straightforward invitation to love, part of a morally degenerate or an elevating cultural revolution, or an opiate to the young who are thus seduced from seeking true political revolution? While many answers have been tendered (Peterson, 1970), the question is still open as can be seen from the articles reprinted in Chapters III and IV.

*   *   *

The selected articles which follow have been grouped so as to bring into focus five different topics. Chapter I deals with the sociopolitical meaning of music for selected broad strata. Chapter II sharpens the focus to look at the deliberate uses of music in specific social movements. Chapter III brings together the diverse interpretations of one recent musical genre—rock. Chapter IV chronicles and evaluates the recent changes in popular musical tastes. Finally, Chapter V explores the diverse ways in which the musical message is shaped by the way it is produced, manufactured, and disseminated.

While most of the authors are academic research scholars, some are journalistic critics and others write for the John Birch Society or for the Communist party. The reader should assume *all* of the authors have some sort of axe to grind. He should read them in a critical spirit in order to whet his intellectual and methodological skills so that he can join the fray.

REFERENCES

Adorno, T. W.
  1941   "On popular music." Studies in Philosophy and Social Science.
            9:17–48.
Albrecht, Milton, James H. Barnett and Mason Griff (eds.)
  1970   The Sociology of the Arts. New York: Praeger.
Aron, Raymond
  1968   Progress and Disillusion. New York: New American Library.
Barzun, Jacques
  1958   Music in American Life. New York: Doubleday.
Bauer, Raymond A., and Stephen A. Greyser
  1968   Advertising in America: The Consumer View. Cambridge: Research
            Publication.
Blumer, Herbert
  1939   "Collective behavior," in Robert E. Park (ed.), An Outline of the
            Principles of Sociology: 221–280. New York: Barnes and Noble.
Boorstin, Daniel J.
  1964   The Image: A Guide to Pseudo Events in America. New York:
            Harper and Row.
Bramson, Leon
  1961   The Political Context of Sociology. Princeton, N.J.: Princeton Uni-
            versity Press.
Burke, Kenneth
  1954   Permanence and Change. Indianapolis: Bobbs-Merrill.
Denisoff, R. Serge and Mark H. Levine
  1971   "The one dimensional approach to popular music: A research note."
            Journal of Popular Culture 6:911–919.
Denzin, Norman K.
  1970   "Problems in analysing elements of mass culture: Notes on the
            popular song and other artistic productions." American Journal of
            Sociology 75:1035–1038.
Duncan, Hugh Dalziel
  1968   Symbols in Society. New York: Oxford University Press.
Faris, Robert E. L.
  1970   Chicago Sociology: 1920–1932. Chicago: University of Chicago
            Press.
Ferris, William R., Jr.
  1970   "Racial repertoires among blues performers." Ethnomusicology 24:
            439–449.
Finkelstein, Sidney
  1970   How Music Expresses Ideas. New York: International Publishers.
Freidson, Eliot
  1953   "Communications research and the concept of the mass." American
            Sociological Review 18:313–317.

Gans, Herbert J.
 1966 "Popular culture in America: Social problems in a mass society or social asset in a pluralist society?" in Howard S. Becker (ed.), Social Problems: A Modern Approach: 549–620. New York: Wiley. [Excerpt reprinted with permission of publisher].
Gillett, Charlie
 1970 The Sound of the City. New York: Outerbridge and Dienstfrey.
Glenn, Norval D.
 1967 "Massification versus differentiation: Some trend data from national surveys." Social Forces 46:172–180.
Greenberg, Clement
 1957 "Avant-garde and kitsch," in Bernard Rosenberg and David Manning White (eds.), Mass Culture: 98–107. New York: Free Press.
Harap, Louis
 1949 Social Roots of the Arts. New York: International Publishers.
Jacobs, Norman (ed.)
 1959 Culture for the Millions? Boston: Beacon.
Kavolis, Vytautas
 1968 Artistic Expression—A Sociological Analysis. Ithaca, New York: Cornell University Press.
Klapp, Orrin E.
 1969 Collective Search for Identity. New York: Holt, Rinehart & Winston.
Krenek, Ernst
 1938 "Bemerkungen zur rundfunkmusik." Zeitschrift Fur Sozial-Forschung 7:148–165.
Kroeber, A. L.
 1957 Style and Civilizations. Berkeley: University of California Press.
Lasswell, Harold D.
 1941 "Radio as an instrument of reducing personal insecurity." Studies in Social Philosophy and Social Science 9:49–60.
Lazarsfeld, Paul F.
 1961 "Mass culture today," in Norman Jacobs (ed.), Culture for the Millions?:9–25. Boston: Beacon.
Lazarsfeld, Paul F. and Robert K. Merton
 1948 "Mass communication, popular taste and organized social action," in Lyman Bryson (ed.), The Communication of Ideas: 95–118. New York: Harper.
Lazarsfeld, Paul F. and Frank Stanton (eds.)
 1944 Radio Research: 1942–1943. New York: Duell, Sloan and Pearce.
Lipset, Seymour M.
 1961 "A changing American character," in Seymour M. Lipset and Leo Lowenthal (eds.), Culture and Social Character: 136–174. New York: Free Press.

Lomax, Alan
    1968   Folk Song Style and Culture. Washington, D.C.: American Associa-
                tion for the Advancement of Science.
Lowenthal, Leo
    1961   Literature, Popular Culture, and Society. Englewood Cliffs, N.J.:
                Prentice-Hall.
MacDonald, Dwight
    1965   "Masscult and midcult." Against the American Grain: 3–75. New
                York: Vintage.
McPhee, William N.
    1966   "When culture becomes a business," in Joseph Berger, Morris
                Zelditch, Jr., and Bo Anderson (eds.), Sociological Theories in
                Progress: 227–243. New York: Houghton Mifflin.
Mendelsohn, Harold
    1966   Mass Entertainment. New Haven, Conn.: College & University
                Press.
Merton, Robert K. and Paul F. Lazarsfeld
    1968   "Studies in radio and film propaganda," in Robert K. Merton
                (ed.), Social Theory and Social Structure: 563–582. New York:
                Free Press.
Northrop, F. S. C.
    1946   The Meeting of East and West. New York: Macmillan.
Parsons, Talcott
    1937   The Structure of Social Action. New York: The Free Press.
Parsons, Talcott and Winston R. White
    1960   "The mass media and the structure of American society." Journal
                of Social Issues 16:67–77.
Peterson, Richard A.
    1970   "Rock as a fad, revolution, moral solvent, opiate, and bread." Paper
                delivered at the Ohio Valley Sociological Society Meetings, Akron,
                Ohio (May 2).
    1971   "A process model of the folk, pop and fine art phases of jazz," in
                Charles Nanry (ed.), American Music: From Storyville to Wood-
                stock. New Brunswick, N.J.: Rutgers University Press.
Randall, Richard S.
    1968   Censorship of the Movies. Madison: The University of Wisconsin
                Press.
Read, Herbert
    1966   To Hell With Culture. New York: Schocken Books.
Riesman, David
    1950   "Listening to popular music." American Quarterly 2:359–371.
Rock and Soul
    1971   "Soul Power." James Brown lyric: 4. Derby, Conn.: Charton
                Publications (July).

Rosenberg, Bernard and David Manning White (eds.)
    1957   Mass Culture. New York: Free Press.
    1971   Mass Culture Revisited. New York: Van Nostrand.
Shils, Edward
    1957   "Daydreams and nightmares: Reflections on the criticism of mass culture." Sewanee Review 65:587–608.
Silberman, Alphons
    1963   The Sociology of Music. London: Routledge and Kegan Paul.
Sorokin, Pitirim
    1937   Social and Cultural Dynamics. Volume 1. New York: Bedminster.
Stanton, Frank
    1959   "Parallel paths," in Norman Jacobs (ed.), Culture for the Millions? 85–91. Boston: Beacon.
Toynbee, Arnold
    1947   A Study of History. New York: Oxford University Press.
White, David Manning and Richard Averson (eds.)
    1969   Sight, Sound and Society. Boston: Beacon.
Wilensky, Harold L.
    1964   "Mass society and mass culture: Interdependence or independence?" American Sociological Review 29 (April): 173–197.
Williams, Raymond
    1961   The Long Revolution. London: Chatto & Windus.
Wirth, Louis
    1948   "Consensus and mass communication." American Sociological Review 13:1–15.

Chapter I

MUSIC AS PROTEST

Over the ages, kings and princes, revolutionaries and priests, peasants and slaves, have expressed their hopes and fears through music. While aiming to convince, they have used music to reassure the faithful as much as to persuade the unbelieving.

Denisoff reviews these various political uses of music in the first article of this chapter. Focusing primarily on the American experience, he shows how protest songs deriving from quite different traditions were infused into mass market-oriented popular music through the medium of rock 'n' roll, beginning in the mid-1950's. As he notes, the rejection of conventional standards and political beliefs inherent in this genre of music was conveyed by its unconventional sound and the irreverent life styles of rock performers as much as by the lyrical content of the music itself. Finally, he points to the important role of the mass media in filtering the content of popular music presented to the public, a concern which is focal in the latter chapters of this anthology.

The second selection deals with the uses of music as protest by blacks in America. Miller and Skipper examine the role of jazz for educated urban blacks. They make clear that a protest message can be carried entirely in the non-lyrical elements of the music and in the life styles of its devotees.

The final selection by DiMaggio, Peterson and Esco deals with country music, which has its roots in the American South and Southwest. They note its growing popularity, examine its lyrical themes, and describe its fans, in order to show how the music expresses the world view of a broad spectrum of the population in the nation at large. This paper should be read in conjunction with the article in Chapter II by Jens Lund, dealing with the ideologically pointed sorts of country music that are not often presented through the mass media of communication.

Taken together, the articles in this chapter, as well as the many sources they cite, suggest a close relationship between a particular social group and its music. Studies which demonstrate the causal connection between protest music and social behavior, however, have yet to be made.

1

THE EVOLUTION OF THE AMERICAN PROTEST SONG

R. Serge Denisoff

While a number of articles have appeared in the popular press on the subject, there are few definitive works dealing with the American protest song. This may well explain much of the confusion surrounding this musical form. A majority of studies dealing with protest songs have focused upon religious, political, and cultural movements which have used music for self-serving purposes. Originally, songs addressed the service of man to God through the Church. After the Reformation, hymns were utilized to bring man into a denomination. Hymns stressed the notion of "them" versus "us" and were basically propaganda weapons. It is well to remember that propaganda is defined as the noun of "to propagate," rather than to protest. In fact, most propaganda songs, such as deodorant commercials, hymns, and patriotic songs are not protest songs.

In the United States, as in Europe, the roots of the protest song are found in the religious sphere. In time, the hymns used by the Methodist revivalists of the 1820's were transformed into vehicles of secular political commentary by the Abolitionists, Knights of Labor, Populists, Grangers, and the Industrial Workers of the World. Even the secular and materialistic movements championing Marx, DeLeon, and Bakunin borrowed heavily from religious movements to politicize the proletariat. The almost exclusive use of political propaganda songs by groups deemed to be radical gave rise to the image of a protest song as being associated with non-conformist movements.

In the context of social movements, songs were characterized as a weapon to achieve a specific goal. John L. Lewis, while leader of the CIO, wrote "a

Reprinted by permission of the author.

singing army is a winning army." The Communist party of the United States
presented the folk song as "a cry for justice." The correlation between the social
movement and the protest song was academically explicated by John Greenway
in his pioneer work, *American Folk Songs of Protest*. Greenway's entire volume
is devoted to various movements and oppressed groups and the songs and singers
they produced. Consequently, he presents a group, or movement, oriented definition of a protest song:

> . . . the struggle songs of the people. They are outbursts of bitterness,
> of hatred for the oppressor, of determination to endure hardships to-
> gether and to fight for a better life. Whether they are ballads composed
> on the picket line, they are imbued with the feeling of communality,
> or togetherness.[1]

Greenway's book aroused considerable controversy since he appeared to restate
the folk song *qua* "cry for justice" thesis. Tristram P. Coffin presented one of the
more cogent critiques, arguing that while many units such as People's Songs,
Inc. did use songs of social reform, they were not *ipso facto* folk songs.
Furthermore, "the desire for change is basically sophisticated and alien to the
folksinger. Protest, which suggests change, appears in folklore much as water
appears in the desert."[2] Ironically, the advocates of the "cry for justice" ideology
also condemned Greenway but for totally different reasons.[3] While folklorists
in many instances questioned the "folk" quality of protest songs, few disputed
the organizational origins of these songs. Edith Fowke and Joe Glazer, in introducing their collection, *Songs of Work and Freedom,* observed: "This book
brings you the songs of the people who have fought for their rights on picket
lines and battle fields, in prison and at the polls . . . Here are the songs of the
oppressed, the downtrodden, the disinherited."[4] Josh Dunson's *Freedom in the
Air* restated the theme that protest songs emerged from "the unshakeable and
immense feeling that the singer had discovered some truth, a plan that was
going to make the world one of bread and roses."[5]

In 1966, I attempted to present a sociological definition of a protest song

[1] John Greenway, *American Folksongs of Protest* (Philadelphia: University of Pennsylvania Press, 1953), p. 3.

[2] Tristram P. Coffin, "Folk Song of Social Protest: A Musical Mirage," *New York
Folklore Quarterly* 14 (Spring, 1958), pp. 3–9. See rejoinder by John Greenway, same
issue, pp. 9–10.

[3] Review of *American Folksongs of Protest* by Irwin Silber, *Sing Out!* 3 (June,
1953), pp. 10–11.

[4] Edith Fowke and Joe Glazer, *Songs of Work and Freedom* (Chicago: Roosevelt
University Press, 1960), p. 9.

[5] Josh Dunson, *Freedom In the Air* (New York: International Publishers, 1965),
p. 45.

tied particularly to the folk song, which has here been expanded to include other musical genres.[6] One type of protest song, the *magnetic,* was outlined as appealing to the listener for purposes of attracting the non-participant receiver to a movement or reinforcing the commitment level of adherents. The structure of this type of song was such that it could frequently be put to familiar or catchy tunes which could be sung en masse either without instrumentation or with a simple piano and guitar accompaniment. Illustratively, most pocket-sized song-books used by radical movements contained no musical notation. Even songbooks including radical lyrics that do have notes are very simple to play, such as three guitar chords in one key. The keys G and D were used by the Almanac Singers and People's Songs, Inc. quite often. The fundamental feature of protest songs has been the recurrent and clear statement of the political message or, as Lenin would have it, music was not to soothe but to arouse the listener to political awareness. In Brechtian terms the ideological message was to be dominant, with the misleading emotional and artistic skill of the performer to be minimized. The most indicative American genre of the agit-prop style of propaganda is the folkish "talking blues" which Woody Guthrie described as "You talk this piece off. They say it's four-four time . . . just play chords and talk."[7] In actuality the "talking blues" is spoken against a steady 4/4 background where the chord progressions are simple and repetitive, usually in the key of G or C. This idiom has been used to address every conceivable subject.

The verbal content becomes primary with the music playing a secondary role.[8] Also, the song stresses the participation notion. The pronoun "we" is frequently used to suggest group solidarity, as well as group participation, as the solution to some real or imagined social problem. This remedy most often was outside of the "common sense world" of the majority, thus placing the group using a protest song in conflict with some or all of the sectors of the legitimate institutions of the social structure. Coser, in presenting his model of social conflict, sees as central to the creation of radical consciousness and group solidarity the notion of non-legitimacy as deviance: "Before a social conflict between negatively and positively privileged groups can take place, before hostile attitudes are turned into social action, the negatively placed group must . . . develop awareness . . . that it is being denied rights to which it is entitled."[9] Within this framework, the competition which succeeds its deviant or non-conformist group is presented as establishing and reaffirming the identity of the

[6] See R. Serge Denisoff, *Sing A Song of Social Significance* (Bowling Green University Popular Press, 1972), Chap. 1.

[7] Woody Guthrie quoted in Alan Lomax, *The Folk Songs of North America* (New York: Doubleday and Co., 1960), p. 434.

[8] Happy Traum, "The Art of the Talking Blues," *Sing Out!,* 15 (January, 1966), pp. 53–60.

[9] Lewis Coser, *The Functions of Social Conflict* (Glencoe, Ill.: Free Press, 1956), p. 37.

group and maintains its boundaries against the surrounding, hostile external world.[10] Lazarsfeld and Merton support this position by adding that propaganda is by itself insufficient for social protest. They write, "Students of mass movements have come to repudiate the view that mass propaganda in and of itself creates or maintains the movement . . ."[11] Instead, they contend that propaganda must also involve "supplementation" through some form of face-to-face or organizational contacts. An outstanding evidence of this phenomenon is the climax of a Billy Graham rally where converts are urged to come forth and make their "Stand for Christ." In the political sphere an ex-Communist describes this mode of the socialization process: "They sang songs, ones that I'd never heard before, folk songs, political agitation songs, but all the songs seemed to reflect my emotions. I thought that these young people were fighting for things I wanted."[12]

The other type of protest song was the *rhetorical* which stressed individual indignation and dissent but did not offer a solution in a movement. The song was a statement of dissent which said, "I protest, I do not concur," or just plain "damn you." Nearly all of Bob Dylan's protest songs were of this nature.[13] Dylan, despite some observers, has asserted on numerous occasions that he was not a member of any specific movement and in time exhibited considerable hostility toward political organizations which made demands upon him. Rhetorical songs placed some emphasis upon lyrics, but allowed for greater musical sophistication and skill, particularly in genres outside of folk music. As will be seen, nearly all of the "protest" songs heard on commercial radio fall into this category.

This typology was applied to four historical periods (1910–1964) to measure the prevalence of these protest song types.[14] The findings indicated a drastic decline in magnetic songs, and a rise in rhetorical songs. Unfortunately, the time span covered ended in 1964, just prior to the emergence of "protest songs" on Top Forty or Boss Radio. Also, it was found that this transformation was linked to the disintegration of the Old Left and the institutionalization of the trade union movement. Only the southern civil rights movement kept the magnetic song going in the 1960's.

[10] Coser, *op. cit.,* p. 38; also see Harry Alpert, "Durkheim's Functional Theory of Ritual," in Robert A. Nisbet, ed., *Emile Durkheim* (Englewood Cliffs, N.J.: Prentice-Hall, 1965), pp. 137–141.
[11] Paul Lazarsfeld and Robert K. Merton, "Mass Communication, Popular Taste and Organized Social Action," in Bernard Rosenberg and David M. White, eds., *Mass Culture: Popular Arts in America* (Glencoe, Ill.: The Free Press, 1957), pp. 457–473.
[12] Harvey Matusow, *False Witness* (New York: Cameron and Kahn, 1955), p. 24.
[13] Given Dylan's demand for a minimum fee of $250 per verse, we cannot present any examples.
[14] See "Class Consciousness and the Protest Song," in Denisoff, *Sing A Song of Social Significance, op. cit.*

Other observers, particularly historian Jerome Rodnitzky, have undertaken similar studies in the postwar era and concluded that the protest song has declined for a number of reasons. Rodnitzky, in one of the more convincing presentations of this thesis, argues that the singers themselves have "outgrown" the folk genre and the protest song. He continues to say that media has become less political and increasingly commercialized.[15] This thesis as far as it goes is empirically sound. The folk music craze of the Hootenanny days is now history. The fact that Dylan, Judy Collins, Arlo Guthrie, and John Sebastian now are "superstars" in the rock genre is equally true. However, one must acknowledge that songs believed to be statements of "protest" are increasingly heard on the radio and written about in various popular and scholarly journals.[16] Citizens' campaigns have been marshalled to help ban "Society's Child," and "Eve of Destruction" from the airwaves. Vice President Agnew has cautioned against the dangers of popular songs. The FCC warned radio stations that they would be held responsible for the lyrical content of the songs they broadcast.[17] Consequently, any pronouncements about the death of protest songs appear premature. It may be more fruitful to acknowledge, as does Rodnitzky, that the "cry for justice" ethos as applied to folk song is no longer valid,[18] if it ever was. The social movement aspect of protest songs is also negated by historical events. The inclusion of protest songs in a highly diverse commercialized medium such as radio has, no doubt, lent an aura of respectability to sociopolitical sentiments that previously had not existed. However, we must avoid the time-bound pit identified by Rodnitzky: "Increasingly, the classic protest song tradition lives not in the folk, but in the memory and articles of academicians and folklorists who continue to inquire about the roots, ideology and continuity of the folk-revival."[19] While this observation has unfortunate implications beyond this discussion (why should scholars not look at the protest songs of past movements?) it does indicate a need for a more contemporary definition of what is a protest song.

The contemporary protest songs are customarily described as containing certain deviant themes. Robinson and Hirsch, for example, present them as those

[15] Jerome L. Rodnitzky, "The Decline of Contemporary Protest Music," *Popular Music and Society* 1 (Fall, 1971), pp. 44–50.

[16] Kurt Korall, "The Music of Protest," *Saturday Review*, (November 16, 1968), pp. 36–39; and John P. Robinson and Paul M. Hirsch, "Teenage Response to Rock and Roll Protest Songs," paper read at the American Sociological Association meetings, San Francisco, Sept. 1969. [Ed. note: See Article 18 in this volume.]

[17] Federal Communications Commission, "License Responsibility to Review Records Before Their Broadcast," March 5, 1971-B FC 71-205.

[18] See R. Serge Denisoff, *Great Day Coming: Folk Music and the American Left* (Urbana: University of Illinois Press, 1971).

[19] Rodnitzky, *op. cit.,* p. 2.

songs which glorify the use of drugs, are anti-war, and generally critical of American society.[20] A less objective critic reacted to the music by writing that it "promotes attitudes and ideas which, if they were aware of the message, would blow the minds of most parents."[21] Indeed, the stage presence of various rock stars beginning with Elvis Presley, through Mick Jagger, Izzy and the Stooges and Alice Cooper has invoked considerable wrath from non-supporters. Originally, it was the visual appearance of performers that offended the sensibilities of observers; today it is the lyrical content. Ed Sullivan, in 1956, showed only the upper part of Presley's famed torso. In 1968, the same television emcee forced the Rolling Stones to change the "suggestive" line in "Let's Spend the Night Together." As these characterizations imply, the lyrics in contemporary rock songs have been viewed as being deviant in nature or, at the minimum, non-conformist. Some of the songs also point to an alternative, albeit not purely political, to the *status quo*. One sociologist spoke of the New Sound as the expression of:

> ...a new culture being born, and its lyrics serve as normative guidelines for youth in the process of defining and establishing a new order ...What they are saying comes through loudest, if not clearest, in their music and it is to the music that we must turn as does youth itself.[22]

Theodore Roszak reiterates this theme by suggesting that "one is apt to find out more about ... youth ... by paying attention to posters ... and dance— and especially to the pop music, which now knits together the whole thirteen to thirty age group."[23] The protest aspect of rock, as in folk music and in Greenway's oppressed groups, is defined by many as indigenous to a specific generational unit. Dylan, rightly or wrongly, has been termed the "voice of a generation." Contemporary topical rock songs do fit many of the criteria enumerated above as being protest songs, at least of the rhetorical variety. The key missing element is the notion of political action. Few selections, lyrically, advocate the type of action found in trade-union or radical songs of the 1930's and 1940's. Instead, the rhetorical songs of the Top Forty look at the life style of the adolescent and the world through his eyes.

[20] John P. Robinson and Paul M. Hirsch, *op. cit.*

[21] Gary Allen, "That Music: There's More To It Than Meets the Ear," *American Opinion* 12 (February, 1969), p. 49. [Ed. note: See Article 12 in this volume.]

[22] Anthony Bernhard, "For What It's Worth: Today's Rock Scene," paper read at American Sociological Association meetings, San Francisco, August, 1967, pp. 1–2.

[23] Theodore Roszak, *The Making of the Counter Culture: Reflections on Technological Society and Its Youthful Opposition* (Garden City: Doubleday and Co., 1969), p. 291.

In the summer of 1965 a number of propaganda songs with socially controversial messages began to appear on the Top Forty charts. Some of these songs
were "covers" of Bob Dylan songs such as "It Ain't Me, Babe" and "Mr.
Tambourine Man." Other songs were written especially for popular consumption, such as "Laugh At Me" by Sonny and Cher, which stressed the teenager's
right to wear clothing different from his parents and accepted adult standards.
Jody Miller's "Home of the Brave" objected to school restrictions dealing with
the length of a student's hair. One verse concludes "Why won't they try to
understand him/Why won't you let him be what he wants to be." These two
songs, labelled deviant or "protest" songs by *Time-Life*, were fundamentally in
keeping with the efforts of Chuck Berry during the 1950's which lamented the
teenage role and the imposition of adult standards. Bob Dylan's first major rock
"hit," "Subterranean Homesick Blues," is a chronicle of the demands of the
adolescent role and the hypocrisy of adult society. As in "Too Much Monkey
Business" and "Almost Grown," Dylan chides the schools, the workaday world,
and warns against many other institutions, for example, "don't follow leaders/
watch the parkin' meters." Once again, the values of the teen culture are lauded
and the notion of postponed gratification questioned; however, this material is
still in keeping with the social commentary of older popular songs.

During this period several other socially significant songs made their way
onto the Top Forty, such as "We Gotta Get Out of This Place," which outlines
the feelings of a slum child who has witnessed his father's unsuccessful struggle
to leave, and who fears a similar fate for himself and his girl friend. The song
ends "We gotta get out of this place/there is a better life for me and you."
Janis Ian's more controversial "Society's Child" is about the intervention of parents in the relationship of a black male and white female. After documenting the
harassments from parents, school officials, and "society" in general, the song
concludes with resignation to the pressures that prevail: "when we're older
things may change/but for now this is the way they must remain . . ." Unlike the
conclusions of the movement-oriented protest song which advocated social action
to create a better society or a "new day," both of these songs are designed either
to "make the best" of what exists or to "get out of this place" in a Horatio Alger
manner.[24] As such, these songs, interpreted as topical commentaries on the world
as the songster perceives it, do not offer any radical solutions or invoke any
sort of political action. The first exception to this rule, it appears, was "The

---

[24] Another category of song frequently labelled as deviant on the Top Forty is the
so-called "double meaning" song which is supposed to have an esoteric meaning, known
only to the "in" people. The author has not included this type of song, such as "Eight
Miles High," etc., since there is a great deal of confusion as to what precisely these songs
mean. Cf., Robinson and Hirsch, *op. cit.*; and "Songs That Have A Double Meaning,"
San Francisco Chronicle, Sept. 25, 1966, p. 13.

Eve of Destruction," which is generally seen as the ideal type of "popular protest song" by all observers.

"The Eve of Destruction" was one of the original overt expressions of political sentiment to reach a Top Forty audience. It was written by a nineteen-year-old, P. F. Sloane, and recorded by Barry McGuire. "Eve" first received air-play in August of 1965 and in five weeks became a national best seller, despite widespread opposition, which included a blacklist of the piece by many Top Forty stations. The American Broadcasting Company also refused to have it played on its affiliates. The song, in narrative style, cited a series of social indignities and hypocrisies, concluding that if social change was not forthcoming, a nuclear holocaust awaited man. Each series of indictments was followed by a warning to look around and see that "we're on the Eve of Destruction." The Sloane composition was a classical rhetorical song using grievances put to an accelerating beat "which slowly developed into the impact of a forceful marching song."[25] Despite its similarity to Spanish Civil War songs and indeed, to Nazi hymns, the song offered no concrete solution outside of the nebulous "truth shall make you free," a cliche found on the walls of most high schools. The success of "Eve of Destruction" on the Billboard Top 100 generated other topical pieces. Decca Records, for example, issued the "Dawn of Correction" by the Spokesmen as an "answer song" to Sloane's composition: "The Western world has a common dedication/To keep free people from Red domination."

Other anti-protest songs have been recorded by Pat Boone, Frankie Laine, and others. None, with the notable exception of the "Ballad of the Green Berets," by S/Sgt. Barry Sadler, based on a Spanish Civil War march, sold well or made any dent upon the Top Forty charts. This fact may not be attributable entirely to ideological perspectives. Nearly all of the aforementioned artists are in the so-called "middle media" of popular music which is addressed to adults over thirty-five or forty years of age who rarely purchase single 45s. On the other hand, topical and protest songs have taken on a "novelty" quality on the Top Forty as well as on the so-called FM "underground stations."[26] Songs such as "Mr. Businessman," "Two Plus Two," "Skip A Rope," "Fortunate Son," "The War Goes On," and "Give Peace A Chance," all have received Top Forty air-play with relatively high sales. Only John Lennon's "Give Peace A Chance," a chant put to music, and Country Joe MacDonald's "Fixin' To Die Rag" have had any success in the American political arena. Both are staples at anti-war

---

[25] Carl Belz, *The Story of Rock* (New York: Oxford University Press, 1970), p. 169.

[26] Underground stations usually concentrate upon playing selections from LP's and choosing a wider range of genre than Top Forty stations. In recent years many FM outlets have drifted toward the "Big Sound" format. Cf., Tom Nolan, "Underground Radio," pp. 337–351 and Harry Shearer, "Captain Pimple Cream's Fiendish Plot," pp. 357–384, in Jonathan Eisen, *The Age of Rock* (New York: Vintage Books, 1969).

rallies. Significantly, "Give Peace A Chance," is the only current political song based structurally on the more traditional format of protest song, being repetitive, easy to sing, and stressing the word "we." The MacDonald composition, also, has a relatively easy-to-learn chorus again underlining the collective: "and it's one, two, three, what are we fighting for/don't ask me I don't give a damn . . . next stop is Vietnam."

FM underground stations, given their relative freedom from some of the economic pressures of Top Forty broadcasting, aptly described by Hirsch, played more protest material than their AM counterparts.[27] For example, Gordon Lightfoot's "Black Day in July," a bitter description of the Detroit riots of 1967, was played on FM stations and generally ignored on AM radio. Material by the Fugs, the Mothers of Invention, and Country Joe & the Fish also is confined to FM outlets, ostensibly because of its use of some four-letter words. Another reason given for the higher proportion of topical songs on FM is the programming format itself. Most current topical songs, following Bob Dylan's innovative lead, are rather lengthy. Consider Eric Burdon's "Sky Pilot," depicting the contradictory role of a military chaplain, which is eight minutes in duration. The "American Eagle Tragedy" by Earth Opera, condemning President Johnson as the "king in the counting house," sending young men off to die, is eleven minutes in playing time. Top Forty songs, in contrast, are customarily three minutes in length.

The length of contemporary political songs is yet another departure from the rather simplistic, easy-to-learn protest songs of religious and political movements. Indeed, many topical song singers today, away from electric current, would be found impotent as propagandists.

Nineteen-seventy found the protest song over-represented on the Top Forty and underground radio stations. Most of these songs revolved around the issue of the Vietnam War. Remarkably, a good proportion of these protest songs were not patterned either on the classic folk song prototype or the "you hypocrites!" posture of the "Eve of Destruction." Instead, "super" groups such as Crosby, Stills, Nash, and Young, and Creedence Clearwater Revival used their own styles and sounds to communicate some form of dissent. CSN&Y recorded "Almost Cut My Hair" and "Long Time Gone" to commemorate the death of Robert Kennedy and to denounce working within the political system. "Ohio" and "Cost of Freedom," by the same group, addressed the murders at Kent State. "Ohio," blacklisted by many radio stations, despite the prominence of the artists, accused President Nixon and his "tin soldiers" of being responsible for the deaths of four students and the wounding of nine others. The song concludes with the chant "Four dead in Ohio, Four dead in Ohio . . . Four . . . Four

[27] Paul Hirsch, "The Structure of the Popular Music Industry," Ann Arbor: University of Michigan, (mimeographed), 1969.

dead in Ohio." Creedence Clearwater, in "Fortunate Son," dissent from the draft and having young men fight the wars of their elders. Their reaction to this situation was "It ain't me, it ain't me, I ain't no military son." The Jefferson Airplane's "Volunteers" was a musical statement of revolutionary goals including many Yippie slogans such as "up against the wall."[28] Perhaps a more significant trend perceivable at this time was the emergence of protest songs both in black popular music and the country and western genre.

Following the lead of the Last Poets, a bitter New York street group, and the more commercial Fifth Dimension, the Temptations wrote a number of protest songs including "Ball of Confusion" which again, chronicled the social and political injustices committed against the black man at home as well as in Vietnam. Their composition of "War," popularized by Edwin Starr, noted "War! HUH! What is it good for, absolutely nothing." A spate of other black liberation songs were issued, such as "Letter From A Black Man," "Power To the People," "We Are All the People," "Unity" and many others. A majority of black protest songs echoed the theme of the James Brown song "say it loud— I'm black and I'm proud." Added to this sentiment was the warning that should integration not be achieved—and soon—crisis was not far behind.

Country music has always exhibited a myriad of protest songs, however rhetorical and conservative.[29] They have nearly always been simplistically patriotic and devoted to simplistic values. In 1970 country music turned its scorn upon Vietniks, as *Time* would have it, hippies, and all of those not adhering to the "virtues which made this country great." Merle Haggard led this assault. Unlike the pseudo-conservative songs of "Johnny Reb" or "Johnny Freedom" (Marty Robbins), Haggard's songs gained popularity with a sizeable population outside the rural South. His favorite piece appears to be "Okie From Muskogee" which is a condemnation of dope-smoking hippies who burn their draft cards. The ideal life style, presented in the chorus of the song, is being an "Okie From Muskogee" where even squares can have fun, and:

> We still wave ole' Glory down by the courthouse
> And white lightning's still the biggest thrill of all.

In the follow-up song, "The Fighting Side of Me," Haggard threatened protesters:

> If you don't love it, leave it
> Let this song that I'm singing be a warning.

[28] For a discussion of the political songs of 1970 see Denisoff, *Sing A Song, op. cit.*
[29] See Jens Lund, " 'The Old Religion's Better After All': Reaction in Country Music," paper read at Popular Culture Association meetings (East Lansing, Mich., April, 1971). [Reprinted in this volume as "Fundamentalism, Racism, and Political Reaction in Country Music," pp. 79–91.]

Billy Anderson, in "Where Have All Our Heroes Gone," laments the loss of individuals of great courage. Guy Drake's "Welfare Cadilac" (sic) attacks recipients of public assistance.

The most spectacular protest song of the 1970's, so far, has come from the country and western firm of Shelby Singleton—"The Battle Hymn of Lt. Calley." The song was released shortly after the conviction of the junior officer for murder in the My Lai massacre of civilian women and children. A spokesman for the Singleton Corporation stated it "was the fastest selling record in this company's history." Considering the successes of the firm, this is not a statement to be treated lightly. The record reportedly sold a million copies in five and a half days. The structure of the song is a traditional one, in that "John Brown's Body" has been used to protest every conceivable cause and injustice known to man. "The Battle Hymn of the Republic" and "Solidarity Forever" are both based on this Abolitionist anthem. The thrust of this ballad is that Lt. Calley was only following orders when he killed the civilians. The song argues that the junior officer was only doing his duty and now "They've made me out a villain and they've stamped me with a brand." The reaction to this song was mixed. Capitol Records declined to release a cover version by Tex Ritter and many radio stations refused to play the song. One disc jockey in Toledo, Ohio was fired for broadcasting the piece. Still, the "Calley" song promises to be the most successful protest ballad in many years, however controversial and divisive it may be.

On the other hand, Johnny Cash recorded a number of songs designed in part to "create understanding" between groups—such as "What Is Truth?" in which the hypocrisy of American society in the trial of the Chicago 8 and other events is evidenced. "The Man In Black" once again echoes the problems of the American system. Cash's conclusions, however, are highly simplistic; he assumes the positivistic stance that knowledge will bring order and consensus. Of all of the songs described, very few suggest any form of political action. Only Merle Haggard comes right out and advocates doing "something" about the dissenters. Songs advocating the opposing position at best are rhetorical, suggesting only that "peace be given a chance."

Since the days of the early frontier circuit rider, the protest song has undergone a number of important changes. It has gone from the religious to the secular, from the sphere of radical political action to the mass media of radio and recordings. This transformation indicates a need for a redefinition of protest songs since at this conjuncture we appear to be in the position aptly described by Steve Stills in "For What It's Worth" :

> There's something happening here
> What it is ain't exactly clear.

2

SOUNDS OF BLACK PROTEST IN AVANT-GARDE JAZZ

Lloyd Miller and James K. Skipper, Jr.

Historians of the future may well view the 1960's as the decade of social protest. Marches, strikes, boycotts, stand-outs, sit-ins, riots have become commonplace. One is surprised if a day passes without the reporting of yet another demonstration by: some group protesting for or against segregation in schools, housing or the labor market; housewives boycotting a grocery chain because of high prices; dairy farmers pouring milk in the street in protest against the low prices they receive for their product; nurses, teachers, and other public servants striking for higher wages; college professors marching in protest against American foreign policy; young men burning their draft cards; college students rioting for more freedom and power. The list could go on and on. Much has been written and will continue to be written about these obvious and conspicuous forms of social protest and what they symbolize.

However, there are other forms of protest which are not so visible or obvious but are nonetheless powerful in their influence and worthy of attention. One of these is the protest represented in the art form of instrumentalized music (instrumentalized in the sociological sense). Music has always been an effective device for the release of cathectic responses relating to controversy, conflict, alienation, and even revolution. As such it often symbolizes the thoughts, feelings, and mood of the times. When we think of protest music today, we usually associate it with the category referred to generically as "Folk." The civil rights song "We Shall Overcome" is a popular and perhaps representative example of this type of social protest music.

However, there is a far less commercial area of contemporary American music which is also producing the sounds of protest. This is the jazz idiom. Jazz music is one of America's unique contributions to world culture, and it is this unique identity which makes jazz of importance in terms of social protest. The roots of jazz are undoubtedly in the rural milieu of the southern Negro, having origins in the field songs and chants of plantation days. Significant as this historical rural setting was vis-à-vis the chant and the blues, the maturity of jazz expression today is a characteristically urban phenomenon. It is an expression of the view from the ghetto, urban tension, alienation, and anomic response. Its bold, lean, and sometimes shocking cacophony lends itself to this purpose. Jazz has never been committed to the preservation of the past, or for that matter to passive acceptance of the present. Its very essence is dedication to outdating itself daily. This does not mean that the projection into the future occurs in limbo but that it represents both functional and dysfunctional values of the present, and at the same time is a reaction to these values as well as a prediction of values to come.

Jazz has always been a disturbing element on the American scene. To the uninitiated ear, its sounds are often strange, exotic, and unpredictable. It commits the sin of nonconformity to the norms of traditional music. In addition, to a large portion of the white community, jazz has been stereotyped as "race music." As such it has been discriminated against in much the same way that the American Negro has himself. For example, the circular that appears on . . . page 28 appeared recently in, of all places, New Orleans, Louisiana.

Finally, the jazz musician is somewhat of a deviant. He is completely dedicated to the small world of his type of music: a "true believer" "with the zeal of a fanatic." He is unconcerned with the demands of those outside his own perspective.[1] His image has been tarnished by an association with drink, drugs, and dives. Many of the early artists grew up around and played in the brothels of New Orleans' infamous red light district—"Storyville." This was the initial association of jazz with sin and sex. The urban working environment of the musician was never very conducive to the middle class standards of the good life. Working almost exclusively at night in smoke-filled clubs in the more seamy sections of major metropolitan areas, surrounded by liquor, and in constant association with underworld elements, often made overindulgence in alcohol and narcotics both feasible and enticing. So great has been the jazz musician's association with drugs that at one time the federal hospital at Lexington, Kentucky

[1] For a discussion of this point see Howard S. Becker, "The Professional Dance Musician and His Audience," *American Journal of Sociology*, 58 (1951), pp. 136–142 [reprinted in this volume as Article 20]; and Alan P. Merriam and Raymond Mack, "The Jazz Community," *Social Forces*, 38 (1960), pp. 211–222.

was able to field an entire all-star band of addict inmates.[2] Primarily for these reasons the Negro jazz musician and his ever changing and evolving music have never been well accepted by the vast majority of the general society.

NOTICE!

STOP

Help Save the Youth of America

DON'T BUY NEGRO RECORDS

(If you don't want to serve negroes in *your* place of business, then do not have negro records on your juke box or listen to negro records on the radio.)

The screaming, idiotic words, and savage music of these records are undermining the morals of our white youth *in America.*

Call the advertisers of the radio stations that play this type of music and complain to them!

Don't Let Your Children Buy, or Listen To These Negro Records

---

For additional copies of this circular, write

CITIZEN'S COUNCIL OF GREATER NEW ORLEANS, INC.

509 Delta Building, New Orleans, Louisiana 70112

[2] Leonard Feather, *Encyclopedia of Jazz* (New York, Bonanza Books, 1962), p. 85.

A Glance at the Past

Most Americans are ignorant of African prehistory and history. There is little realization that the American Negro was brought to this country from societies whose culture placed great emphasis on social change, especially in the verbal arts. Topical songs, for example, are common in African cultures. Although they may be based on old rhythms and melodies, their texts are composed for specific occasions and are essentially creative commentaries on the present social scene. When an African dons a mask and performs certain dances or sings about people and events, he is no longer acting as a person but as a being or spirit. In this role, he often has freedom for comments on social relations and for actions that, if unmasked, would produce social friction or hostility.

It may not be an exaggeration to observe that when the African Negro came to America he brought this cultural trait with him. In the work songs and chants of the plantation fields, when he cried out to his brothers, "Ahm tired a dis mess/Oh, yes, Ahm tired a dis mess," he was commenting on society, but now as an American. This tradition has remained with him. While he no longer hides behind a tribal mask, to commune with spirits, he may symbolically take refuge behind a horn, a drum, a piano, or a voice to give expression to his deepest thoughts and feelings. These expressions take many different forms. Examples are the "shout" (to utter a sudden loud cry), the "shout song" (a rhythmic religious song characterized by responsive singing between leader and congregation), and the "moan" (to make a low, prolonged sound of grief or pain). These utterances represent the beginnings of Negro protest under the bonds of slavery. However the "cry" (an inarticulate utterance of distress, rage, or pain; to cry out for help or to proclaim publicly) is unique, because it is the quintessence of the new sound of protest in avant-garde jazz today.

The bondage of slavery evoked the cry, as represented in the work songs, and the shouts and moans were strident laments. They were also chronicles, but of such a mean kind of existence that they could not assume the universality any lasting musical form must have. The work songs and later blues forms differ profoundly, not only in their form but in their lyrics and intent. Since most Negroes before and after slavery were agricultural laborers, the corn songs, the shouts, and hollers issued from this kind of milieu. Some of the work songs used as their measure the grunt of a man pushing a heavy weight or the blow of a hammer against rock to provide the metrical precision and rhythmical impetus behind the singer. Probably one of the best known examples, is the traditional "Take This Hammer."

> Take this hammer, uh;
> Take it to the captain, uh;
> Take it to the captain, uh;
> Tell him I'm gone.

Because of his status as a slave, there were lyrics to some of the songs that the Negro could not sing in front of his master. The protest was there, nonetheless, and while it could not be given free and strong expression, its importance as a mechanism for cathectic release cannot be underestimated. As the slaves were introduced to Christianity, gospel singing also served the same purpose. The Negro's religious music and spirituals were possibly the first completely native American music.

The church was an important part of the slave's life. For the white masters who had "given Christianity to the heathens," it was seen as a socializing influence and a means of social control. For the Negro, it was to become the one institution where he could escape, momentarily, from a subhuman existence.

It was not until well after Emancipation that the Negro experienced any real secular life. Often the churches considered "fiddle songs," "devil songs," and "jig tunes" of the period sinful. Certain musical instruments such as the violin and banjo were also thought to be "the devil's invention."

As the Negro church became institutionalized in the image of the white model, a definite social hierarchy developed. Ministers, deacons, elders, trustees, and even the ushers of the Baptist and Methodist churches formed a definite social hierarchy which dominated the whole of Negro society. In the new theocracy, the "backslider" (the sinning churchgoer) and the "heathen" became the lowest rung of the social ladder.

With the end of slavery there was less dependency on the church as arbiter of the Negro's life style. As the alternatives of secular life began to take shape, there were more and more "backsliders" and, consequently, more and more of the devil music was heard. With emancipation came increasing mobility. The Negro began to leave the plantation for the city in hopes of finding work and a better way of life. In many respects his rural background left the Negro ill-prepared to adjust and adapt to the more complex patterns of urban living. The frustrations, tension, and anxieties encountered in these new settings were symbolized in a new style of music—"the classic blues."

Louis Wirth classified minorities into four basic types: (1) pluralistic—live and let live, (2) assimilationist—desire to join the dominant group, (3) secessionist—rejection of the values and norms of the dominant group, and (4) militant—desire to dominate. It is our contention that jazz today, in its most progressive form, is rapidly becoming instrumentalized as protest and that its evolution as such conforms to the Wirth paradigm with a surprising "goodness of fit."[3]

[3] Louis Wirth, "The Problems of Minority Groups," in *The Science of Man in the World Crisis,* Ralph Linton, ed. (New York, Columbia University Press, 1945), pp. 347–372.

Pluralistic Stage

Classic blues is called "classic" because it was the music that seemed to contain all the diverse and conflicting elements of Negro music, plus the smoother emotion of the performance. It was the first Negro music that appeared in a formal context as entertainment. It is probably the end product of more diverse sociological, as well as musical, influences than any other music with the exception of jazz. In contrast to primitive blues, which emerged from the worksong era and was characterized by the mastery of simple musical instruments such as the banjo and guitar, classic blues became more stylized and reflected many changes that were taking place in the life of the Negro. It also reflected the urban way of life, in contrast to the rural environment of the past. The blues communicated the pluralistic desire to be accepted, of a people free, but still in economic bondage. Blues are simple and elemental, but they express the profound depths of suffering, sense of defeat, and down-heartedness of the Negro. Yet they are not intrinsically pessimistic. In many of the blues, there is a steady, throbbing undertone of hope. "Times is bad, but they won't be bad always" is the lyric carried in a score of blues songs. For example, in the classic "Trouble In Mind," regardless of the specific troubles the performer may be singing about (women, money, liquor, unemployment, etc.), the last lyric always centers on the theme that someday the sun will shine on the individual again.

Blues are also characterized by lusty vulgarity, sensuality, and exuberance for life, love, and sex. The suggestive titles of many popular blues songs hint at these themes: "She Can Love So Good," "Drive Me Daddy," "Don't Come Too Soon," "Cherry Red," "Feather Bed Mama," "Let Me Play With Your Poodle," "Mother Fuyer." From "barrel-houses" and "honky-tonks" came many of the descriptive words which were applied to the music played there. Included were such graphic terms as "gulley-low," meaning, as its name implies, low as a ditch or gulley; hence, "low-down" and "gut-bucket." This was in reference to the bucket which caught drippings or "gutterings" from the barrels. Invariably, a pastiche for all this was provided by a small band, notable for their lack of restraint.

Assimilationist Stage

The emergence of classic blues and the popularization of jazz occurred at approximately the same time. Both were the results of social and psychological changes within the Negro community as it moved toward the mainstream of American society. By 1914 masses of Negroes began to move toward the northern industrial centers such as Chicago, Detroit, and New York in hopes of high-paying jobs and a better way of life. But the urban milieu proved harsh, and invariably Negroes received the lowest wages and the most debasing jobs. For many it was simply a new form of slavery. World War I played an important role in the assimilation of the Negro into secular life. It tended to broaden his horizons to the world beyond America and the realization that the inequalities he experienced were not necessarily the inevitable lot of the Negro.

It was during this period that jazz began to develop in New Orleans and other sections of the South.[4] As the Negro migrated north, the influence of this new music spread to the major metropolitan areas, but especially Chicago, Kansas City, and New York. Jazz was not so much a successor to the blues as it was a seminal music that developed out of, but independent of, the blues. It was an artistic form of expression, a type of communication between those experiencing the plight of existence in big-city slums.

During the late 1920's and 1930's the white community came in contact with jazz and a number of white musicians began to learn and imitate this music.[5] White bands were formed and gained a high degree of proficiency, popularity, and financial success during the "Swing era." However, inevitably, the feeling of rejection the Negro was experiencing in the urban milieu and society at large began to manifest itself in his music. At about the time white musicians began to understand and master the new type of music, the form of jazz changed radically. It turned its back on the past.[6] The new sounds of the 1940's began to evoke strange, sympathetic, and to many, mystifying vibrations. The incipient pitch of protest, a musical harbinger of things to come, had begun.

Secessionist Stage

The emergence of identifiable alienation in jazz began in the middle 1940's. It was known generically as "bop" and became a movement of major proportions. Charlie Parker and Dizzy Gillespie were the major innovators of the period and usually receive the lion's share of credit for its development.

The two main alienating factors in the bop era were the growing complexity of the music which many musicians did not understand, let alone the general public, and the bop artist's quest to individualize his own identity. Acceptance *per se* was no longer a goal. He began to "de-minstrelize" himself. Gillespie launched a broadside against Negro stereotypes. He began wearing sneakers,

[4] Barry Ulanov, *Handbook of Jazz* (New York, Viking Press, 1959), pp. 5–6.

[5] However, a few white musicians were playing a *type* of jazz almost from the beginning. See Joachim Berendt, *The New Jazz Book* (New York, Hill and Wang, 1962), pp. 10–12.

[6] John S. Wilson, *Jazz: The Transition Years 1940–1960* (New York, Appleton-Century-Crofts, 1966), p. 26.

baseball cap, goatee, and heavy horn-rimmed glasses. Between trumpet excursions into regions of startling technical brilliance, he quoted Shakespeare extensively and accurately, both on and off the bandstand.[7]

Parker in his own way was even more deviant than Gillespie. Musically he was a genius. He attempted to translate everything he saw and heard into music. He set new standards on every level: harmonic, rhythmic, tonal, and melodic. His ability to improvise influenced almost all musicians who heard him. Parker's haunting solos with their plaintive cry established him as the reigning jazz musician of the era. His recordings have been re-released and his stature continues to grow. Like many of the bop artists, Parker's life was plagued by alcoholism, drug addiction, and mental illness. He died in 1955 at the age of thirty-five of a complex of illnesses including ulcers and cirrhosis of the liver. However, to many jazz men the cause of Parker's death was simply "too much Soul."

Along with the development of bop emerged another music termed "cool." It was characterized by restraint, depersonalized and introverted sound, suppressed cathexis, and sociologically speaking, incipient alienation. Vestiges of the cool school are still part of the jazz colloquy today. In the 1950's a new musical current began to flow from "cool" musicians located on the West Coast. It formed a direct link betwen earlier, more traditional jazz forms and what in the 1960's became the violent protesting of avant-garde jazz.

Representing a major stream in jazz today, it is sometimes referred to by such patois as "hard bop," "roots," and "funky," which means hard-driving, blues-infected jazz. The term which enjoys the most currency today and subsumes all of the above designations is "soul," a word rapidly becoming semantically overloaded. In today's racial disturbances its mere presence on a store window—it connotes black ownership—may save an establishment from destruction. In nonmusical terms, the chief quality of "soul" music is ingenuousness, or honesty, both in its musical content and its rubric and dialogue. In reverting to earlier jazz forms, spirituals, and blues, soul music symbolizes a growing disenchantment and rejection of contemporary values.

The rejection may take many forms. Trumpeter Miles Davis often shows his contempt and disdain for an audience by not facing them while playing. Saxophone Virtuoso John "Soultrane" Coltrane sometimes left the bandstand before his group was through playing so that he did not have to accept applause from the audience. Drummer Max Roach composed the "We Insist: Freedom Now Suite," one part of which, "The Protest," consists of several minutes of

---

[7] Wilson comments: "The only aspect of bop that had real appeal to the public was its decor—the beret, dark, heavy-rimmed glasses and goatee that were publicized as the standard bop garb. Bop kits, consisting of a real beret, empty glasses frames and false goatees enjoyed a brisk sale. (More than a decade later the same equipment was being peddled around San Francisco as a 'Beatnik Kit.')" *Ibid.,* pp. 22–23.

unaccompanied screaming by vocalist Abbey Lincoln.[8] Nina Simone's hostility
to both audiences and co-artists is legendary. She has been known to leave the
stage during her own numbers, and upon returning, deliver a tirade against
the audience, whose attention had waned. The title of her own composition,
"Mississippi God Damn!"[9] symbolizes her uncontained rage about racial
conditions existing in the South.

Finally, Archie Shepp, a complete avant-garde saxophonist, is also a
merciless parodist. He has been known to make appearances in a World War I
officer's jacket, tan glen plaid pants, knitted cap, and tinted Ben Franklin
spectacles. Thus a bit of American culture becomes instrumentalized. But the
protest is by no means confined to the instrumentalization of jazz as parody.
Parody is muted protest, but the new jazz is being used as a forum for protest
of the strongest kind—complete secession. In addition, avant-garde jazz is
proving to be a fountainhead of secessionist jargon, a jargon which is the
essence of the "black power" concept. Rarely in history has a relatively small
metronymic compound evoked so much hue and cry.

Militant Minority

At the far end of the continuum lies Wirth's fourth type of minority,
which he designates the militant:

> Its goal reaches far beyond toleration, assimilation, and even cultural
> and political autonomy. The militant minority has set domination over
> others as its goal. Far from suffering from feelings of inferiority, it is
> convinced of its own superiority and inspired by the lust for conquest.
> While the initial claims of minority movements are generally modest,
> like all accessions of power, they feed upon their own success and
> culminate in delusions of grandeur.[10]

The new music indeed reaches far beyond toleration and assimilation, and
certainly it suffers from no apparent inferiority complex. Aggressive tendencies
are already manifest in its willingness to offend most tastes and obliterate old
musical norms.

On February 23, 1965, playwright-critic-author LeRoi Jones announced
the opening of the Black Arts Repertory Theatre School in Harlem. This
marked Mr. Jones' emergence as one of the chief spokesmen for Black Power

[8] Max Roach, *We Insist: Freedom Now Suite,* Candid Records, 8002 (1960).
[9] Nina Simone, *Mississippi God Damn!* Phillips Records, 200–135 (1965).
[10] Wirth, *op. cit.,* p. 363.

through the mediums of jazz criticism and the theater. Mr. Jones has been warming to his assignation for some time. Although his primary concern has been with jazz, he has enjoyed considerable notoriety, as well as artistic and commercial success with his plays, *The Dutchman, The Slave,* and most recently, *The Toilet.* Jones writes for several influential publications including *Downbeat* which is circulated in 142 foreign countries. Like other advocates of black power, Jones' commitment is to black culture only; he rejects all white culture. Among his favorite artists are: Ornette Coleman, John Coltrane, Archie Shepp, the Ayler brothers, and Sun Ra.

Ornette Coleman was one of the original innovators focusing on his new styles as early as 1954. His music is completely atonal and lacks the conventional patterns of improvisation based on chord patterns. He plays a *plastic* alto saxophone which in itself is deviant. Of his music Coleman states he can "groove myself by finally saying something since nothing says nothing to me."[11] In an attempt to expose his own personality, each member of Coleman's group at times appears to go his own way paying little attention to what the others are playing. A critic was once reported to have inquired as to whether listening to Ornette Coleman was covered by Blue Cross.

John Coltrane died at the age of forty in July of 1967. He was probably the best known, most influential, and most financially successful avant-garde musician. Originally a "hard-boppist," before his death Coltrane had moved into a musical realm quite unconnected and almost antithetical to the work of other bop artists. Coltrane was accused of playing "strings of meaningless notes," and playing his tenor saxophone as if he were trying to "blow it apart." Yet LeRoi Jones said of Coltrane that "when he speaks (plays) of God, you realize it is an Eastern God, Allah perhaps."[12]

Archie Shepp's saxophone screams and rants in imitation of the human voice. LeRoi Jones calls him "the age of cities, an urbane traveler with good senses (heart and ear)."[13] Shepp is an outspoken advocate of black culture and black power.

> Jazz is the product of the whites—the ofays—too often my enemy. It is the progeny of the blacks—my kinsmen. By this I mean, you own the music and we make it. By definition, then, you own the people who make the music. You own us in whole chunks of flesh—I play about the death of me by you. I exult in the life of me in spite of you—

[11] A. B. Spellman (liner notes), *Ornette Coleman On Tenor,* Atlantic Records, 1394 (1963).

[12] LeRoi Jones (liner notes), *The New Wave in Jazz,* Impulse Records, A = 90 (1965).

[13] *Ibid.*

That's what the avant-garde is about. We're not simply angry young
men—we are enraged, and I think it's damn well time.[14]

The Ayler brothers, Donald on trumpet and Albert on tenor saxophone
are second only to the fabled Sun Ra in their jazz extremities. Often their
music sounds like squawks, screeches, moans, and human cries. They emphasize
the feeling, the sound, and not the musical notes. Albert insists that their
music comes from the black ghetto: "Why should I hold back the feeling of
my life, of being raised in the ghetto of America?"[15] Both men attempt to
emphasize their own consciousness, strength, and pride in being black.

Sun Ra is fervently anti-white. His music reflects the ultimate militancy
in jazz. He calls his group of ten to twelve musicians a Solar Arkestra, and
even denies that they play jazz. Supposedly the music is other-worldly, played
on a plane beyond everyday consciousness. When performing the men dress
in shining tunics and gold cloth or velvet headbands or hats. On some tunes
the only lights are those flashing off the costumes of the musicians and especially Sun Ra's headband. On others, the group marches in a long line
playing and chanting as the lights flash on and off. Although Sun Ra plays
regularly on the south side of Chicago, the actual time and place of his gigs
are not publicized, and only a small circle of his followers are allowed to hear
him. Even his recordings are almost impossible to obtain through conventional
channels. He records on the most esoteric label in the United States—E.S.P. with
liner notes in Esperanto!

These men and their music are deviant; not only in the general society, but
also to the mainstream of jazz. Undoubtedly they have been caught up in the
civil rights movement and the thrust for black power. They form a perfect
example of Wirth's militant minority. The musical sounds of protest by this
new breed of musicians are many and varied. They range from the protest
against an obsequious self-image to the vigorous protest which perceives the
white man as the devil. To what extent they represent and symbolize the feeling,
thought, and mood of the new generation of American Negroes is still problematic. But the avant-garde jazz musician just may be the revolutionary
intellectual communicating to all who have ears to hear. Steve Young, Music-
Art co-ordinator of the Black Arts Repertory Theatre School has said: "These
men are dangerous and someday they may murder, send the weaker hearts and
corrupt consciences leaping through windows or screaming through their
destroyed dream world."[16]

[14] Nat Hentoff, "The New Jazz—Black, Angry and Hard to Understand," *New York
Times Magazine,* December 25, 1966, p. 10. Copyright © 1966 by The New York Times
Company. Reprinted by permission.

[15] *Ibid.,* p. 38.

[16] Steve Young (liner notes), *The New Wave in Jazz,* Impulse Records, *op. cit.*

Without a "critical mass" of social protest of some form, few basic structural changes take place in society. The radical, yeasty element in the "new music" may be one manifestation of this "critical mass." At what point do the elements of social fermentation reach the proper proportions for fusion? It appears that the threshold was approached in the recent riots in the Negro ghettoes of New York, Cleveland, Chicago, Los Angeles, Newark, Detroit, and a host of other metropolitan areas.

This, then, is protest. Protest with a sound. A sound with a semantic thrust which demands to be heard, will not be silenced, and should not be overlooked.

3

COUNTRY MUSIC: BALLAD OF THE SILENT MAJORITY

Paul DiMaggio, Richard A. Peterson, and Jack Esco, Jr.

In concluding his scholarly history of country music, Malone (1968:359–360) notes country music's expanding popularity despite the increasing complexity and urbanization of the nation. The music has remained vital, he concludes, because it mirrors the social mores of a broad stratum of people today, thus both reflecting and shaping their values.

This paper will examine country music lyrics in order to better understand the world view of its fans. First, we will *demonstrate* the growth in country music's popularity. Second, we will *examine* four distinctive themes in the lyrics. Third, we will *assess* the available information on the music's audience. And finally, we will *discuss* the link between lyrical themes and audience characteristics.

THE GROWING POPULARITY OF COUNTRY MUSIC

Country music was first recorded just after World War I (Green, 1965) and the first successful country music artist, Vernon Dalhart, had a number of recordings which sold several million copies apiece during the 1920's (Haden, 1970); but until the end of World War II, mass media-disseminated country

This article was especially prepared for this book. The authors would like to thank R. Serge Denisoff, Mark Gowin, Terry Fain, William Ivey, and John D. McCarthy for their comments on an earlier draft of the paper. Part of the research reported here was supported by the National Science Foundation, Undergraduate Research Participation Program; part was supported by a grant to the Vanderbilt Urban and Regional Development Center from the Ford Foundation.

music[1] consisted of several small traditional forms with largely regional markets (Malone, 1968:80–84; Russell, 1970:59–70). The country songs which sold widely outside of these markets were novelty tunes such as "Pistol Packin' Mama" and "Jambalaya," love songs sung in a country mood by Eddie Arnold and others, or genre songs which fit some popular fad such as the cowboy songs of Bob Wills, Gene Autry, and Tex Ritter (Malone, 1968:185–193; Russell, 1970:78–92). In each of these sorts of music, success outside the country music markets was obtained by diluting the essential country elements. A more recent example of the same tendency can be found in the rockabilly style of the early Elvis Presley, Jerry Lee Lewis, and the Everly Brothers during the mid-1950's (Belz, 1969:66–74). Many writers in country music fan magazines including Ike Everly (father of the Everly Brothers) feared in 1956 that country music might disappear in the diluting flood of pop-rock styles. But this did not prove to be so.

To the contrary, through the entire 1960's and particularly during the latter half of the decade, country music enjoyed greatly increased popularity. In 1961, for example, there were just 81 fulltime country music AM radio stations in the United States. By 1970, their number had increased to over 650 with 1200 more stations programming country music for part of the day (CMA, 1970a). In addition, by 1970 there were 18 syndicated country music TV shows (CMA, 1970b), six of which reached over a million households each week (CMA, 1970a). What is more, this increased mass media exposure has come primarily in cities outside the South—the traditional home of country music (Hall, 1967, 1970, 1971; McKinnon, 1967; Sponsor, 1967; *Billboard,* 1969, 1970, 1971a; Rowlett, 1971).

Another indicator of popularity is record sales; unfortunately, no figures on country music sales are available which cover the entire decade. Between 1961 and 1970 the dollar sales of the entire music industry combined tripled (*Billboard,* 1971b) and the dollar sales of country music records have apparently increased at an even faster rate. Knowledgeable industry people estimate that during the decade country music record sales have increased at least fourfold in their *share* of the total record sales, and industry data show that between 1967 and 1970 country music's share nearly doubled, so that only the pop-rock category (including country-rock) accounted for a higher proportion of total record and tape sales (CMA, 1970b). Thus, country music reaches a much

---

[1] All forms of popular music are now disseminated over radio and TV but these media place limits on the sorts of lyrical themes that can be conveyed, both because of possible censorship and in order to "popularize" the music in an attempt to broaden its audience. The bifurcation between a more conventional and ideologically pallid mass media *commercial* music and a more ideologically rich *communal* music presented primarily in live performance to committed devotees can be found not only in the country field but also in rock, rhythm and blues, jazz, and gospel music.

wider range of fans than it did half a century ago when mass media dissemination was just beginning.

COUNTRY MUSIC LYRICS

The "country" music of this broad new generation of fans is different from that of 1920—the banjo and fiddle have faded while drums and electrified instruments have been added. Purists insist that this is killing country music (Gentry, 1969; Hemphill, 1970; Bart, 1970; Grissim, 1970:296–299; Soelberg, 1970), but, as Malone (1968:239–304) has shown, for the first time in this century the wide commercial success of a country music song does not depend on trivializing its lyrics. Rather, the new broader acceptance of country music has been built on a reassertion of many traditionally important themes in country lyrics.

The analysis of lyrics which follows is based on two formal samples of song lyrics published in *Country Song Roundup,* a fan magazine, which publishes those songs that are popular on the country music hit charts at the time of publication. This method of selection insures that songs analyzed will be those popular in the country music market, not those defined as "country" by some esthetic criterion.[2] Forty songs were drawn randomly from every fifth year between 1950 and 1970. Each of these 200 songs was classified separately by at least two different coders.[3] Love themes were coded by using the scheme devised by Horton (1957) and later used by Carey (1969a) and Peterson and Berger [see chapter V]. In addition, songs were coded for three other themes found to be important in country music by McCarthy, *et al.* (1972); these are drinking, work, and "way of life" themes. Another sample of 80 songs was drawn from the years 1965 and 1966. It was subject to more detailed analysis, focusing on the relationship between the sexes (DiMaggio, 1971). In

---

[2] Some records which are popular by the market criterion (in that they are often requested at country-oriented record stores, jukebox outlets, and radio stations) would not be defined as "country" by purists because of non-country elements of instrumentation, arrangement, tonal quality, rhythm, lyric, accent of the singer, or even the group performing the rendition (Malone, 1968; Grissim, 1970; Govani, 1970). We do not employ these esthetic criteria because we are interested in what the fan chooses through his patronage rather than in the musical form *per se.*

[3] Each of the authors was engaged in the coding of songs and we would like to thank Edward Dell who helped in this process. In addition, we are grateful to the Country Music Hall of Fame and Museum for graciously loaning us back-issues of *The Country Song Roundup,* the Country Music Association which provided information on the growth of the industry, and Gregory Daniels who provided part of the data on radio listenership.

addition to the formal samples, a number of other popular songs will be cited because they illustrate particular themes in country music.[4]

Interpreting the lyrics of any musical genre is difficult (Denzin, 1970; Denisoff and Levine, 1971), but it is less difficult to interpret country lyrics for at least three reasons. First, themes tend to be stated unambiguously. There is little difficulty, for example, in interpreting songs like "I Wouldn't Live in New York City If You Gave Me The Whole Damn Town," or "Thank God and Greyhound You've Gone." Pop and soul lyrics may also be unambiguous, but country songs have a second characteristic which makes them easier to interpret. They tend to tell a complete story embellished with particularistic detail (Bart, 1970). Thus, while the pop song typically deals with abstracted, if common, situations, as in "Tea for Two" or "Light My Fire" (Riesman, 1951; Carey, 1969b), and soul music tends to set a mood with a cliche such as "Soul Power," or "Make It Funky" (Shaw, 1970), country lyrics typically detail an individual situation and play it out as a three-minute soap opera, secular sermon or as country music songwriter John Hartford (1971) calls them, "Word Movies." Finally, country songs accent the words at the expense of melodic, rhythmic, and tonal complexity, so that these latter elements do not color the meaning or popularity of the song as they usually do in other sorts of commercial music (Coker, 1971). It is notable in this regard that, while pop music producers are constantly looking for a "commercial sound" (Peterson and Berger, 1971), country music producers are on the lookout for a "commercial lyric" (Grissim, 1970:185–187).

Most country lyrics deal with one or more of the four following topics: love, liquor, work, or the passing of the good old ways. Though often woven together in songs, these four topics are discussed separately, with the final theme receiving the greatest attention because it contains the most directly political themes.

Home Is Where the Heart Is. Love themes are found more often than all others, but they carry a different message in commercial country music than in pop, rock, or soul music. The joys of love anticipated or consummated are less often celebrated than is the anguish of love on the decline or love already dead; 75 percent of our 120 sample songs of 1960, 1965 and 1970 deal with love themes and just over two-thirds of these deal with these latter

[4] The picture presented in the lyrics is incomplete for at least two reasons. First, commercial country music lyrics are confined by standards of "good taste" because this music must be played over the air. While conventions have changed rapidly since 1955, aspects of sex, politics, and racism are still taboo. Second, lyrics are set in conventional situations, using words which have symbolic significance, thus limiting the range of ideas that can easily be expressed.

phases of love.[5] Love themes in the 80 songs of the 1965–66 sample were analyzed in detail. They reveal a view of love that complements the country music ethos to be described below.

While the male conquest is sometimes accomplished with the bravado of a "truck drivin' son-of-a-gun," the woman is more often sought in the mood that a wounded soldier seeks a nurse. Defeated or, at least, frustrated and confused by the larger world beyond the home, men who sing country songs turn to women for comfort, stability, and strength. Lines from three songs tell this story. "You make the world go away"; "It's another world when I'm with you"; and "Everything went wrong 'til you came along, bless your heart."

If a woman's love can revivify a hollow man, its loss is absolutely shattering. As one man laments, "You tore me up in little bitty pieces, you drug me all over the ground, I was a big man but now I ain't nothing" and "what man wants a woman who won't satisfy his heart and soothe his ego?" Fearing withdrawal, men often test their women for signs of disaffection. One man notes, "Something's wrong, I can feel it when I hold you." Men commonly express anxiety over their dependence on a "cat-like" female who enjoys a magical power over them and who delights in making them suffer. Men rarely "love 'em and leave 'em" without looking back. Rather, seduced or drunk, they jilt and feel remorse. As Hank Thompson sings, "Every man must leave his footprints on the shifting sands of time, but I'll just leave the mark of a heel."

Women singers often feel victimized in the love relationship, "You've left me with two kids, three dogs, and a house full of dirty wash." But the woman often expresses dignity and stoicism in holding a home together in spite of her foolish man's silly behavior. The tool is her sexuality. Addressing her man who is about to leave, Brenda Lee says, "Lay down here beside me, and love me like you never have before"; in a lecture to women entitled "Good lovin' keeps a home together," Tammy Wynette advises, "You got to be just a little bit better than her, a whole lot warmer in the night," and Leona

---

[5] While 80 songs from 1950 and 1955 were coded, they will not be discussed in detail here because the renascence of country music noted by Malone (1968: 271–304) and others began after 1957. These changes are reflected in our data. The 1950 sample contains a mixture of cowboy ballads, barn dance novelty tunes, and love songs, most of which could have been sung by a crooner like Bing Crosby as effectively as by Ernest Tubb, Eddy Arnold or some other country artist. In sharp contrast, the 1955 sample shows the great incursion of rockabilly and teen-oriented popular songs. A higher proportion of the 1955 songs deals with the stages of the conventional courtship cycle than those of any other year and the greatest proportion of these deal with the travails of finding love rather than with love's loss. Our 1955 sample closely duplicates the findings of Horton (1957) for the same year.

Williams hopes to outstrip the rivals for her husband's attention by "sewing all day long . . . so tonight you'll see a country girl with hot pants on." While the man never does, the woman often addresses her rival, asking her to see the home she is "wrecking" or even boasting that the rival isn't woman enough to steal her man. Thus, while love and marriage may make for great happiness in which the man finds nurturance and the woman can build a stable household, the songs taken together suggest that a battle betwen the sexes is inevitable. In this battle, the man is weakened while the woman, though hurt, is ennobled.

Drunk Again. Liquor is mentioned only three times in the 80 songs of the 1950 and 1955 samples and then it is mentioned twice in connection with barroom killings. Yet it appears twelve times in the songs of 1965 and 1970. The increase in such songs, noted by both Grissim (1970) and Malone (1968), is interpreted by them as illustrating the new frankness which has become possible in music lyrics in the last fifteen years and signaling a return to classical country music concerns.

Fully half of the songs in our sample which mention liquor see it as a means to enjoy life and feel good. The rest portray it as a means of drowning disappointment, loneliness, and failure. As the mixer of the "Loser's Cocktail" says, "Some of the losers come here to forget, while the rest still haven't found out yet." There is a cycle in these songs quite parallel to the love cycle in which the male sings the female part in the battle. He is, first of all, fascinated by liquor, then seduced and overcome with delight, then deserted, and finally left with a hollow or bitter feeling of "Sunday morning coming down." Again, as with love (with which liquor songs are usually mixed), the accent is on the latter *problem* phases of the affair with liquor. Even when sought in the joyful mood of "Let's get drunk and be somebody," for example, it most often leads to violence, economic irresponsibility, or marital infidelity.

Alcohol is probably such a tool of devilish temptation in country music, of course, because it long had that symbolic meaning in fundamentalist Protestant religion (Denisoff, 1970). A new note enters into a number of these lyrics such as Roger Miller's "Dang Me," however. In these, being "under the influence" of liquor is seen as the cause of economic, job and family problems thus *absolving* the singer of responsibility for his actions, if not dissolving his felt guilt.

Work Freedom and Alienation. Lyrics often focus on an occupation (but never on school). Fully twenty of the 120 songs in our 1960, 1965, 1970 samples are of this sort. The cowboy, farmer, rancher, and outlaw are still idealized because of their job freedom, strength and resourcefulness. But some songs now lament the passing of their era. Truckers, taxi drivers, entertainers, and those with outdoor blue-collar jobs (such as telephone linemen) are replacing rural occupations as the heroic ideal, though their virtues are much the same.

These work songs celebrate the victory of the strong self-reliant worker over all obstacles of nature, the body, technology, and modern organization. In the stereotypic trucking song such as "Truck-drivin' Son-of-a-gun," "Blazing Smokestack," and "Big Wheels Sing For Me," for example, the driver may be described as leaving a girlfriend, driving a malfunctioning and overloaded truck too fast through an ice storm in defiance of company orders while high on pep pills in order to get home to his wife. Lowly occupations such as those of odd jobber and prostitute are glorified as being resourceful means of coping with adverse circumstances.

Factory work and mining are not glorified. They are seen as man-killing, routine, and exploitative of the working man in the long-standing folk music tradition (Joyner, 1964; Denisoff, 1971). In "Cotton Mill Man," for example, the millhand notes that he lives in a shack while the son of the mill-owner drives a big car around town. Two popular songs not in our sample best illustrate this theme. They are the mining song, "Sixteen Tons" which notes, "you load sixteen tons and what do you get?/another day older and deeper in debt," and "Detroit City" told by a homesick Southerner on an assembly-line who expresses classic job alienation and escapism (Israel, 1971): "By day I make the cars, and by night I make the bars."

Politics: Not Just On the Right. Songs with ideologically tinged lyrics which imply political or social criticism total just over 10 percent of our 120 songs from 1960–1965–1970. Such songs, however, receive a much greater amount of attention, both from the country music fans and from general commentators as well (Ackerman, 1966; Maxwell, 1967; Silber, 1967; Reagan, 1969; Reed, 1970; Dickson, 1970; Gottschalk, 1970). Songs like the super-patriotic "There's a Star Spangled Banner Waving Somewhere" (1942) or "Okie from Muskogee" (1969) continue to be remembered far more than the equally popular love songs of the same year. In order to better interpret ideologically tinged songs, a number of those beyond the ones in our sample will be considered.

Merle Haggard's "Okie from Muskogee" and his follow-up song of two-fisted patriotism, "Fighting Side of Me" have led popular commentators to see all country music as right-wing know-nothingism. But this is a simplistic interpretation of the available facts. For example, most of Haggard's songs such as his "My Momma's Hungry Eyes" recount problems of common people trying to survive with dignity in a harsh and complex society. What is more, while Haggard's "conservative" recordings were popular in 1970, Johnny Cash's "What is Truth?" a plea for tolerance of the different ways of youth, and his brother Tommy's "Six White Horses," an expression of grief over the killings of Jesus, the Kennedy Brothers, and Martin Luther King, were also high on the country music hit-tune charts. It would be more accurate to say that country music changes with the mood of the nation at large, expressing popular opinion quite accurately—if in its own terms—as can most clearly be seen in the songs dealing with war.

Country Music Goes to War.   During the patriotic World War II period, country lyrics joined the fray with gusto and some songs were tinged with "get the dirty little Jap" type of racism. Such songs include "Cowards Over Pearl Harbor," "Smoke On the Water," and "Stars and Stripes on Iwo Jima."

In the Cold War and McCarthy eras songs portrayed an apocalyptic struggle between our side and Godless Communism. Examples include "No, No, Joe (Stalin)," "The Voice of Free America," "They Locked God Outside the Iron Curtain," "The Red that We Want is the Red We've Got in the Old Red, White, and Blue." In a number of these songs of the 1950's, the atom bomb figures as an instrument of God's judgement, as in "The Great Atomic Power," and "When the Hell Bomb Falls." The Korean War was begun in the jingoistic spirit of "Korea, Here We Come," "From Mother's Arms to Korea," and "Douglas MacArthur," but the national lack of resolve was reflected in such songs as "A Heart-sick Soldier on Heartbreak Ridge." And songs about personal problems of returning home of the "will she still be waiting when I get out" and "there's a gold star in the window" variety soon came to predominate as they have at the *end* of every American war since the Revolution (Ewen, 1961).

Beginning in 1965, the Vietnam War has inspired a spate of songs representing each of the types already discussed, from "Hello Viet Nam" (1965) to "Little Johnny from Down the Street" who made the "biggest sacrifice" (1970), but few of the many "give 'em hell" or "It's for God, country and you, Ma" types have been very successful with the exception of the 1965 hit "Ballad of the Green Beret," which, while not explicitly a country music song, was played most often on country music radio stations. A number of songs written in personal terms have made it clear that the war was *not* worth while. This theme includes a letter to "Dear Uncle Sam" by Loretta Lynn who says to Uncle Sam, you didn't need my man as badly as I did; "Ruby Don't Take your Love to Town" (1969) sung by a disabled veteran, and "Congratulations, You Sure Made a Man Out of Him" (1971) sung to the United States Marine Corps by a woman about her newly returned husband who no longer prays, now drinks gin instead of root beer, is cold to the touch, doesn't play with the kids, no longer sings or laughs, and keeps things inside —like there are some things that happened in Viet Nam that he wants to hide. Songs such as "Mama, Tell Them What We're Fighting For," have defensively justified our involvement while many more have paired this sentiment with a total condemnation of war protesters, hippies, and ghetto rioters—who are characterized as the enemy within. Other songs in this vein include "The Minutemen are Turning in their Graves," "Is This War a Useless War?" "Viet Nam Blues," and "Wish You Were Here, Buddy," the latter sung by a soldier to his long-haired, war protesting high-school classmate.

These Are Not My People. A number of songs contrast Godless, unclean, foul-mouthed, dope-taking, unconventional, educated, complex, urban youths with their virtuous small town counterparts without focusing directly on the war. "Okie from Muskogee" is not only the most popular of this genre, it is also one of the least virulent. The number of these songs, together with their general lack of commercial success, suggests that the country music fans, much like the nation at large are quite divided on these issues.

Rather than seek confrontation, a number of songs strike a note of fatalism in wishing for a simpler time when heroes made issues seem clearcut. The most popular of this sort is Bill Anderson's "Where Have All Our Heroes Gone?" His heroes include General MacArthur, Roy Rogers, Charles Lindbergh, Jesse Owens,[6] John Wayne, the Kennedys, Martin Luther King, the astronauts, Joe DiMaggio, and Winston Churchill. They are characterized as "men who don't mind putting on a white hat and saying 'thank you'."

The classical American "know-nothing" urge to escape from problems by anti-intellectual retreat is most forcefully portrayed by the 1969 country hit "Sing a Song about Love." It lists numerous disasters of the sort seen on television from self-immolation and war to car wrecks and advises, "shut it off, sing a song about love," echoing the feeling of many that the war atrocities committed by American soldiers should never have been disclosed (Dickson, 1970). A similar theme is expressed in "None of My Business." After recounting problems ranging from rats on a baby's bed to a girl screaming for help, the singer concludes, "That stuff about a fellow man's fate, Lord, it's none of my business."

This Is Not My Home. Popular songs of a century ago such as "The Old Oaken Bucket," which nostalgically recall rural ways of a day gone by, can

---

[6] The inclusion of black heroes is interesting to note because a number of songs in the communal side of country music are specifically hostile to blacks (Lund, see chapter II). No songs in recent mass media-disseminated commercial country music have had anti-black lyrics and Charlie Pride, the one major black country music performer is extremely popular. Pride's acceptance may be due in large measure to down-playing his "blackness." His recordings are in the classic country mold and sung with an impeccable country accent. Interviewed the day after receiving the Country Music Entertainer of the Year award in October, 1971, he answered the question, "Do you see yourself as a leader for your race in this field?" by paraphrasing the lyric of his current hit, "No, I'm just me."

still be found in country music, but this genre is increasingly explicit in its criticism of urban ways. City life is seen as lonely, so unsafe that police cannot walk their beat, corrupting of women, materialistic, and Godless. As in Joe South's 1969 song, "Don't it Make You Wanna Go Home?" a number of songs express the wish of those on assembly lines and in office jobs to leave the big city and go back to the small town in Alabama or Oklahoma. Other songs show that it is impossible to "go home" because the old ways are being destroyed *everywhere*. Often, the federal government is seen as the agent of undesired change as in "Don't Bus Them Kids," and "Welfare Cadilac" (sic). Even the outhouse, that minor rustic symbol of self-reliance, is drawn into the polemical struggle with the Sanitation Department in the "Ode to the Little Brown Shack out Back." But even this is a losing battle, for as one song notes, "I got the Interstate running through my outhouse."

THE COUNTRY MUSIC AUDIENCE

As early as 1926 a writer asserted that country music was fast becoming the music of all America (*Radio Digest*, 1926) and this assertion has been repeated almost every year since. But, there still has been no systematic study of the country music fan. Nonetheless, it is possible to put together a composite picture from a number of special studies.

The primary source of data for the characterization which follows is the "Local Qualitative Radio: VIII" study made in 1970 by the Pulse Corporation. They report data on radio listeners, eighteen years of age or older in ten metropolitan areas distributed across the country. Using their tabulations, we have compared the characteristics of listeners to the major fulltime country music stations (at the time of the study) with the characteristics of the general radio audience in each of these ten cities. The cities studied, the country music station used, and the number of persons interviewed are shown at the top of Table 1. The responses of interviews were weighted to reflect the absolute amount of radio listening *and* the amount devoted to particular stations. So, for example, if an assembly line worker listens to station WXYZ for an hour in the morning and station WABC for two hours in the evening, one unit is placed in the WXYZ category on occupation for semi-skilled workers and two units are placed in the analogous WABC category (Pulse, 1970).

To evaluate the country music listenership we have compared the characteristics of listeners to the country music station in each city with the listeners to all stations in the metropolitan area combined. To simplify these comparisons for presentational purposes, the equal sign ($=$) is placed in each cell in which the listenership of the country music station is not 25 percent more or less than that which would be expected from the total radio listener-

MUSIC AS PROTEST

Table 1

CHARACTERISTICS OF THE COUNTRY MUSIC AUDIENCE IN TEN CITIES

Country Music City and Radio Station	Baltimore WBMD	Cincinnati WUBE	Dallas KBOX	Denver KLAK	Detroit WDEE	Fresno, Calif. KMAK	Jacksonville, Fla. WQIX	Kansas City KCKN	Minneapolis WMIN	Providence, R.I. WHIM
Audience Characteristics										
Age of Audience										
18–24	+	−	−	=	=	+	=	=	=	=
25–34	=	++	++	++	++	=	−	+	++	++
35–49	=	=	++	+	=	+	++	+	++	+
50–64	−	−	−	−−	−	−	−	−	−−	−−
65+	−	−−	−−	−−	−	−−	−	−−	−−	−−
Education										
grade school only	+	++	+	++	++	−	=	+	=	++
at least some high sch.	=	=	=	+	+	+	+	+	+	+
at least some college	−−	−−	−	−−	−−	=	−	−−	−	−−
Occupation										
professional, technical	−−	−−	−−	−−	−−	−−	−−	−−	−	−−
executive, managerial	−	−	+	−−	=	−	−−	=	−−	−−
clerical, sales	−	=	=	−	=	=	−−	−−	−	−−
semi-skilled, skilled	++	++	++	++	++	++	++	++	++	++
unskilled, service	+	+	=	+	=	=	+	++	+	++
Family Income										
less than $5,000	−−	+	−−	=	−−	−−	−	=	=	−
$5,000 to $10,000	+	=	+	+	=	+	++	+	+	=
$10,000 to $15,000	=	−−	+	+	++	+	=	=	=	=
greater than $15,000	−	−−	−	−−	−	−	−	−	−	−

Key:
The proportion of listeners to a country music station who have a particular characteristic (such as ''income less than $5,000'') is compared with the proportion of the total radio listenership in the city having that characteristic.

= means the proportion of the country music station listeners is within ± 25% of the expected.

+ means the proportion of country music station listeners is 25–50% more than expected.

++ means the proportion of country music station listeners is greater than 50% more than expected.

− means the proportion of country music station listeners is 25–50% less than expected.

−− means the proportion of country music station listeners is more than 50% less than expected.

ship. A second plus or minus sign is added if the country music listenership is more than 50 percent greater or less than would be expected from the total sample characteristics.

Age. The Pulse survey reports only the ages of women listeners, 18 or older. As Table 1 shows, the female audience for country music stations is generally concentrated in the 25- to 49-year-old range and country music is avoided by those over 50 years of age. An independent study of radio listeners in Chicago (AEB, 1971) showed that the country music station WJJD, which held nearly 5 percent of the total market, attracted only a bit over 1 percent of teenage listeners. Studies by Hall (1969) and Robinson and Hirsch [see Chapter IV] which have data for both sexes corroborate the finding that country music fans are neither old nor young, but are concentrated in the 25 to 45 middle-age range.

Race. The Pulse survey has no data on race of listeners but all observers agree that country music's audience is almost exclusively white. The small group of black country music fans found by McCarthy *et al.* (1972) were older blacks raised in the South and Southwest.

Region. The national dispersion of country music radio and TV programs, noted earlier, suggests that country music is not purely a regional music. The Country Music Association (1971a) study of country music record sales indicates that this music is still most popular in its Tennessee–Kentucky homeland but sells well in all areas except the states along the Atlantic coast. Studies of attendance in Nashville, at the Grand Ole Opry illustrate the same pattern (Wells, 1968). Fans travelled an average of 480 miles to the Opry and were much more likely to drive from the Midwest or West than to drive comparable distances from the Northeast.

City Size. The saturation of country music radio stations tends to be greater in small than in large cities, but there have been no national studies of residence patterns of country music fans. The McCarthy *et al.* (1972) study of Nashville working-class whites shows, however, that country music fans are more likely to agree with the statement that "life in a small town is better, even though there may not be as many good jobs as there are in the city."

Education. Our analysis of data from the Pulse survey of ten cities in Table 1 shows quite clearly that country music fans are less well-educated than the average radio listener. They are more likely to have completed grade school only, and much less likely to have attended college.

Occupation. Table 1 shows that country music's male fans are greatly overrepresented in the lower prestige occupations. Country music fans are nearly absent from professional occupations, and are underrepresented among executives, managers, clerical and sales personnel. They are generally overrepresented among unskilled and service workers and are *predominant* in the skilled and semi-skilled blue collar occupations. These findings closely parallel the national survey of 30,500 persons reported by Hall (1969). A majority of country music listeners are workers in skilled or semi-skilled crafts—47.1 percent as compared with 27.4 percent for total radio.

Income. Except for WUBE–Cincinnati, whose listeners have a relatively lower total family income than the rest, country music fans are concentrated in the lower half of the middle-income ranges while being underrepresented among the poor who make less than $5,000 per year and nearly absent among the well-to-do who make over $15,000. A concentration of country fans in the $5,000–$10,000 range was also found by Hall (1969). Considering the data on income together with that on occupation and education, country music fans appear to be "status inconsistent," in that they have low-education and low-prestige jobs while enjoying relatively higher incomes.

CONCLUSION: POPULISM IN RETREAT

Having shown the increasing popularity of country music, examined its lyrics, and described its fans, it remains for us to show the link between these elements. Such a venture is speculative, for no one has made a study which pinpoints why certain people like the music, but there is a suggestive correspondence between the lyrical themes in country music and the life situation experienced by most of its fans. Taking the data already reported and framing a composite, country music fans are urban-living, white adults with rural roots who are established in home, family, and job, but are content with none of these.

There is some evidence for the assertion that country music fans are discontented. McCarthy *et al.* (1972) found that work is the source of special tensions for country music fans. More often than others they agreed both that "the most important qualities of a real man are determination and ambition," and that "the best way to judge a man is by success in his work." Yet, they most often held low-prestige jobs and more often than others felt that they could not improve their jobs over the next five years. In the light of these findings, it may be that the lyrical insistence on the heroic qualities of blue-collar jobs may be an ideological assertion of working-class worth in the face of urban white-collar ways.

A person's fate is more completely under individual control in the domains of sex, family, and home and, as we have already seen, these areas are a great focus of attention in country music lyrics. Here the woman is ultimately in the stronger position within the working-class culture. She has greater control over sexual gratification and nurturance while the man is less able to provide social status and economic security which derive from the world beyond the family. Unable to keep his wife "barefoot and pregnant," in the modern urban setting, a man can show his prowess only by extra-marital adventures and drinking, which in turn threaten the stability of the home.

These things considered, it is not surprising that male country music singers cry out for a return to the idealized "good old days" when there was dignity in physical labor and the man was master of his household. It is also understandable that they heap invective on the apparent causes of their travail. Taken together, the love, work, liquor, and way-of-life themes point to a world which could be beautiful but isn't. Country music expresses a modern version of the *populist* world in which God's promise of freedom is land for the homesteader and his descendents (Hofstadter, 1955; Nugent, 1963). But the agrarian way of life is no more, few jobs are really heroic, liquor becomes a way of retreatist escape, and love more often brings new pain rather than shelter or fulfillment.[7] The music which underscores these realities might help develop revolutionary discontent (Greenway, 1953) but country music not only depicts the promise-and-denial tragedy, it also provides several means of rationalizing failure short of questioning the American dream itself.

Five sorts of accommodation can be seen in the lyrics already discussed.[8] The first is simply to verbalize the problem in hopes of thus transcending it. This tactic can be seen in the 1971 hit, "There Must Be More to Life Than Growing Old." The second accommodation identifies some malevolent force which is to blame. At the national level, such scapegoats include Communists, hippies, big cities, big government, and big business while at a personal level there are home-breaking love rivals, and the overpowering compulsions for sex, liquor, or the freedom of the road. Many of the same personal accommodations are put in yet a third way, fatalism. Here the individual rationalizes failure by appealing to common beliefs about what alcohol does, how women are, etc. or a belief that "What will be, will be." A fourth sort of accommodation suggests a flight from the world of unfulfillable responsibilities into a frontier land of freedom from social bonds of any sort—an American version of the "escapist" quest for freedom analyzed by Fromm (1941). A number of songs depict men as prisoners of the law, family, or job who have been trapped by their own desires to do right (by marrying the girl, holding the family together, keeping quiet about some heinous crime), but who wish to "fly over prison walls" and cry "release me." Epitomizing this fantasy accommodation, one man asks himself while driving to work, "left or right at Oak Street?" The one way means the routine of job, family, small town, and debts while the other means the freedoms and uncertainty of the road. The final accommodation involves perseverence. A good

---

[7] Add drugs and this same tragedy of promise and denial animates many recent films such as *Midnight Cowboy, Easy Rider, Alice's Restaurant,* and *Medium Cool* (Holton, 1970).

[8] A more detailed analysis of parallel mechanisms which help blue-collar workers rationalize their own failure short of revolution can be found in Peterson (1972).

number of country songs radiate quiet pride in "getting by," in spite of all the emotional ravages, economic privations, and moral temptations.[9] Describing himself as a loner living off the fat of "our great land," Merle Haggard concludes, "I take a lot of pride in being what I am," and Charlie Pride echoes this sentiment in his 1971 hit, "I'm Just Me."

REFERENCES

Ackerman, Paul
   1966   "The poetry and imagery of country songs." Billboard: The World of Country Music. 78, 44:14–16, 20.
American Research Bureau
   1971   "1971 ARB shares and cume ratings, Chicago metro area." New York: American Research Bureau.
Bart, Teddy
   1970   Inside Music City USA. Nashville, Tennessee: Aurora Publishers.
Belz, Carl
   1969   The Story of Rock. New York: Oxford University Press.
Billboard
   1969   "Howdy neighbor: corn country radio gets fond good-bye." April 12:27.
   1970   "Network TV boom in 1969." April 25: N-18.
   1971a   "Country radio spells national success story." October 16: CM-28-30.
   1971b   "Record and tape sales up 4% to $1.660 billion in '70," August 7:1.
Carey, James T.
   1969a   "Changing courtship patterns in the popular song." American Journal of Sociology 74:720–731.
   1969b   "The ideology of autonomy in popular lyrics: A content analysis." Psychiatry 32:150–164.
CMA
   1970a   "The growth of country music stations." Nashville, Tennessee: Country Music Association.
   1970b   "What you don't know about country music is probably costing you money." Nashville, Tennessee: Country Music Association.

---

[9] Another way of understanding the world view embedded in country music is to see how its performers are characterized by their fans. Of course, all are defined in one way or another as "country" but several distinct types emerge. There are the classic losers (Jimmy Rodgers and Hank Williams), the rakes (Jerry Lee Lewis), the reformed losers (Johnny Cash), and the bitter but resigned rebels (Merle Haggard). Beyond these are the many who have tasted fame and fortune while enduring great personal tragedy through divorce and the death of close relatives. In spite of expensive clothes, Cadillacs, and visits to the White House, they all remain models for their fans in being "just plain folks."

Coker, Wilson
1971   Music and Meaning. New York: Free Press.
Denisoff, R. Serge
1970   "The religious roots of the American song of persuasion." Western Folklore 29:175–184.
1971   Great Day Coming: Folk Music and The American Left. Urbana: University of Illinois Press.
Denisoff, R. Serge and Mark H. Levine
1971   "The one dimensional approach to popular music: A research note." Journal of Popular Culture 6:911–919.
Denzin, Norman K.
1970   "Problems in analyzing elements of mass culture: Notes on the popular song and other artistic productions." American Journal of Sociology 75:1035–1038.
Dickson, Paul
1970   "Singing to silent America." The Nation (February 23): 211–213.
DiMaggio, Paul
1971   "Content analysis of eighty country-western songs," Unpublished manuscript, Nashville, Tennessee.
Ewen, David
1961   The History of Popular Music. New York: Barnes & Noble.
Fromm, Eric
1941   Escape from Freedom. New York: Holt, Rinehart and Winston.
Gentry, Linnell
1969   A History and Encyclopedia of Country, Western and Gospel Music. Nashville, Tennessee: Clairmont.
Gottschalk, Earl C., Jr.
1970   "Love it or leave it: New patriotic music wins fans, enemies." Wall Street Journal (August 18): 1, 12.
Govoni, Albert
1970   A Boy Named Cash. New York: Lancer Books.
Green, Archie
1965   "Hillbilly music: Source and symbol." Journal of Amerian Folklore 78:204–228.
Geeenway, John
1953   American Folksongs of Protest. Philadelphia: University of Pennsylvania Press.
Grissim, John
1970   Country Music: White Man's Blues. New York: Paperback Library.
Haden, Walter D.
1970   "Vernon Dalhart: His rural roots and the start of commercial country music." Paper presented to the Association for Recorded Sound Collectors (October).
Hall, Claude
1967   "KRAK 'crakling' with success as modern country play clicks." Billboard (March 25): 34.

1969   "Country bears strongly in pulse of nation listeners" (sic). Bill-
        board (January 27): 18.
1970   "Country radio—some giant steps." Billboard (October 17):
        CM-62.
1971   "Country makes WBAP shoot to second." Billboard (January
        16): 33.
Hartford, John
1971   Word Movies. Garden City, N.Y.: Doubleday & Co.
Hemphill, Paul
1970   The Nashville Sound, Bright Lights and Country Music. New
        York: Simon and Schuster.
Hofstadter, Richard
1955   The Age of Reform. New York: Knopf.
Holtan, Orley I.
1970   "The agrarian myth in 'midnight cowboy,' 'alice's restaurant,' 'easy
        rider,' and 'medium cool.' " Journal of Popular Culture 4: 274–285.
Horton, Donald
1957   "The dialogue of courtship in popular songs." American Journal
        of Sociology 62 (May): 569–578.
Israel, Joachim
1971   Alienation: From Marx to Modern Sociology. Boston: Allyn and
        Bacon.
Joyner, Charles W.
1964   "Up in old Loray: Folkways of violence in the Gastonia strike."
        North Carolina Folklore 12 (December): 20–24.
Malone, Bill C.
1968   Country Music U.S.A. Austin: University of Texas Press.
Maxwell, Neil
1967   "The bigotry business: Racist records, books are hits in the south."
        Wall Street Journal (April 20): 1–12.
McCarthy, John D., Richard A. Peterson and William L. Yancey
1972   "Singing along with the silent majority." In George E. Lewis
        (ed.), Popular Culture Today. New York: Goodyear.
McKinnon, Dan
1967   "KSON an instant country success." Billboard (April 8): 47.
Nugent, Walter T. K.
1963   The Tolerant Populists. Chicago: University of Illinois Press.
Peterson, Richard A.
1972   The Industrial Order and Social Policy. Englewood Cliffs, N.J.:
        Prentice-Hall.
Peterson, Richard A. and David G. Berger
1971   "Entrepreneurship in organizations: Evidence from the popular
        music industry." Administrative Science Quarterly (March): 97–
        106.

Pulse
   1970   "Pulse interviewer's manual." New York: Surveys Unlimited.
Radio Digest
   1926   " 'Hill billies' capture WRC: Boys from Blue Ridge Mountains
             take Washington; open new line of American arts." (March 6):
             3–6.
Reagan, Mike
   1969   "The pious rhetoric of country music." Music Journal 27 (Jan-
             uary): 50, 67–70.
Reed, Ray
   1970   "Country music becomes concerned." New York Times. April 16.
Riesman, David
   1950   "Listening to popular music." American Quarterly 2: 359–371.
Robinson, John and Paul M. Hirsch
   1969   "It's the sound that does it." Psychology Today (October): 42–45.
Rowlett, Darrell
   1971   "Hee haw: The CBS reject that refused to die!" Country Song
             Round-up (December): 12–14.
Russell, Tony
   1970   Blacks, Whites and Blues. New York: Stein and Day.
Shaw, Arnold
   1970   The World of Soul. New York: Cowles.
Silber, Irwin
   1967   "Songs to fight a war by: A study in illusion and reality." Sing Out!
             (August): 20–25.
Soelberg, Paul W.
   1970   "Modern country radio: friend or foe?" Billboard (October 17):
             CM-44, 46.
Stambler, Irwin and Grelun Landon
   1969   Encyclopedia of Folk, Country and Western Music. New York: St.
             Martin's Press.
Sponsor
   1967   "Two country outlets in the big apple." Sponsor—The Magazine of
             Broadcast Advertising (August): 5.
Wells, Emily
   1968   "Change in country music and its listening audience." Unpublished
             manuscript, Nashville, Tennessee.

Chapter II

MUSIC IN SOCIAL MOVEMENTS

"Why should the devil have all of the good tunes?" exclaimed the founder of the Methodist church, John Wesley, when asked about his incorporation of barroom tunes in church services. For Wesley, music was the most potent weapon in the arsenal of methods used for religious conversion. Music-making, he urged, ought to have loftier purposes than just sensual entertainment.

The use of hymns based on popular tunes was pioneered by the revivalist Methodists. In time, the hymns themselves were adapted and given new lyrics by social reform and revolutionary movements. The Salvation Army, which was oriented toward the "social gospel," the Volunteers of America, and the Young Men's Christian Association (YMCA) all patterned their songs after the Methodist revivalists. In like manner, the secular Populist movement, the Grange, and other agrarian-based protestors wrote new lyrics to hymns extolling the yeoman farmer and his virtues while castigating the "demons" running the banks and railroads on Wall Street. Just as the Populists borrowed from the Revivalists, the Socialist party of America took many songs from the Populists, introducing them into urban centers where their political strength was based.

The social movement best known for its musicality was the Industrial Workers of the World (IWW) or the Wobblies. The movement song-writers such as Joe Hill, Ralph Chaplin, and others produced many parodies and agitational songs which would permeate the labor struggle of the 1930's. Nearly all of the ditties of the Wobblies, such as "Hallelujah,

I'm A Bum," ("When the Roll Is Called Up Yonder"); "Onward One Big Union," ("Onward Christian Soldiers"); "Dump the Bosses Off Your Back," ("Take It To The Lord in Prayer"); and "The Preacher and the Slave," ("In the Sweet Bye and Bye") were based on hymns. In Article 4 Richard Brazier, from his own personal experience in the movement, tells of the uses of music in the organizing drives of the Industrial Workers of the World.

The movement most influenced by the Wobbly model, yet highly innovative in its own right, was the Communist party of the United States. The Left's interest in folk music is analyzed in Article 8 by Denisoff. During the first stormy decade of its existence the Marxist-Leninist movement in America primarily sang revolutionary songs from the Soviet Union, Europe, and from the United Kingdom. The "Internationale" opened and closed Party rallies. Occasionally, several Wobbly songs were sandwiched in. In 1936, however, the Americanization phase of the Communist apparatus caused the movement to politicize various native musical genre. Traditional country and folk ballads and tunes were given lyrics condemning capitalism, and espousing "people's causes." The plight of migratory workers, Jim Crow in the South, and unionization, all were subjects for "people's singers." The advent of the cold war and McCarthyism drove the Communist party and its front groups increasingly into political isolation, and finally, in 1956, into a small political sect. As Denisoff concludes, when this genre of protest music was revived in the 1960's by Bob Dylan, Phil Ochs, Tom Paxton and others, it focused less on collective means of overthrowing the capitalist system than on vague hopes for a better day and finding personal fulfillment.

The various studies of the use of music in social movements taken together suggest that quite different social movements employ music which is comparable in many ways. Such a comparative perspective is provided by Roland Warren in his examination of the lyrical themes in the Nazi propaganda songs and those in Christian hymns. He finds that both are designed to state a problem, make an indictment, and present a collective solution which promises a glorious future—in a dramatic way—to enhance ideological commitment.

The popular image of a "protest song," especially in the folk genre, is that it is left wing; yet protest songs are far from being the exclusive property of the Left. The Radical Right has spawned a number of songs, many based on hymns and popular tunes. The Ku Klux Klan is a prime example of a conservative movement utilizing songs, most of which have been in the country music mode. Focusing less on a social movement *per se*, Jens Lund looks at the ideological elements in the country music genre not often heard outside the South. These include religious fundamentalism, anti-black racism, and right-wing superpatriotism.

The Black Freedom movement in the Southern states revived singing in American social movements in the 1960's. The Southern Christian Leadership Conference, Student Non-Violent Coordinating Committee, and other civil rights groups combined the Negro spiritual with some labor songs and produced the unifying and uplifting "freedom songs" heard on many a dusty Main Street south of the Mason–Dixon line. "We Shall Overcome," the song most associated with civil rights, represents many of the characteristics of "freedom songs." It began as a Negro spiritual and was changed into a labor song during the Depression years. In the 1950's, at Highlander Folk School, the song was adapted for the civil rights movement. This song is significant in that it brings together the entire protest song tradition in America: religion, workers' songs, and, finally, civil rights. While noting the importance of music as a part of the politically oriented freedom marches, Rochelle Larkin suggests that the soul music of Nina Simone, Ray Charles, James Brown and Sly Stone and their like have done much more to lift the racial self-consciousness and pride of blacks. Hers is one of the few analyses that views the evolution of soul music out of rhythm and blues as a kind of social movement—one which is roughly parallel to the evolution of rock, on which we focus in Chapter III.

4

THE INDUSTRIAL WORKERS OF THE WORLD'S "LITTLE RED SONGBOOK"

Richard Brazier

I first came to Spokane, from the Cobalt section of Northern Ontario, in 1907. Even before arriving there, I had learned of the I.W.W. and its songs from the Ontario miners, who had flocked to the area in and around Cobalt when large-scale deposits of cobalt and silver had been found. The I.W.W. was active in Spokane and my curiosity was aroused, for I remembered the miners' friendly comments about this organization. So I began to attend its meetings.

What first attracted me to the I.W.W. was its songs and the gusto with which its members sang them. Such singing, I thought, was good propaganda, since it had originally attracted me and many others as well; and also useful, since it held the crowd for Wobbly speakers who followed.

The I.W.W. had no official songbook at that time. All they had was a song-card—a small, four-page card brochure—which they sold for five cents a copy. It was apparently very popular, or at any rate it sold very well at all meetings I attended. The song-card contained some of the classic songs of revolt, such as "The Red Flag," "The Marseillaise," and "Hold the Fort." It also included poems: Shelley's "Men of England," and William Morris' "Hear a Word, a Word in Season," among others. From time to time a new song would come along and, after achieving popularity, would replace an older one on the song-card. As new songwriters developed among the Wobblies, the song-card became —with the exception of two or three of the old standbys—a small, nearly complete Wobbly songbook. Despite its size, this songbook blazed the trail for the larger songbook to come, a songbook of lasting fame—and one that would make the I.W.W. known in all corners of the earth.

Reprinted by permission from *Labor History* (Winter, 1968), pp. 91–104.

It became obvious that a larger and better songbook was needed for the many new songs of Wobbly songwriters, even though the song-card had always been a best seller. If enlarged to a full-size songbook priced at ten cents a copy, it was thought, it would sell even better. Much discussion took place. But nothing could then be done owing to the poor financial condition of the Spokane Branch of the I.W.W., which had been hit hard by the 1907 panic. So an enlarged songbook had to wait for a better time.

That time came nearer when J. H. Walsh blew in from Alaska. He came as a National Organizer to the Spokane Branch of the I.W.W., after Alaskan activities which included the founding of a Wobbly paper, *The Nome Industrial Worker*. After spending some time on the West Coast he came to Spokane, which would be just a stopover for him en route to the 1908 I.W.W. Convention. He was then recruiting his famous "Overall Brigade," which would (by "riding the rods") beat their way with him to the Convention. By the time Walsh returned to Spokane, where he would continue his work, the worst effects of the 1907 panic were nearly over.

This Panic came without advance warning. It was caused, some said, when Eastern bankers withdrew financial backing from railroad construction. Thousands of men who had been secure in their jobs, sure employment would last long enough for them to make a "stake," became jobless overnight. They were transformed into a penniless and homeless army, travelling in a disorderly, directionless, vain search for jobs. Most of them had been paid off in fake currency— something they called "Scrip Paper"—which neither bank nor merchant would cash (or, if they later did, it would be for a 50 percent charge).

The roads were black with jobless men. They rode the trains in such great numbers that it was impossible to "ditch" them all. They were chased and harried at every railroad stop, and in some places rounded up like cattle by mounted police and citizens, and driven away. There was no welfare in those days; only a few bread lines and soup kitchens in a few larger towns. Mostly these men had to fend for themselves, and live off the country as best they could.

The worst was over when J. H. Walsh returned from Spokane. Employment-sharks were beginning to display their job signs again, and getting ready to continue the old custom of "gypping" workers who bought their non-existing or short-lived jobs.

Having been hard hit by the Panic, Spokane's I.W.W. was not too strong at the time. But it was now beginning to build up strength, and Walsh was just the man to help get things rolling again. He saw at once that the main local issue would be the employment-shark; and never neglecting the class struggle, he made this issue the target of his heavy guns.

It did not take Walsh long to gain the membership's confidence in the ideas he advanced. We want a larger and more commodious hall, he would say, and we want it as near to the Slave Market as we can get it, as close to the workers as possible. We must not hide from the "stiffs" on some obscure side street; we are missionaries in the class war and we have a message for them; we want to deliver it. That's why we want our hall near the Slave Market, he explained; then hundreds can attend, instead of mere handfuls. We want a hall that will accommodate all our members, that will have a baggage room where the men can safely leave their bundles and other property, and that will also include a reading-room, employment office, and offices for our officials.

Walsh also favored a new and larger songbook. He visualized it as a real Wobbly creation done up in a distinctive red cover with the I.W.W. label emblazoned upon it, so that it could be recognized at a glance. We already have, he would say, our own songwriters; and others, when we get a new and larger songbook, will also send in their poems and songs. How prophetic he was! Joe Hill, Ralph Chaplin and Covington Hall were all contributing their songs to the *Little Red Songbook* within a few years and helping to make it world-famous.

Walsh also noticed how the "Starvation" (Salvation) Army and the "Vultures" (Volunteers of America) delighted in trying to break up the I.W.W. street meetings with blare of trumpet and banging of drum. He would form an I.W.W. band in order to give these organizations some competition, he declared: we have as many tunes and songs as they have hymns; and while we may borrow a hymn tune from them, we will use our own words. If they do not quiet down a little we will add some bagpipes to the band, and that will quiet them. We do not object to religious bodies, as such, but when they try to hog the streets for their own use we do object—and most vigorously so.

J. H. Walsh was one of the best street speakers I've ever heard. He could be heard even above the din of the Salvation Army's drum and trumpets, which were deliberately trying to drown him out. Yet he never shouted. He talked in an easy conversational way, as though he was speaking man to man with each individual in his audience. He knew how to handle a crowd. On at least two occasions he stilled audiences bent upon destroying the offices of employment-sharks, and led them instead to the I.W.W. hall, where he explained the uselessness of violent action. The only effective way to fight these robbers, he said, was through a union, such as the I.W.W. Mob action will get you nothing, he stated; build your union so strong that it will force the bosses to come to your Union employment office for the men they need, and make your Union card the guarantee of a job. Then clamp a tight boycott on all the employment-sharks and don't allow any workers to buy their jobs. The police and the local press freely admitted that Walsh had saved a touchy situation from turning into a violent riot.

From the very beginning, employment-sharks had planted their stooges in Walsh's audiences to ask loaded and foolish questions. Being used to heckling, he was able to put them to rout with wit and sarcasm. There was one time when an employment-shark in person ventured to cross swords with Walsh. Standing on the edge of the crowd—where a path of retreat was open—he yelled, "Mr. Speaker, when and where did you last do any work?"

> Why [said Walsh], I'm working now. Trying to show these workers what suckers they are to buy jobs from robbers like you. Later on I'll give you this soapbox and let you defend yourself and your evil practices. And I'll promise you that you will find it the hardest work you have ever done. And you have the nerve to use that honest word 'work.' You that haven't done a day's useful work since the day you were born and, on that day, your poor mother done all the labor bringing a rat like you into this world. Come on now, and take this soapbox and defend yourself. These men won't hurt you—although they have good cause to give you your lumps. They'll listen to you with attention, for they believe in free speech, even for robbers like you. They want to hear your defense of your evil practices. Come on, hop up here and let's have your story.

But seeing the crowd edge towards him, as though to force him on the soapbox, the "shark" beat it away to the accompaniment of boos. This was a favorite tactic of Walsh's: to offer hecklers the use of the soapbox to state their cases. But I never heard a single acceptance of his offer.

I have said a good deal about J. H. Walsh because he was a remarkable man in many ways. His unremitting support of the new songbook helped to make it possible; he might well be called the "Father of the *Little Red Songbook*." His idea of the format being done in such a way as to make it obvious that it was indeed a true Wobbly creation was embodied in its first edition. And shortly after he returned from Chicago the *Songbook* was nearly ready for the printers. Thus he was able to see come into being something for which he had fought.

Then, to his great satisfaction, the crusade against employment-sharks and their practices gathered momentum in his absence. Entering the fray with renewed vigor, he helped turn the spotlight of publicity upon them which, in some degree, reduced their loathsome practices.

Finally, the idea of moving to a larger hall, which he had proposed earlier, materialized before his return to Spokane. The I.W.W. was now in a fine hall—in the Slave Market section, just as Walsh desired. It was on Front Avenue—and it was ideal for I.W.W. purposes. This new hall, furthermore, had all the improvements Walsh had asked for, and it was here that the Wobblies first introduced entertainment as well as propaganda into their meetings.

After the street meetings were over, the Wobbly band would strike up a lively tune and lead the crowd into the hall. Here it would play a medley of

Wobbly and rebel tunes to which the audience would sing the words (in those days almost everyone in Spokane knew one Wobbly song or another); then a short talk or some announcements would be made. Many new songs eventually got into the *Songbook* in this way. But the original idea was to intersperse a little entertainment in order to break the monotony of long-winded speeches. It was a successful formula and drew large crowds. Walsh was one of the prime movers, but he did not, to be sure, make all these changes single-handed. He had the backing of a large and enthusiastic membership, and good teamwork all around made such changes possible.

It was in this atmosphere of growing strength that the birth of the *Little Red Songbook* took place. Now that the I.W.W. had weathered the Panic, gained in membership, and augmented its funds, it was in a position to take up the songbook issue. Although generally union sentiment favored it, there still were questions about the benefits to be expected. Some thought that the new edition would not catch on or, if it did, its popularity would not last long. They argued that people would soon tire of singing or of hearing the same songs, and also saw little propaganda value in songs or songbooks. Instead, they favored the old line doctrinaire leaflets and pamphlets as being the best form of propaganda to educate and attract new members. Besides, they feared a flop, in which case the I.W.W. would be stuck with large quantities of unsold and unsellable songbooks. Hence, they said, if the members approved, the first edition should be small—about two or three thousand copies. If it went well the order could be repeated on a larger scale. Songs could be one of the strong arms of our propaganda. The songbook's champions pointed out that workers had used songs to relate their grievances and make their demands known through all recorded history. The folklore of all lands was filled with songs of discontent; some were world-famous, like "The Marseillaise," "The Red Flag," and "Hold the Fort." The I.W.W. would be blazing a trail as the only union with its own Songs of Discontent, they argued, and other unions might follow. Songs are easily remembered but dull prose is soon forgotten, they claimed, and our aims and principles can be recorded in songs as well as in leaflets and pamphlets—in some cases even better. For songs for workers will be more apt to reach the workers than any dry-as-dust polemic. Note how to-day's popular songs sweep through the land, they declared, and how some never die. We do not know what songs our composers may write, but they will be working-class songs and perhaps one among them will be worthy to be called "Labor's Anthem." Whatever our poets may write and our minstrels sing will reach a world-wide audience. For their songs will be sung wherever there are Wobblies to sing them—and that will be everywhere.

The *Little Red Songbook* will be a distinctive creation of the I.W.W., its advocates continued. It will serve to make the I.W.W. known and to propagate its ideas and principles. Thus it will be a great propaganda medium. It is a new idea, one necessary to destroy the old myths that have enslaved us for so long. We want to rend the curtain of falsehoods that stand between the workers and truth. We think our songbook will help us in that task.

We shall run the gamut of emotions in our songs, the argument went on. We shall have songs of anger and protest, songs which shall call to judgment our oppressors and the profit system they have devised. Songs of battles won (but never any songs of despair), songs that hold up flaunted wealth and threadbare morality to scorn, songs that lampoon our masters and the parasitic vermin, such as the employment-sharks and their kind, who bedevil the workers. These songs will deal with every aspect of the workers' lives. They will bring hope to them, and courage to wage the good fight. They will be songs sowing the seeds of discontent and rebellion. We want our songs to stir the workers into action, to awaken them from an apathy and complacency that has made them accept their servitude as though it had been divinely ordained. We are sure that the power of song will exalt the spirit of Rebellion, and we want that new and better songbook. On this note the debate ended.

The General Executive Committee, after a short discussion, accepted the proposal for a new songbook. It suggested that a songbook committee, composed of two members from each of the local unions of the I.W.W. branch, be elected for the purpose of compiling the songbook's material. This committee was given full power to study ways and means of getting out the new edition. It would look over all materials proposed for the songbook—all songs, poems, ideas and suggestions—and these would be included only upon its approval. The committee also was responsible for the songbook's format. Because of the migratory work of most committee members, its personnel changed frequently. The tenure of a committee member, like his stay in town, depended upon his "stake." If it was small, then he would soon be moving along in search of a job—"beating his way" to warmer climes, generally California.

On the other hand, a Wobbly who had made a good "stake," and who liked the town, might decide to remain through the winter. In some towns men could "shack up" all year round if they wished. Spokane had such a place, the "Peaceful Valley"—where for $5 a month, one could obtain a fully equipped shack for "batching up." Four men, pooling their stakes, could live comfortably all winter and still have some of their stakes left when work began to open up in the spring, and a "road stake" was necessary.

There were, therefore, very few "Home Guards." Some, however, were on the songbook committee. They kept their stake "alive" by doing odd jobs around town and they—all old-timers—formed the committee's core. Among them were T. H. Dixon, Fred Fisher, Otto Nelson and Louis (Papa) Gatewood. Tom (Scotty) Borland and Richard Brazier were on the committee, but having submitted songs to the committee, they were not allowed to have any voice in the selection procedure. But they did vote on all other matters concerning the songbook.

Preparation of the new songbook was the work of the committee alone. No elected official of the Spokane Branch officially interfered. And, since committee members had been elected by the various local unions that made up the Spokane Branch of the I.W.W., it could be truly said that the *Little Red Songbook* was a creation of the rank and file itself. If it had not favored a new edition, it could have killed the idea, but being for it, the idea survived; and, after some forty or more editions, it is still doing quite well.

Of course branch secretary Jim Wilson, branch treasurer C. L. Filigno, and J. H. Walsh all aided with suggestions. But they were, in effect, just committee assistants who advised upon request. Walsh, for instance, offered advice which was adopted on the *Songbook's* cover; but he left the selection of the songs to the committee. He would offer no suggestions, except to say that the *Songbook,* once it is born, would transcend Spokane's boundaries. It would be seen and heard in every town and village in the land and in far-off lands; and wherever there is a Wobbly, it would go with him.

The committee had been elected in mid-December 1908, just before Walsh returned from the I.W.W. Convention with his Overall Brigade; and it began to hold meetings immediately. Its objective was to get the *Songbook* ready for the printers early in 1909.

The first order of business was the cover design. Many ideas were discussed; some were too drab, some too flamboyant, and others not colorful enough. Eventually they followed Walsh's idea of a red cover, with the I.W.W. official label emblazoned upon it, and at the top in small print would be two Wobbly slogans: the first being "An Injury to One is An Injury to all" and directly underneath, "Labor is Entitled to All It Produces." Just below would be the songbook's title: SONGS *of the Industrial Workers of the World.* Then followed the official I.W.W. label. At the bottom of the cover page was the address of the Spokane Branch of the I.W.W. The Preamble of the I.W.W. was printed on the inside page of the cover. On the outside page would be the names of all the local unions of the Spokane Branch as well as the time, place, and days of their meetings.

Selection of the songs was, of course, the hardest job. What the committee looked for—from among the forty or more songs before it—were songs written to the more popular melodies of an era of sentimental ballads and good vaudeville tunes. Many tunes were borrowed from the oldtime favorites and, with Wobbly words, became popular Wobbly songs. Some of Stephen Foster's tunes were so used. Nor did we hesitate to take over religious hymns and substitute our own words. At times we would sing note by note with the Salvation Army at our street meetings, only their words were describing Heaven above, and ours Hell right here—to the same tune.

As a matter of fact the first edition of the *Songbook* was composed largely of songs written by the local Spokane talent—in agreement with Walsh's statement: "Let the local talent pave the way." He knew that publication and wide distribution of the *Songbook* would encourage others to try writing for it, and that it would only be a short time before the *Songbook's* size would have to be enlarged. Walsh had a prophet's eye: in a year or two an influx of new song-writers began to appear, and some made the *Songbook,* and others appeared in the *Industrial Worker* and later in *Solidarity*. But the committee, at the outset, selected the best songs in the old four-paged song-cards which had been their earlier mainstay. In addition they had some twenty-two songs which were submitted by Spokane Wobblies. There were also several songs by unknown authors and, of course, most of the classical rebel songs. There were only two new songs by non-Spokane Wobblies—"Workingmen Unite" by E. S. Nelson, who wrote it to the tune of a very popular song, called "Redwing," and "The Hope of The Ages" by E. Nesbit, to a patriotic tune called "Three Cheers for the Red, White and Blue." Shelley's great poem of revolt "Men of England" was also included. Of the twenty-two songs submitted by the Spokane Wobbly songwriters, seventeen were accepted and five rejected.

The new songbook was twenty-eight to thirty pages in length, which looks small compared to the size of the *Songbook* today, some of whose editions have reached sixty-eight pages. But compared with the four-paged song-card, the songbook's predecessor, it was large indeed. Besides, it grew in size with almost every new edition, until it is now settled at about sixty-four pages.

Having completed its task of compiling the new songbook and of accepting the cover design, the committee now turned its attention to printing costs. They agreed on a first order of 10,000 copies, and a standing order of 10,000 more on demand. And by the first weeks in January 1909, the songbooks were being sold at all meetings. Members bought them in quantities—in order to take them on the jobs and, as they said, to "wise-up" the men, and to enliven dull hours of camp life.

That first order was sold out before the end of the month. But the standing order of 10,000 kept us fully replenished all the time. While Spokane's demand died down somewhat, there was always a steady and profitable demand for the *Songbook*. New members would buy it, sometimes in lots to give to friends or to men on the job; and I.W.W. unions were growing and they bought it in increasingly large lots. So the demand did not slacken at all, and the *Songbook* remained one of the best-selling pieces of I.W.W. literature.

Its amazing success was a hard blow to those who believed that the theory of industrial unionism could only be explained by pamphlet and book couched in language beyond the average workingman's comprehension. They had forgotten the little couplet that Wat Tyler's peasants used to sing: "When Adam delved and Eve span/Who was then the gentleman?" The Wobblies would express the same sentiment. They would sing: "When Adam delved and Eve span/Who then robbed the workingman?" That bit of a song stirred up a Peasants' Revolt in England. Perhaps some Wobbly song might do the same for American workers or at least bring home to them a truth they never knew.

Two committee members, both rather colorful figures, deserve special mention; one was a young Scottish lad, and the other an older veteran—a onetime Western Federation of Miners' member and now a Wobbly. "Scotty" Borland had a lot to do with popularizing many a Wobbly song. He had a naturally fine voice, and was easily the best Wobbly singer I ever heard. He would open meetings with a Wobbly song, very often a new song that had not been heard before, and also lead the mass in singing. He was a songwriter as well and one of his songs, "Unite, Unite," written to some Scottish tune, was in the *Songbook* for many editions. His career was cut short when he went to Montana, caught the tick-fever and died. I have often wondered how he would have belted out Joe Hill's and Ralph Chaplin's songs if he had only lived to sing them. He would have made their songs famous long before they became so. "Scotty" Borland was truly one of those who helped to bring the *Little Red Songbook* into existence, made its first edition a great success, and popularized many of its songs.

Louis Gatewood, called "papa" because of his age and appearance, was no singer. He was an old-time circuit rider who used to preach the Gospel to what he called the Southern "white trash." Judging by his eloquence, he must have been a real soul-stirrer in his preaching days. After circuit-riding for a time, he went West, became a miner, joined the Western Federation of Miners, became active in many of its strikes—especially those in Idaho—and underwent the horrors of the bullpen. Coming to Spokane, he had joined the I.W.W. and became one of its popular soapboxers. He had a habit of dressing up for a speech, and would wear a long-tailed coat, a vest with a gold watch and chain stretched across it, and a wide, soft hat, which made him look like the circuit rider he once was or a Kentucky Colonel. He was an eloquent extemporaneous speaker. He never sought to hide the fact that he had been a Gospel preacher in his early years. He always declared that his young years had been wasted in efforts to save the souls of the white trash, for they had neither souls to save nor brains to reason with. They were just soulless animals tied to the land and, like the Negro, exploited by the big landowners. Yet they looked down upon their colored brothers. Gatewood's mission, then, became an exercise in futility and giving it up, he got away from it all.

> Yes [he would say, opening a speech], I used to preach the
> Gospel of St. John and try to show the way to Heaven to all. I still
> preach the Gospel of St. John, only now it is the Gospel of Vincent St.

John of the I.W.W. And the heaven I want to show you the way to, is the one you will create right on this earth, just as soon as you get wise to organize together to bring it down from the sky to here where we can see it and live in it. Never mind looking upwards to the sky to find it, you'll never find it there. The only hell there is, is the one you are already in. We aim to organize all workers, not just the workers in Spokane, or in this land, but in all lands. Then we will change the hellish conditions under which we now live, so change them that, compared with the way we live now, the world then will seem like heaven itself.

When he was asked why he wore the circuit-rider's outfit just to talk to a bunch of working stiffs, he would say:

I'll tell you. This is what I call my hellfire and brimstone suit. When I was preaching to that white trash down south, I used to give them the Gospel red-hot. That was the way they wanted it. They loved to be bawled out. None of those mealy-mouthed, milk-and-water sermons for them. They wanted to hear the worst. So I gave them hellfire and brimstone, I really threw the Good Book at them—and they lapped it up. But they must have thought that my sermons cleansed them of their sins—gave them absolution, so to speak, for they became more sinful after my sermons than they were before. I give the working stiffs hellfire and brimstone in order to wake them up from their sinful ignorance, their apathy and their indifference to the necessity of organizing to fight for more of the good things of life. I'm not interested in their sins—or in religion—I'm only concerned with the fact that they are not organized to fight for better conditions, and a better way of life. Until they do wake up they will hear a lot of hellfire and brimstone in my talks.

He became a veteran of the Spokane Free Speech fight, and he served his thirty days on bread and water. Then he was re-arrested as one of the ringleaders in that fight, charged with conspiracy, and sentenced to six months in the county jail. Later he, with all the other so-called conspirators, was pardoned by the governor.

The Little Red Songbook is still in the field, bigger and better than ever, a living tribute to the committee that helped create it and to the Spokane membership who supported the original idea. It has been damned, banned, and spat upon by its enemies—yet it survives and despite parlous times for the I.W.W., it still sells well. No one knows how many copies have been sold in its fifty-six years of existence—perhaps millions; no one can say how many different songs have been carried in it, but they must run into hundreds. Many of them are still being sung. No worker, once having read it, can forget Ralph Chaplin's "Solidarity Forever." Considered by many to be America's best labor song, it has been a union marching song and is truly labor's anthem. Ralph Chaplin was essentially a poet, but the few songs he wrote were all first-class. Those in the *Songbook,* "The Commonwealth of Toil," and "May Day Song" are, together with his "Solidarity Forever," worthy of being ranked alongside the finest songs of revolt. His poems in the *Songbook,* "To Joe Hill" and "November," dedicated to Wesley Everett, are touching tributes to two of labor's martyrs. His well-known anti-war poem "The Red Feast," coupled with John F. Kendrick's "Christians at War," form one of the most slashing indictments of Christian cruelty and hypocritical morality ever penned.

It is nearly fifty years since Joe Hill was railroaded to his death before a Utah firing squad. Yet his songs still live, and some of them have become embodied in the folklore of the land. Hill is perhaps best known for "Casey Jones" and "The Preacher and the Slave." I believe it was their lilt that made these songs so popular. The coining of the "Pie in the Sky" phrase made "The Preacher and the Slave" very popular. But I would rate three others better in quality and subject than his two most popular songs: "Workers of The World Awaken," "The White Slave," which, sung to the sentimental ballad called "Meet Me Tonight in Dreamland," shows the effects of paying starvation wages to girl workers, forcing them into prostitution, and "Should I Ever Be a Soldier," which, sung to the tune of an Irish song—"Colleen Bawn" (that is little known here)—is a bitter protest against the arms race and the ever-growing power of militarism. Joe Hill, like most Wobbly troubadours, adopted popular tunes, for he had a good gift of parody and could fit words to any tune. But he also knew something of composition and did write his own words and music for a few songs—none of which, however, were as popular as those written to borrowed tunes.

Joe Hill, to be sure, was not around when the *Songbook* was first launched, but he was largely responsible for its success and expansion in size. Regarding the latter, only one other Wobbly songwriter exceeded him in the number of songs in the *Songbook,* but none exceeded him in quality.

Others also wrote real good songs: Joe Foley, with his "Are You A Wobbly?" and "Everybody's Joining It"; August Walquist's "Workingmen of The World, Unite"; Pat Brennan's "Coffee an'" and, in 1914, his "Harvest War Song." There were other one-song contributors, all of which went to prove Walsh's prediction: "Once you get this songbook launched, there will be no dearth of songwriters, and no shortage of songs." I think Walsh was right. Even in recent times "T-Bone Slim" has come through with several songs that have infused new blood into the *Songbook.*

I think *The Little Red Songbook* will live if it can supplant some of its dated songs with those written to fit the changing conditions of today. Songs dealing with automation are needed; songs that depict the problems of the unorganized workers and the submerged fifth of the nation; songs about the war on poverty and the Great Society which, I am afraid, would have to be written with cynical humor for, to the Wobblies, such ideas cannot flourish within the profit system; songs on Civil Rights, for which we fought for a half century, though in those days, we bore the cross alone.

The *Songbook* still lives, having become a repository of rebel songs of Labor and Freedom and while it does, the name of the I.W.W. will not perish from the earth.

5

THE NAZI USE OF MUSIC AS AN INSTRUMENT
OF SOCIAL CONTROL

Roland L. Warren

National Socialism as a movement has depended from the beginning on the sustained emotional appeal of a crisis psychology. Stirring speeches, repetition of emotionally toned slogans, breath-taking visual displays, mass meetings, press propaganda, and the appeal to German history, tradition, and legend have all been exploited as instruments for maintaining the necessary morale to support the movement. An important source of emotional support is also furnished by group singing, a fact which has received little attention in the United States, perhaps because group singing in this country does not play as important a role as it does in Germany.

In times of war crisis, it is true, songwriters rise to the occasion by contributing their bit to national defense. There are many significant differences, however, between the fighting songs of the United States and those of National Socialist Germany. Perhaps the greatest difference is that most of the American songs are ragtime or jazz, designed for dancing as well as singing. The National Socialist songs, on the other hand, are designed to be sung, rather than to be listened to or danced to. Many are designed to be sung without accompaniment, and resemble the simplicity of the folk song.

Further, American "morale songs" arise generally during limited emergencies. So it was with the World War I songs, most popular of which was probably George M. Cohan's "Over There," so it was with depression songs such as "Marching Along Together," and so, more recently, with the host of

Reprinted by permission of the American Psychological Association, from "German Parteilieder and Christian Hymns as Instruments of Social Control" in *Journal of Abnormal and Social Psychology,* 38 (1943), pp. 96–100.

morale songs which stemmed from the success of "God Bless America." A counterpart for "The White Cliffs of Dover" and "Remember Pearl Harbor" cannot be found in the National Socialist songs. The first is too manifestly sentimental, the second too "football-ish." "My Buddy" and "Ich hatt einen Kameraden," both popular in World War [I] days, point the contrast. The former was composed during the war, was a dance tune, and was designed to meet the current market for sentimental war numbers. The latter went back for its tune to 1825, and for its words to Ludwig Uhland, a famous German poet who composed them in 1809. It is more rigorous, and, although equally sentimental, it is almost "marchable" and tells a story.

Indeed, the National Socialist songs are more comparable to Christian church hymns than they are to American war songs. They occupy a place of permanence in the national life, they depend upon the same psychological mechanisms of mass singing, they are highly symbolic, and are inspired by a similar prerogative of eternity. The "Horst Wessel" song is in many respects more similar to "Onward, Christian Soldiers" than it is to "Marching along Together." The last-mentioned shows the characteristic football derivation of most American marching songs, while the first two have in common their broader, slower rhythm, their implications of eternity, their appeal to dead heroes, their reference to "the foe," and their urging on to victory.

The National Socialist and Christian hymns have a double purpose. Their *primary* function is to arouse the emotions of the singers to a point where they are more sensitive to the impact of the words (sermon, political address) of the speaker. But they also fulfill the *derivative* function of exercising a lasting influence over the attitude of the individual participants after they leave the group.

Interstimulation is the key process which transforms a mere group of people in close physical proximity into a crowd. Psychologists have analyzed the techniques employed by religious leaders in furthering this process. The use of symbols encrusted with emotional meaning, the performance of hallowed rituals, the group recitation of the creed, the singing of hymns—all help in the primary function of breaking down resistances which inhibit the desired responsive attitude in the members of the fold.

Seashore has emphasized the "feeling of freedom, luxury, and expanse" created by the rhythmic qualities of music, tending to neutralize inhibitions and make the individual feel "as if one could lift oneself by one's bootstraps."[1] Pratt has reported the increase in suggestibility brought about by group singing of hymns.[2] The individual, as he repeats the words borne up by the compelling

[1] Carl E. Seashore, *Psychology of Music* (New York: McGraw-Hill, 1938), p. 142.
[2] James B. Pratt, *The Religious Consciousness: A Psychological Study* (New York: Macmillan, 1921), p. 172 ff.

urge of the melody, affirms his faith, and that in a loud voice. Through singing he can say things which it would embarrass him to repeat in his more inhibited moments. And, hearing his own uninhibited confession on the lips of those surrounding him, he is led to an even deeper affirmation of faith in what he is reciting. It was this insight which led William James to speak of "faith in someone else's faith." Common affirmation of faith, supported by rhythm and melody, is an important factor in "whipping up a crowd," as any evangelist will testify.

The derivative function of hymns is that of conditioning attitudes which will remain with the individual after the group has dispersed. As such, their verbal content can be analyzed in terms of "the control of opinion by significant symbols," as Lasswell has succinctly put it;[3] and consequently many of the better known propaganda techniques apply to these hymns as well as to other instruments of controlled attitude-formation. Propaganda must be considered in its context. To be successful, it must meet the level of interests and prejudices of those whom it is to influence, as well as adjust its appeal to their degree of emotional excitement. Religious leaders have sensed this condition, as evidenced by the care which they use in selecting hymns appropriate to the main theme of the sermon or to the festival which the church is celebrating. The Nazi hymns are also selected according to the "message" to be implanted and the state to which the emotions of the singers are expected to be aroused.

A careful analysis of the hymns included in the National Socialist party songbook indicates that certain clearly discernible appeals occur with unusual frequency.[4] The appeals most frequently employed are to the following motives: loyalty, eternity, dead heroes, self-sacrifice, the leader, freedom, chief symbols, the fatherland, nearness of victory, "everybody's doing it," not too much questioning of goal, enemies, youth, and "all together in the cause." It will be shown below that the Christian church hymns are replete with substantially the same type of leading motives.

The National Socialist songs are an excellent example of the efficient adaptation of means to ends in the formation of group sentiment. This is not to imply that in every case a song fulfilling certain definite functions was made to order for the Party. Indeed, some of the songs antedate the National Socialist movement. Three generalizations would appear to be warranted, however:

[3] Harold D. Lasswell, *Propaganda Technique in the World War* (New York: Knopf, 1927), p. 9.
[4] Liederbuch der nationalsozialistischen deutschen Arbeiterpartei, herausgegeben vom Kulturamt der Reichspropagandaleitung. München: Franz Eher Nachfolger, 1939. Landsknecht and Soldier Songs have been omitted from the following analysis for two related reasons: First, most of these songs have an origin independent of the National Socialist movement, many of them antedating the first World War, and, secondly, the Party has had a particularly difficult problem in transforming the army ideologically, so that even those songs of recent origin have little direct reference to the current situation.

(1) The songs which were either "pushed" by the Party or came more naturally to popularity were those which, as a matter of fact, had high functional value in strengthening the National Socialist cause. (2) The songs which were purposely written to bolster Party solidarity employed, as a matter of fact, those techniques of appeal which were already apparent in the movement and which were potentially effective in the social milieu from which the songs arose. (3) As a result, the songs, partly by deliberation, partly by accident, became an integral part of the total propaganda effort on the home front.

Typical quotations from the party songs are given below under the heading of the leading motive of the appeal. Accompanying each set of quotations are corresponding quotations from a representative Christian hymn book.[5] The comparison serves to illustrate the similarity of appeal, and affords another interesting example of a remarkable correspondence between certain appeals used by the Church and the National Socialist Party.[6]

> *Loyalty:* (17)[7] Though all should grow disloyal, we shall still remain true. . . . Defiantly waved their flags as they lowered him into the grave, and they swore eternal loyalty for the Hitler-comrade. . . .
>
> Am I a soldier of the cross, a follower of the Lamb? And shall I fear to own His cause, or blush to speak His name? (488) I bind this day to me for ever, by power of faith, Christ's Incarnation. . . . (525)
>
> *Eternity:* (17) . . . Germany, the proud manor, carries thy countenance, carries thy spirit into all eternities. We shall hold thee, flag . . . high over death's rule into eternity.
>
> Breathe on me, Breath of God, so shall I never die; but live with Thee the perfect life of Thine eternity. (380) . . . To Him that overcometh, a crown of life shall be; He with the King of glory shall reign eternally. (538)
>
> *Dead heroes:* (15) . . . Marching on before us, with battle-scarred flags, are the dead heroes of the young nation. . . . Comrades shot by Red Front and Reaction march in spirit with us in our rows.

---

[5] A Hymnal: as authorized and approved for use by the General Convention of the Protestant Episcopal Church in the United States of America in the year of our Lord 1916. . . . (New York: Gray, 1916).

[6] In an earlier study, the writer compared fascism and the Church from the standpoint of structure and techniques of appeal. See "Fascism and the Church," *American Sociological Review,* 6 (1941), pp. 45–51.

[7] Under each topic, quotations from National Socialist songs will be given first, and underneath them quotations from Christian hymns. Seventy-six National Socialist songs were examined for this study. The number in parentheses after each topic refers to the frequency with which the topical motive is employed. The number in parentheses after the quotations from the Christian songs refers to the number of the hymn.

For all the saints, who from their labours rest, who Thee by faith before the world confessed, Thy Name, O Jesus, be for ever blessed, Alleluia. (295) The martyr first, whose eagle eye could pierce beyond the grave; who saw his Master in the sky, and called on Him to save. ... Who follows in his train? (85)

Self-sacrifice: (23) ... We are faithfully devoted to Hitler, faithful unto death. ... Heart that has loved only Germany, heart which in battle never degenerated, heart which gives itself to the people.

Fight on, my soul, till death shall bring thee to thy God. ... (118) Yea, let Thy cross be borne each day by me; mind not how heavy, if but with Thee. (163)

The leader: (18) ... we come like a storm, the *Führer* has called. Soon Hitler flags will flutter over every street, the oppression will last only a little while longer.

Jesus calls us; o'er the tumult of our life's wild restless sea, day by day His sweet voice soundeth, saying, "Christian, follow Me." (268) Jesus shall reign wher'er the sun doth his successive journeys run; His kingdom stretch from shore to shore, till moons shall wax and wane no more. (480)

Freedom:[8] (14) ... the day of freedom and bread is dawning. ... Father, in life and death help us to win freedom. ...

(Such quotations as "Lord make us free!" could be given. No word, however, seems to be the counterpart. Rather, a variety of words and ideas would correspond):

"Salvation, glory, honour!" I heard the song arise. ... (542)

Chief symbols: (40) Leader, carry the flag before us into clouds and sun. ... The flag stretched high, the rows formed close together, S.A. [Storm Troop] marches with a quiet, firm step. ...

Onward Christian soldiers, marching as to war, with the Cross of Jesus going on before. ... Forward into battle see his banners go. (530)

The fatherland: (26) ... Germany, in flowering beauty you ever rise up anew. Germany, Germany above everything, above everything in the world. ...

Jerusalem! high tower thy glorious walls. ... (543) Glorious things of thee are spoken, Sion, city of our God. ... (468)[9]

Nearness of victory: (11) Soon Hitler flags will flutter over every

---

[8] Offhand, it might be thought that the word "freedom" would be conspicuously absent from these songs. Perhaps the best hint to its meaning in the ideological context of National Socialism can be drawn from Immanuel Kant: "... therefore, a free will and a will under moral laws are one and the same thing." But in National Socialism, of course, it is Hitler, not Reason, who dictates the "moral laws."

[9] To the same tune as "Deutschland, Deutschland über alles."

street, the oppression will last only a little while longer. . . . One day shall come the day of revenge, one day we shall be free. . . .

What rush of alleluias fills all the earth and sky! What ringing of a thousand harps bespeaks the triumph nigh! (541) At last the march shall end; the wearied ones shall rest; the pilgrims find their Father's house, Jerusalem the blest. (537)

"Everybody's doing it": (6) . . . Millions are already looking to the swastika full of hope. . . . . . . no one can stand idle along the way, everyone must come along with us. . . .

Onward, then, ye people! Join our happy throng! Blend with ours your voices in the triumph song! (530) Come, labour on. Who dares stand idle on the harvest plain. . .? (497)

Not too much questioning of goal: (2) . . . and no one is here who in cowardice despairs or tiring, questions the way. . . . How stupid to ask, how small to ask why we are marching!

I do not ask to see the distant scene; one step enough for me. (244) How blest are they who have not seen and yet whose faith has constant been. . . . (555)

Enemies: (18) . . . Day and night let us guard the flag against all enemies. . . . . Judah appears, to win over the Reich. . . .

Principalities and powers, mustering their unseen array, wait for thy unguarded hours. . . . (128) Christian! dost thou see them on the holy ground, how the powers of darkness rage thy steps around? (126)

(Indeed, the Jews come in here, too, for hostile reference in one hymn): Have we no tears to shed for Him while soldiers scoff and Jews deride? (153)

Youth: (10) . . . We (youths) are the glory of our times. . . . . . We youths stride through the German land full of faith facing the sun; we are a sacred Spring. . . .

O Thou Whose feet have climbed life's hill, and trod the path of youth . . . Thy Name, proclaimed on every lip, the Master of our schools. (365) . . . In every tongue and nation she (the Church) calls her sons to pray. . . . (352)

"All together in the cause": (12) . . . Youth and aged, man for man, embrace the swastika banner. . . . Brothers of spade, desk, and hammer silently shake each other's hand.

Bright youth and snow-crowned age, strong men and maidens meek. . . . (537) Brother clasps the hand of brother, stepping fearless thro' the night. (539)[10]

---

[10] One cannot but recall a simple children's hymn in this connection, which does not limit the in-group to the Aryan race: ". . . Yellow, brown and black and white, they are precious in His sight. Jesus loves the little children one and all."

The Church hymns come closer to being the American counterpart for the Party hymns than any other group of songs in America. This is not only because they are the only sizeable body of songs built around a cause familiar to great numbers of Americans, but because they use a similar technique in their emotional appeal. The similarity can be over-emphasized, however. First, although they employ similar psychological means, their ideological ends are vastly dissimilar. Secondly, and more important for this study, they make appeals on a social psychological level which are employed to a certain degree by all social movements: The appeal to enemies to solidify the in-group, the appeal to dead heroes, the sanction of eternity, the employment of symbols, the imminence of victory as a bolster to morale,[11] the rallying around a leader, etc. Thirdly, although the theme has not been fully exploited in this paper, the Party songs, despite their employment of the sanction of eternity, emphasize deeds and this-worldliness, while the Church hymns emphasize faith and the world to come.

---

[11] Interesting was the use of this technique by Jesus in proclaiming that the kingdom of heaven was at hand. St. Paul and other enthusiasts, as is well known, took this appeal too literally, and much of St. Paul's writings can be understood only in this light.

6

FUNDAMENTALISM, RACISM, AND POLITICAL REACTION IN COUNTRY MUSIC

Jens Lund

Country music is a product of the American South, which has long been the area of the United States most supportive of political reaction. Not suprisingly, therefore, numerous examples of religious fundamentalism, racism, and right-wing political ideology can be found among the songs in the country idiom which have been recorded over the past half century. While love is the most common theme in all types of popular music, the growing popularity of country music outside the South suggests that this form of music expresses an important element in the American ethos. *Washington Post* columnist Kevin P. Phillips suggests that as youth-oriented pop music has come to express "anti-establishment" values, country music has been embraced by somewhat older and conservative "common people" from both North and South.[1] Looking behind the country songs which are now widely heard on the radio and TV, this paper examines the religious, racial, and political themes which have been expressed in country music during this century.

FUNDAMENTALISM

Much of America's rural religious tradition was established by the great religious revivals of the nineteenth century. The emphasis was upon personal salvation through an emotional conversion experience. Calvinist elitism was

---

This revised version of a paper read at the Popular Culture Association meetings, East Lansing, Mich., April 1971 was prepared especially for this book.
[1] Kevin P. Phillips, "Revolutionary Music," *The Washington Post* (May 6, 1971).

replaced by Methodist free grace, making Christian witnessing of utmost importance.[2] The camp meeting was utilized as a mass-conversion instrument. Religious singing schools taught the rudiments of harmony to the nineteenth-century Southerner through *The Sacred Harp* and its shape-note technique. The close harmony characteristic of country polyphony is a direct descendant of the shape-note tradition.[3] The Southerner inherited a vast store of hymns, particularly through the songbooks of the singing schools.

The first major challenge to fundamentalist interpretation of the Bible in the South was the famous 1925 trial of John T. Scopes for teaching evolution in the public school of Dayton, Tennessee. Scopes's trial immediately became a cause-célèbre for preachers and songwriters throughout rural America. The most popular song about this event was written by Carson Robison, recorded by Vernon Dalhart, and titled "The John T. Scopes Trial." Dalhart sang that "Mr. Scopes' house was built on sand," praising "the folks of Tennessee, they're as faithful as can be," and ending in the refrain, "the old religion's better after all!"[4] A number of other songs praised William Jennings Bryan's fatal effort on behalf of the prosecution, including Dalhart's "Bryan's Last Fight," Rev. Andrew Jenkins' "Evolution—Bryan's Last Fight," Charles Nabell's "Scope's Trial" (sic) and Charles J. Oaks's "Death of William J. Bryan," which interestingly depicted Bryan as an antagonist of "the capitalists" as well as evolution.[5] The Scopes trial found its way into other songs as well. Fiddlin' John Carson's humorous "There Ain't No Bugs On Me" stated that there "may be monkey in some of you guys, but there ain't no monkey in me."[6] Uncle Dave Macon and Sam McGhee recorded "The Bible's True" with a spoken introduction: "Now I don't believe in evolution or revolution...," and the Gentry Family's "You Can't Make A Monkey Out Of Me" debunked various scientific theories in favor of Biblical literalism.[7]

A literal interpretation of the Bible is still quite widespread in the South. A survey conducted in 1962 included the statement: "The Bible is God's word and all it says is true." Of the lower-middle-class respondents, 80 percent

    [2] Thomas R. Ford, "The Passing of Provincialism," in Thomas R. Ford (ed.), *The Southern Appalachian Region: A Survey* (Lexington, Ky.: Univ. of Kentucky Press, 1962), p. 22.
    [3] Bill C. Malone, *Country Music, U.S.A.: (A Fifty-Year History)* (Austin, Tex.: Univ. of Texas Press and the American Folklore Society, 1968), p. 16.
    [4] Marcello Truzzi, "The 100% American Songbag: Conservative Folksongs in America," *Western Folklore,* 28:1 (Jan. 1969), pp. 37–38.
    [5] Norm Cohen, "Scopes and Evolution in Hillbilly Songs," *John Edwards Memorial Foundation Quarterly,* 6:20 (Winter 1971), p. 177.
    [6] John Cohen and Mike Seeger (eds.), *The New Lost City Ramblers Songbook* (New York: Oak Publications, 1964), p. 242.
    [7] Norm Cohen, *op. cit.,* p. 179.

of the rural residents agreed, along with about 70 percent of the small-urban and metropolitan respondents. The upper-middle-class responded with 70 percent of the rural and metropolitan respondents agreeing, to 55 percent of the small urban population. Among the lower class, about 75 percent of the rural residents agreed, but about 90 percent of the metropolitanites and 98 percent of the small urbanites agreed! The comforting assurances of fundamentalism die hard.[8]

Typical of Protestant fundamentalism is an apocalyptic vision which interprets all modern misfortune as the Biblical "time of tribulation," which is supposed to precede the millenial Second Coming of Christ. Fundamentalists are fond of emphasizing the Biblical books of Daniel and Revelation and interpreting worldwide events as fulfillments of their prophecies. The Carter Family recorded a song which was a reaction to the Depression in these terms. In "No Depression In Heaven," the economic disaster is seen as a harbinger of the apocalypse. "No Depression In Heaven" offers no solution to the Depression other than, "I'm going where there's no Depression, to that Happy Land that's free from care."[9] Topical themes, often of a "doomsday" nature, continued to be used to reinforce the relevance of country gospel songs through the 'forties and 'fifties, particularly in the religious songs of the Louvin Brothers. Among their original compositions were "God's Great Atomic Power," "The Weapon Of Prayer," and "They've Got The Church Outnumbered," which deplored the fact that ballparks and theatres are more crowded than churches. Also prominent in the technique of fundamentalist interpretations of modern events were some of the songs of Roy Acuff. Acuff justifiably assailed drunken driving in "Wreck On The Highway," asking, "Did you hear anyone pray?" Acuff also used a rather farfetched metaphor in "The Automobile Of Life," suggesting letting, "Jesus take hold of the wheel, so you'll make it to Heaven on high."

The dawn of the Atomic Age reinforced apocalyptic visions among Christian fundamentalists. The Biblical idea of the world ending in fire has considerable impact in a world threatened with nuclear holocaust. The immediate postwar era also experienced a rash of sightings of unidentified flying objects— the "signs in the sky" of the Book of Revelation?[10] Twentieth-century totalitarian movements, particularly Communism, were interpreted in terms of the prophesied Antichrist. Fundamentalist views of these events were common in the country music milieu, for neither the Southern performer nor his audience was cut off from mass communication any longer. "Are you ready for God's

---

[8] Thomas R. Ford, *op. cit.*, p. 23.
[9] John Cohen and Mike Seeger (eds.), *op. cit.*, p. 261.
[10] Rev. 15:1 (authorized version).

great atomic power?," asked the Louvin Brothers; the Buchanan Brothers warned, "you'd better pray to the Lord when you see those flying saucers, it may be the coming of the Judgement Day"; Little Jimmie Dickens lamented that "They Locked God Outside The Iron Curtain"; Wayne Raney, troubled by rising crime statistics, deduced that "this world is about to go," and recommended "We Need A Lot More of Jesus (And A Lot Less Rock 'n' Roll)." Apocalyptic interpretation of current events had its musical heyday during the postwar period.

Secularization, urbanization, and political liberalism were also decried by fundamentalist songwriters. Lamenting the secularization of modern life, the Bailes Brothers' "Dust On The Bible" evoked an image of an old family Bible neglected in the living room of a modern home.[11] The U.S. Supreme Court angered many Southerners by banning prescribed prayers in the schoolroom, raising the ire of religious and political conservatives alike, and "Don't Let Them Take The Bibles From Our Schools" was associated with the movement to impeach Chief Justice Warren.[12] The musical idiom of Bluegrass, which became the "ethnic" music of the Southern migrant in the Northern city, contains a large percentage of fundamentalist gospel material.[13] According to a study by sociologist Lewis M. Killian, the urban "hillbillies" rarely attend urban churches, in spite of their strong religious backgrounds. A number of reasons are cited, including feelings of inferiority, distrust of the liberal urban churches, and the inability of the urban church to play the cohesive social role that was so much a part of rural religious life.[14] Consequently, big-city social life centered around the "hillbilly tavern," where "hillbilly" music, both live and jukebox, was played.[15] The gospel song had to fill the religious gap in this environment, replacing the "old-time" religious service for the displaced Southerner. Secular protests against urbanization are even more common, the best example being Bobby Bare's 1957 hit, "Detroit City." Most of the urban factory hands, both in the Northern Midwest and the South, were recruited from among low-income farm-dwellers,[16] who tended to think of themselves as "in," and not "of" their

[11] Bill C. Malone, op. cit., p. 271.

[12] Marcello Truzzi, op. cit., p. 27 (fn.).

[13] Russell B. Nye, The Unembarrassed Muse: The Popular Arts in America (New York: The Dial Press, 1970), pp. 346–347.

[14] Lewis M. Killian, "The Adjustment of Southern White Migrants to Northern Urban Norms," Social Forces, 32:1 (Oct. 1953), p. 68.

[15] Lewis M. Killian, loc. cit., and Albert N. Votaw, "The Hillbillies Invade Chicago," Harper's Magazine, 216:1293 (Feb. 1958), p. 65.

[16] Harold Kaufman, "Social Class in the Urban South," in Rupert B. Vance and Nicholas Demerath (eds.), The Urban South (Chapel Hill, N.C.: Univ. of North Carolina Press, 1954), p. 174.

new environment,[17] and who have consistently displayed a penchant for frequent trips back home to the South on the slightest pretext.[18] Today, even the most sophisticated "uptown" country artists are still recording songs affirming rural conservative religious practices, such as Johnny Cash's "Daddy Sang Bass (Mama Sang Tenor)," which extols the old-fashioned virtues of the family gospel-sing.

RACISM

Considering the depth and viciousness of racism in American society, it is not surprising that it is represented in America's music. Stephen Foster's happy darkies are well-known, and the minstrel show and the "coon" song did have their heyday. Yet, *The Victor Master Book (1925–1936)*, which consists of about one-quarter country material, lists fewer than ten songs with overtly racist titles, out of thousands of entries.[19]

The loss of the Civil War, the shock of Reconstruction, and the conservative Democratic restoration reinforced traditional Southern genteel conservatism, particularly with reference to the race question. The careers of the first and second Ku Klux Klan are legendary, and such venerable institutions as lynching are described in the pages of the South's leading author, William Faulkner. The Populist movement was both radical and conservative, and it used traditional musicians to draw crowds for political events. Georgia's Populist Senator Tom Watson, who was intimately connected with the lynching of Leo Frank, a Jewish factory manager, for the murder of a child, was a close friend of Fiddlin' John Carson, the first generally acknowledged country recording artist.[20] Carson also often played for Ku Klux Klan events.[21] He reportedly played, "The Christian doors of Heaven had sent Leo Frank to Hell," on the courthouse steps after the infamous lynching,[22] thereby originating the song "Little Mary Phagan" which is still encountered today by folklorists.[23] Carson is better known for his recording of the Populist anthem, "The Farmer Is

[17] Thomas Ford, *op. cit.,* p. 22.

[18] Ellen J. Stekert, "Focus For Conflict: Southern Mountain Medical Beliefs in Detroit," *Journal of American Folklore,* 83: 328 (Apr.–Jun. 1970), p. 123.

[19] Brian Rust (ed.), *The Victor Master Book, Vol. 2 (1925–1936)* (Stanhope, N.J.: Walter C. Allen, 1970).

[20] Archie Green, "Hillbilly Music: Source and Symbol," *Journal of American Folklore,* 78:309 (Jul.–Sept. 1965), p. 208.

[21] Tony Russell, *Blacks, Whites, and Blues* (New York: Stein and Day, 1970), p. 23.

[22] Mack McCormack, "The Damn Tinkers," in Chris Strachwitz (ed.), *The American Folk Music Occasional, No. 1* (Berkeley, Calif.: American Folk Music Occasional, 1964), p. 13.

[23] Marcello Truzzi, *op. cit.,* p. 27.

The Man Who Feeds Them All," a protest against middlemen and credit foreclosure.[24] The Ku Klux Klan sponsored fiddlers' conventions, including a huge one at Mountain City, Tennessee in 1925 at which the original Al Hopkins' Hill Billies ("the band that named the music") received a great deal of publicity.[25]

The problem of dealing with folksongs of the right wing has often been skirted by folklorists and "folk" enthusiasts, misled by their own romantic or ideological considerations. For instance, the ancient anti-Semitic ballad "Sir Hugh or The Jew's Daughter" (Child 155), which deals with the medieval ritual murder allegation, has been collected in the Southern United States.[26] Racism is a cultural "fact of life" in the South, particularly among poor whites, and to represent the "folk" as ideologically "pure" or class-conscious is to misrepresent the truth. Sociologist Marcello Truzzi has in several instances pointed to the heritage of right-wing folksong material only to find himself criticized by indignant letter-writers.[27] Folk music may well be "people's music," but if "the people" are reactionary, their music is bound to reflect this fact. A number of traditional Southern fiddle tunes had racist names, such as "Nigger In The Woodpile" and "Run, Nigger, Run," and traditional views of blacks existed in such folksongs as "The Henhouse Door Is Always Locked," "Nigger Be A Nigger," and "Watermelon Hanging On That Vine."

Much of the racist material in Southern tradition originated in the minstrel show and "coon" song. The big hit of the year 1900 was Ernest Hogan's "Every Race Has Its Flag But The Coon" which later found its way into tradition.[28] "The Henhouse Door Is Always Locked" and "Shanghai In China" (where "people chase a nigger just like he was a squirrel") were among the folk material recorded during the 'twenties by Doc Walsh and Garley Foster. Dr. Smith's Champion Hoss-hair Pullers had "Nigger Baby"; the Georgia Yellow Hammers and Charlie Poole's North Carolina Ramblers, "Tennessee Coon"; and Fisher Hendley, "Nigger, Will You Work?" The five-string banjo was associated with the minstrel show—indeed it is believed to have been patterned after plantation folk instruments of African origin by Joel Walker Sweeney, himself a minstrel performer during the 1850's.[29] The most

[24] Archie Green, "Politics and Country Music," lecture at the Univ. of Chicago Folk Festival, Jan. 31, 1971.

[25] Archie Green, "Hillbilly Music," p. 214.

[26] Marcello Truzzi, "Folksongs On the Right," *Sing Out!* 13:4 (Apr. 1955), pp. 51–52.

[27] Marcello Truzzi, "The 100% American Songbag," p. 33.

[28] Harriet Janis and Rudi Blesh, *They All Played Ragtime* (New York: Oak Publications, 1965), p. 100.

[29] Pete Seeger, *How To Play The Five-string Banjo* (Beacon, N.Y.: Oak Publications, 1962), pp. 68–69.

famous country performer in the minstrel tradition was Uncle Dave Macon, who performed continuously from 1917 until his death in 1953. Macon is often best remembered for his version of "Run, Nigger, Run," which is usually ignored by urban compilers of Macon anthologies.[30] This song is not really anti-black; it advises a presumably escaped slave to run before the ".patterollers" (Southern slave-catching patrol) catch him. Among Macon's more racist songs were "New Coon In Town" and "The Coon That Had A Razor." "Coon" songs and humor were often purveyed in actual blackface, as when Mainer's Mountaineers performed a skit entitled "Sambo Suing Liza For A Divorce."[31] Appearing on the Grand Ole Opry were 'Lasses White and Honey Wild, and Charles Correll and Freeman Gosden began their famous Amos 'n' Andy career on Chicago's National Barn Dance.[32] Recordings of "coon" material began to decline by the 'thirties although Bill Cox recorded "Nigger Loves A Watermelon" in 1930, and the Monroe Brothers' version of "Watermelon Hanging On That Vine" appeared in 1936. Racist songs during the 'forties were mostly anti-Oriental, their racism being secondary to a characteristic wartime nationalism.

Although racism has not been peculiar to any one region of the United States, its overt expression has occurred primarily in the South. There are a number of historical reasons for this fact, the most obvious ones being the Confederate heritage, and the residence of many more blacks in the South than in other regions. But the recording companies that made racist songs available were the major Northern firms, such as Columbia, OKeh, Victor, Vocalion. Music historian Bill Randle reports that the Columbia 15000 and OKeh 45000 series contain over 150 references to "nigger" or mentionings of black people in the pejorative. He also discovered 134 songs by Southern writers favorable to the Ku Klux Klan during the period from 1922 through 1927.[33]

Racist songs experienced a minor renascence during the 'sixties as a consequence of present-day racial tension. Such politicians as George C. Wallace, Lester Maddox, and Orval Faubus continued the tradition of using country music bands in their campaigns. The well-known country entertainers who lent their talents usually stuck strictly to conservative or pseudo-conservative expressions. An exception to the "play down the hate" theme are the recordings on the Reb Rebel label out of Crowley, Louisiana. A well-known Nashville personality, who has successfully remained anonymous under the pseudonym, "Johnny

---

[30] Mack McCormack, "The Damn Tinkers," op. cit., p. 12.

[31] Chris Strachwitz, "Mainer's Mountaineers," in Chris Strachwitz (ed.), op. cit., p. 52.

[32] Burt Goldblatt and Robert Shelton, The Country Music Story: A Picture History of Country and Western Music (Indianapolis: Bobbs-Merrill Co., 1966), p. 197.

[33] William M. Randle, History of Radio Broadcasting And Its Social And Economic Effect On The Entertainment Industry, 1920–1930 (unpublished dissertation, Western Reserve University, 1966), p. 468.

Rebel," has recorded such grotesque absurdities as "Nigger Hatin' Me," "Looking For A Handout," and "Kajun Klu Klux Klan." (sic)[34] In the minstrel black-impersonation tradition, a number of comedy narratives have been released, including "NAACP Flight No. 105" which reportedly sold a million copies and was advertised in *Billboard*.[35] The deliberate viciousness of these Southern "underground" records is often so extreme as to defy description. In spite of recent conflicts, racist records have remained relatively esoteric in appeal and circulation. They are distributed by mail-order (especially through advertisements in *The Fiery Cross,* United Klans of America's official organ), under-the-counter sales at record shops (not unlike "dirty" records), and at local general stores and truck stops run by outspoken Klan sympathizers.[36] Country and western radio stations do not play them, although less specific right-wing material is often heard on the air, including some with racist overtones, such as "Bus Them Here, Bus Them There."[37] Jukeboxes in isolated Southern towns still occasionally include a few racist songs as "novelties."[38] A recent civil rights case in Mount Airy, North Carolina involved a luncheonette where such records were used to discourage blacks from entering the premises as customers. The proprietor was ultimately enjoined by the U.S. District Court from, "playing or using any instrument, equipment or other device for the purpose of or with the effect of intimidating or discouraging Negroes. . . ."[39] Racist periodicals, such as Savannah, Georgia's *The Thunderbolt* touted the case briefly as a First Amendment issue.[40]

SUPER-PATRIOTISM

America's wars have been inspiring patriotic songs ever since the fight for independence. World War II was the country music industry's first opportunity to contribute to a "war effort." Wartime shellac-rationing did not affect country music as much as the other parts of the industry, possibly because of the average country song's staying power on the charts in comparison to

[34] Tony Russell, *loc. cit.*

[35] *Ibid.*

[36] The presence of such a store near the main entrance to the U.S. Marine Corps Base at Parris Island, S.C. has been related to me by former U.S.M.C. S./Sgt. Robert Conlin of Eagleville, Conn., who was stationed at Parris Island as a drill instructor.

[37] Marcello Truzzi, "The 100% American Songbag," p. 27.

[38] Christopher S. Wren, "Country Music: the Great White Soul Sound," *Look* 35:14 (July 13, 1971), p. 13.

[39] *U.S.A.* vs. *Wiser Lee Shaw, d/b/a Bill's Lunch,* U.S. District Court, Middle District of North Carolina C-25-WS-70 (Jan. 14, 1971), *Order,* p. 2.

[40] "Atty. Gen. Mitchell Sues To Stop White Records," *The Thunderbolt: The White Man's Viewpoint* 123 (March 1970), p. 2.

other types of music.[41] Country music was also popular among servicemen, many of whom were rural Southerners away from home for the first time. The Special Services Division of the European Theatre of Operations and the R. J. Reynolds Co.'s "Camel Caravan" purveyed "hillbilly" bands to those in uniform. Pearl Harbor spawned a rash of "Jap" songs, many of which were recorded by Carson Robison. Among them were "Remember Pearl Harbor," "Cowards Over Pearl Harbor," "We're Gonna Have To Slap That Dirty Little Jap (And Uncle Sam's The Guy Who Can Do It)," and "The Modern Cannonball." Roy Acuff also recorded "Cowards Over Pearl Harbor," and Red Foley's "Smoke On The Water" proposed making Japan a graveyard, "when our army and our navy overtake the enemy." The use of the atomic bomb was celebrated in Riley Shepard's "Atomic Power" ("Hiroshima, Nagasaki paid a great price for their sin...."), and Karl and Harty's "When The Atom Bomb Fell" ("when the smoke had cleared away, there the cruel Jap lay, the answer to our fighting boys' prayer"). Gene Autry's "Don't Bite The Hand That's Feeding You" called into question the loyalty of aliens living in the wartime United States, and Bob Wills' popular Texas Playboys recorded a number of songs about specific events in the Pacific Theatre. Typically, anti-German sentiments never flourished in songs, except those of the left, although Elton Britt's "There's A Star Spangled Banner Waving Somewhere" pleaded, "let me help to bring the Axis down a peg," and Carson Robison recorded a number of satirical "last letters" from Hitler to Hirohito and Mussolini. Britt's song may have been the most popular item, both in and out of the country idiom during the Second World War, as it was popularized by many urban recording artists as well.[42] In all, most of the country music's World War II songs dealt with homesickness and the girl left behind, rather than hatred of the enemy, and even those that were angrily militant were not particularly reactionary. They merely reflected the determined mood of a mobilized nation.

The Cold War and the Korean conflict spawned a new series of militantly nationalist country songs. For Gene Autry, the answer lay in "The Bible On The Table And The Flag Upon The Wall." Hank Williams denounced Soviet expansionism in his narrative, "No, No, Joe." Jasper Blake paraphrased the classic "Deck Of Cards" narrative with "The Red Deck Of Cards," which concerned atheistic brainwashing performed upon American prisoners-of-war. Cowboy Copas changed parts of Red Foley's "Smoke On The Water" directing it against Khrushchev and Castro instead of Hirohito. Roy Acuff's "Advice To Joe" foresaw the day "when Moscow lies in ashes," and his "Doug MacArthur" warned against those who would, "let the Communists take over all creation." Other anti-Communist songs included Jimmie Osborne's "Thank God For

[41] Bill C. Malone, op. cit., p. 101.
[42] Ibid., p. 193.

Victory In Korea," the Louvin Brothers' "From Mother's Arms To Korea," and Elton Britt's "The Red We Want Is The Red We've Got (In That Old Red, White, And Blue)."[43]

It was not until the controversial Vietnam War that country music began taking a warlike stance to the right of the nation in general. On the back of the Starday record album *Country Music Goes To War,* Don Pierce (president of Starday, Inc.) wrote, "It is significant that Country Music artists have never been identified with the so-called 'protest songs' or 'peace marches' . . . right or wrong, Country Music stands with our Country. When America goes to war— Country Music also Goes To War(sic)."[44] In a similar vein, Buck Owens' fan club magazine, *The All-American,* begins its first issue with a harangue about support for God and country, concluding with a call for "All-American music for All-Americàns."[45] Several recording companies have issued "theme" albums concerning the Vietnam War, including King's *Country Music Goes To Vietnam* performed by Charlie Moore and Bill Napier. For several weeks in 1966 S/Sgt. Barry Sadler's "Ballad Of The Green Berets" was the number-one-selling record. Although it was not particularly country-styled, it was widely played on country radio stations, and it was followed by an album by Sadler of similar material in a more country vein.

The efforts of the peace marchers must have inflamed the ire of a number of country songwriters, because many of the Vietnam War songs refer to the demonstrators, and in such terms as "cowards," "bums," "beatniks," "traitors," and "scum." Pat Boone's "Wish You Were Here, Buddy" took the form of a letter to a college-student protester with a "when I come back, I'll come a-lookin' for you." Loretta Lynn recorded "Dear Uncle Sam"; Johnny Sea's "Day for Decision" (seemingly an answer to the pacifist pop song "Eve of Destruction") warned that the demonstrations were the enemy's plan for "wearing us down." Stonewall Jackson's "The Minute Men Are Turning In Their Graves" ironically decried the lack of principle in those who would "rather go to prison than heed their country's call." In Autry Inman's "Ballad of Two Brothers," a protesting college student "sees the light" after losing his brother in Vietnam and enlists, in spite of the advice of his left-wing economics professor. Dave Dudley contributed "Tell Them What We're Fighting For" and Mother Maybelle Carter, by now performing at colleges and "Folk festivals," replied with "I Told Them What You're Fighting For." Merle Haggard's "The Fightin' Side of Me," although written during the de-escalation, was said by

    [43] *Ibid.,* p. 229fn.
    [44] Don Pierce, on liner notes to Starday 12" 33 rpm record *Country Music Goes To War* (SLP 374).
    [45] *The All-American* I (Oct. 1964), no page number.

Ernest Tubb to express "the way all of us really feel."[46] The racist Reb Rebel label also got into the act with its "Birthday Thank You Tommy From Viet Nam," to a "real 100 percent American boy," and a double-barrelled "A Victim of the Big Mess (Called the Great Society)," ostensibly the story of a black soldier ("who doesn't resent bein' called 'Nigger'") back home from Vietnam to find that "the Commies" have poisoned race relations in the South.

A number of political songs not specifically about the war have resulted from the Vietnam era's political and cultural polarization. Merle Haggard's "Okie From Muskogee" is by far the most popular of these. Beginning with "We don't smoke marijuana in Muskogee...," it strongly lambasts the most visible attributes of the present-day "youth culture," and reaffirms the superiority of small-town "square" values. During the 1968 presidential campaign, country performers lined up, to a man, for Nixon and Wallace.[47] Marty Robbins (under the pseudonym Johnny Freedom) recorded "Ain't I Right?" for the Wallace campaign. This song was directed primarily against the "suffering" caused by "outside agitators." The other side of this record was "My Native Land," which attacked the foreign aid program, another issue frequently raised by Wallace. Victor Lundberg's narrative "Open Letter to My Teenage Son" warned, "if you burn your draft-card, then burn your birth certificate at the same time, from that moment I have no son." Guy Drake's controversial "Welfare Cadilac" (sic) was directed against welfare recipients, and won the heart of President Nixon, who asked to have it performed at the White House by Johnny Cash. (Cash refused.)[46] Cash's own conciliatory "What Is Truth?" has been parodied by Ben Colder as "What Is Youth?" which advocates giving malcontents forced haircuts. Bill Anderson's "Where Have All Our Heroes Gone?" has raised a great deal of controversy within the country music right wing itself. Typically, it lambasts draft card burners, non-tax-paying "Folk" singers, and riot agitators. But among its long-gone heroes are black athlete Jesse Owens, President Kennedy, and even the late Martin Luther King, Jr.! According to *Billboard,* some parts of this song have regularly been "bleeped" out by Southern radio stations, but in spite of criticism by fans and associates, Anderson stands by the song, as is.[49] Other militantly pro-Vietnam and anti-protestor songs include Kris Kristofferson's "Vietnam Blues" (recorded by Dave Dudley), Moore and Napier's "Is This A

[46] Ernest Tubb, on National Educational Television Network program, "An Evening With Merle Haggard," Jan. 24, 1971.
[47] " 'Name' Artists Come To Aid Of the Party," *Billboard* 80 (Nov. 16, 1968), p. 38.
[48] R. Serge Denisoff, "Kent State, Muskogee, and the White House," *Broadside,* 108 (Dec. 1970), p. 2. An expanded version appears in R. Serge Denisoff, *Sing A Song of Social Significance* (Bowling Green, Ohio: Bowling Green Popular Press, 1972).
[49] "Hero-Hitting Tune Stirring Rhubarb," *Billboard* 82 (Oct. 10, 1970), p. 72.

Useless War?" and "Dear Mr. President." Harlan Howard's "Mister Professor," recorded by Leroy Van Dyke, blames atheism, draft-dodging, protest-marching, and even arson, on liberal college professors.

The acceptance of Bluegrass music by the urban "Folk" revival has caused it to be looked at askance by many people within the country music industry. According to Bill Vernon, "several prominent modern country performers have denounced Bluegrass and urged its extinction."[50] In a letter to *Bluegrass Unlimited* magazine, Don Pierce of Starday Records explained that he will no longer promote and record Bluegrass music because of its recent ties with "people of doubtful loyalty."[51] Who these people are, he does not explain, nor does he elaborate upon his criteria for determining loyalty. Ironically, Bluegrass music has also been promoted by Wallace campaigners in the South as "White Folks' Music."[52]

The popular support for Lt. William Calley which appeared after his conviction in April 1971 was immediately transformed into a country song. "The Battle Hymn of Lt. Calley," sung by Terry Nelson, was quickly released on Shelby S. Singleton's Plantation label. It reportedly broke numerous short-term sales records, but it also generated a storm of controversy.[53] Country "star" Tex Ritter petitioned Capitol Records to record his version of the song, but was overruled by the company's executives.[54] The Nelson version was originally released for jukebox-play but was later withdrawn after it reportedly caused a number of fist fights.[55] It was first played extensively, then banned on the U.S. Armed Forces Network.[56]

The racism, fundamentalism, and political reaction of country music are really quite expectable, considering its primarily working-class and rural—or rurally derived—audience. In Lipset's famous sociological study, "Working-class Authoritarianism," racial intolerance, religious chiliasm, and political misoneism

[50] Bill Vernon, "Bluegrass Stands the Test," *Billboard: The World of Country Music* 79, Section 2 (Oct. 28, 1967), p. 80.

[51] Don Pierce in "Letters," *Bluegrass Unlimited*, 2:4 (Oct. 1967), p. 3. On Bluegrass's actual relation to the "Folk revival" see Jens Lund and R. Serge Denisoff, "The Folk Music Revival and the Counter Culture: Contributions and Contradictions" (in progress).

[52] "Bluegrass is White Folks' Music," bumper-stickers distributed by mobile "Wallace for President" headquarters at Carlton Haney's Fourth Annual Blue Grass Festival, Berryville, Va., Sept. 1–3, 1968.

[53] "Calley Disk Stirs Market: Supply Runs Behind Demand," *Billboard* 83 (Apr. 24, 1971), pp. 3, 62.

[54] "Cap Nixes Disk; Seeks Not To Glorify Calley," *Billboard* 83 (Apr. 24, 1971), p. 3.

[55] Earl Paige, "Jukebox Programmers Putting 'Calley' On Request-Only Basis," *Billboard* 83 (Apr. 31, 1971), pp. 1, 36, 38.

[56] "U.S. Command in Vietnam Bars 'Battle Hymn of Calley' From Radio Network, Citing Pending Appeal," *The New York Times* (May 1, 1971), p. 4.

were found to be highest in those classes throughout the Western world.[57] In the United States, the rural and lower classes have traditionally been hotbeds of conservatism and reaction. Their music, both folk and commercial, has consistently reflected such themes. When not overtly expressed, as in the above examples, these traits have been manifested in the vocal and instrumental styles of their musical performance. Indeed, country music's distinctive "sound" reflects its conservative and discriminatory make-up, even when a given song has no overt political or religious message. Country music has thus reacted to the social changes of the twentieth century by rooting itself ever more firmly in the past. As Richard Hofstadter observed, "the development of a retrospective and nostalgic cast of mind has gone hand in hand with the slow decline of a traditional faith ... as opportunity has gone into decline, men look wistfully back toward a golden age."[58] Like it or not, country music has always reflected a part of Americans' emotions. If Americans are often bigoted, country music is often bigoted. If America looks too much to its past, so does country music. Consequently, Hofstadter's "nostalgic cast" has proved to be one of the most profitable traits of American society from the entertainment industry's point of view. The "good old days" are always marketable, whether on Currier and Ives prints or on grooved disks of celluloid, and, like a Currier and Ives print, country music presents a picture of how many people see the world.

[57] Seymour Martin Lipset, *Political Man: The Social Bases of Politics* (Garden City, N.Y.: Doubleday and Co., 1959), pp. 87–126.

[58] Richard Hofstadter, *The American Political Tradition and the Men Who Made It* (New York: Alfred A. Knopf, 1948), p. vi.

7

THE SOUL MESSAGE

Rochelle Larkin

As the condition of the black man in America has always required protest, so has his music mirrored that protest. During slavery, the call to freedom was wrapped in religious guise; the rise of the blues echoed the pangs of new problems. The protest wasn't always pointed, but it was always there. One of the most vivid and pointed of all protest songs came from the deeply emotional, divinely talented, tragic Billie Holiday. The song was written for Billie, and it was called "Strange Fruit." The strange fruit it referred to were the dead bodies of the lynched, and Billie sang it everywhere: in clubs, theaters, wherever she appeared. (Sometimes her audiences were so stoned they didn't know what she was singing; in her autobiography she tells about the woman in a nightclub who asked her to do "that sexy song about the people swinging in the trees.") But to those who listened, and most importantly, to Billie herself, the song was a very strong statement. As one who came up the hardest way possible, all her life Lady Day suffered the inequities heaped upon the outcast. Indeed, it cost her her life. If her other songs reflected her personal blues, "Strange Fruit" was her universal black blues.

In terms of the songs of its day (1939) as well as in terms of what white America was willing to hear black America say, "Strange Fruit" was far ahead of its time. Probably only Billie Holiday could have gotten away with it. (She had already been so damaged by what she had gone through, there was little else for her to lose.) It wasn't until the emergence of the civil rights movement of the early 1960's that musical protest began to be heard in any great volume.

From "The Music is the Message" in *Soul Music* by Rochelle Larkin. Copyright © 1970 by Lancer Books, Inc. (New York: 1970), pp. 166–180. Reprinted by permission of publisher.

There had been some off-handish kinds of rumbling in some of Chuck Berry's lyrics, especially "School Days," with its complaints against overcrowding, irrelevance of subject matter, and the white image of teacher (who didn't know "how mean she looks"). But this was in a musical context that kids, black and white, could dance and relate to without giving it too much thought.

The protest music of the civil rights movement, on the other hand, quite accurately mirrored that movement, both its strengths and weaknesses. As noted before, most of the "freedom songs" were church songs that usually dated back to slavery days. They were valid enough, but scarcely what you would consider dynamic new forms. And much of the new stuff was being done by folksingers, mostly white, mostly sincere, mostly young. The sight of a girl, on vacation from an exclusive eastern college, perched on a stool in a Greenwich Village coffee house, singing about the "Chain gang-*uh*" (even with the emphasis on the work syllable "uh") is scarcely the sort of thing to bring down the bastions of bigotry.

There were some strong, black voices being raised against injustice, notably Odetta's and Harry Belafonte's, but they too were in the folk bag, a musical expression of limited effect in the black communities. It remained for the time of affirmation, the day of "Black is Beautiful," for a popular music proclaiming that fact to win the hearts and the ears of the people. The new anthem for black people was James Brown's "Say It Loud—I'm Black and I'm Proud." (By 1969 the Catholics of Northern Ireland did their own bloody cover on "We Shall Overcome," which no longer was a contender on the musical or political charts of black people.)

Other singers had been voicing protest and identity before "Say It Loud," but the floodgates of popularity had never before been opened wide enough to admit a broad-based acceptance of commercial importance. For instance, few people ever heard of "Mississippi Goddam," although most of the public was familiar with the name, at least, of Nina Simone, its composer and singer. Even those familiar with her work never quite knew how to classify her. Folk singer, jazz singer, blues singer, pop singer? Her range of material and complete command of any musical idiom made it impossible to cubbyhole her. A country that likes all its products, including human beings, neatly packaged and labeled couldn't find a single musical shelf broad enough to contain Nina Simone. She was idolized by a small coterie of knowledgeables, hip to her undeniable talent; her records sold and her appearances were well attended. All along, her mixed bag included songs of more than personal meaning. She was one of the very few who could do a new reading of "Strange Fruit" and make it happen all over again; make it as devastating in its way as Billie's original had been.

Then, Martin Luther King, Jr. was assassinated, and not even trying to hide her bitterness, Nina Simone asked, "Why? (The King of Love is Dead)." That question reverberated throughout the country.

As her public grew, and listened, and learned, Nina Simone became the voice of the black revolution. Nobody else could provide as encompassing a musical backbone. She wrote and sang of "Revolution," where once it had been "Backlash Blues" that occupied her mind; and the "Four Women" who previously had symbolized for her the conditions forced upon black women gave way to the "Young, Gifted, and Black," who had, after all, had the most to learn from Nina Simone. Her person and voice were as black and beautiful as anyone could wish. Her message was as fiery and outspoken as anything that could be heard argued on a ghetto streetcorner. Her artistry was as great as a people drenching themselves in the floodwaters of a found identity could wish one of their own to be. After years of other-imposed twilight, the sun was shining, and Nina Simone was high noon.

Born Eunice Waymon in a little town called Tryon in North Carolina, she became Nina Simone when she took her first job singing in a night-club. Her parents were church-connected (naturally!), and she didn't want to associate the family name with the booze-blues-dues atmosphere of her new way of livelihood. That wasn't the only change that occurred the eventful evening she reported to work at an Atlantic City nightspot; the manager informed her that she was expected to sing, and all of her training had been as a pianist. Once again, we owe three hosannas and a hallellujah to the splendors of that old-time religion and the choirs it trained. Nina, née Eunice, didn't have just another job. The conservatory-trained piano teacher had a whole new career. And the world was soon to have a major new artist to touch first its heart, then its mind and, ultimately, its soul. For Nina has been aptly titled the "High Priestess of Soul," and her music transcends any barriers or limitations that other artists or the public may place on this art. Her voice soars as her spirit soars, and her ideal of soul is as pure and strong as any. She is a culmination of all black music, and possesses a good deal of black magic as well; (anyone who has seen her spellbinding performance can attest to this). But magic comes naturally to a high priestess-conjurer anyway, and Nina Simone is all of that and more. She carries her celebration as a right and a challenge, and she ain't about to lay that burden down. No other artist comes to mind from whom we can expect more exciting and important work in years to come.

We have already talked about James Brown, our Soul Brother Number One and the validity of that designation for him; however, it's impossible to discuss R & B [rhythm and blues] with social content without mentioning the enormous part he has played in tuning in great masses of listeners to songs that have something to say. If he hadn't proven that such material could and would sell, the "money changers" of the music business would not have let other artists record significant songs. The recording industry depends on mimicry for much of its success; the ability to spot a trend and latch onto it quickly counts much more by far than, say, the ability to read music or recognize talent. (These assets are at most "sometime" things.) If J. B. hadn't told (and sold!) the kids "Don't Be a Drop Out," they never would have let Sly Stone tell them simply to "Stand."

But tell them he did, and in this and other songs lies the heart of what may well be the most dynamic group in popular music today, Sly and the Family Stone. No one can touch them, but they have touched not only the young audience in this country, but other performers as well. The organization and instrumentation of the seven-member Family is as original and complex as is its sound. Members cross all lines of color and gender: Cynthia Robinson plays trumpet, Freddie Stone is lead guitar, Larry Graham is on bass, Jerry Martini is saxophonist, Gregg Errico is drummer, Rosie Stone, in a blond Shirley Temple wig, plays electric piano, and Sly's orgiastic organing charges the whole congregation. Lyrically as well as musically, it is the most sophisticated sound being pounded out by any group today. What makes it all so wonderful is that, in all its sweet complexity, it is grasped and appreciated by an audience of, in Sly's own words, "everyday people." The group doesn't cater to the jaded tastes that require sophistication for their entertainment. The art of the Stone is as broad as it is deep. "Stand" implored its listeners to do just that: "Stand/You've been sitting much too long . . . "

"Stand," Sly insists, "They will try to make you crawl"; in so insisting, he sold well over a million records; a million everyday-people bought that tune. That so strong a fusion of music and message as the Stone belt out is so damned attractive to so many people is enough to make you start believing in something again.

That Sly Stone believes in something is obvious from talking to him. The something is dual: people and music. What Sly wants to achieve, and has achieved, is peoples' music. He explains it this way:

> I want everybody to understand my songs. I want even dummies to understand so they won't be dumb anymore. And you got to talk to them in a way that they can understand. And those people that get bugged by being talked to loud, then you've got to talk soft; if you can still tell the truth and talk soft.

He has always been involved with music; his churchy beginnings go back to age four. While still in his teens, he was a top-rate disc jockey in his native San Francisco. He was already producing and writing (remember Bobby Freeman and "The Swim"?), and more than anything else, wanted to form his own group, a group that would be able to give full expression to the songs and sounds that Sly Stone was already hearing in his head. (A member of the group says that Sly always has at least fifty tunes in his wig that nobody else has heard. That's why they never run out of material.) Sly put a group together, but they weren't marching to his drummer and he disbanded that first band; his second attempt resulted in the Stone exactly as it stands today. At that time, 1966, Sly was twenty-two.

It has been a steady climb since then. The only time the group was inactive was when Cynthia Robinson was seriously ill and Sly cancelled all engagements. One of his firmest rules is that when the sign says Sly and the Family Stone, that's exactly who you're going to see. Sly accepts no substitutes, and he doesn't expect his audience to either. This is one group that has integrity, not just integration. Too, their sound is so tight, so stringently worked out, so unified, there is no way to shuffle pieces and still achieve exactly what the perfectionist Sly demands. He feels that there has been an evolution of his music and of his group; they aren't just a bunch of musicians out there gigging. Each set they play is a statement and a declaration.

He started with music for the body to groove to. The swim was a big dance craze, "Dance to the Music" a big Sly hit. This in turn led to music to turn minds on ("Life," with its admonition, "You don't have to die before you live," "Don't Call Me Nigger, Whitey," and "Jane is a Groupee," with its cutting indictment of a segment of the audience). The messages were strong, but simply stated, and wedded to irresistable music. Depending on the type of hall, the music could mesmerize the audience, set it dancing (or at least swaying, given the packed conditions of a sell-out concert). Sly is concerned with personal freedom, as in "You Can Make It if You Try." "Stand" is a call with broad social implications. He has run the gamut of subject matter from the personal to the cosmic; his keen ability to see the smaller concern within the context of the larger and illuminate both without ever talking down to his audience is his greatest gift. Couple this with his fantastic musicality, and his complete grasp of the dynamics of performing, and the $250,000 worth of electrical equipment he has towering onstage seems superfluous. But as Sly himself said, can you still talk soft when you're telling the truth. If he feels that all that hardware is necessary, then so be it. (It forms the damnedest background for his free-free-free group. There they are, dressed in the most extraordinary clothes, beaded, feathered, fringed, furred to a fare-thee-well, and there, lurking behind them are absolute mountains of grey steel that look like King Kong's file cabinets. Cold, mechanical, IBM-looking things that are inhuman, and would seem to negate the life and life-style that Sly sings of and seems to embody. Well, if that's what he needs to get the music out, it must be okay; but maybe the girls could hang flowers or drape chiffon or do *something* to the machinery to get that death-pallor, insurance company look, off the stage.) That's really the only nit I have to pick with this group; its fantastically talented leader is

certainly going to keep it at the forefront of everything that is musically important for years to come.

Sly's influence is not confined to the Family Stone. He has strengthened
the commitment of other musicians; given them confidence to say and sing what
was really on their minds. My soul stirrer has taught me that you can take the
boy out of the ghetto, but you can't take the ghetto out of the boy. Indeed, it
is one of the great strengths of R & B that it has always stayed as attuned to the
people as the people are tuned to it. No matter how successful and rich a singer
becomes, he cannot forget his roots. No matter how green the money, the skin
stays black. Or as James Brown put it on one occasion, "Money Won't Change
You But Time Will Find You Out." (How does he know *everything*?) Thus,
singers who had stayed on a safe, comfortable, "I-want-my-baby-back" niche
strayed to thoughts of where the problems were really at. The Temptations could
leave that smooth "middle-of-the-road" Motown route, take off on "Cloud
Nine," that junkie's dream, and without ever mentioning "drugs" in the lyric,
touch every nerve in the ghetto. They could then follow with "Message From
a Black Man," "Slave," and others.

A careful examination of the repertoire of the most respected and important
names in R & B will show that awareness of the problems afflicting the people
was always there, and found its way into musical expression; before, however,
this expression was not always as explicit as a Sly Stone song.

Ray Charles did it, when he sang the sharecropper's lament, "Busted,"
which depicted the travails of those who work so hard for so little. Aretha
Franklin did it, when she wrote one of the best double-meaning songs of all
times, "Think." Taken on one level of meaning, it can be just another lover's
lament, with a very powerful beat. But a closer listening to Aretha's inspired
interpretation reveals that she is addressing herself to anyone who has been
putting her down, since she was, according to the lyric, about ten years old.
This was probably the age Aretha awakened to the fact that she was "different"
from many of the other kids she knew. A rude awakening it must have been
too, considering the cruelty of children. It was strong enough to survive in her
memory and appear as a deeply moving song.

Those Motown mainstays, the Supremes, did it with two brilliant tunes
of the Diana Ross era, "Love Child" and "I'm Livin' in Shame." The former
was the plea of a girl who was an illegitimate child to her boyfriend to understand why she wouldn't risk raising a child under the same conditions. The
second tune is a perfect delineation of a member of the "Black Bourgeoisie," a
young girl who goes to college, marries well, and completely turns away from
her background and a mother who wore rags and scrubbed floors in order to
put her through school. It is so accurate an indictment that a sociologist would
need a volume to get across what the composer got across in the sixty-four bars

of an R & B song. It's dangerously close to poetry, an art form that says much in few words. Rock is the living literature of an oppressed people; a poetry with its own music, an art form which must be judged by its own standards.

Classically (European) trained musicians and critics could not understand or evaluate jazz because its source was different from the solely-European based music they knew. A musician who could interpret the profoundest ideas of Bach would be completely helpless in doing the sort of improvisation that any jazzman worthy of the name did. Blue notes sounded flat and foreign to them, and so they scorned the possibility of jazz being art. Yet, those who live outside the experience that produced both R & B and jazz have neither the right nor the way to judge these art forms. The oppressor cannot understand the art of the oppressed; unless he can stop being an oppressor and learn to understand the testimony of those he has been tyrannizing. (The drawings of the concentration camp survivors would have seemed like meaningless scratchings of demented children to their former captors, the "elite" SS guards.) And when a classical performer (like Jose Iturbi) would, in a rare instance, tackle jazz, it sounded like a bad joke.

R & B, as an art, has already produced some major and minor masterpieces. What must be remembered is that although its origins can be traced to antiquity (in fact farther back in time than the European tradition), its present form has been around for only a few decades. To date it precisely is almost impossible; as any art, it is a constantly growing, developing, changing form. Sometimes long buried, forgotten pieces come forth and seem as fresh and new as the latest flowerings of the branches of the soul tree. (African sculpture was also scorned and forgotten for centuries till Picasso and the post-Impressionist painters "discovered" it and were deeply influenced by it in the early 1900's.)

An art object, be it music, painting, or drama, may be so-called primitive in form, and yet be very profound in its interpretation of human emotion, and capable of creating a very immediate reaction on the viewer or listener. The "primitiveness" may enhance the intrinsic value of the object; it may even, when our eyes and ears have become educated, be found to possess a sophistication far beyond our own. It is this open-mindedness that is essential if we are to enjoy and understand the art or thought of other peoples. (Back to Picasso for a moment: when a viewer announced that he didn't understand the master's paintings, Pablo retorted, "I myself do not understand a single word of Greek. Should I suggest that all the books in Greek be destroyed?" 'nuff said.)

The R & B tradition draws heavily on its African traditions in ways that even its practitioners may not be consciously aware of. African literature, folklore, and mythology were not written art. They were spoken and sung, played and danced. European culture, which leans so heavily on the use of pen and pencil when dealing with everything from art to arithmetic, conquered a continent that knew no books. Close-mouthed, thin-lipped, the Europeans could not evaluate a living tradition that had passed intact from father to son over the centuries. They put the value of a written culture above an oral one; this assured them of their own superiority. With a book in one hand (the Bible, which is not European, but originated in Asia Minor), and a gun in the other (gunpowder also did not come from Europe, but from China), they robbed, divided, enslaved, and killed, all in the name of a man-made, not a God-given, superiority. (That crazy idea has survived to this day.)

Dismissing all prejudiced judgments, it is enough to say that R & B today has not broken with its ancient traditions, even as it has expanded into a form and content that were undreamt of by the ancestors. Continuity on the one hand, and viability on the other, are both necessary requirements of any art. Another necessity of an art form is an audience. The old-timey arguments about art for art's sake are of no interest to anyone anymore; dusty and dated, they serve no purpose here or anywhere else. And no art being practised today is closer or more meaningful to its audience than is R & B.

Books by black writers are not, for the most part, massively read by black people. This is true especially of fiction, where black writers have yet to give us great works that mirror the lives of the people. (After forty years, Claude McKay's novel, "Home to Harlem" is still the best book on the life in that community.) Black drama, when it is found, is most often to be found along the theater belt traveled mostly by white liberal ticket-buyers; relatively few blacks can afford the prices. Ghetto-based theaters have not had a continuous existence. They too have not mirrored the lives of the "people" to merit broad-based support. The reasons for these and other failures of the "arts" are analyzed in great detail in . . . *The Crisis of the Negro Intellectual,* by Harold Cruse (New York: Morrow, 1967). Interestingly, in all its massive detail and information, this almost six-hundred-page book makes no mention of anyone in R & B, except that the name of Nina Simone appears on a list with no comment of any kind. Perhaps this points up the first fact of the intellectuals' problem: failure to stay close to the people and *their art.* Only now are black writers beginning to discuss the R & Beautiful people; the only exception has been LeRoi Jones, who has a great affinity for *all* black music and writes about it beautifully and brilliantly. Initially a lover of jazz and historian of blues, he recognizes the value and vitality inherent in R & B that might be beneath the notice of a more narrow-minded critic. No one can fault his ears, or his endeavors as a dramatist bringing theater right into the community. His book, *Blues People* (published by Morrow), is the best and most readable account of the history of black music in America.

Movies and television as media of black art simply do not exist. In movies, there has been one very conspicuous development: Sidney Poitier; damn little else. But a performer, even a good one, doing the work of white writers, directors, producers, cameramen, and owners can scarcely create a black art form. Television's most notable breakthrough to date has been an educational program for preschool children called Sesame Street. It uses many black talents well; but, this is education, and not art.

What then is it we hear, pouring out of window radios and record shops all over the ghetto? Whose latest performance is being lauded and analyzed on all the street corners, in the bars and barbershops, in the schoolyards and at parties; in short, wherever people gather? It is the art of the singer and the song, who together are telling it like it is; who are commiserating and communicating; celebrating and vindicating the sweet-and-sour mysteries of life. One with their Afro ancestors, the singers tell their tales not in the empty vapidity of lined-up prose, but with much clapping of hands, beating of drums, and moving of feet; testifying as the preachers still do, with the wailing, sighing, shrieking affirmation of the congregation-chorus; invoking in the listener a want to weep, a need to sing, a desire to dance. The artist who works his rootsy, bluesy, mojo magic on the heart of the listener is perhaps the most important artist of all, for he speaks to us and he speaks to today. Not for him the musty museums, a Sunday showcase, or the silence of centuries before he will be heard. He is now.

That nowness is perhaps the greatest strength of this art form. When church and field were the only workshops of song, the gospel grew and the work shout flourished. As black people moved out of the South, the blues went with them. To the promised land came men of musical promise and jazz began. All through the long struggle, there was song to help sustain the spirits of a put-upon people. Dinah Washington cried out against "This Bitter Earth." Sam Cooke knew that "A Change is Gonna Come," and Otis Redding demanded "Respect." These three are gone but their messages are still thrillingly clear. They each had the ability to sing of personal trials, and at the same time, express a universal message that became a haunting search for freedom, understanding, and the recognition of a hard-won dignity. This quality of the personal-made-universal is another important aspect of art, and one that exists in abundance in R & B.

This is not to say that every song that hits the R & B charts is a real or potential work of art. Far from it. That would be tantamount to saying that great paintings are created every time a brush and oils hit canvas. But R & B is an art form by every criterion supplied by those who measure such things for the benefit of the rest of us. Although we might accept their vocabulary in defining our art, it is the standards of the community from which the music comes that are to be applied in judging the art itself. For far too long, white standards have been used against black art forms; the word "against" is precisely the right one, because the result has too often been total negation of black art. The society whose standards can tolerate the ineptness of a Leslie Uggams on a weekly basis but needs to space out visits by Aretha Franklin to a twice-a-year thing is obviously not one whose judgment can be relied upon. Nor have its faculties been sharpened by the hardness of ghetto life to provide a critical ability precise enough to appraise R & B.

As the day of the white hunter in Africa is quickly fading, and white mastery of the continent is shrinking, the white "expert" of black art in America is fast passing away. This "white" expert often has black skin. See Franz Fanon, *Black Skin, White Masks* (New York: Grove Press, 1967). In the past, this "expert's" job has been to analyze all things black and explain black people to white people, and to black people themselves. However, a writer like Nat Hentoff will continue to be respected in both communities because he has impeccable credentials, hard won, and he is worth listening to. There aren't many others. The younger black critics and writers who have come along since LeRoi Jones, men like A. B. Spellman, Carman Moore, Charles Wright, and others will help to develop the necessary new critiques, standards, and vocabularies for writing about R & B. There will be mistakes (e.g., the writer who interpreted Martha Reeves and the Vandellas' "Dancing in the Streets" as a call to urban rioting), as with anything new, but at least they will be honest mistakes and not mistakes inspired by the churlish negation or, equally bad, the mindless and patronizing adoration that has been true in the past.

As the audience also grows in education and cultural maturity, it will make more discriminating demands on the music, and art and audience will reinforce each other. The artist who falls behind his audience is always in big trouble, never more so than now with the "Black-is-Beautiful" generation. No amount of hype in the world is going to be able to buy these kids; the artists and their labels had better get hip to that, and quick. These kids have changed and are changing the image of the black man in America. Dig this: the only multiple murder of unknown innocents by a demented black killer took place not long ago on a Pennsylvania highway. (This sort of crime is not the usual black style.) The assailant turned out to be the son of the old movie stereotype, Stepin Fetchit. The new generation simply cannot live with that image, although the forms of dissociation are not always that extreme. But it is a case in point, and a strong enough one to stick in the memory and jab the consciousness. "Is he down?" you'll hear kids asking each other, "is he for real?"

The artists who survive and flourish under the demanding conditions that the new generations will impose will probably fall into four non-rigid and often overlapping types. First, the undeniable talents, those whose gifts are unmistakeable, the Dionne Warwicks, Ray Charleses, Aretha Franklins. Second, those who, with searing truth of vision, testify about the experience of black America:

artists like B. B. King, John Lee Hooker, and the great gospel voices. Third, those who have something new to say, and dynamic ways of saying it: Nina Simone, Sly Stone, Taj Mahal. The fourth group will embody artists who are so uniquely representative of the voices and emotions of the community that they will always stand at its heart. Such ones today are James Brown and Tina Turner. The names cited are but a very few who qualify; of course there are many others.

As to the music itself, the trend towards more meaningful songs is undeniable. On a given week in early 1970 (according to *Record World,* January 24, 1970), soul music's top 50 hits included the following which can clearly be classified as music with a message: "Everybody Is a Star," "Thank You," by Sly and the Family Stone; "Is It Because I'm Black?" by Syl Johnson; "To Be Young, Gifted, and Black," by Nina Simone; "Message From a Black Man," the Whatnauts; "Compared to What," by Les McCann and Eddie Harris. (This last is a top-notch jazz composition, as are two other chart items, "Electric Surfboard," by Brother Jack MacDuff and "Preacher Man," by Cannonball Adderley.) Then, there are two James Brown tunes back-to-back, and two blues greats, B. B. King and Bobby Bland. There are two entries by the perennial, ultimate soul exponents, Ike and Tina Turner; two supergroups, Supremes and Temptations, with superlative songs. Eight more spots are occupied by some of the top male vocalists in popular music: Wilson Picket, Walter Jackson, Brook Benton, Joe Simon, David Ruffin, Jerry Butler, Johnnie Taylor, and Marvin Gaye. This accounts for almost half of the chart action, and there are also contributions from such outstanding performers as the Miracles, Sweet Inspirations, Mary Wells, the Dells, Jr. Walker, and others.

As an interesting corollary, it might be noted that of the 50 tunes on the R & B chart, 30 are on the 100-top-hits pop chart for the same week, and together with four other sides that have already moved off the R & B list, comprise one-third of all the pop tunes. This is a pretty good gauge of the importance of soul music on the entire pop scene.

Should one examine the R & B charts of all of 1960, just ten years earlier, the enormous progress that soul music has made in the past decade is very apparent. Sam Cooke and Dinah Washington were doing "Chain Gang" and "This Bitter Earth," respectively; those were the only two songs that had a serious lyric content. There are no titles that contained the words "black," or "soul," or even "funky." The greatest significance of the R & B hits of 1960 lies in the performers themselves. In addition to those two departed artists mentioned above, some artists who appear on the 'seventies chart had already established their importance in the 'sixties. For example, Brook Benton, Ike and Tina Turner, Jerry Butler, the Miracles, and B B. King have never stopped happening. That's a pretty good record of longevity for the area of popular music which is notorious for its one-hit performers and rapid change in taste and fads. The singer, not the song, seems to be the message here.

Besides the songs mentioned, 1960 and 1970 both had excellent entries that were never intended by their creators or performers to do anything other than entertain. In terms of art, it is probably too early to attempt an evaluation of those songs; however, it should be remembered that much of what is considered serious and almost sacred art today was originally meant merely to entertain. (The works of painters like Daumier and Rowlandson were classed as cartoons when they first appeared. The posters of Toulouse-Lautrec weren't even designed to entertain; they just told the public where the entertainment was being held. Have you tried to buy an original Lautrec lately?) We can let the future determine the value of such songs as "The Twist," by Chubby Checker, which highlighted the year of 1960, and "Georgia On My Mind," by Ray Charles, the big hit of that year. It is especially fascinating to conjecture how fate will handle the Genius in years to come. Or vice versa.

It has been suggested by a critic that the dominance of European music has passed its apex, and that the new influence will come from Africa. This idea was mentioned in connection with "serious" music, not popular music. The international acceptance of R & B was merely mentioned to bolster the idea. But instead of putting down pop music simply because it is pop, the reverse approach should be taken. Soul music is the sound of today; it does reach out and touch more people than any other music being played today. Its use is so widespread as to be all but immeasurable. Television commercials rock along to the strains of R & B to sell us everything. (Schaeffer Beer in New York is especially hip to soul music; they even sponsor contests to discover new talent, which they then hire to get the message across. And it swings!)

The musical comedy of Broadway, which white middlebrow critics like to think is America's main thrust at culture, was long immune to soul music. A musical educator produced a complex diagram showing the points of African and European influences on various stages and phases of American music; Broadway was the point furthest of all from Africa on this musical map. This was changed for all time with the production of *Hair*. After decades of dominating popular music in America, the musical theater went into a decline as far as its influence on hits is concerned. (Before, the "standards" of the ballad singers and even many of the greatest jazz works came originally from the Broadway scores.) While rock and R & B were on the rise during the 'fifties, not one Broadway tune became a number one song. Even shows purporting to be as contemporary as *West Side Story* and *Bye Bye Birdie* (with its rock idol hero) didn't make it. But *Hair,* with its hippie-type cast, its mixture of black and white youngsters, its parodies of 1950's R & B hits,

its take-off on the Motown product, its use of current soul stirrings, made it; and made it big. It became a million-seller album, and at least three of its songs have hit the number one spot so far. The best of these hits is the rollicking "Age of Aquarius," as done by the Fifth Dimension. Broadway will never be the same, thank God.

And so the soul goes on and on. Here and abroad, R & B artists and their music play all the best clubs and concert halls. College audiences demand the sound. Television has had to bring back black artists into the nation's homes with a now taken-for-granted frequency.

There are no limits to the talents who create soul music. Soul will no doubt go on to conquer whatever portions of the globe it hasn't conquered already. While many classics of this most unclassic art have already been produced, the best is certainly yet to come. And come it will, its blues and gospel and shout reworked to today's themes; its rhythms and beats turning on today's needs; its finger-poppin', foot-stompin', knee-slappin', hand-clappin' sound will go on, and on. And so on and so on and scooby dooby doo-bee.

8

FOLK MUSIC AND THE AMERICAN LEFT

R. Serge Denisoff

Andre Malraux once wrote: "Folk art no longer exists because 'the folk' no longer exists." Despite Malraux and critical observers of the so-called urban folk movement such as Wilgus and Stekert (who adhere to the traditional criteria of Redfield) concert posters and record jackets repeatedly announce the latest manifestation of urban "folksinging." In the common-sense world any performer playing a guitar and singing certain types of material, be it country-western, folk in origin, or political in nature, is a genuine folksinger. Folklorists and other serious students of traditional music, of course, know that a definitional comparison of Emma Dusenberry and Tom Paxton or Peter Seeger would produce highly different results. Paxton and Seeger are "city-billies," "imitators," "folk entrepreneurs," or whatever category one wishes to apply to the urban songster who uses the folk genre. Yet, as Malraux suggests—with considerable support from the demographers and urban sociologists studying industrial and population shifts—the folk in the classical sense are generally nonexistent in the urban centers of the United States. As such, the urban folk-music progression is generally aberrant from other societal trends such as the growth of mass communication and culture. Numerous proponents of urban "folk music" have argued that cosmopolitan utilization is merely a continuation of the "folk memory" of the people, or a musical search for national identity. Empirically, these hypotheses are difficult to substantiate. Studies of the artistic tastes of urbanites prior to the "commercial revival of the 1960's" leave little doubt that the offerings of the mass culture predominate in popularity.[1] Hoggart, for

From "The Proletarian Renascence," in the *Journal of American Folklore* (January/ March, 1969), pp. 51–63. Reprinted by permission of the American Folklore Society.
    [1] Arlene Kaplan, "Folksinging in a Mass Society" (M.A. thesis, U. of California, Berkeley, 1952).

example, in an examination of the tastes of the English working class, a group steeped in tradition, found that folk music played an insignificant role in their musical preferences.[2] Other discussions suggest that in the United States "folk material" was a novelty item in the mass culture, or generally confined to the Library of Congress archives, to folklore journals, and to social movements. In the context of social movements, the use of the folk genre by the American Left during the 1930's and 1940's was a deviation from general practice. One of the Almanac Singers stated: "We think this is the *first time* there has ever been an organized attempt of this kind actually to sing the folk songs of America . . . We are trying to give back to the people the songs of the workers."[3]

Social movements have historically used song to put forth their belief systems and to gain internal unity. To accomplish these ends functionally reformers and radicals, by and large, have drawn upon the musical idioms recognized by their potential and actual constituencies. Until the 1920's the Wobblies used hobo ditties and religious material. The Southern Tenant Farmers Union employed spirituals and hymns, and nearly every singing social movement has added one lyric or another to the music of "John Brown's Body." "John Brown's Body," like other well-known American favorites, has undergone numerous alterations and treatments in keeping with what Greenway and others have labeled "ease of communication," that is, familiarity of the material.[4] However, the political use of the folk genre in the urban metropolis was a deviation from this pattern. Except to a handful of the followers of concert performers such as John Jacob Niles and Carl Sandburg, "folk music," until its injection into the mass media in the 1950's, was little known outside of left-wing circles in the urban milieu. The Industrial Workers of the World evidently disdained folk music and rarely used it in their organizational efforts. It logically should follow that left-wing social movements in the 'thirties and 'forties in New York and in other urban enclaves should employ the mass culture or the popular-music idiom to inculcate class consciousness. As the history of the American Left, especially the Communist party, indicates, popular music was rejected and "folk music" style incorporated as a primary propaganda vehicle to create Folk Consciousness.

Folk Consciousness is an awareness of folk music which leads to use of the music in an unnatural environment, such as the metropolis, in the framework of social, economic, or political activity. This concept is regarded as a gestalt

---

[2] Richard Hoggart, *The Uses of Literacy: Changing Patterns in English Mass Culture* (Boston: Oxford U. Press, 1957), 184–191; and David Riesman, "Listen to Popular Music," *American Quarterly*, 2 (1950), pp. 359–371.

[3] Don Russell, "Meet the Almanac Singers: They Sing Hard-Hitting Songs That Belong to the People," *Daily Worker*, August 14, 1941, p. 7.

[4] See John Greenway, *American Folksongs of Protest* (Philadelphia, 1953, reprinted 1970 by Octagon Books); and R. Serge Denisoff, "Songs of Persuasion," *Journal of American Folklore*, 79 (1966), pp. 582–583.

in that it is a product of a number of variables such as ideological, tactical, organizational, and psychological variables. The affecting of rural clothing, the addition of ideological messages to folk tunes, and the use of rural jargon by middle-class dropouts and intellectuals are all aspects of this phenomenon. The genesis of Folk Consciousness was political-ideological and primarily manifest in the Communist party (CPUSA) during the 1930's and 1940's. Unfortunately, because of the political climate of the McCarthy period, very few writers outside the extreme Right have attempted to deal with the role of the Stalinists and folk material. It should be noted in the ensuing discussion that not all of the individuals and groups treated were holders of Party cards, despite Mr. Noebel's contention to the contrary.[5]

Karl Marx, in formulating his theories of social change, presented two concepts which later were to weigh heavily in the use of the folk genre by the Communists and other radicals. The first notion was that of "class consciousness"; that is, the working class or the proletariat had to be aware of their plight in the capitalistic system and be willing to change these conditions. Awareness, for Marx and later for Lenin, in the form of political or class consciousness was the key to social change. The essence of social movements, vehicles of change according to these theorists, was to inculcate political consciousness. The communication of ideas is not limited to pamphleteering or speechmaking. Art, literature, posters, music, and the like are all equally, if not more, effective. During the October Revolution the Bolsheviks used the culture of the Russian populace at all levels to inculcate political consciousness, which they assumed would lead to revolutionary action. One Soviet scholar noted that "They found a fountain of inspiration in folk songs and fairy tales, in proverbs and adages."[6] The Leninists employed this folk material in dramas, songs, cartoons, and political posters. The dramas and songs, being oral, and the cartoons and posters, visual, eliminated the need for literacy. Similar usages of recognizable art by social movements of a non-Marxian persuasion are found throughout the nineteenth and twentieth centuries in the United States. Marx's theory of "class struggle," however, added a new dimension to this utilization. Marx and his successors argued that there exists a class struggle and that every form of art becomes a tool or weapon in this conflict. Albert Rhys Williams, for one, states categorically: "There can be no music without ideology. The old composers whether they knew it or not were upholding a political theory—for the most part bolstering the rule of the upper class."[7]

Numerous Marxist writers continued this argument, stating that classical

---

[5] See David Noebel, *Rhythm, Riots, and Revolution* (Tulsa, 1966).

[6] Galina Demusfenova, "The Revolutionary Art Poster," *USSR* (November 1963), p. 32.

[7] Albert Rhys Williams, *The Soviets* (New York, 1937), p. 405.

music as well as popular music was wedded to the ruling class and obscured the dialectic system of reality. Lenin is reported to have said that "classical music was too nice" and only mellowed the political consciousness of the masses. Popular music, similarly, was viewed as a tool of the "bosses" or the bourgeoisie and unworthy and unrepresentative of the cultural orientations of the working class. One member of the Almanac Singers, in discussing the jazz form of "boogie woogie," commented: "The form is excellent, but the bourgeoisie have taken that form and used it in a different way for a wrong purpose. That form can be and has been used for genuine music of protest."[8] On another occasion the Almanacs wrote: "People know inwardly that these 'hits' are no part of their working, slaving, worrying, and no solution to their troubles."[9]

Folk music, on the other hand, was perceived as "people's music." Harap, in *Social Roots of the Arts,* suggested:

> . . . folk song . . . exhibits the general characteristics of a genuine people's art in class societies. Folk art serves the interests of the common people; its subject matter arises out of their everyday life; it is practiced by the people as participants and not merely as spectators; its individual exponents spring from the people themselves.[10]

Another writer during the mid-thirties suggested that proletarian music must be national in form, revolutionary in content. One of the few musical genres fitting these criteria was the folk-styled song of persuasion. Ideology in the set of Folk Consciousness as such can be interpreted as directive and definitive in that it suggests a musical idiom for political activity.

The variable of tactics partially based on ideology contributed to the awareness of folk music by the American Left. In the 1920's a great deal of Communist strategy was based on the Bolshevik model of revolution. The Russian followers of Lenin and Trotsky achieved success and therefore were emulated in all areas of political activity, including music. Because of the preindustrial structure of tsarist Russia, folk music was an important national art form. Given this structure, folk music was extensively used by the Octobrists for propaganda purposes. Their American counterparts as well as other leftists used this material despite its foreign origins. Although this type of propaganda song appealed to adherents of the Third International, it did little to increase the ranks of the Communist movement. Indeed it violated Lenin's definition of art: "It [art] must be intelligible to these masses and loved by them. It

[8] Russell, "Meet the Almanac Singers," p. 7.

[9] Almanac Singers, "Songs of Work, Trouble, Hope," *People's World,* October 28, 1941, p. 5.

[10] Louis Harap, *Social Roots of the Arts* (New York, 1949), p. 127.

must unite the feeling, thought, and will of these masses; it must elevate them."[11]

As one of the cofounders of the Southern Tenant Farmers Union, H. L. Mitchell recalled after a Communist organizer attempted to teach the "Internationale" to rural farmers, "It didn't go over very well."[12] Mitchell's comment can equally be applied to the Party as a whole, in that its dependence on the Bolshevik model greatly hampered its American organizational drives. One of these organizational campaigns, under the banner of "dual-unionism," did introduce the Stalinists to the folk-music genre. From the Gastonia textile strike came the "ballats" of Ella May Wiggins, described by Margaret Larkin in a number of articles appearing in the *New Masses* and the *Nation*. One article concluded with the following statement: "These songs that begin 'Come all ye workers' and end 'Let's stand together, workers, and have a union here' are destined to be the battle songs of the coming industrial struggle."[13]

The rural industrial conflicts of the late 'twenties and early 'thirties were one of the major preconditions for consolidating the traditional folksong with the ideology of the Left. During this half-decade the rural enclaves were perceived as providing the greatest potential for the organization of dual unions and for some trade-union activity. The classic conditions of class conflict did indeed exist in small company towns sprinkled throughout the South. This new focus of northern radicals exposed them to a new subculture, far different from the halls of ivy or the *la Boheme* of Greenwich Village. Consequently, the relationship of the northern organizers to these mountain regions was varied and often haphazard and confused. Frequently ideology shaded their ability to accommodate and relate to specific strike situations. The experiences of Commonwealth College testify to the pitfalls of extrapolating the model of the October Revolution to the Cumberlands. These ideologically oriented outsiders redefined reality for the residents of many a mining and textile town. Solutions taken from the works of DeLeon, Marx, Lenin, and the social philosophy of A. J. Muste were injected into the poverty-ridden South. Some miners and textile workers did indeed accept these remedies, but the majority did not, preferring to return to the respectability of the New Deal and the conservative United Mine Workers and Textile Workers. With the exception of the Highlander Folk School, most labor colleges and similar institutions had either collapsed or were on their last legs by the last half of the 'thirties. Lenin's view of "trade union consciousness" as opposed to "political consciousness" prevailed. The lack of the "solidification" of the rural masses, however, did

[11] V. I. Lenin quoted in Harold Swayze, *Political Control of Literature in the USSR: 1946–1959* (Cambridge, Massachusetts, 1962), p. 10.

[12] H. L. Mitchell, *Oral History of the Southern Tenant Farmers Union* (New York, 1956–1957), p. 70.

[13] Margaret Larkin, "Ella May's Songs," *Nation,* October 9, 1929, p. 283.

not reduce the musical significance of this period. Jim Garland, Aunt Molly Jackson, and others merged their music with social action. Larkin's articles introduced the Gastonia "ballats" of Ella May Wiggins to the urban readers of the *New Masses*. The New York appearances of Aunt Molly and Garland served a similar function. These visits and the writings of Margaret Larkin were situational and issue oriented. The presence of Garland at the funeral of Harry Simms at the Coliseum, and Aunt Molly's appearance before an estimated twenty thousand persons, also at the Coliseum, heralded the struggle in Harlan County. Larkin's exposition of Ella May Wiggins was of interest only during the Loray strike. As such, the impact of these singers and songs in the early 'thirties was similar to the headlines of a daily newspaper.

While the attention span of radicals shifted away from the issues of the Loray Mills and the mines of J. H. Blair to Scottsboro and other proletarian struggles, the folk genre was introduced into the milieu of New York City. This process can best be pictured as one of cultural filtering by *carriers* of songs. Organizers and journalists assumed this functional role on several occasions. Archie Green in his analysis of "The Death of Mother Jones" presents an example of this interactional set:

> In his constant travel between southern textile and mining areas and Brookwood Labor College, Tom Tippett carried hill-billy records north and union songbooks south . . . Brookwooders were teaching "Solidarity Forever" in West Virginia in 1931; Seacrist [a Musteite organizer] in turn moved "The Death of Mother Jones" into urban circles.[14]

This interchange of song style between the traditional singer and the urban organizer is equally present in the Larkin article and in the Harlan campaign visits of Molly Jackson and Jim Garland to New York. The rural-industrial conflicts of the late 'twenties and early 'thirties were empirical factors in consolidating the traditional folk idiom with the left wing, especially the Stalinists. This period, however, was more innovative than assimilative, or discovery rather than acceptance. A side effect of these campaigns which later colored the proletarian renascence was that hamlets of conflict afforded the opportunity for rural people to hear solutions taken from the works of Marx, Lenin, Thomas, and Muste. A handful accepted these remedies on a long-term basis and became functionaries in the "hootenanny" scene of the late 1930's.

Another consideration in the development of Folk Consciousness was organizational pragmatism.

[14] Archie Green, "Death of Mother Jones," *Labor History*, I (1960), p. 6.

Richard Wright, in recalling his affiliation with the John Reed Clubs, quoted a Party leader as stating: "We've got to crash out of our narrow way of working and get our message to the church people, students, club people, professionals, middle class."[15] The method of doing this, although not totally by design, was the *front populaire* or the Fourth Period. As Howe and Coser note in their critical analysis of American Communism: "The Popular Front was not merely a political tactic, it was also, and in the United States even more importantly, *a kind of culture* . . . applicable to almost any intellectual area . . ."[16]

One illustrative article of the time was to state that Communists are the "guardians of American traditions."[17] Americana was enthroned and injected into the intellectual milieu of the period. The "Internationale" was de-emphasized in favor of the "Star Spangled Banner" and Walt Whitman became the litterateur par excellence. The Stalinists in part became the American *narodniki* of the "red decade." In 1934, Richard Frank, in a piece in the *New Masses,* urged the adoption of Negro music for "revolutionary" purposes.[18] Frank argued that a large portion of the American proletariat could be mobilized and made politically conscious through the use of music as opposed to pamphleteering. He also noted that a significant minority of the Negro population was illiterate but had a strong musical tradition that could be politicized. He concluded that Negro music was popular with the patrons of mass culture and therefore would serve a dual propaganda purpose. Half a decade later Woody Guthrie, in the *People's World,* used the same argument in urging the use of song in mobilizing migratory workers.[19]

The concept of "Communism is twentieth-century Americanism" did not lead directly to the native folk idiom. Rather, outside of New York City the Stalinists followed in the footsteps of the Wobblies and drew from American standards. The *Western Worker* columnist Michael Quin wrote revolutionary lyrics to "Dixie" ("There's A Way, Working Man"), "She'll Be Coming 'Round the Mountain" (She'll Be Selling Western Workers"), "Battle Hymn of the Republic" ("Battle Hymn of Labor") and the IWW-inspired "Tramp, Tramp, Tramp" ("Someday We'll Pay Our Debts"). Other lyricists took up the religious hymn, once again, to attack the system with ditties such as "His

[15] Richard Wright, *The God That Failed,* R. H. Crossman, ed. (New York, 1950), p. 130.

[16] Irving Howe and Lewis Coser, *The American Communist Party: A Critical History* (Boston: Beacon Press, 1957), p. 363.

[17] Miriam Bonner, "Communists Are Guardians of American Traditions," *Western Worker,* October 17, 1935, p. 5.

[18] Richard Frank, "Negro Revolutionary Music," *New Masses,* May 15, 1934, pp. 28–29.

[19] Woody Guthrie, "Woody, Dustbowl Troubador, Sings Songs of Migrant Trails," *People's World,* April 19, 1940, p. 5.

Majesty, the Capitalist" put to "When the Roll Is Called Up Yonder." "Some-day We'll Pay Our Debts" is illustrative of the material of this period:

> Bills, bills, bills are piling high, boys
> Cheer up comrades, there is hope
> And someday we'll pay our debts
> With our worker Soviets
> We will give the boss what's
> Coming to him then.[20]

The similarity of these songs to Wobbly material suggests that the previous affiliations of a number of Stalinists may have influenced their propaganda songs. A disproportionate number of Party officers and native-born members were ex-Wobblies who had witnessed the effectiveness of propaganda songs in organizational drives and strike situations. Writers such as Edwin Rolfe and Mike Gold in *Daily Worker* columns pointed to the IWW as a model of how songs should be used to change the world. Gold once wrote that the Stalinists needed a "Communist Joe Hill."[21]

The search for a CPUSA counterpart to the Wobbly bard, however, was hampered by the European style of propaganda song and the so-called "chorus movement" typified by the Workers' Music League. The short-lived Music League's dominant orientation was to develop a proletarian music *for* the workers. Indeed, the use of folk-styled "proletarian" songs as manifested by Aunt Molly Jackson and later Ray and Lida Auville was generally ignored or criticized. One League member, Carl Sand (a pseudonym), rejected the efforts of Ray Auville as a "hybrid mixture of jazz and balladry."[22]

Mike Gold, the chief spokesman of American "pro-cult," challenged this stance as "too intellectual," and "difficult," and basically a "desertion of the masses."[23] He continued to suggest that the work of the Auvilles provided the needed guideposts for future proletarian music. Gold's position prevailed and the WML became the American Music League. Equally, many musical idioms reflecting Americana were transformed into "folk music." For example, any picket-line ditty printed in the Communist press was a "folk expression of the people." While Americanization in the New York area pointed the revolutionary movement in the direction of "folksongs," several events of the Fourth Period further enhanced the idiom.

The most significant event of the Popular Front era was the Franco rebellion in Spain. It was during the hostilities between the *Falange* and the

[20] Michael Quin, "Seeing Red," *Western Worker,* June 22, 1936, p. 5.
[21] Mike Gold, "What A World," *Daily Worker,* October 19, 1933, p. 5.
[22] Mike Gold, "Change the World," *Daily Worker,* January 2, 1936, p. 5.
[23] *Ibid.*

Loyalists, with their cohort International Brigades, that folk material received another boost in left-wing circles. New York became the hub of Stalinist activity in the midst of a semi-Bohemian political subculture which romanticized the use of folksong as well as any artifact associated with "the people." The war to repel Franco and "Fight Fascism" was carried on in a nation rich with peasant myths and songs. From the Jarma Front and other military encounters came songs such as "Los Cuatro Generales" and "Viva La Quince Brigada," repeatedly sung by Communists and other supporters of the Loyalist cause. It was this war more than any other historical event which legitimized the CPUSA in intellectual and Bohemian circles. Despite Oscar Brand, the war did not cause the Left to "swallow folk music," but rather further popularized the idiom and attracted personnel who would later play important roles in the "people's revival."

The idealization and mythology of labor lore has frequently presented a portrait of a so-called singing union comprised of class-conscious characters from a Hugo Gellert sketch harmonizing songs decrying the abuses and suffering of their socioeconomic position. As one observer and participant of labor-song organizing has recalled, a great deal of this stereotype falls into the area of mythology.[24] The amount of propaganda-song activity that did exist in the urban-industrial labor movement, the CIO, was owing in great part to several influences such as the United Mine Workers of America and the American left wing. The old veterans of coal conflicts were unable to speak well but could sing songs. Communists, Trotskyites, and Socialists could do both and were willing to undertake the dangerous role of labor organizers. Despite many treatments to the contrary, it now appears that labor songs were generally confined to strike situations, and other vocalizing in this area was done by colonizing political partisans. For example, in 1942 four members of the Almanac Singers were hired by the UAW to perform at union meetings to "keep the members from leaving during intermission." In 1939 Zilphia Horton of Highlander Folk School was employed by the Textile Workers Union to compile the songbook, *Labor Songs,* with an introduction by John L. Lewis. This is not to say that the labor movement of the 1930's did not use song, but rather that accounts stressing the role of this movement during the Depression decade appear overstated.

In discussing the last half of the "red decade," Lipton stated, "Anyone who could sing 'The Four Insurgent Generals' in Spanish was sure to be the life of the party."[25] In other words, a person playing a guitar and presenting a working-class front could find social and economic acceptance in the milieu of Folk

[24] Peter Seeger, "Whatever Happened to Singing In the Unions?" *Sing Out!* 15 (1965), pp. 29–31.
[25] Lawrence Lipton, *The Holy Barbarians* (New York: Messner, 1959), p. 290.

Consciousness. One hypothesis accounting for this phenomenon is found in the literature of social psychology. The key variable here involves identificational interaction, that is, the patterning of attitudes and style of life on a specific model. The first model was manifested by the Lincoln Battalion of the International Brigade. The war in Spain was for many a holy crusade with which those unable to cross the Pyrenees identified. Song was one method of expressing one's commitment and support of the Loyalists. One Communist publication, in praising this material, exclaimed, "They bring the point home, and they keep the lesson alive."[26]

A complementary aspect of this was the "cult of Preacher Casey" which emerged during this period. The model man became a character from a Hugo Gellert drawing. Overalls and blue jeans became the uniform of the time. One middle-class artist during this period insisted on wearing blue jeans to union meetings even if his working-class audience came dressed in their Sunday best. Middle-class dropouts and refugees from the "capitalist system" gathered together to create a new social order and a "new folk community" comprised of all of the elements of Folk Consciousness. The effort among middle-class intellectuals and artists to erase their personal identity and class origins, coupled with a new and "instinctively sound" identity in the proletariat, is frequently found in the literature of the "red decade." Almond relates the story of a San Francisco fashion designer who carried a bag to change into blue jeans after work.[27] One of the prime movers in the proletarian renascence recalled, "There I was trying my best to shed my . . . upbringing, scorning to waste money on clothes other than blue jeans."[28] Into this "scene" came the Garland clan—Molly Jackson, Jim Garland, and Sarah Ogan—and also Leadbelly, Woody Guthrie, Earl Robinson, Will Geer, Burl Ives, the "amorphous aggregate" called the Almanac Singers, and many others.

An elaborate ethos evolved around this milieu and the use of the folk genre. In part the ethos was that folk music was the idiom of the people and mirrored the stratification dichotomy presented by Karl Marx. Folk music was proletarian music and therefore a suitable weapon in the class struggle leading to social change. Proponents of this view saw the Almanac Singers and Woody Guthrie as continuations of a people's "folk memory," a sort of Jungian archetype. Others saw this enclave of Folk Consciousness as a sort of new folk community—an aggregate of persons singing so-called folk material and therefore a new folk culture. One observer stated that this phenomenon was "a new

[26] "Spain Lives In the Great Songs of the Thaelmann Battalion," *People's World*, November 5, 1940, p. 5.

[27] Gabriel A. Almond, *The Appeals of Communism* (Princeton, 1954), p. 284.

[28] Moses Asch and Alan Lomax (eds.), *The Leadbelly Songbook* (New York: Oak, 1962), p. 7.

folk community composed of progressives, anti-fascists, and union members."
Siegmeister, for example, saw Josh White, Aunt Molly Jackson, Woody Guthrie,
and others as giving birth to a "new kind of folk music."[29] Accounts of the
assimilation of Aunt Molly Jackson, Leadbelly, and Burl Ives all suggest that
these songsters, at least for a time, accepted the political ideology of the milieu
of Folk Consciousness.[30] This historical manifestation, the proletarian renascence,
is arbitrarily dated from the advent of the Spanish Civil War to the demise of
the Almanac Singers as a functioning unit in the summer of 1942.

The essence of the proletarian revival can be presented by briefly treating
Woody Guthrie and the Almanac Singers as ideal types of this phenomenon—
"ideal type" in the Weberian sense of a typical pattern of action and underlying
attitudinal orientations. Guthrie and the Almanacs are seen as typical manifestations of Folk Consciousness and the proletarian renascence.

Woody Guthrie, as a majority of his biographers note, was psychologically
far from typical, yet his role in the proletarian renascence embodied a number
of general social patterns found during this period. Woody was a product of
both the economic hardships of rural America and the radical tradition of
Oklahoma. His father, Charles Edward Guthrie, was a Socialist leader and
possessed one of the largest radical libraries in the Sooner State. In the late
'thirties Woody obtained a job on a Los Angeles radio station owned by a campaign manager of Culbert B. Olsen and the "Ham and Eggs" movement. Here
Guthrie wrote for the Olsen magazine, putting forth the merits of the "Ham
and Eggs" program. After a brief sojourn in Mexico, where he got into trouble
with the Mexican police over his political orientations, Woody returned to
KFVD, Los Angeles, where he was heard by Mike Quin, a *People's World*
columnist. At KFVD he also made the acquaintance of another *People's World*
writer, Ed Robbin, who introduced Guthrie to Will Geer. Shortly after this
time Guthrie began his "Woody Sez" column for the *People's World*. Guthrie's
prose in this column, as in a number of his songs, was marked by a Will Rogers
type of Marxism, peculiar to the author rather than to any social movement.
For Guthrie, "historical materialism" was "a Blow by Blow write up of the
Match Between the Money Folk and Workin Folks."[31] On the class struggle
he wrote, "Until you workin folk all get together to beat Wall Street, the bean
will be a subject of popularity."[32] From these and many other excerpts from
Guthrie's column one finds a ruralized native political interpretation of the

[29] Elie Siegmeister, *Music Lover's Handbook* (New York: Morrow, 1943), p. 51.
[30] See, for example, Charles Seeger, "Folkness of the Non-Folk," in *Folklore and Society*, Bruce Jackson, ed. (Hatsboro, 1966), p. 4.
[31] Woody Guthrie, "Woody Sez," *People's World*, August 18, 1939, p. 4.
[32] Guthrie, "Woody Sez," *People's World*, June 5, 1939, p. 4.

contradictions of American capitalism. The prose also idealized Mike Gold's many urgings for "working class jargon."

Will Geer left Southern California to work in New York and wrote to Woody urging him to come East. From New York Guthrie resumed his *People's World* column and wrote for the *Daily Worker.* He went on an organizational tour of the nation and became part of the Almanacs until drifting away in the summer of 1942. Despite Guthrie's personal idiosyncrasies, his career is not unrelated to that of many of his cohorts. Like the Garland clan and Leadbelly, he experienced the privations of the rural social order and the oppression of "gun thugs" and police officialdom. Like most folk entrepreneurs in the 1930's he found in Communists and radicals an audience for his product, the song of persuasion, which also shared his semipersonalized contempt for "Rich Folks." As one member of the Almanac Singers stated, Guthrie was well read and grammatically literate, despite the sentence structures of "Woody Sez." As such, Woody idealized many of the currents noted in the proletarian renascence. He was a cultural transplant who directed his material in the context of Folk Consciousness. He was an intellectual of sorts, who dissociated himself totally from this position, not unlike many of his urban middle-class counterparts. He accepted, in varying degrees, the values of the Stalinists and other radicals and used folk material as a weapon in the "Battle Between the Rich Folks and the Workin' Folks." In essence, Woody manifested for the Left what a "folksinger" should be: working class in appearance and language, radical in thought and action, a weapon in the class struggle, and a means of relating urban radicals to the people. "Folksinger" therefore equaled "people's artist" and "people's artist" equaled "folksinger."

The Almanac Singers, even more than the Dustbowl Balladeer, personified this ethos. The Almanacs were a coalescence of the events of the 'thirties and the first formalization of Folk Consciousness. The nebulous personnel of the "amorphous aggregate" reflected the Southern labor-college tradition in the persons of Lee Hays and Sis Cunningham; the civil-rights campaigns of the period were reflected by Josh White, and middle-class intellectualism was manifested by Earl Robinson, Millard Lampell, Peter Seeger, and the Lomaxes. The hootenannies at Almanac House further represented the dual union campaigns of the TUUL and other drives with performers such as Jim Garland, Aunt Molly Jackson, Sarah Ogan, Leadbelly, and Burl Ives, who mirrored the anti-Fascist ideology of the Spanish conflict.

The function of the Almanac Singers was propaganda, which was not limited to ideology but also referred to a musical genre. The following quotations are illustrative: "Say the truth as simply as you can and repeat it as many times as it has to be repeated"; and, "They're just conversations that you say over and over without getting tired of it—till you hammer some single lesson home."[33] One evidence of this structure is the "Ballad of October 16th," which repeats many times the chorus that FDR hates war and "so does Eleanor/But we won't be safe till everybody's dead."[34] Related to the message was the media of transmission. As a number of writers have suggested, a secondary function of the group was to popularize the folk genre, thus replacing the bourgeois products of Tin Pan Alley. In one article, "Like a Grass Fire in a Gale," the Almanacs wrote:

> So they . . . [workers] reach in the other direction, toward rough, tough, hard hitting, brave and fighting forms of folk music that are a part of their very blood. And a song like "Talking Union" will take in wagonloads of nickels, for ten times as long as 90 per cent of the popular weekly hits.[35]

The group functioned to proselytize both the means and the ends of ideology and folk material. The ideology found in the songs of the Almanacs reflected many of the social concerns of the American Stalinists. The albums *Songs For John Doe* and *Dear Mister President* illustrate these parallel concerns. However, the question as to the number of Almanacs who were official members of the CPUSA has never been satisfactorily answered. Suffice it to say that the commitment to sectarian ideology is manifest in their songs. In sum, the Almanacs were evidences of the proletarian renascence, drawing from the ideological and political orientations of the period, the techniques of the early dual union campaigns, the task of labor organizing, the Loyalist struggle, and finally, the United Front of World War II. The advent of World War II terminated the proletarian renascence, eventually leaving one Almanac Singer temporarily to mind the store. By January of 1943 the "hoots" and the Almanacs were past history, to be taken up again by People's Songs Inc. in 1946.

Of the artistic artifacts of the "red decade," the song of persuasion literally was the only leftist preference to survive time and the fragmentation and suppression of the sectarian Left. Of the plethora of left-wing publications only *Sing Out!* magazine, a continuation of *People's Songs Bulletin,* withstood Walter, Wood, and McCarran, the 1956 "cult of personality speech," and the Gates-Foster debate. The legacy of the proletarian renascence is predominantly in the definition of the social role of the urban political folksinger. Social role

[33] "Almanac Singers: Four Young Men With a Lot to Sing," *People's World,* August 1, 1941, p. 5.
[34] *New Masses,* May 20, 1941, p. 20.
[35] Almanac Singers, "Like A Grass Fire in a Gale," *Daily Worker,* October 20, 1941, p. 7.

generally refers to an ascribed position in a social system, that is, a blueprint for behavior. Consequently, an occupant of the role of urban "folksinger" finds that certain expectations go with the role—for example, the ability to play a musical instrument passably well and sing songs in the folk idiom. Coupled with these expectations are those contributed by the proletarian renascence. The first of these can be labeled "the ideology of folksinging." The main tenet of this ethos is that urban songsters must be "socially significant." Chad Mitchell, for one, stated the argument as follows: "The topical song is truly the folk music of today . . . it is the song whose content deals with contemporary issues that are most meaningful to people."[36] Or, "Songs are best . . . when they move people to action of a more significant character than that of the squealing teen-agers' orgasms over false images conned off as 'folk singers'."[37] This last reference, of course, is to the defection of Bob Dylan from the ranks of the socially significant. The Dylan controversy, which raged in the pages of *Sing Out!* and *Broadside,* highlighted this issue of political import. In November 1964, Irwin Silber published an "open letter to Bob Dylan" condemning his lack of social concern: ". . . any song writer who tries to deal honestly with reality in this world is bound to write 'protest' songs. How can he help himself?"[38] [Ed. note: See Article 11 in this book.] Another proponent of the art-is-a-weapon school, in comparing Phil Ochs and Dylan, used the following adjectives: ". . . the difference between the two performers became manifest; *meaning* vs. innocuousness, *sincerity* vs. utter disregard for the tastes of the audience, *idealistic principle* vs. self-conscious egotism."[39]

The political urban folk entrepreneur should therefore exhibit the qualities of social meaning, ideology, and sincerity. These criteria, in part, explain the contemptuous role given the Kingston Trio, whose prime function was entertainment. Social significance, however, does not in itself involve a general awareness of society, but rather a specific political orientation. Joan Baez at one time commented, "There's never been a good Republican folk singer," to which Pete Seeger added, "All folklore music by its very nature is anti-fascist." While empirically these positions are difficult to sustain (note for example the use of folk material by the Third Reich and American right-wing movements), they are a basic tenet in the ethos of the urban songster. Woody Guthrie's guitar, to illustrate, had carved on it the slogan "This Machine Kills Fascists." In a sample of songs of persuasion in *Broadside* magazine, a predominant number of compositions were found to deal with themes of world peace, civil rights,

[36] Chad Mitchell in "A Symposium/Topical Songs and Folksinging, 1965," *Sing Out!* 15 (1965), p. 14.

[37] Don West in "A Symposium," p. 10.

[38] Irwin Silber, "An Open Letter To Bob Dylan," *Sing Out!* 14 (1964), p. 22.

[39] Paul Wolfe, "The 'New' Dylan," *Broadside,* 53 (1964), p. 2.

and opposition to the Vietnam war.[40] Social significance assumes a specific ideology or political orientation ranging from liberal to New Left. Nevertheless, these songs had little structural connection to the magnetic songs of the renascence. The compositions of Dylan, Ochs, Paxton, and their followers did not offer organizational solutions such as those of the labor movement or the Young Communist League.

A corollary to this political stance was the related issue of "commercialism." As noted, one of the ideological elements of the renascence was an anti–mass-culture stance. Guthrie, Seeger, and others derided Tin Pan Alley and its products on many occasions.[41] Commercial success was viewed as "selling out." Woody Guthrie, for example, several times turned down high-paying media jobs which did not afford him total freedom of expression. During the revival, a similar phenomenon could be observed in Bob Dylan's refusal to appear on the Ed Sullivan program because of the censorship of "Talking John Birch Society." Equally, a large number of performers rejected offers to appear on the Hootenanny television program for ethical reasons. The social role of the urban folksinger, then, requires specific sets of attitudes to be in vogue. The Kingston Trio have historically been renounced by folkniks as "crude commercialists" despite their prominent role in setting off the college-based revival.

Another ramification of the proletarian renascence can be seen in the area of "style of life." In the 1930's the Depression confirmed a high value on the work ethic. As one observer noted: "The workingman was the ideological hero of the time. Carl Sandburg could give to a poem the title *The People, Yes,* with no obscurity intended or inferred."[42] Hollywood made movies about miners, factory hands, and the migrants of the Dustbowl as captured by Steinbeck's best-seller *Grapes of Wrath*. In a word, the working man was enshrined. The proletarian renascence equally exhibited the "working-class" style of life and the middle-class refugees and rural migrants living at a subsistence level. Friesen, in his series of articles on the Almanac Singers, documents the struggle for near-survival at Almanac House.[43] Woody Guthrie tells a similar tale in *Bound For Glory* and *American Folksong*. Biographies of contemporary songsters fit into a similar tradition. Bob Dylan is romantically described: "With holes in his shoes, with a corduroy Huck Finn cap topping his red-brown mop, with

[40] R. Serge Denisoff, "Protest Movements: Class Consciousness and the Propaganda Song," *Sociological Quarterly,* 9 (1968), pp. 228–247.

[41] A number of articles decrying commercialism are collected in David A. DeTurk and A. Poulin, Jr., eds., *The American Folk Scene* (New York, 1967).

[42] Alistair Cooke, *A Generation On Trial* (New York: Penguin, 1952), p. 23.

[43] Gordon Friesen, "Winter and War Come to Almanac House," *Broadside* 8 (1962), pp. 1, 4–6.

his guitar and his two harmonicas, he headed East."[44] Similar accounts are to be found of urban songsters such as Jack Elliot, Pat Sky, and others, despite the fact that the 'sixties exhibit few of the migratory trends found in the decade of the Depression.

A related feature of "style of life" is that New York City remains the mecca of urban political folksinging. Greenwich Village, until the advent of folk rock, remained the citadel of hootenannies and folk-music clubs. Just as Guthrie, Hays, Seeger, the Garland clan, and an army of others came in the 1930's, so did the Dylans, the Paxtons, and the Chandlers come to "Greenrich" Village to find truth, fame, and fortune, thus adopting many features of the socially defined role of urban folk entrepreneur. To summarize these points, the social role of the political urban folksinger is primarily based on previous urban usage rather than on actual folk tradition. These cultural filtrations nevertheless have not advanced the functions of urban folk usage.

[44] Sy and Barbara Ribakove, *Folk-Rock: The Bob Dylan Story* (New York, 1966), p. 25.

Chapter III

ROCK IS A FOUR LETTER WORD
WHICH MEANS....

No one has totally escaped rock music. The young, the old, the cosmopolite, the Lawrence Welk fan, and even plants and monkeys have been subjected to the big beat sound. Yet, beyond the assertion of David Laing (1970) that rock is the sound of our time, there is little consensus on what exactly rock music is. In his aptly titled book *The Rock Revolution,* Arnold Shaw (1971) lists nineteen specific ways in which rock is different from the older generation's popular music, while Jerry Hopkins (1970) and Charlie Gillett (1970) present the best analyses of how it emerged.

New York music critic Richard Goldstein defines the "new rock" as being a "mulatto: . . . born of an unholy alliance between white country music and rhythm and blues. At first a hybrid called 'rockabilly,' it consisted of brisk and brittle songs, laced with fiery verbal cadenzas and was meant to be belted across, with a whole lotta shakin' goin' on." (1968: 67).

Goldstein's definition asserts that rock music has absorbed the poetry of Dylan and others, thus combining experiential and intellectual elements. Many students and critics of rock writing in the various fan magazines such as *Crawdaddy* and *Rolling Stone* reject the intellectual side as unnecessary for understanding the genre. Even art historians sometimes lapse into such a stance, as when Carl Belz asserts "Any listener who wants rock defined specifically is probably unable to recognize it" (1969: vii). This anti-intellectual stance may be justified when trying to evaluate the artistic or esthetic qualities of the music. But, it is completely inappropriate when trying to discover the political, social, and cultural meanings rock music has had for people over the several decades of its existence.

While social commentators disagree on most other things about rock's influence (Peterson, 1970), all of the authors whose work is reprinted in this chapter would agree with Theodore Roszak (1969: xii) that rock music and its associated life-ways have been central to the emergence or at least the appearance of a youth-oriented "counterculture" which "radically diverges from values and assumptions that have been in the mainstream of our society at least since the Scientific Revolution of the seventeenth century." Article 9 by Greil Marcus which opens this chapter most clearly reflects the thinking of the counterculture. In the spirit of the New Left, he argues that the protest songs of older social movements such as the IWW and the Communist party are ineffective because they so directly *preach* a line to the listener. In focusing on the events surrounding the 1968 Democratic Party convention in Chicago, he shows how the less "preachy" rock music helped to create and articulate the consciousness of the New Left.

Ralph Gleason, longtime jazz critic and social commentator, author of a book on the Jefferson Airplane based on his involvement with the San Francisco rock scene, elevates the ideas expressed by Marcus into a manifesto for a rock-based cultural revolution. Many who shared Gleason's view in 1969 when he wrote the article reprinted in this chapter have since become disillusioned with the "Woodstock Nation." They have been disheartened by events like those which took place at the December, 1969 rock concert at Altamont, California where four were killed—one murdered by Hell's Angels, one drowned in a puddle, and two killed by hit-and-run drivers (Eisen, 1970). But Gleason still remains optimistic, if rather defensive, in asserting "the dream simply isn't over" (Gleason, 1971).

Both the Old Left and the Radical Right have attacked rock music and those who perform it as corruptive influences upon the young. Gary Allen (Article 12) and Jere Real (1964), in *American Opinion,* the monthly journal of the John Birch Society, have denounced folksingers and rock 'n' roll artists for subverting American teenagers as part of the international Communist conspiracy. David A. Noebel, of the Christian Crusade, has been especially vocal about the "narcotizing influences" of rock music in general and the Beatles in particular. In *Rhythm, Riots and Revolution* (1966) he portrayed a rock song's lyrics as being:

. . . . obviously aimed at instilling fear in our teenagers as well as a sense of hopelessness. Thermonuclear holocaust, the button, the end of the world, and similar expressions are constantly being used to induce the American public to surrender to atheistic, international Communism. (1966: 229).

While this description of Barry McGuire's "Eve of Destruction" may have some semblance of fact, since it is an anti-war song, Noebel's treatment of the Beatles is purely ideological in nature:

Throw your Beatle rock and roll records in the city dump. We have been unashamed of being labeled a Christian nation . . . let's make sure four mop-headed anti-Christ beatniks don't destroy our children's emotional and mental stability and ultimately destroy our nation . . .

Noebel's attacks on the Beatles are generally in keeping with right-wing ideology as described by Rush, Denisoff, and others, that is, fearfulness of the decline of traditional values which stress individual morality. Noebel's thesis is simply that modern technology, when placed in the hands of the immoral, will be used to seduce American youth in Pied Piper fashion. This view is forcefully put by Susan Huck in "The Great Kid-Con" (Article 13).

Such a conspiratorial view is, however, hardly the exclusive property of the Radical Right. Political commentators on the Left see Machiavellian maneuverings which are aimed at thwarting their cause. Rock musicians such as the Beatles and particularly Bob Dylan, who "defected" from the more proletarian genre of folk music, have been cited as creators and possessors of "false consciousness." For example, A. Martynova writing in *Sovetskaya Kultura,* the official organ of the Ministry of Culture of the Soviet Union, denounced the Beatles as perverters of class consciousness. The Beatles are pictured as "creators of a fairy tale," who:

. . . . have always been proud of their being apolitical and of their non-participation in the governmental machine. They invite one into the world of love, nature, and pure feelings, in short, into another world, one separated from the surrounding . . . political . . . one . . . they didn't find such a world, even with the help of

narcotics. Instead, they became the property of another world—
of pop-art, the market, and business. (1969:4).

In an analogue to the right-wing perspectives of Allen and Huck,
Michael Lydon (1969), writing from a leftist perspective, argues that rock
is an opiate of the young which seduces them from the true path, but, unlike them, he defines the ideal path as political revolution.

In the United States Bob Dylan, the moving force behind the emphasis
on lyrics in rock music, has been roundly condemned for this lack of
political commitment. Irwin Silber in *Sing Out!*, Paul Wolfe in *Broadside*
(*NYC*) and Peter Aceves in *The Spectator* all have attacked Dylan for
leaving the "protest song" genre and becoming more abstract in lyric and
submersed into the rock music style. This upset a good number of former
People's songsters who had seen Dylan as a sort of reincarnation of Woody
Guthrie, which of course, he was not. Others, particularly in the New York
folk scene, felt personally betrayed. Pete Seeger, reportedly, wept when
Dylan appeared, rock band and all, at Newport and was booed off the stage.
Paul Wolfe's *Broadside* article, reprinted here, provides a vivid illustration
of the reaction to Dylan's artistic changes, which Aceves sums up as: "In
abandoning his socially conscious fans, Dylan has paid the price of becoming just another product of mass culture."

Marion Meade is a rock music lover who finds much in the music
scene to criticize. Her *form* of argument is a severe castigation of rock for
furthering a cause which it outwardly condemns—male chauvinism. She
notes that rock's "rebellion against middle-class values, its championing of
the unisex fashions, and long hair styles for men, seem to suggest a blurring
of the distinctions between male and female. But for all its hip camouflage,
sexism flourishes." The several letters to the editors of the *New York Times*
in response to the Meade piece add more voices to the cacophonic commentary affirming that rock's influence on our times is a variously interpreted thing.

Rock music, then, is many things to many people who tend to interpret
it within their particular frame of reference. The acidhead and the speed
freak may experience the Jefferson Airplane or the Grateful Dead in a
totally different way than the occasional visitor to the Fillmore West.
Dancers will feel the loud pulsating rhythms of a rock band, while sta-
tionary concertgoers may evaluate intellectually the material they are hearing. So it is in the political arena. The "radical consciousness," the imposition of a logically closed system of thought, of those on the Right and the

Left, leads them to conclusions which most non-political individuals would miss. For example, few rock fans seriously believe that the Beatles are Kremlin agents attempting to enslave their minds. Nor do most rock music enthusiasts see their favorite artists as tools in a class struggle between the establishment and the oppressed. Instead, each social group envisions rock music in a way compatible to its frame of reference and particular ideology.

Taken together, the readings in this chapter demonstrate the sociological principle that "being"—an individual's status, education, occupation, age, etc.—determines his consciousness; what W. I. Thomas called the "definition of the situation," or Harry Stack Sullivan termed "selective perception." Thus, rock is a four letter word which may mean nothing more or less than what you think it does, and your opinion tells much about *who* you are.

REFERENCES

Belz, Carl
  1969   The Story of Rock. New York: Oxford University Press.
Denisoff, R. Serge (ed.)
  1971   The Spectrum of Political Nonconformity In the United States. New York: Harcourt, Brace, and World.
Gillett, Charlie
  1970   The Sound of the City. New York: Outerbridge and Dienstfrey.
Gleason, Ralph
  1969   The Jefferson Airplane and the San Francisco Sound. New York: Ballantine.
  1971   "The Dream Simply Isn't Over." Rolling Stone (October 28): 30.
Goldstein, Richard
  1968   "The New Rock: Wiggy Words That Feed Your Mind." Life (June 28): 67–68, 70.
Hopkins, Jerry
  1970   The Rock Story. New York: New American Library.
Laing, Dave
  1969   The Sound of Our Time. Chicago: Quadrangle Books.
Lydon, Michael
  1969   "Rock for Sale." Ramparts Magazine (June): 19–24.
  1971   Rock Folk. New York: Dial Press.
Martynova, A.
  1969   "Beatles as Cinderella: A Soviet Tale" (trans. by Ieva Vitins). Rolling Stone (February 15): 1, 4.

Melly, George
    1971   Revolt into Style. New York: Doubleday.
Noebel, David
    1965   Communism, Hypnotism and the Beatles. Tulsa: Christian Crusade
              Publications.
    1966   Rhythm, Riots, and Revolution. Tulsa: Christian Crusade Publica-
              tions.
Peterson, Richard A.
    1970   "Rock as Fad, Revolution, Moral Solvent, Opiate, and Bread."
              Paper delivered at the Ohio Valley Sociological Society Meetings,
              Akron, Ohio (May 2).
Real, Jere
    1964   "Folk Music and Red Tubthumpers," American Opinion 7 (De-
              cember): 19–24.
Roszak, Theodore
    1969   The Making of a Counter Culture: Reflections on the Technological
              Society and Its Youthful Opposition. Garden City: Anchor Books.
Rush, Gary B. and R. Serge Denisoff
    1970   A World To Win: A Social History of Ideological Movements.
              New York: Appleton-Century-Crofts.
Shaw, Arnold
    1971   The Rock Revolution. New York: Macmillan.
Yinger, J. Milton
    1960   "Contraculture and Subculture." American Sociological Review 25
              (October): 625–635.

9

A NEW AWAKENING

Greil Marcus

If there is anything definite that can be said about today's music, it is that the old-fashioned protest song has been junked, relegated to the godforsaken past. There is a reason for that: protest songs, when they were bad, were preaching songs, instant pulpit, instant Billy Graham. They refused to allow the listener to make any decisions; they took away his freedom by telling him that if he liked the song he was right, and if he didn't like it he was wrong. There isn't any way one can talk about "digging" a protest song—first off, you had to *agree* with it. That style made "content" obnoxious, and it still does.

There are many ways to get something across, though; and if the artist has any respect for his audience, and any respect for his art, he'll not make it too clear what he means, because he probably isn't too sure himself. There's just a feeling, a sense, and it's that hint of certainty against a conversation of emotions that forms the basis for the best rock 'n' roll stories: the stories Dylan tells, that his band tells, that the Stones told in "Play with Fire" and "I Am Waiting" and "Who's Been Sleeping Here," that the Beatles told in "Girl" and "Norwegian Wood" and "A Day in the Life." A situation is created, and the music makes it real, gives it immediacy, drawing the listener in, and as the story ends, the mind is reaching, and will return for another try, not to "interpret," most likely, but to get close to the stories our music tells us.

It was a very depressing time. The Democratic party had just presided over its incredible black mass in Chicago. They had given the American public its first view of the American police state in all its grisly omnipotence. In depressing times, I listen to music. I put on an old Pete Seeger song I used to love, called "Hold On." The song was once an ancient gospel chant, a biblical challenge of sin and retribution, but Seeger had changed the lyrics to straight protest: "United Nations make a chain, every link is freedom's name." It's a good song, the music, Seeger's banjo, his singing; but the words are flat, and they have no power of motion. They are incapable of taking the listener beyond himself. The lyrics, holding the "message," are the weakest part of it all; they pull the experience of hearing Pete Seeger sing "Hold On" down to sterility, while his voice and his music try to pull one out of oneself into the transcendental experience that is the miracle of any sort of music at its best.

It's the smugness that destroys the art. Believing in, say, racial harmony, another of the causes listed in "Hold On," needn't be smug, but when Seeger sings out in its defense, and the audience cheers, they cheer not only, not even principally for the affirmation of a "good," but for themselves, because they recognize that the black and white politics of "Hold On" divide the world into two sides, right and wrong, and they're right. It's Lenny Bruce's story all over again: "Yeah, Joe Louis was a hell of a fighter . . ."

There is nothing to understand in message lyrics of this sort, lyrics that are afraid to admit to the element of uncertainty and unpredictability that gives art—music, painting, poetry—the tension that opens up the senses. There is nothing to keep the mind alive; there is just something to undercut and perhaps even destroy the music that "goes with" the message. Singing protest songs on a sit-in or on a demonstration can be different; sometimes you have to applaud yourself just to keep going. Even then, I think, the words are irrelevant. They are an excuse to start singing, to have "something to sing," because people still think that words are "something," and that music is what you hang that something on. But it's the experience of letting the rhythms of the music capture you, together, that affirms the group, strengthening the will to fight and keeping the struggle going. It is the act of singing, not the message mouthed as the words are sung. That's why when Phil Ochs gets up to sing protest songs to people getting ready for a demonstration, to tell them that they are right and that their opponents are wrong, he always sounds flat and empty compared to the singing that begins when the cops move in. That's why no one ever argues about what song to sing when the time for singing comes. And that is why I can't listen to a message song, that tells me that I'm right and the world is wrong, when I'm depressed and disgusted with the politics that these songs try to sing about.

To clear my head, I put on Dylan's "Absolutely Sweet Marie," a great rock 'n' roll song, and then I put on "Memphis Blues Again." I've heard that song hundreds of times before, but this time it was different. It became a journey, a rite of passage, a struggling effort to pass out of an inexplicable contradiction, only to find another, with no escape, only a change to a new chord, a new movement of the guitar or organ, intensifying the desire that it all be over, if only on a crude level of time. And then it was all there, all in front of me—that incredible black mass had been captured, framed, and punctured.

I didn't "interpret" the words to "Memphis Blues," they interpreted my situation. They existed to act on me, not for me to figure out "what they mean." They'll mean something else the next time I hear them. The music carries those words—I might never have heard them without the jangling of the guitar that caught my ear and made them jump. But the words don't exist as statements; they exist as part of a song, as a moment on that journey I was trying to get through.

The words of a message song just lie on the floor, dragging the music down. You don't have to go to them, they don't have to go to you. There is nothing to reach for. "Message," in music, isn't "meaning"—what is meaningful has powers of its own, powers that aren't carefully explained out of a fear that someone might miss something. There is a recording of Dylan's "Blowin' In the Wind" by Peter, Paul, and Mary, in which they very conscientiously inform the audience that "this song asks nine questions—we hope, as we ask them, you will ask them of yourselves." That's a lot different from the Grateful Dead yelling to the audience: "Let's get up and dance!"

If music is "meaningful," its meaning must be free enough to depend on how one hears it. "Shooby shooby doo wah," heard in the right mood, has more meaning than a flat-out protest song ever does, because by definition when you listen to a protest song absolutely nothing is in doubt; the listener is in a box. There isn't any movement. But Dylan told me a little story, and where he got it I don't know, and it doesn't matter at all, because that story keeps finding new ways to tell itself to me.

That was my best response to the dismal events of the political week; but in Berkeley, in the middle of August, two sets of events, "political" and "musical," set to work on one another. The "newspaper" we were reading had stories in it other parts of the country missed; our newspaper had the Rolling Stones and the Beatles right next to Hubert Humphrey, and Country Joe & the Fish along with Mayor Daley.

As thousands of demonstrators and onlookers and even a score of convention delegates were beaten and busted by the Chicago police, the Fish, our very own hometown big-time rock 'n' roll band, in town for the big week, were given theirs by a few of Chicago's law-abiding citizens, veterans of Vietnam to boot. Law and order is where you find it. These fellows found it in the lobby of the hotel where the Fish were staying. Screaming, "Why don't you like America, you dirty hippies!" they knocked Barry, the lead guitarist, into an elevator, and as it shot up four stories, they took on Country Joe and David, the organist. By the time Barry had made it downstairs, armed with a fire extinguisher, the veterans had split, leaving the cops who were called with an unsolvable mystery. It seemed that "to live outside the law" you not only have to be "honest," but fast on your feet. The Fish, one of the country's most political rock bands, who dedicated an album to Bobby Hutton, an eighteen-year-old Black Panther shot by the Oakland police, were our Marx-Brothers-reminder that youth is the enemy, not only to the police, but to the nation. Their troubles made us realize, in the midst of Chicago's enforced vision of crime and brutality, that political terror is random as well as institutional; that risk is becoming less a matter of commitment than of age.

The day after the convention, people in Berkeley took to the street. It wasn't nearly as dramatic as it sounds. We went to Telegraph Avenue to show sympathy with the kids in Chicago, to flaunt the police, to see what would happen at the latest of Berkeley's innumerable illegal rallies. We had something to talk about there on the street, beneath the speech-making and outside of the slogans we'd all heard too many times before. For in the midst of this incredible week of cops and hatred, with our memories of the Paris students' rebellion in the spring and the Berkeley police riots of early summer, the Beatles and the Rolling Stones had released new singles. There we were on the Avenue, not really knowing why we were there, waiting around for the cops who were staying away, both jealous and relieved that we hadn't been in Chicago, but listening in our minds to John Lennon singing "Revolution" and Mick Jagger screaming "Street Fighting Man."

The Beatles were ordering us to pack up and go home, but the Stones seemed to be saying that we were lucky if we had a fight to make and a place to take a stand.

"The Beatles are preaching again," remarked a disk jockey, as he played "Revolution" along with the Stones' "Street Fighting Man." "You *know* which one of these they aren't playing in Chicago this week."

> But when you talk about destruction
> Don't you know that you can count me out.

A lot of the people were mad at the Beatles because their "politics" didn't agree with ours. We felt tricked, because we had expected the Beatles to be *our* spokesmen (whoever "we" were), to say what we wanted to hear, what we wanted to learn about. We had taken the Beatles for granted, and if we felt tricked, it was probably our fault. There was, though, a lot more involved.

The Beatles were giving orders and setting up rules, singing words that were perfectly intelligible, making sure nobody missed anything, singing a song that neatly caught the listener in a logical trap. No one takes sides with the "minds that hate" that the Beatles were singing about. "Revolution," though hardly a protest song, worked like one. It set up all the old barriers, retrieving all the abandoned assumptions about life: the world divided into two sides, right and wrong, one side indefensible, the other unassailable. And who wants to be wrong, especially when the magic Beatles are beckoning?

. . . The lyrics John Lennon was singing had no space for doubt or illusion, no space for the listener if he happened to be different. They had no space, for that matter, for fun. Nothing was left to the imagination. The words delivered a straightforward message, a strict command.

The best songs the Beatles write add dimensions of experience and imagination to our lives, revealing new realms into which we might not have entered without a little help. It is done in such a simple and inscrutable way that we find ourselves with epigrams and epitaphs for every season of the year. In "A Day in the Life" the Beatles strung out the cliches of anyone's morning routine, and then exploded them, opening up the possibility that the tying of one's shoe might reveal terror and impotence, or power and grace. In "Penny Lane" they built and dismantled a theatre without ever interrupting the comedy in progress: "And tho' she thinks she's in a play, she is anyway." I could walk through a whole day with that phrase in my head and watch everything and everyone bloom like a charming flower. A line like that sticks in one's memory and tempts it; a singer cannot touch its power by declaiming "Love is all around" or by barking "Free your mind."

The words to "Revolution" close down the theatre instead of opening it up, denying the imagination in favor of a tangible opinion. There are no elusive secrets, only phrases that keep company with those slogans we ignored that night on Telegraph Avenue after the Convention. "Revolution" speaks a language that destroys the relationship between performer and listener that the Beatles created with songs like "Penny Lane"; with that, they gave us a mirror, but they didn't tell us we had to look in it.

But rock 'n' roll is not the polite, quiet, cerebral music of the protest song, and "Revolution" isn't the strumming of a folk guitar, it's full of the crashing explosions of a great rock 'n' roll band. There is freedom and movement in the music, even as there is sterility and repression in the lyrics. Music takes risks that politics avoid, and that is why "Revolution" isn't simply a collection of pronouncements and rules. Years ago, with the words fitted to another idiom, it might have been, but it isn't now. It is a wild, shouting song that is so immediate and ecstatic that I find myself singing along as my fingers pound out the beat. The music makes me feel happy even though the lyrics depress me. John Lennon's singing possesses all the thrill of rock 'n' roll, his voice as full of the humor of his wonderful grin as the words he sings are empty of it. Nicky Hopkins, sitting in, hits the piano like nobody since Huey "Piano" Smith and Frankie Ford teamed up on "Roberta" and "Sea-Cruise"; like the frantic piano player on "One Fine Day," only better. George Harrison and John Lennon are playing unfettered and incredibly loud guitars, mad with the freedom of making music on the spot, sounding like the best guitarists in the world.

Eyes brighten, bodies move. If you're reading a newspaper, that music says put it down, listen to me; if you're driving a car, you put your foot down on the accelerator and beat your hand on the roof and all over the dashboard.

The radio executives ought to be more careful, those men that smugly program "Revolution" every hour in the hope that it will keep the kids off the streets. Those men like the "message," but there is a "message" in that music which is ultimately more powerful than anyone's words. The music doesn't say "cool it" or "don't fight the cops." Rock 'n' roll music at its best, and it's at its best in "Revolution," doesn't follow orders—it makes people aware of their bodies and aware of themselves. Lyrics like . . . "free your mind instead" can't make people forget the beat they feel in their hearts or the confidence in themselves they sense when the beat is translated into a personality of movement.

I can dig "Revolution," and get beyond the level of right and wrong that the lyrics try to impose, because it's a great rock 'n' roll song before it's a "message." There is too much to listen to for the obviousness of one element to triumph. A great rock 'n' roll "protest" song can't be written or sung, because if it is great rock 'n' roll the music dodges the message and comes out in front, especially if the message is clear and unmistakable. The idea must be virtually lost in the music before it is worth reaching for, or be so simple and emotional that "words" and "idea" become music themselves, as they do in the songs of Otis Redding.

So coming out of a few windows that night was this great obnoxious rock 'n' roll song. It was hardly enough. We wanted to hear the rest of the story. We wanted the Stones there with us as well; but "Street Fighting Man" was invisible except for the title. It had been banned in the Bay Area as well as in Chicago. We kept talking, though; it is amazing how people can speculate on a song they've never even heard.

There's Just No Place for Street Fighting Man

The Stones broke in looking tough and angry and hungry, even though Mick Jagger had just dropped out of the London School of Economics. They became a vehicle for everyone's petty rebellions, and when they got a chance to catch their breath, they set about giving those rebellions a little content. The Stones were each of us when we were mad at our parents, at society, at our friends. They came on hard, not kidding around, with their first real hit, "I Wanna Be Your Man."

They had a little help from some slightly less outrageous friends in those days. The Beatles wrote that song for them, and it fit, far better than when Ringo recorded it some time later.

We didn't know about any of that when the Stones hit America in 1964. All we knew was that they had a driving, bluesy record, with their dark, menacing figures on their album cover. The pictures on the back of the record looked like mug shots of back-alley hoods, not friendly, almost as if they were daring you to play a game of "chicken" out of *Rebel Without a Cause.* Except that they didn't look as if they'd feel too bad if you happened to go over the cliff. The Stones were hardly that evil and cruel, of course; but it's easy to lose a little of one's perspective when for years all there had been to hear was the crooning of well-groomed Bobby Vee.

The notes to the first album seemed ridiculous: "The Rolling Stones are more than a group; they are a way of life." It turned out to be true, truer than any press agent or any fan could have guessed. More than anyone else, more than the Beatles, more than Dylan, the Stones created an image of a style of life, and put together a musical and verbal language with which to express that style. It is ever-changing, but always tough and humorous. Just listen to Keith Richard's playing on "Miss Amanda Jones" or "Ride On Baby." The only way I can describe his guitar on these songs is to call it "Ugly Throw-Up"; he has more jokes to tell than a stand-up comedian, all of them sarcastic, until he seems to be cracking up over his own tag lines.

When the Stones find themselves trapped in a story they're telling, such as their attempt to get across the uselessness and the confusion of the guy trying to save the girl in "The 19th Nervous Breakdown," they don't sit down and keep calm, as our Boy Scout Handbook told us to do when we got lost in the woods—they pick up their instruments and make hard, scary, exhilarating music, and break out of it.

The Rolling Stones aren't "liberal," in the classical sense of the word, in the way that British (and American) politics are "liberal." As "Street Fighting Man" went on sale in the record stores, the cop-killing trial of Oakland Black Panther leader Huey Newton resulted in a verdict of "voluntary manslaughter," not murder, not acquittal, but a carefully balanced "liberal" decision, "taking two positions, either of which might be true, and arriving at a compromise that could not possibly be true." The Stones aren't "liberal." That doesn't mean they always have to win; they can accept something that can't be won, that can't be understood. In "Ruby Tuesday" they sang about a girl that no one could "hang a name on," that no one could conquer or pin down. But they aren't interested in compromises.

Their "politics" would always be confused, because they would never bother to separate "politics" from life, in the bedroom or on the streets. The characters in the stories the Stones tell accept problems that can't be easily adjusted to protect one sphere of experience from another. Their "politics" might be like the politics of Parnell, the great Irish nationalist leader, who survived prison and a charge of treason only to destroy his career and his life when he stole the wife of his most fervent supporter. A man like Parnell would have loved the Stones singing, "Let's drink to the hard working people, let's drink to the salt of the earth," not just because of the song's "politics" but because it's a song one could sing in a pub just before closing time.

Out of the pubs and into the streets. "Street Fighting Man." Listen to it. There will be an automatic "political" response, if one is expecting a wax manifesto: "What the hell is going on? I can't understand anything but the title! I can't hear a word Jagger's saying!"

That is as it should be—a confusion for the listener, so he has to pull out of it himself. Words not too clear, so there is an incentive to go further into the song, to become more involved with the rhythm and the chords. Mick Jagger takes his cue from early rock 'n' roll: he has said that the words should never be sung too neatly—yell out a motif or a phrase so everyone can hear it, giving people a place from which to start, but let them figure out the rest for themselves. The Stones have never fallen into the arty trap of printing their song lyrics on their albums, as have the Beatles, the Doors, Jimi Hendrix, and others. The first rock 'n' roll game, if one wants to play it, is figuring out the words, just for fun. In a sense, each listener virtually writes his own song when he hears great records like "Street Fighting Man," records where music overpowers lyric. Getting a hint of an idea across *is* important, if it is a song with a story to tell, a story with an idea that wants to be placed in front of a listener; but a signpost is all that is needed to begin.

The people on Telegraph Avenue knew nothing of the Stones' new song save for the title. If it *had* been coming out of the windows of the apartments facing the street, along with "Revolution," the only words we would have understood would have been "street" and "fighting" and "man"—our place to start.

This motif stands in the middle of a very powerful sound. It is held up by a strong, strong combination of bass and drums, driving harder and harder, fighting the limits of the instruments, until finally the chorus comes back again and the Stones are ready for another try at answering their own question: "What can a poor boy do?... sleepy London town, it's just no place..."—asking the question, but smashing forward once again, because there's no time to reply when all one can hear is "the sound of marching, charging feet."

That question is very important, both for our own feelings when we have finally heard the song enough times to understand it, and for what the Stones themselves are doing with their music.

The Stones ask both us and themselves a question, injecting a humorous element of uncertainty into a situation that is really as confusing as a street riot. There is no doubt as to which side we're on, "of course," but what is really happening? "Nowhere to run to, nowhere to hide." Why not? What does "side" mean, anyway? It all has to come apart before it can come together; and *we* have to put it together. Someone might say, "Great! The Stones are telling us to go out and fight the cops! They're on our side!" but it's hardly that simple. If you can imagine the Stones' record personified, marching down the street, it might talk like this: "Yeah! I'm a Street Fighting Man! But who stole my paving stones? Who forgot to build the streets with them in the first place? My God, what am I doing here?" It gets complicated. The Stones create a situation that seems absolutely clearcut, but they accept just a hint of doubt, and that situation dissolves and becomes a challenging emotional jigsaw puzzle, not congratulations for being on the right side.

The Stones won't do our thinking for us, as the Beatles tried to do with "Revolution." They aren't giving orders, but describing a very simple situation that is possessed by an unexpected complexity. The tension rises, created by the band, as it fights the doubts of the lyrics with tough musical emotion, the tension created by Jagger's singing, angry and self-deprecating at the same time. What's going on?

> 'Cause summer's here and I think the time is right
> For fighting in the streets.

"Summer's here. . . ." It's almost a rock 'n' roll tradition to have a new summer-song every year. Usually, these June-to-September songs bounce gaily back and forth to nowhere, affirming the great good of summer as opposed to the unspeakable evil of school, in the vein of, "No more pencils, no more books, no more teacher's dirty looks." There are dozens: "Summer's Here," "Here Comes Summer," "Summer Set," "Summertime Summertime," "Summer in the City" (written by a boy who was still in high school), and to finish it off, the quaintly melancholy "Summer's Almost Gone." All of these songs were teenage paeans to the joy of release from bondage, replacing homework with "drive-in movies every night." Eddie Cochran sang the only summer-song about the problems and hang-ups of the off-season, with the great "Summertime Blues." A job to do while the sun was out, a boss who made you work overtime, a car you couldn't get, the fun the other kids were having while you baby-sat to earn money for gas. "There ain't no cure for the summertime blues!"

Like "Summertime Blues," "Street Fighting Man," our summer-song for a year of police riots and violence, catches the listener, not in a trap, as did the Beatles with "Revolution," but in a paradox. Summer is the time when all the problems are supposed to float away, but there are more problems than ever, because we're free of the usual mild slavery, with time on our hands, and they still won't leave us alone. Summer is a practical joke. Putting "Summertime Blues" or "Street Fighting Man" into the midst of the usual summer ditties is like inserting an obscene sculpture by Keinholz into a cheap copy of a landscape by Monet. It works that way. The Democrats weren't kind enough to hold their convention in February, and they didn't even call off the draft in honor of the baseball season.

The songs don't give answers. The Stones keep trying to find a place for their Street Fighting Man to catch his breath, and Eddie Cochran makes it all the way to Washington, D.C., in a hilarious state of innocence. Cochran's line about his Congressman tells us more about "politics" than any protest song, because its absurdity comes out of self-conscious humor. It isn't self-righteous; there is no desire to kick out the dirty old man and sit in his chair, to prove who is good and who is bad, an impulse that seems to underlie the spirit of most message songs. "Street Fighting Man" reveals an idea about Chicago or Paris or San Francisco or Berkeley that no learned article or New Left polemic has ever understood—that once one goes beyond an appeal to "our democratically elected representatives," and stands in the streets to represent oneself, the first flush of mastery and self-confidence dissolves into a confusion of very real doubts. It is hardly just a fear of the cops. Representing oneself is a very old idea that is suddenly very new, and the streets of "sleepy London town" (or any other town) were not built for its expression. "Street Fighting Man" is a musical confusion of feeling in a political context—very simply the context of our daily life—not a list of priorities or a secret map of battle plans. It is not a call for a revolution, but in a natural and necessary way, a part of one that is already in progress.

Rock 'n' roll is not a means by which to "learn about politics," nor a wavelength for a message as to what is to be done or who is to be fought. It is, at times (especially in such moments as August, 1968), a way to get a feeling for the political spaces we might happen to occupy at any particular time. Rock 'n' roll music and a rock 'n' roll song—a record—keeps those spaces open. That record holds back, for a moment, the tangible weight of enemies and outrages and violence, allowing us to move within a situation we create with a rock 'n' roll band, out of its response to our lives and our response to its song. Questions and humor, grafted on to the irresistible beat of exciting music, allow us to form that fleeting personality of movement. If we can keep moving in that space, opened up by a song that brings us a joke on ourselves and a sense of the doubts we might try to hide, we have a chance at an honest response to the coldly serious New Left and the fascism of the old guard. When doubt disappears, there is only bitterness and a desire to control everything that might offend. A "personality of movement" is just another way of saying that I heard a record, and it let the movement of my body open up a situation within which, for a moment, my mind could watch my emotions create my own song. It was this summer's gift from the Rolling Stones, just a "singer and a rock 'n' roll band."

10

A CULTURAL REVOLUTION

Ralph J. Gleason

Today, all over the United States, American young people are being spoken to by revolutionists in words they understand, in a style that makes those words acceptable, and through an invisible medium that old professional politicos have not yet picked up on.

This medium is the phonograph record, purveyor of bubble gum music and symbol of Elvis Presley's "Houn' Dog" and the celebrated "Get off of my Blue Suede Shoes" (which John Lennon once called a protest song). One of the leading manufacturers, Columbia Records, runs a series of advertisements in the underground press, the theme of which is "The man can't bust our music" and "Know your friends." The implication aligns "us" against "them," and the context of the advertising design and illustration is interracial, hippie, pot-smoking youth.

Is Columbia for legalization of marijuana? No. Columbia is for making money. Thus the investment in music aimed at long-haired youth. The music speaks directly to them, it leaps past all barriers and is justified by the sacred principles of the true religion of the United States, making money. Would Columbia invest in an advertising campaign for a product that did not make money? Would it sign a young Texas blues guitarist and singer for a guarantee of $300,000 if there were not millions to be made? (In February 1969 it did so.)

The popular music business—records and personal appearance—is a multi-million dollar proposition, yet the messages it sells to young people imply a

First published as "The Greater Sound" in *The Drama Review,* Volume 13, Number 4 (T44) (Summer 1969), pp. 160–67. Copyright © by *The Drama Review.* Reprinted by permission. All rights reserved.

distinctly different way of looking at the world than that which is held by their parents—or by the owners of the record companies. The economic momentum of the medium confounds old Marxian analysis. It's possible to say that the expression of youth's disaffiliation through pop music merely siphons off rebellious feelings and makes them assimilable and in the long run harmless—but surely this is offset by the fact that unarticulated protest is made specific, and applied to political subjects like Vietnam, for kids in remote towns who wouldn't otherwise know that they are part of a vast movement or wouldn't connect their discontent to its sources in our social-political setup.

A fallible but useful gauge of the efficacy of a movement may be the degree of reaction which it provokes. Military scientists are fond of looking at "the other side of the hill," as Wellington put it, to see how their situation appears to those they are fighting. To Republican Congressman James Tustin of California, the Beatles and the other rock musicians "use Pavlovian techniques to provoke neurosis in their listeners." Congressman Tustin also believes that rock 'n' roll and sex education (he combines them; a view not far from the mark) are a Communist plot to destroy our nation. *American Opinion* and other organs of the radical right, as well as fundamentalist religious publications, are vehement in their protest against the music of electric guitars. When radical rightists talk about telstars and satellite H-bombs hung in the sky by Russia, when they discuss George C. Marshall as a Communist, they are hallucinating. When they talk of the Beatles as Communists, they are not hallucinating—they are merely mislabeling the contents. They correctly define the Beatles as their enemy.

A new philosophy has been articulated and communicated. And, as Plato warned,

> Forms and rhythms in music are never changed without producing changes in the most important political forms and ways . . . the new style quietly insinuates itself into manners and customs and from there it issues a greater force . . . goes on to attack laws and constitutions, displaying the utmost impudence, until it ends by overthrowing everything, both in public and in private . . .

The content of rock lyrics has had the most obvious effect on our "customs and manners"—and these lyrics are always meant to be heard, although technology trips them up sometimes. But the movement in pop from foxtrot rhythms to black variants of 6/8 time or triplets over a 4/4 beat has brought blues, always an underground communication against the oppressor, overground. There's been a parallel development in dancing, from the rigidity of Arthur-Murray-type box-stepping to a sensuous, individual expression. Dylan's message is in his lines, the Grateful Dead's is in the form of their music, its relation to drug and sexual experiences, its improvising freedom—and in the way that's shown through their collective movements and creation on stage.

The 12-inch long-playing vinylite phonograph record, with its half-hour to 45 minutes of songs, is an intellectual time bomb—even if bought primarily for a hit song heard on thousands of radio stations (and radio means *only* pop music to all those Americans under 25 who will add up to more than 50 percent of the population in another year). The album brings to its purchaser other songs as well. They are all heard. Even though Mick Jagger of the Rolling Stones was forced by the Ed Sullivan TV show producers to change "let's spend the night together" to "let's spend some time together," none of the young people who saw the show were fooled. The millions who own the disc, and the millions upon millions who have heard it in the original version on radio stations, know the right words. (Ironically, it was radio's desperate reaction after TV came on the scene which started the stations bringing rhythm and blues—"nigger music"—to white ears which previously had at best heard Basie and the swing bands.)

The Rolling Stones attack sexual taboos and endorse the directness of today's young people. Not an overtly revolutionary act but one which—when coupled with the Beatles singing "I'd love to turn you on" and "I get high with a little help from my friends" and Grace Slick in "White Rabbit" advising listeners to "feed your head" (after telling them about "pills which make you large and pills which make you small and the ones that mother gives don't do anything at all")—challenges fundamentals of American behavior. Once you set up a situation in which sacred tenets of the social fabric are treated as obsolete or irrelevant, anything may be questioned. There are also the more directly political songs of Bob Dylan, Country Joe & the Fish, and other groups. Dylan is central. His songs provide phrases to be quoted in political tracts of the underground and college press as well as in conversation. Even American adults have heard of Bob Dylan.

Country Joe & the Fish, with three best-selling albums last year, have a song called "Fixin' to Die Rag." Country Joe comes right to the point, "Put down your books and pick up your gun/we're gonna have a lot of fun." In the last verse, using a Brechtian image with parallels going back to "When Johnny Comes Marchin' Home," the group sings, "You can be the first ones in your block to have your boy come home in a box." That song has been heard and understood by millions. It is heard by someone every day in all probability. Is there any comparable medium?

In Iowa and Minnesota, in Arizona and Florida and Washington—as well as in Central Park—Country Joe & the Fish sing that song and lead their audience in the "Fish Cheer"—"Gimme an F! Gimme a U! Gimme a C! Gimme a K! All right, F!U!C!K! Fuck!" After they did that in Central Park the vice presidents of their booking agency, which handles talent for all the best places and all the best TV shows, staggered unbelievingly back to their plush offices. But they did not stop arranging concerts for the band.

The Democrats in the last election were aware of some of the power of this music. Johnson and Humphrey tried to reach people through James Brown and the Supremes. Coca-Cola sells its product via the pop stars. But the James Brown government-sponsored message, "Don't Be a Drop Out," had not one-tenth the effect of his ghetto hit, "Say It Loud, I'm Black and I'm Proud." The "sell" is easy to detect in music.

Today there are almost one hundred FM stations all around the country constituting what the radio trade calls "underground" radio—they play adult rock music, not the teeniebopper music of the Monkees and Nancy Sinatra and the plastic contrived rock groups who play the discotheques and dominate the Top 40 radio station play-list. Buffy Sainte-Marie's records get played a good deal on these stations. One of her songs is called "My Country 'Tis of Thy People You Are Dying," a bitter indictment of United States society, which she accuses of lying, of censoring history books, of untrustworthiness ("see what our trust in America brought us"), of genocide, and of ghoulishness ("the graves have been robbed"). Then she applies a fundamental Marxist thesis—"Can't you see that their poverty is profiting you?"

The Mothers of Invention is a group of electronic music experimenters from Los Angeles who along with creating very serious music, indulge in an all-out satirical commentary on American society rivaled only by that of Lenny Bruce. Their first album for Verve, which made their reputation, sold more than 300,000 copies and is still selling (when a *book* sells 300,000 copies it is news; a point to be remembered in this discussion). "Who Are the Brain Police?" and "Trouble Every Day" are on this album and both are sharp, insightful attacks on the structure of the society. Students in schools and universities where the SDS hasn't a slim chance of penetrating hear this message loud and clear. And they believe it as they do *not* believe the history books in their classes and will never again believe their teachers.

Some radical politicos have sensed the importance of this medium, though perhaps not considering it either as revolutionary or as useful as I do. As I see it, the situation is plain: if you want to reach young people in this country (and revolutions are made by the young; the old make counter-revolution) then write a song, don't buy an ad or issue a statement. In the early 'fifties, Tennessee Ernie Ford made a hit out of "Sixteen Tons," a song that was a pure economic determinist account of the reality of coal mining life, but nobody took it seriously. At that point in time, American song hits were generally written *for* someone else to sing and not sung by the man who wrote them. Carl Oglesby of the SDS is writing songs and playing with a rock band. Hubert

Humphrey had songs written and played for him. We do not know yet what Oglesby's songs are like, but they are his own. One's imagination may stagger at the sight of Hubert Humphrey arm in arm with the Supremes, but mine, at least, simply will not accept HHH writing and singing a song.

Dylan, of course, set the mold for all of this. He showed the record companies that there were huge profits to be made with songs that might be labeled controversial and which *said things,* instead of using innocuous or euphemistic lyrics. And the record companies, discovering he was right, dropped the taboos. It was not only his issue-oriented, topical songs which were effective —such as "Who Killed Davey Moore" (about the death of a boxer; in it, after enumerating those who denied responsibility, he pointed out that boxing was illegal in Cuba) or "The Lonesome Death of Hattie Carroll" (the story of the brutal murder of a Baltimore house servant by a white employer, in which Dylan named the names); it was the trio of unofficial anthems of the movement: "Blowin' in the Wind," "The Times They Are a Changin'," and "Chimes of Freedom": sung by Dylan and by others, they became a propaganda campaign that shames the Voice of America. It is no wonder that right-wing congressmen and clergy attacked Baez and Dylan and Pete Seeger and the others who sang the songs. But it was when Dylan abandoned his topical "folk" songs and devoted himself to composing a series of State-of-the-Union addresses describing the American social and cultural landscape that he made his deepest and most important impression on American youth.

Dylan made a record called "Subterranean Homesick Blues," backed by an electric rock 'n' roll band. It was an instant hit and he became a pop star. Kids scribbled the words on scraps of paper and duplicated them on high school ditto machines to pass around. In "chains of flashing images" Dylan described a world in which young people are monotonously advised to "please her, please him," urged to be a success, told "don't steal, don't lift," and as a reward after "twenty years of schoolin' . . . they put you on the day shift." The repeated theme of the song was "look out kid, it's something you did, God knows when but you're doin' it again." Dylan hit on the mindless drive to blame the young, the new, and the different, and on the true hypocrisy of the American dream.

"Subterranean Homesick Blues" was a single 45 disc. Dylan's next hit was "Like a Rolling Stone," one of the best-selling records of 1965. In it he spoke directly to young people, assuming their isolation from the adult world. "Like a Rolling Stone" was in an album, *Highway 61 Revisited,* in which there were two other seminal songs, "Ballad of a Thin Man" and "Desolation Row." "Ballad of a Thin Man" is Dylan's indictment of the liberal intellectual adult. Its refrain, "something is happening and you don't know what it is, do you, Mr. Jones?" has become a catch phrase to describe the generation gap. Huey P. Newton, the Black Panther leader jailed for the killing of an Oakland policeman, says he could not have written his "Papers from the Minister of Defense," the ideological framework of the Panther party, if it had not been for that song. "Desolation Row" is a poet's prophetic vision of the reality of America. The villains are "the agents" (after all, Dylan lives in a world of show business with concert, recording, and booking agents). At the fatal hour of midnight they appear "and round up everybody that knows more than they do."

In that verse, as well as in others in the same song and in other similar songs ("Maggie's Farm" and "It's Allright Ma" especially), Dylan lays out a view of American society as valueless, its institutions as rotten, and its leaders as immoral and without any motive but greed and power. The body of Dylan's work (and familiarity with it is a prerequisite for political activity in America) adds up to the starkest analysis yet of the poverty of the system, of Orwellian submission to the machine in its anti-human, anti-artist drive, and of the impossibility of change until the entire structure is revised—*and until the way in which such change is thought about is revised.*

Dylan's poetry is studied today in some university English classes and in many high schools. Sometimes it is part of the established curriculum, but generally it is included either because of a conviction by the teacher of its importance or as a response to the demands of students. In either case, it is being done. The millions who bought the Dylan albums (and a best seller in 1968 was *The Best of Bob Dylan,* which had "Rolling Stone," "Subterranean," "The Times They Are a Changin' " and "Blowin' in the Wind" on it) have heard and absorbed all the lyric content.

In Europe last summer Danny Rifkin, one of the managers of the Grateful Dead, a San Francisco rock group, was hitchhiking through Germany. Everywhere he stopped for the night, in camps, in fields, in hostels where young people gathered, he reports they had miniature tape recorders with cassettes of Dylan music which they played at night, their ears pressed to the tiny speakers. In this country, innumerable people in high school and college (and some older) go to bed nightly, their phonographs playing with the automatic turn-off devices set. It is sleep-learning of a kind. As they drift off to sleep, the words of the prophet ring in their ears.

Timothy Leary captured the mass media with his "Turn On, Tune In, Drop Out" slogan, but the Beatles made it stick with their songs of love and pleasure. If Dylan and the Stones represent a relentlessly real (though poetic) description of the world around us, the Beatles speak of hope ("Hey Jude" is almost religious in tone) and of a glorious future ("All we need is love").

The argument over activism in the American Movement has been summed up in music. The Beatles in "Revolution" said "if you want money for people with minds that hate, all I can tell you is brother you have to wait" . . . Nina Simone, the black American singer, sings a response to the Beatles which is currently widely played on radio. "Sing about a revolution because I'm talking 'bout a change. . . ."

But beneath the struggle in the Movement today is the central fact that if you accept Dylan you can never again see America as Jackie Gleason or Governor Rockefeller or even, on the good guy scale, as Mayor Lindsay or the textbooks see America—nor, especially, as the *New York Review* or the *Nation* see it. Young politicos know Dylan's songs and dig them. Yet the implications of his truths contradict the imperative of their ideology which, despite its radical nature, is imbued with the concept that the engine *can* be made to work, if only the tracks are changed and the power supply altered. Dylan says flatly it won't work because it is by its nature corrupt and corrupting. The Beatles say it won't work and that we have to walk away from it and change our heads (i.e., change the way we think about all of it, including change itself). "Lighting a joint is a revolutionary act," Leary says, and there is deep truth in this, since the act puts the actor outside the law from that time on. But I think that the whole body of rock music, spreading out from the center, with Dylan, the Beatles, and the Stones, involves its audience in an even more fundamental confrontation with the society. It says you are, all of you, wrong.

Rock music has involved young people as no other pop or elite art has ever done. In fact, it has involved young people as nothing else at all, aside from sex, has done in generations. It has made poetry real to them. It has given them the vision that they can literally take over the world, as they see members of their own generation seizing the means of production in one area— concerts, dances, record companies run by under-25's. It has firmly allied youth, bound them together with an invisible chain of sounds and a network of verbal images in defense against the Elders. No amount of public (free) appearances by Jackie Gleason and drummed-up Kids for Decency crusades will diminish the actual popularity of the Doors or Jim Morrison. There are short-term pragmatic objections to Jim Morrison of the Doors unzipping his rig and shaking it out for the audience in Florida to see. But as Lenny Bruce said, if you find something wrong with the product complain to the manufacturer. The rock bands, their life style and their music, say the human body—and hence each human being—is beautiful. American morality to the contrary notwithstanding.

There is as yet no program. But there is intuition that there will be one. In a midwestern university where the few activist students were depressed about the barren cultural landscape and the dim prospect of getting students politicized, they finally decided that the opening wedge would be a series of rock dances and/or concerts. The Living Theatre appeared this winter in Berkeley, where there have been free rock concerts in the park on sunny Sundays for two years and rock dances most weekends. The Living made little impact. "The rock 'n' roll showcase has eliminated all this with swinging music and lots of people," R. G. Davis of the S. F. Mime Troupe commented. Some weeks earlier a benefit for the Oakland Seven, on trial for leading anti-draft demonstrations against the Oakland Army Base, drew more people than the Living Theatre by presenting a series of rock bands plus speeches by Black Panther Bobby Seale and Kathleen Cleaver.

In the program for the Living Theatre, it is stated that the group is "in the vanguard of a new phenomenon in theatrical and social history—the spontaneous generation of communal playing troupes sharing voluntary poverty, making experimental collective creations and exploring time, space, minds and bodies in manifold new ways . . ." The rock groups have been doing this since 1965 and reaching an audience infinitely greater. It also might be noted that when asked by *Time* what Aretha Franklin's music (i.e., soul/gospel) was about, Godfrey Cambridge said "Fucking." Julian Beck squats morosely on stage and cries "fuck for peace" like a sentence imposed by a Kafka judge. The rock bands sing "fuck for joy" in every line, as an invitation to beatification and a command to a state of grace.

The radical movement in the United States has always seen music as an arm of the revolution. Radical sympathy supported the folk music revival, beginning with Leadbelly and Woody Guthrie and coming on down to Peter, Paul, and Mary. But radical theoreticians mis-assessed the phenomenon of pop music. Pop music meant mass culture and mass production and was, *de facto,* anti-art and anti-culture and manipulated by perverted money-makers. Beatle records are smuggled into Russia from East Germany, where they are available principally because the Beatles are slightly associated with Germany, having lived and worked (and first recorded) in Hamburg. Nobody ever smuggled Woody Guthrie records across any curtains, iron or otherwise.

The missed point is not that there is a line from Guthrie to Dylan (of course there is) but that in order to make money, corporate American enterprise will, in a kind of autolysis, allow its own destruction to be preached via a product that is profitable. Marx was not faced with this alternative. None of the radical bards from Guthrie on through the Weavers have had the benefit of the mass audience that Dylan has.

The rock groups reflect something else long alien to American culture. This has been a nation of individualists, of iconoclasts (mythologically, at least), of "I'm from Missouri, show me" loners, and "group" meant conspiracy and cooperation and hence distrust. Beginning with the Free Speech Movement at Berkeley and the San Francisco Mime Troupe before that, the concept of activity in which individuals were submerged in the group effort became a part of the political scene and, more importantly at that point (and more quickly, too), part of the music world. Previously music was individual-oriented. Even the most prominent groups (i.e., the big bands of the 'thirties) were individual-oriented. They consisted of employees who worked for one leader (star) employer. The labor union for musicians accepted this as such a fundamental that it is built into the union rules and practice. The union actively opposed cooperative groups for years and only now has accepted their reality, while still demanding that one man be responsible and sign the contracts. The Casa Loma band in the 'thirties and the Modern Jazz Quartet in the 'fifties were the only two successful major musical groups operating without using the name of a single leader. The rock bands are cooperative. They are also to a large degree communal. They live together.

The Young Rascals, a real, real version of the West Side Story musical group, have announced that they are not interested in playing the Ed Sullivan show and that they won't appear on a concert bill unless there are also black artists presented. The San Francisco bands inaugurated a novel idea—playing for free. They have been appearing in the parks in San Francisco, Palo Alto, and Berkeley for over two years, a practice that has now spread wondrously as far as London. In concerts organized by rock fans and absolutely free, bands such as the Jefferson Airplane (which regularly turns down offers of up to $15,000 for a single night's engagement) play.

The support which has been given all radical causes by rock groups (particularly in San Francisco) is incalculable. Benefits for everything from Newsreel to the San Francisco State College defense fund have been freely held. I mention this not to lavish credit on the bands but to point out that every cause goes to them for help. The reason is the power of the music.

In a culture of noise—not just the jets roaring overhead and the trucks thundering on the streets, but the psychic noise of the crashing of institutions and assumptions and conventions, the whole crescendo of a collapsing civilization —the only peace seems to be in the middle of an even greater sound in which a special kind of sonic high is produced and a new kind of one-to-one communication occurs. As for the physical effects of the volume: no rock musician I know has gone deaf, no matter what Ralph Nader says.

Wearing all or part of a costume that identifies them, and using ritualistic pass words ("what's your sign?" is only one), the members of the New International reach out to one another in a gigantic conspiracy of feelings, a network of common understanding. They have seen the empty values of patriotism; they would rather be alive red, white, or blue than dead and there is no cause worth dying for. Dylan has told them "don't follow leaders" and the only leaders they *will* hear are those who are determinedly not leaders, a reality which has been appreciated so far only by some of the New Left. They are learning to trust their intuitions and their feelings (two untrustworthy weathervanes by Aristotelian standards), but then again, as Dylan says, you don't need a weather man to know which way the wind blows.

Art is always ahead of culture. The rock musicians have made music out of noise, art out of what began as teen-age exploitation and meaningless money-making. In the process, they have begun to rethink the premises of Western society, I believe, and the end product, while not clearly in sight, looms. "We have to make politics groovy," Country Joe said in discussing why political rallies were a drag. The poetry of politics is rock music. Once we begin to think of it this way, the power and direction of the music begin to make sense.

11

DYLAN'S SELLOUT OF THE LEFT

Paul Wolfe

The Newport Folk Festival of 1964 formed an important milestone in the resurgence of topical music. It brought many of the younger performers into first contact with large segments of the folk music world; it proved that topical music, when delivered with artistry and sincerity, can be heartily appreciated by a wide and diverse audience; it outlined many of the goals toward which the various writers must strive.

But the Festival's most significant achievement was specific and twofold: it marked the emergence of Phil Ochs as the most important voice in the movement, simultaneous with the renunciation of topical music by its major prophet, Bob Dylan. It was the latter event that proved most surprising.

Dylan's "defection" into higher forms of art was predicted. His preference for free-verse, uninhibited poetry over topical songs has been apparent for quite a while; his dissatisfaction with concert tours and the adulation of fans is also no secret. But his new songs, as performed at Newport, surprised every-one, leaving the majority of the audience annoyed, some even disgusted, and, in general, scratching its collective head in disbelief. The art that had, in the past, produced towering works of power and importance, had, seemingly, de-generated into confusion and innocuousness. "Your new songs seem to be all inner-directed, inner-probing, and self-conscious," wrote Irwin Silber, editor of *Sing Out!*, in an open letter to Dylan. "You seem to be relating to a handful of cronies behind the scenes rather than to the rest of us out front."

From "The 'New' Dylan," *Broadside* Magazine (New York: December 20, 1964). Reprinted with permission of publisher.

This disappointment in his new songs was heightened by their juxta-position, on the stage of Newport, with the eloquent musical force of Phil Ochs. While Dylan was telling his perennial, anonymous girl friend, "All I really wanna do is, baby, be friends with you," Ochs was informing the leaders of the government "I ain't marchin' anymore!" While Dylan sang "It Ain't Me, Babe" and, in the guise of rejecting a persistent female, told his thousands of worshippers to look elsewhere for someone to walk on water, Ochs took the time to denounce the labor unions for their betrayal of the civil rights movement; in "Links On The Chain"—Ochs' supreme artistic achievement —and perhaps the most important topical song of the year—he calls upon the "ranks of labor" to ponder their own "struggles of before" and tell, ironically, which side *they* now are on in the Negro struggle for equality.

Thus, the difference between the two performers became manifest: meaning vs. innocuousness, sincerity vs. utter disregard for the tastes of the audience, idealistic principle vs. self-conscious egotism. And even in his attempts at seriousness Dylan was bewildering. "Hey, Mr. Tambourine Man," while under-lain by a beautiful poetic idea, must be termed a failure; somehow, a forced monotony of rhymes seemed much more effective in "Only A Pawn In Their Game." And in his other song "Chimes Of Freedom," the bewilderment is raised to the highest degree. In this incredible jumble of confused, obscure images piled atop one another, Dylan traces the pursuit for higher forms of freedom, spanning a human lifetime, encompassing all of human life. This probing journey through anguish begins "far between sundown's finish and midnight's broken toe" and ends, some eight grueling minutes later, with the chimes of freedom flashing "for every hung-up person in the whole wide universe." The fallacy inherent in the concept of chimes flashing is annoyingly obvious. It is also obvious that Dylan was too enmeshed in his own ego and seeming adoration of words (no matter how meaningless his combinations of these words renders them), to consider the absurdity of treating a subject of such scope in a song. As Irwin Silber said, the Dylan we once knew, the author of "With God On Our Side" and "Hattie Carroll," "never wasted our precious time." "Chimes of Freedom" brings to mind once again the fable of the Emperor's new clothes; and a short story entitled "Face In The Crowd" by Budd Schulberg (it was made into a noted movie). The protagonist of that story is a hillbilly singer who, through publicity, slick management and an over-powering ego, rises to such heights of stardom and popularity he thinks he can get away with anything on the public. The tragedy is that he cannot, and, in the end, is ruined.

Does Bob himself give a concrete reason for the emergence of the "new" Dylan? One might be found in the song "My Back Pages" in his latest album *Another Side Of Bob Dylan.* It is an intensely honest, revealing self-portrait, indeed a brutal denunciation of the "old" Dylan. It characterizes the latter as a deceived, impotent "musketeer" whose main stimuli to action were confusion and immaturity, rather than a fiery poetic spirit reacting to the injustices he saw all around him. Thus a seeming disillusionment with both himself and the ideals he fought for looms as a factor.

Other forces shaping his new posture include his own artistic drives and capabilities (which are indeed considerable), running headlong into the limitations of the musical form. As Phil Ochs said in the 1964 Newport brochure:

> I think he's slowly drifting away from song-writing because he feels limited by the form. More and more of his work will probably come out in poetry and free verse, and I would not be surprised if he stopped singing altogether, considering the over-adulation of his fans and the lack of understanding of audiences that identify with him.

Indeed there are reports not only that he is working on a book of his own poetry but that he plans to start a poetry magazine (further Dylan artistic endeavors include a motion picture, which Dylan has written, is directing, and stars in himself). These varied artistic projects imply his abandonment of topical song writing; an artist must express himself through the most effective media at his command. But they do not explain his new songs; nor, if he is so discontented with singing, why he continues to give concerts; nor why he is still cutting records. Contradictions have followed Bob Dylan from the time his folksinging career began. Now, seemingly at the end of it, they have yet to be dissipated.

The paths of Bob Dylan bear extreme relevance to the course of today's topical songwriting. For instance, take Phil Ochs. His career is still evolving and expanding, but considering what has happened to Bob, an inevitable question arises concerning Phil: will he follow in the footsteps of his predecessor? Will Phil too eventually be disillusioned, or in some other way become discontented, with his personal messages of protest, and abandon them? Only time—of course—can tell. But an analysis of the facts renders this unlikely. The differences between Ochs and Dylan, both as artists and personalities, are striking. Ochs is much more deeply committed to the broadside tradition; to news and politically oriented songs, most of which are focused on specific events and do not range into the wide scope of human events and variegated problems that characterize so many of Dylan's more famous works. In addition, Dylan has undergone repeated metamorphoses as a performer; each of his four albums differs radically from the others. This has not been so with Ochs, whose second LP (by Elektra) plainly will be a continuation of the work foundationed by his first . . . Quite to the contrary, Phil's basic melody and lyric patterns have remained constant from the very beginning; indeed, many of his first songs, notably "William Worthy" and his talking analyses of Cuba and Vietnam, occupy important positions in his current repertoire. Thus, the constant change of character and outlook, the reluctance to stay in one "bag" of song-writing for an extended period of time, that have engendered Dylan's renunciation of topical music, are not evidenced in Ochs. Nevertheless, the influences of Dylan have found their way into several of Ochs' new songs. In "In The Heat Of The Summer" and "The Hills Of West Virginia," Ochs has attempted subtlety and poetry where before he used power and irony. Thus, these two songs differ artistically from all his previous ones; indeed in the first song, dealing with the recent riots in various Negro ghettos, he goes so far as to abandon rhyme scheme altogether. It is a novel artistic experiment; but, unfortunately, this first attempt at poetry-in-song is unsuccessful; "In The Heat Of The Summer" emerges as little more than an exercise. But in "The Hills Of West Virginia," some reflections during an automobile trip, Phil's simple, unpretentious, easy-flowing imagery, encased in what could be his most beautiful melody, weaves a sharp and colorful tapestry of observation. It is certainly one of his best songs and proves Ochs doesn't have to protest to be good. It also proves that one can absorb the good influences of Dylan without being affected by the non-artistic sides of the latter's enigmatic career.

Many talented people today are writing topical songs. But, to me, Phil Ochs stands virtually alone in his field; very few writers are even close to him in quality and productivity. This is a happy fact for topical music. However, the cash registers are ringing in his ears more and more; legions of adulating fans and his identity as a "celebrity" grow larger as time goes by. Thus, one final question must be posed in connection with the path of Phil Ochs, hence the path of topical music. Can he overcome the pressures, the lures, the rewards and the egotism attached to being a celebrity? Can he maintain a sincerity of principle despite material prosperity? It is evident that he will continue writing protest songs; the question now is whether he will continue meaning them. For Phil Ochs, on whom the future of topical music rides, "these are the days of decision."

*   *   *

12

MORE SUBVERSION THAN MEETS THE EAR

Gary Allen

All across America parents are throwing up their hands in exasperation and despair—the universal complaint being that they are unable to communicate with their teenage sons and daughters. One reason they are finding it so difficult to get through to the "turned-on" generation is that today's young people so often have a blaring transistor radio plugged into one of their ears. Such electronic paraphernalia seems, alas, to have become a part of the teenage anatomy. No wonder our teenyboppers appear so vacuous—they are in shell-shock from having tuned in the local rock-music stations blasting out the latest revolutionary horrors on the "Top Forty."

While the youngsters groove on the cool sounds, parents avoid such rock music—considering it a cacophony of piercing sounds, and screeching, garbled voices, guaranteed to send anyone over thirty scrambling for the Excedrin. Besides, the lyrics often feature words and references no more meaningful to the Geritol set than a lecture on Homer in Swahili. Should they "tune-in" and listen, however, parents might learn why the generation gap is fast becoming an unbridgeable canyon.

Rock music, universally in high regard among a whole generation of adolescents, has somehow evolved as one of the major influences on our children —and, through them, on our nation's future. Rock singers are in constant communication with our teenagers—promoting attitudes and ideas which, if they were aware of the message, would blow the minds of most parents. The

From "That Music, There's More To It Than Meets the Ear," in *American Opinion* 12 (February, 1969), pp. 49–62. Reprinted by permission of the publisher, Robert Welch, Inc., Belmont, Mass.

adulation by young people of rock bands and singers has reached fanaticism, and is fed by a bevy of magazines aimed at teenagers which cover the lives, promote the attitudes, and sell the radical political views of the new "gods" in hoary detail.

More goldfish swallowing?

Hardly.

Turn on your radio, tune in a rock station, and listen to The Beatles' new hit about how great it is to be out of America and "Back In The U.S.S.R." Pretty crimson propaganda to be coming from Capitol Records, isn't it? Still, if that little ditty leaves you "uptight," and you vent your displeasure about it to your local mod squad, a dime will get you a dollar that the song will be defended and your complaints made the object of ridicule. That's the degeneration gap, Baby, and it's no accident. Paul Cantor [sic], of the wildly popular acid-rock group called The Jefferson Airplane,[1] admitted recently on the Les Crane television show that the new rock music is *intended* to broaden the generation gap, alienate parents from their children, and prepare young people for revolution. Clarifying this, the "underground" *San Francisco Express Times* carried in its issue for November 13, 1968, a "White Panther Manifesto" which declared:

> With our music and our economic genius we plunder the unsuspecting straight world for money and the means to carry out our program and revolutionize its children at the same time. And with our entrance in the straight media we have demonstrated to the hunkeys that anything they do to f*** with us we will expose to their children. You don't need to get rid of all the hunkeys, you just rob them of their replacements and let the breed atrophy and die out, with its heirs cheering triumphantly all around it.[2]

Of course, "Liberals" become giddy sniffing the fumes of such glue. *McCalls* magazine, for example, enthused in its issue of November, 1967:

> Pop is music to be alive by, right now. It's music to make the mind and/or the body dance. It's the cutting edge of today's youth culture, the beat of the Sixties, the new language of the contemporary state of mind. It contains freedom, participation, energy, love, sex-

---

[1] The Jefferson Airplane takes you on a "trip," *i.e.* it simulates a drug experience.

[2] Editor of the *Express Times* is Marvin Garson, one of the originals from the Free Speech Movement at Berkeley. Marvin is married to Barbara Garson, author of a scabrous play called *MacBird!*—the story of a smalltown boy who made good by murdering his way to the Presidency.

uality, honesty and rebellion. It scorns convention, pretense, sentimentality and false patriotism (p. 78).[3]

The *Saturday Review* (of Leftwing Literature) registered even more moisture over the new revolutionary music in its issue of August 26, 1967:

> Music and songs are the new youth's primary tools and means of expression . . . . The drive is away from a general sense of hypocrisy in diverse areas of life—a separation from older values. Existing circumstances are source material for comment. The threat of the Bomb and fighting unnecessary wars to stalemate, keeping us constantly on the precipice of disaster, fan the flames.

Of course, the announcements of the Far Left that music is being used as a powerful political weapon hardly amount to the revelation of a new concept. The culturally sagacious have for centuries recognized that as music can be used to produce a powerful effect on the emotions, it can be a powerful propaganda agent.

Music is both an art and a science. Eugene Helms noted in *The Scientific American* of December 1967:

> What is seldom appreciated, even in the musical world, is that the roots of the relation between music and mathematics stem deep into antiquity. The roots of these relationships were understood by the Chaldeans, the Egyptians, the Babylonians and the Chinese. The rules of harmonic proportions were worked out by Pythagoras.

And, it was Pythagoras who first noted that music was an exact science which could be used to produce profound and disturbing atonal effects. Plato went farther in *The Republic* and warned that "the introduction of a new kind of music must be shunned as imperiling the whole State; since styles of music are never disturbed without affecting the most important political institutions." Emil Neuman, in his *History of Music,* summarizes Plato's ideas concerning music this way: "He insisted it was the paramount duty of the Legislature to suppress all music of an effeminate and lascivious character, and to encourage

---

[3] *McCalls* is owned by Hunt Foods (no connection with H. L. Hunt) which recently bought a vast store of vegetable oil from the Soviet Union. The magazine came out editorially, in its issue of July 1968, for World Government. President of Hunt Foods is Leftist Norton Simon, a member of the Board of Regents of the University of California who has consistently supported appeasement of revolution on California's campuses.

only that which was pure and dignified . . . ." Many philosophers have shared this opinion. Henry David Thoreau prophesied in *Walden,* more than a hundred years before The Beatles made their first record: "Even music may be intoxicating. Such apparently slight causes destroyed Greece and Rome, and will destroy England and America."

When words are combined with music the emotional and political effect may be heightened. As Andrew Fletcher observed:

> I knew a very wise man who believed that if a man were permitted to make all the ballads, he need not care who should make the laws of a nation. And we find that most of the ancient legislators thought they could not well reform the manners of any city without the help of a lyric and sometimes of a dramatic poet.

One would have to be naive in the extreme to think that the Communists, master propagandists that they are, could ignore a field with so much influence as music. They haven't. Vladimir Lenin, speaking to the Third All-Russian Congress of the Young Communist League on October 2, 1920, informed the assembled young Comrades that they must "rework culture"—that only by so doing could they hope to build "a proletarian (Communist) culture." A part of that "reworking" was the subversion of music.

By 1929 the Russian Association of Proletarian Musicians had been formed. Its purpose, according to Nicholas Slonimsky in *Music Since 1900,* was the "extension of the proletarian Communist influence to the musical masses, re-education and reorganization of these masses in order to direct their work and creative talents toward . . . ultimate victory of the proletariat as builder of Communist society."

Sidney Finkelstein, described by the House Committee on Un-American Activities as "the cultural spokesman for the Communist Conspiracy" in the United States, made Lenin's "rework culture" speech the theme of his book, *How Music Expresses Ideas.* Finkelstein called for breaking down the barrier between classical music and "popular" music. Realizing that the proper sort of music could be used to sell a revolutionary message in the same manner that a singing commercial sells soap, Finkelstein called for the replacement of classic symphonic music by revolutionary music with a jungle beat.

The Communists have made extensive use of such music in America, where they were early successful in the field of folk music. (See Jere Real's "Folk Music," *American Opinion,* December 1964.) Such talented Communists as Pete Seeger, Leadbelly, Malvina Reynolds, and Woody Guthrie, popularized songs of class warfare and subversion for millions. Now, the New Left crowd has taken folk music, combined it with rock and roll, and turned it into folk-rock—with revolutionaries like Phil Ochs and Bobby Dylan projecting the philosophy and songs of Communist Woody Guthrie into the protest music of the 'sixties.

Writing in the Communist *Mainstream,* Comrade Ochs has noted: "I have run across some people who seem to consider Guthrie solely a writer of great camp songs. They cannot fathom or don't want to fathom the political significance of a great part of his work." We should certainly not have too difficult a time "fathoming" the significance of Ochs's work. One of his latest albums features poetry by Mao Tse-tung on the back cover.

Phil Ochs's newest hit is called "Rhythms of Revolution" (*Only the dead are forgiven as they crumbled inside the rhythms of revolution*). He is, however, more famous for "I Ain't Marchin' Anymore" (*Call it "Peace" or call it "Treason,"* . . . *But I ain't marchin' anymore*), and the "Draft Dodger Rag" (*If you ever get a war without blood and gore, Well, I'll be the first to go*).

Anti-war songs, aimed at helping to defeat our men fighting and dying in Vietnam, are Comrade Ochs's bag. Declaring "The Viet Cong are right . . . . We should support Ho Chi Minh," he has created such popular horrors as: "White Boots Marchin' In A Yellow Land." . . . As Phil's songs all follow the same theme on the Vietnam War, they are obviously very big with that great poet, Chairman Mao. Unfortunately, they are now also very big with America's teenagers.

While Phil Ochs specializes in the mad dog approach, Bob Dylan is smoother and even more influential. *Look* magazine has said of the latter that "Dylan is unchallenged as the teen and college crowd's Absolute Hipster, their own 'hung up' idol, the singing analyst of a jingle-jangle reality that makes more sense to them than any square, whitewashed American dream."[4] *Look* also tells us that Dylan's heroes are "Woody Guthrie, Leadbelly, and Pete Seeger." The *Look* editors, of course, forgot to mention that Dylan's trinity of favorites are all Communists.

The Establishment's other mass slicks have gotten into the act of promoting Dylan. *Life* calls him "a major poet of his generation," and the *Saturday Evening Post* says that he is "probably the most influential voice in contemporary music." Even two years ago it was estimated that over 10 million Dylan records had been sold.

What were the songs which made this crimson troll the "spokesman for his generation"? One of his first hits was "Masters of War," an attack on

[4] This about a creature who told another national magazine: "I want my woman dirty, looking as though I'd just found her in some alley. Dirt is very attractive. It triggers animal emotion. I want dirty long hair hanging all over the place." Bobby's thousands of fans among adolescent females no doubt took notice.

general officers and those who manufacture our nation's defense equipment. Even more potent was "Blowin' In The Wind." The latter song became an unofficial anthem of the Communists' "Peace" Movement, and the answer that was blowin' in the wind was Revolution and support of the Vietcong. Fifty-eight different versions of this tune have now been recorded.

Since the revolutionary Bob Dylan is the "certified spokesman" for his generation, it is not surprising that his "The Times They Are A-Changin' " has become a sort of theme song on the road to the generation gap.

No wonder the Communists' *People's World* and *The Worker* and *The Guardian* have called Dylan "America's greatest poet," and the Communist Party has given him a "Tom Paine" Award, and published one of his "poems" in a revolutionary anthology. He has, after all, become the most successful proponent of the new class war: Youth versus Age. Of course, Dylan has become a millionaire while singing about the poor overthrowing the rich ("the first one now will later be last").

Bob began at the top, with Columbia Records, where the godfather of his career was one John Hammond, an extreme Leftist who just happens to have regularly stumbled into a number of officially cited Communist Fronts. Yes, Dylan got off to a flying start, thanks to Hammond and an expensive Establishment promotion job. Promoter Hammond, who has been affiliated with the Communists' notorious Highlander Center, also served as the producer of Communist Pete Seeger's albums.

Isn't it a small world!

Since it is now against the law of the land to discriminate because of sex, I am required to mention at least one of the female revolutionary singers— someone like Judy Collins. Miss Collins was named as a member of the Communist DuBois Clubs at a special workshop on the arts during the D.B.C.'s summer 1966 convention. An activist in "Civil Rights" and "Peace" demonstrations, Judy sings one of the most violent of the hard-core songs, called "Marat/Sade"—a popular contemporary shriek about the glories of the French Revolution. The content of the lyrics makes it obvious that it is a call for a repetition within our own country of that bloody Revolution.

As the pop cycle has evolved from folk-rock to the hippy-oriented acid-rock, the theme of revolution has evolved with it and is now accompanied by the piercing twang of amplified electric guitars. To start the new year right "The Lovin' Spoonful,"[5] a group heard thousands of times a day on rock radio

---

[5] A spoon is used to cook heroin or to mix amphetamines with water before "shooting" them into the vein.

across the nation, has released an album entitled *Revolution '69.* The lyrics to the title song are reprinted on the back of the album lest anyone miss them in the din of the screaming electrified instruments.

While revolution[6] is a favorite theme of the rock-music groups, it is by no means the only one. The theme most often heard, outside the wide range of songs which deal with boy-girl love, is that of *drugs.* Drug lyrics are a mystery to most adults because of the Aesopian language used by the singers. Teenagers have always seemed to have a code language all their own, and no adult can hope to understand the lyrics on the "Top Forty" unless he is familiar with that jargon. The current adolescent vernacular, however, is simply incredible. Only if you have served time in a state penitentiary, or been a prostitute or a junky, would you fail to need an interpreter. For, alas, it is just such an underworld which is the source of most of the current hippy language.

Youngsters pick up the meaning of the argot through disc jockeys, conversation with their peers, and the teenage and "underground" newspapers and magazines. The hippy vocabulary allows verbal communication in code and separates those who are hip from the squares. Our teenagers, not wanting to feel isolated from their fellows, pick up and use the hip vocabulary. The result is more generation gaposis between parents and their children: Youth versus Age.

As New York music critic Richard Goldstein has observed: "Rock lyricists today try to invest their slang with a depth of ambiguity that allows the words to be heard equally well on all levels right down to the [revolutionary] underground. No one doubts that the purpose of so-called psychedelic rock is to reconstruct an actual drug experience." That is why it is often called "acid-rock." *Acid* is slang for LSD. By making the lyrics deliberately ambiguous and couching references to drugs in code and double-entendres, it is generally possible for the musicians and the radio stations to avoid complaints from irate parents. The evil, they piously maintain, is in the ear of the listener.

When Gordon McLendon, owner of thirteen radio stations, tried a while back to eliminate the playing of the drug-cult music on his network, he was subjected to national ridicule (including a blast from *Newsweek,* which has often run articles downgrading the harmful effects of marijuana). McLendon nonetheless had the courage to object to the "songs that glorified dope addiction . . . ," and raised the question nationally. Bill Young, program director at Mr.

[6] Other contemporary popular songs having to do with revolution include: "My Back Pages," The Byrds; "Chimes Of Freedom" and "My Generation," The Who; "The Cities Are Burning," Frederick Douglass Kirkpatrick; "War Blues," Ronnie Petersen; "Burn, Baby, Burn," Bill Frederick; "Hell No, I Ain't Gonna Go!" Matthew Jones and Elaine Laron; "My Country 'Tis Of Thy People You're Dying," Buffy Sainte-Marie; "The Time Will Come," Elaine White; "Sounds of War," Ricardo Gautreau; "I've Got To Have Peace On My Mind," The Outlaw Blues Band; "There's A War On," The Rainbow Press; "Street Fighting Man," The Rolling Stones; and, "Ballad Of Ho Chi Minh," Ewen MacCall.

McLendon's radio station KILT in Houston, remarked: "The hippies know what they are saying on these records, but old John Q. Public doesn't. We're tired of them putting it over on John Q."

The intent of the lyrics of acid-rock is carefully obscure—often bathed in the mysticism associated with Zen, Hinduism, and other Eastern religions which have been affected by the followers of the drug culture. Few of the young people understand all of the lyrics to the songs played on the rock stations, of course. Indeed, some of the lyrics are so obscure as to defy interpretation by anyone this side of the Himalayas.

One can conjecture that many of these songs are written under the influence of drugs, as has admittedly been done on a number of occasions by The Beatles.[7] The carefully coded promotion of narcotics in The Jefferson Airplane's "White Rabbit" is all too typical [in its allusion to the pills that make you larger or smaller,[8] hooka-smoking,[9] and feeding your head.][10]

The Beatles are still the Number One pop group. According to their authorized biography, by Hunter Davies, they started using drugs at the beginning of their career together. They have during the past two years popularized many songs which have been interpreted by young people as dealing with drugs. For example, "Lucy In The Sky With Diamonds" is advertised on posters with the letters L,S,D underlined. While the Beatles have dismissed charges that the song deals with drugs, teenagers who buy the record know better—claiming that the lyrics don't make sense unless one interprets the imagery as a "trip" on LSD.[11]

[7] See Hunter Davies, *The Beatles,* p. 268.

[8] The pill that makes you larger is an amphetamine or "upper" (a stimulant), and the pill that makes you smaller is a barbiturate or "downer" (a depressant).

[9] Marijuana is sometimes smoked through a water pipe.

[10] Drug users refer to taking drugs as "feeding your head."

[11] A "trip" to your local record shop will reveal that there are now literally hundreds of songs designed to be interpreted by those who speak the language as promoting the use of drugs. A sample includes: "Colored Rain" (methadrine), The Wichita Falls; "Mary Jane" (marijuana), Willie and the Rubber Band; "Jumpin' Jack Flash" (when methadrine, taken intravenously, hits the brain it is known as a "flash"); "Lady Jane" (marijuana), "You Turn Me On," "Eight Miles High," and "You've Got Me High"—all by The Rolling Stones; "Rainy Day Woman" (a marijuana cigarette), and "Mr. Tambourine Man" (drug peddler), Bob Dylan; "Mainline Prosperity Blues" ("mainlining" is shooting drugs directly into the vein), Richard Farina; "Puff The Magic Dragon" (smoke marijuana) by Peter, Paul, and Mary; "You Turn Me On" by Ian Whitcomb; "Yellow Balloon" (drugs are often carried in a balloon so that they may be swallowed and later retrieved in the event of imminent arrest) by The Yellow Balloon; "Up, Up And Away" (which sold 875,000 copies, won a Grammy Award, and was adopted by Trans-World Airlines as its theme song) by the Fifth Dimension; "Along Came Mary" (marijuana) by The Association; "Bend Me, Shape Me" by The American Breed; "Acapulco Gold" (a particularly fine grade of marijuana) by The Rainy Daze; "Get On Up" by The Esquires; "Full Measure" by the Lovin' Spoonful; "Express To Your Head," Soul Survivors; "I Had Too Much To Dream," The Electric Prunes; "Faster Than The Speed (methadrine)

"Yellow Submarine" has been one of The Beatles' biggest hits and has been called by *National Review* "a beautiful children's song." Those who are a little more hip than the crew at *Buckley Review* know that in drug terminology a "yellow jacket" is a submarine-shaped barbiturate, seconal, or "downer" (a "downer" submerges you). Among other Beatle songs generally interpreted as referring to drugs are "Norwegian Wood" (British teenagers' term for marijuana), "Strawberry Fields Forever" (marijuana is often planted in strawberry fields, in order to avoid detection, because the plants are similar in appearance), and "Magical Mystery Tour" (*Roll up, roll up [your sleeve] for the mystery tour . . . .*), and "A Day In The Life" (*I'd love to turn you on*).

The music reviewer for *Holiday* magazine in its issue for October of 1966 deals with whether all of these lyrics promoting use of narcotics have been sneaked onto the records because those in the business are naive:

> Is it possible that record producers have been fooled by the jargon of the songs—have put out such discs not knowing what they mean? It is unlikely because it is impossible to be in the music business long without seeing pot smoked . . . the terminology of narcotics is widely known and understood in the industry, both by artists, recorders and producers. Some publishers shrug off the drug songs by saying, "These songs are a reflection of our times." In songs meant for children of 12 or even younger they proclaim that it is wise and hip and inside to dissolve your responsibilities and problems of a difficult world into the mists of marijuana, LSD or heroin (p. 130).

No, Virginia, it is not an accident that a generation of young Americans is being pushed toward drugs.

A third major category of songs (besides drugs and revolution) has to do with glorifying sexual union between teenagers. Just as the songs of revolution have served to mentally condition many young people to accept the ravings of the New Left, and the myriad drug songs are doubtless a factor in the skyrocketing use of narcotics by teenagers, so the open exhortations to indulge in illicit sex acts are also a factor in the demoralization of youth—helping to produce unprecedented numbers of illegitimate children and an unparalleled rise in venereal disease among teenagers.

Of Life," "Magic Carpet Ride" by Steppenwolf; "Journey To The Center Of The Mind," Amboy Dukes; "Connection" (drug peddler), "She's A Rainbow" (Rainbows are nembutals or seconals), "2000 Light Years From Here" by The Rolling Stones; "Merry-Go-Round," The Youngbloods; "Rose Colored Glasses," Lothar and The Hand People; and, "Buy For Me The Rain" (methadrine) by The Nitty Gritty Dirt Band.

As with the drug songs, some of the sex songs are blatant, but most are couched in ambiguous double-entendres. Music critic Richard Goldstein puts it this way: "Rock and roll has always been raunchy. That's what it's all about. It's got a special code and a lot of kids understand it. It's made for that purpose."

Many would dismiss the importance of sneaking raw lyrics into popular songs on the basis that it has been going on for years. Admittedly it has, but fifteen years ago songs like "Work With Me Annie" and "Light My Fire" were heard on "rhythm and blues" stations by a comparatively small number of young people, most of them over sixteen. Today, however, the audience is at least fifty times as large, with children as young as eight becoming regular listeners. Today some $60 million worth of such recordings are sold yearly—with the biggest group of purchasers being girls from nine to thirteen years of age.

With this enormous audience of highly impressionable young people, it is not surprising that the Far Left has been so successful in selling the line of a number of contemporary songs directly promoting alienation between young people and their parents. This theme, as I have noted, is often found woven through the lyrics of songs about drugs and revolution. Some come right out and urge teens to run away from home to join the New Left. The Beatles' hit "She's Leaving Home" may have been instrumental in causing many a youngster to run away to the hells of Hippieland.

But, for sheer gall and a solid one-two punch, you can't beat Scott McKenzie's "What's The Difference," with "San Francisco" on the flip side. These tunes were at the top of the hit parade last year for nearly six months. One side tells the young person to run away, and the other side tells him where to go. Unlike many of the acid-rock records in which the words are badly garbled, both of these are very plainly enunciated. . . .

Other examples of generation-gap music are those songs which depict adults, particularly businessmen, as shallow hypocrites. Probably the most vicious in this category is Ray Stevens' "Mr. Businessman."

While the lyrics of these songs speak for themselves, the music is at least as important as the words. Practically anyone can deduce the significance of the lyrics, while only those trained in music will understand the significance of the contemporary use of rhythms.

Cheetah, one of the burgeoning magazines aimed at teenagers, quotes a New York musician as noting: "If the establishment knew what today's popular music really is saying, not what the words are saying, but what the music itself is saying, then they wouldn't just turn thumbs down on it. They'd ban it, they'd smash all the records, and they'd arrest anyone who tried to play it."

Frank Zappa, leader of a rock group called Mothers Of Invention, adds:

The loud sounds and bright lights of today are tremendous indoctrination tools. Is it possible to modify the human chemical structure with the right combination of frequencies? . . . If the right kind of beat makes you tap your foot, what kind of beat makes you curl your fist and strike?

Zappa, whose group has recorded some lollapaloozas in the fields of sex, drugs, and revolution, knows what he is talking about. Despite the mangy beard, long hair, and hippie costume, Frank has a Master's Degree in music.

Possibly the country's number one expert on music subversion is Joseph Crow of Seattle, who lectures extensively on the subject. Dr. Crow, who now operates a custom jewelry business and is an Associate Professor of Sociology at Pacific Western College, was a professional trumpet player for fifteen years —during which he did a stint with the famous Stan Kenton Band. He also studied music composition at the University of Washington and the Westlake College of Modern Music in Hollywood. Professor Crow explained it to me this way:

> The harmonic and rhythmic fabrics of rock music are critically important. Only someone trained in music can *fully* comprehend the import of this music, but it is not necessary to understand the intricacies of music to understand what is being done with it. You can understand the impact of television without completely comprehending the laws of physics involved.
>
> When I was studying composition we learned almost mathematically to utilize orchestration, sound, and timbre to really give foundation to a concept. You can write music to tell a story with it. Ferde Grofé's "Grand Canyon Suite" is a beautiful example. With rock music they are using a musical and lyrical formula for selling ideas. With the right musical background the lyrics take on more profound meaning.

The changes in rhythm and other musical techniques used to sell attitudes and concepts are not unrelated to brainwashing. As Dr. Crow informs us:

> Many of Pavlov's experiments were conducted with a metronome to research the effects of rhythms as a conditioning agent. His famous experiment done with lights, controlling the salivating of a dog, was repeated with metronomes. A dog was conditioned only to eat his food when the metronome was playing at 60 beats per minute, and not to eat his food when the metronome was set for 120 beats per minute. By switching back and forth, or playing both rhythms simultaneously, an artificial neurosis was created.

By changing the rhythm within a musical piece you can have a strong impact on the listener and the subliminal effect is to push the "message" much more strongly. Some people actually have a physiological response when, for instance, a beat is switched from three-four time to five-four time. Pop music now does this type of poly-rhythms all the time, because it accentuates the message. We were taught never to do this in music school, but we were not trying to use music for mind conditioning.

As has been noted again and again by scientists and psychologists, the use of a rhythmic beat is also related to hypnotism. "All you have to do is attend a rock dance and watch the people to observe that they are in an almost hypnotic trance while the music is playing," notes Dr. Crow. He continues:

A young person may hear the same song hundreds of times. As Madison Avenue has proved, that constant repetition sells products. Repetition is the basis of hypnosis. When a person is under hypnosis, or something approaching it, he is highly suggestible. This means that the message contained in the lyrics is recorded deep in the listener's subconscious mind. He may not even be aware of it. If I asked you to write down the words to 'Little Brown Jug' you probably couldn't do it; but if I played the music you could recall the words. Everything you hear is stored in the memory banks inside your brain and may be brought out under proper stimulus—which is why this music is dangerous whether the young person fully understands the words or not.

Music can stimulate the emotions and penetrate the mind in ways that seem incredible. Famous composer-conductor Dimitri Tiomkin puts it this way:

The fact that music can both excite and incite has been known from time immemorial. That was perhaps its chief function in prehistory, and it remains so in the primitive societies which still exist in the far reaches of the world. In civilized countries, music became more and more a means of communicating pleasurable emotions, not creating havoc.

Now, in our popular music, at least, we seem to be reverting to savagery. And the most dramatic indication of this is the number of occasions in recent years when so-called concerts of rock 'n' roll have erupted into riots.

Those riots, however, are only the obvious manifestations of what I mean. More to the point is the fact that youngsters who listen constantly to this sort of sound are thrust into turmoil. They are no longer relaxed, normal kids.

They will tell you they get a "charge" out of rock 'n' roll. So do the kids who smoke marijuana and shoot H[heroin].

Professor Crow believes that without question the most important group now setting the trends in pop music is The Beatles. They began with standard Elvis Presley-style rock 'n' roll and evolved into presenting drug and other message-lyrics in a highly sophisticated way. The Beatles have even changed their appearance, from smiling mop-tops to serious, bearded, and mustachioed hippies. They deny that they have used drugs since adopting Buddhism, but Beatle John Lennon was recently arrested along with his mistress [Ed. note: now his wife], Japanese film star Yoko Ono, for possession of marijuana.

The song at the top of the hit parade as this is written is The Beatles' "Hey Jude," which is widely interpreted as being a song about methadrine. . . . The song reaches crescendo with great screaming as the drug produces a "flash." On the flip side of the single is a little ditty called "Revolution," which has been widely misinterpreted—and nowhere more grossly than by the *National Review Bulletin* of November 12, 1968:

> The International Communist enterprise may at last have met its match: The Beatles. Radical sorts anxious to preempt the Beatles' creative and immensely popular music for the Left have found little or nothing in it to comfort them over the years.[12]

The *coup de grace,* according to the swingers at *National Review,* is that "Revolution" puts down the Maoists. In this one, of course, The Beatles are simply telling the Maoists that Fabian gradualism is working, and that the Maoists might blow it all by getting the public excited before things are ready for "Revolution." The song makes it perfectly clear that The Beatles are on the side of, and working for, "Revolution"—and that their war is going to be successful (*it's gonna be alright*). In short, "Revolution" takes the Moscow line against Trotskyites and the Progressive Labor Party, based on Lenin's *Leftwing Extremism: An Infantile Disorder.*

The new Beatles album, containing "Revolution" and "Back In The U.S.S.R.," is, according to a Capitol Records spokesman, "the fastest selling record in the history of the record industry." No wonder the Communists have had some very good things to say about The Beatles, who rated a feature article in Volume 1, Number 1, of *Insurgent*—the Communist DuBois Clubs' official

---

[12] Will someone please play "Back In The U.S.S.R." for the Billyboppers?

magazine. It was there that Communist Carl Bloice wrote: "If we are to be partisans of our generation in this chaotic world we can only cheer four guys from Liverpool who made it to the top and made so many of us feel more alive in the process."

Among themselves, the young Reds tell it like it is. After attending a workshop on the arts conducted by *Insurgent's* managing editor Celia Rosebury, Chicago Police Department undercover operative David Gumaer reported to his superiors:

> It was mentioned that the reason the Beatles and other folk-rock groups received such success in the music field was because they were backed by the Entertainment Section of the Communist Party, and that music was a weapon used to win children and young adults to Marxism. It was also stated that Paul McCartney of the Beatles was a member of the Young Communist League.

McCartney is credited with being the co-author along with Lennon of both "Revolution" and "Back In The U.S.S.R." Professor Crow told me, however, that he has serious doubts that The Beatles really do write all their own songs, as is claimed. Speaking frankly, he explained:

> Some of the newer Beatles songs are the same simple types they were doing four years ago, but other songs are of a very high quality and show an acute awareness of the principles of rhythm and brainwashing. Neither Lennon nor McCartney were world-beaters in school, nor have they had technical training in music. For them to have written some of their songs is like someone who has not had physics or math inventing the A-bomb. It's possible, but not very probable. Because of its technical excellence it is possible that this music is put together by behavioral scientists in some "think tank."
>
> I know from personal experience that it takes a great deal of time to create complicated music and lyrics, and I don't know when The Beatles would have the time to put this kind of stuff together. They are always on tour, vacationing, or making a movie. The puppy-love songs go together pretty rapidly, but not the kind of intricate songs they have been coming out with lately.

Another important point concerning The Beatles, according to Crow, is the technical excellence they have developed and the phenomenal care taken in the production of their records. He notes:

> In the last two years The Beatles and many other groups have evolved from being technically awful to being very good. It has been

published that they spent $50,000 on engineering for the *Sergeant Pepper* album alone. That's a lot of bread. Most people wouldn't have been able to tell the difference if they had spent half that much, but someone feels that it is important to have the message presented perfectly.

The Beatles are no longer just four kids thumping away on their instruments. In "Eleanor Rigby" (which is about the death of the Church) they used a string quartet; and, on their newer records, a 120-piece band.

The high quality of their recent recording almost scientifically creates a mood for them to push home the message in their songs. I have no idea whether The Beatles know what they are doing or whether they are being used by some enormously sophisticated people, but it really doesn't make any difference. It's results that count, and The Beatles are the leading Pied Pipers creating promiscuity, an epidemic of drugs, youth class-consciousness, and an atmosphere for social revolution. What The Beatles begin is imitated, and often expanded upon, by literally hundreds of other groups who in turn reach tens of millions of young people.

Clearly, the generation gap has now been magnified and distorted into class warfare in the Marxist mould. Youth versus age, along with black versus white, has largely superceded labor versus management as the premier target of leftist propaganda.

It would be ludicrous to contend that Communists, Fabian socialists, or Establishment *Insiders* (who manipulate the aforementioned groups) invented the tensions between parent and teenage offspring. Such pressures have always existed. But, much of what we call the generation gap *has* been manufactured in an attempt to exploit natural problems. Today, it is considered "hip" for a young person to be disillusioned, lost, confused, and bitter. There have always been such disturbed teenagers, but never before have the Establishment media extolled them and cast such outcasts as models to be imitated. Never before has the Establishment sought to make idols of the pathetic worst of a whole generation.

Music is now the primary weapon used to make the perverse seem glamorous, exciting, and appealing. Music is used to ridicule religion, morality, patriotism, and productivity—while glorifying drugs, destruction, revolution, and sexual promiscuity.

Youth believes it is rebelling against the Establishment. Yet the Establishment owns and operates the radio and TV stations, the mass magazines and the record companies, that have made rock music and its performing artists into a powerful force in American life. Without the Establishment media, the Beatles would still be twanging away in some dingy Liverpool cellar, and their hundreds of imitators would be students, workers, or legitimate artists.

Without the Establishment's mass media, LSD would be just three random letters in the alphabet to most people, and marijuana would be a problem confined to jazz musicians and criminals instead of a national campus fad. Does it not seem strange that the same Establishment which has used the mass media to ridicule and denigrate the anti-Communist movement should open its door to those who think they are the Establishment's enemy?

It is the major Establishment record companies which have merchandised acid-rock music to millions of teenagers.[13] And, it is the full-page ads from these recording giants which keep many of the so-called "underground" newspapers financially solvent. It is now usual to find squeezed between the pornography, drug pushing, and shouts for revolution found in the "undergrounders," the full-page spreads purchased by Capitol Records, MGM, RCA Victor (the holding company for NBC), Columbia Records (owned by CBS), and ABC records (owned by the American Broadcasting Company). These vicious anti-American "underground" newspapers, in short, are financed by the Establishment they claim to be attacking. And, they are so financed to sell the music of illicit sex, drugs, and revolution.

Our teenagers would do well to ask why the Establishment would finance those claiming to seek its own demise?—unless what is happening is all part of a single revolutionary thrust, of which America's youth is to be the ultimate victim.

---

[13] While some of the rock groups appear on lesser labels, many of the smaller recording companies are subsidiaries of the major recording firms.

13

THE GREAT KID-CON

Susan Huck

America seems to remain full of people who consider it pretty paranoid and extremist to note the role of pop records in promoting dissension and the rhetoric of "revolution." Yet there is no particular reticence about aims to be found either in the actual words of so many currently "popular" songs, or in the views broadcast by their performers. In fact, the revolutionists—the professionals, that is—flaunt their pop-singer and folk-rock allies as openly as said performers flaunt their Marxism in song and interview.

That bit of Living Theater called the Chicago Conspiracy Trial has even been scored for music as defense strategist William Kunstler parades performing "artists" into the courtroom. He knows that they are not going to be allowed to sing in there, but he is eager to let the younger generation know where some of their idols stand.

On January 22, for example, Judge Julius Hoffman refused to allow Judy Collins to sing for the jury, "Where Have All the Flowers Gone?", which dwells upon the theme of dead soldiers—American dead, of course. Previously Mr. Kunstler, the professional defender of professional revolutionists, had brought to court Phil Ochs, Arlo Guthrie, and "Country Joe" McDonald.

Phil Ochs, to judge by his latest "songbook," does not entertain a single non-Communist thought. Kunstler wanted him to sing his masterpiece, "I Ain't Marchin' Any More" (except in leftist demonstrations). "Country Joe" was supposed to perform "Vietnam Rag" for the jury, and Arlo Guthrie, son of Communist Woody Guthrie, offered to run through "Alice's Restaurant." For

From *Review of the News* (February 11, 1970), pp. 17–24. Reprinted by permission of the publisher, Robert Welch, Inc., Belmont, Mass.

some reason, Judge Hoffman did not choose to endure revolutionary pop concerts during working hours.

Kunstler was arguing, all the while, that such songs are "directly relevant to the protests during the (Democrat) Convention"—the "protests" which erupted into planned rioting and violence in August 1968.

Singer Judy Collins, incidentally, helped Jerry Rubin and Abbie Hoffman to form the so-called Youth International Party, or "Yippies," which they all agree was never a "party" nor openly "international." Since its leaders are thirty-ish, it may not even be "youthful." But it *was* a group formed to participate in *apparently* mindless and zany violence.

But to return to the role of popular music in promoting (they hope) a revolution to destroy America as we know it . . . you will be glad to know that Ralph J. Gleason, a Berkeley-based music critic, writing for the *Drama Review,* takes it all very seriously. In the issue of *Drama Review* for Summer 1969 he begins his article, "The Greater Sound," [Ed. note: reprinted in this book as "A Cultural Revolution." See pp. 137–146] as follows:

> Today, all over the United States, American young people are being spoken to by revolutionists in words they understand, in a style that makes those words acceptable, and through an invisible medium that old professional politicos have not yet picked up on . . . .
>
> It's possible to say that the expression of youth's disaffiliation through pop music merely siphons off rebellious feelings and makes them assimilable and in the long run harmless—but surely this is offset by the fact that unarticulated protest is made specific, and applied to political subjects like Vietnam, for kids in remote towns who wouldn't otherwise know that they are part of a vast movement, or wouldn't connect their discontent to its sources in our social-political setup.

At least Ralph Gleason is able to see the conscious and sustained effort which is being made—more than can be said for *National Review's* "former" Maoist Phillip Abbott Luce, for example. And Gleason, while ritualistically ridiculing the "radical right" (that's us), does state that "they correctly define the Beatles as their enemy." While, unfortunately, Californian Gleason mis-identifies California Congressman James Utt as "James Tustin," he does agree with him that rock music and sex education *are* interconnected campaigns.

Mr. Gleason knows that all this is intended to destroy America as we know it, and he even sounds uneasy about it, like an overage "liberal" overtaken by events. But, you see, it couldn't possibly be a *Communist* enterprise. The ritualistic "liberal" mind is closed to that notion!

Nevertheless, critic Ralph Gleason is an informed and, within the limits of his ideological framework, an honest observer of the rock-music politics-and-revolution campaign, and makes a number of very valuable observations.

He knows what the aforementioned "Country Joe" McDonald is talking about when he sings to millions: "Come on mothers throughout the land, pack your boys off to Vietnam." (And Gleason is probably quite old enough to know that no such songs were allowed during World War II, when American troops were, as it turned out, dying in order to deliver half of Europe to our wonderful Red "ally," Josef Stalin.)

Unlike *National Review's* Phil Luce, Gleason knows exactly what Grace Slick means when "advising listeners to 'feed your head' "; he knows she's drug-peddling, as usual, and that "once you *set up a situation* (italics ours) in which the sacred tenets of the social fabric are treated as obsolete or irrelevant, anything may be questioned."

He mentions an album by the group calling itself the Mothers of Invention, which he describes as "an all-out satirical commentary on American society rivaled only by that of Lenny Bruce," and which has sold 300,000 copies—pointing out that this would be a very respectable number of copies of a *book* to be sold. Pop records, you see, *are* a "mass medium." True, they are "invisible" in the sense that the words are heard, then gone, and it takes a little doing to get hold of written copies of them. But that just makes it difficult to wave the actual words under the noses of doubters.

(Incidentally, we have found that printed versions of popular songs are frequently "cleaned up"—if you listen to the record and compare, you notice the difference right away. And for some weird reason, records with really foul "lyrics" do not seem to be played on AM radio stations, but are sometimes broadcast over FM. A spokesman for the Federal Communications Commission with whom we spoke could not understand this, since the laws and regulations apply equally to both types of stations. However, he dodged almost instinctively, even while stating that federal law prohibits "obscenity" on the air. "But what is obscenity?" he added at once. Obviously he didn't know.)

As an example of the sort of "popular" music you are more likely to hear on FM radio stations, Gleason cites a typical hate-America ditty by Buffy Sainte-Marie entitled, "My Country 'Tis Of Thy People You Are Dying." (Buffy's people? Yes, maybe we are dying of *them*.) According to Gleason, "She applies a fundamental Marxist thesis" in this opus.

Another singer, Nina Simone, extols the virtues of self-brainwashing; or "change your molecules" as Grace Slick put it in our interview for the March 1970 issue of *American Opinion.*

The link-up with the promotion of indiscriminate and public sex, and drug use, is perfectly clear to critic Ralph Gleason. "Stars" of revolutionary rock do not content themselves with merely uttering the hoary four-letter words, or embellishments thereof. Being performers, you see, they have to find ways to flaunt sex as well. Gleason mentions "Jim Morrison of the Doors unzipping . . ." before a Florida audience and doing what exhibitionists do. Then there was "Country Joe" cheerleading the kiddies in those easy-to-spell words. Gleason's article was written before "Beatle" John Lennon's id reached full flower. Did you know, dear reader, that for little over $1,000 you, too, can possess fourteen priceless lithographs of John and his wife Yoko, "performing" on their honeymoon?

As for drugs, there's a tendency to flaunt that, too. The inimitable Dr. Timothy Leary said it out loud in his widely-quoted interview with the *Berkeley Gazette* last year: "Drugs are the most efficient way to revolution." Leary frankly wants to see the entire nation "dropped out" to a complete preoccupation with drugs and sex, and reduced to a primitive tribal existence by the year 2000—he has made that as clear as his somewhat muddled mind can make anything clear any more. Another overage hippie, Paul Goodman, had expressed his "dream" of the future, years ago, in somewhat the same way—from sea to shining sea, Americans reduced to a Neolithic culture, laboring communally in the pot and poppy fields.

It is interesting to note that, while Grace Slick of the Jefferson Airplane is obviously all for mind-zapping drugs, Ralph Gleason, speaking in her defense, said that she is fighting valiantly against *one* drug—methadrine, or "speed." As the saying goes, "Speed kills." That seems to be the only objection to it (although other drugs "kill," too). It's hard to imagine what Grace has against "speed." Maybe whoever winds her up feels that enslaved addicts and mind-blown cripples are of more lasting use to the "Movement" drive to enfeeble America than young people who are merely dead.

Gleason makes another point about drugs, too: *"Lighting a joint* (of marijuana) *is a revolutionary act,"* Leary says, and there is deep truth in this, since the act puts the actor outside the law from that time on.

We of the "radical right" have said that too—and we know that this is precisely the intent of the "drug culture." Certainly "liberalizing the marijuana laws" will not solve the problem. It will simply move the playing field further to the left, and the revolutionary Left is already miles out of *that* ball park, too, now peddling heroin like there's no tomorrow.

Continuing, critic Gleason says:

> I think that the whole body of rock music, spreading out from the center, with (Bob) Dylan, the Beatles, and the (Rolling) Stones, involves its audience in an even more fundamental confrontation with society. It says, *you are, all of you, wrong* (Emphasis ours).

Yes, that's the standard line for the pitifully ignorant young—*Everything* is rotten about America, so *everything* has got to go. Then, out of the shambles, by some miracle only the ignorant and credulous could possibly believe in, there will arise a world of infinite beauty created by drug-sex-and-rock nuts instead of old fuddy-duddies who *work*.

Lots of people in this country are "fundamentally wrong"—mainly our "liberal" leaders. But it takes a special kind of blinders to conclude that the fundamentally right people are the electric-guitar twangers.

"The radical movement . . . has always seen music as an arm of the revolution," Gleason observes flatly. "Radical sympathy supported the folk-music revival, beginning with Leadbelly and Woody Guthrie and coming on down to Peter, Paul, and Mary." Gleason fails to note the ideological uniformity of those he mentions, as well as that other resurrected Old Communist, Pete Seeger. Possibly the "folk-music revival" occurred because those boys represented an investment, after all. Gleason thinks that the "radical theoreticians" were late in climbing aboard the boat. It's hard to imagine what he's talking about. Those old-time Communists were aboard the boat the last time it pulled out, too, in the "People's Song" and "Hootenanny" days of the late 'forties. Some of them rode the same boat even in the 'thirties. That's how *new* all this is to the unnamed "radical theoreticians" who, according to Gleason, stood back fastidiously from folk-rock because it was "manipulated by perverted money-makers."

It's the radicals who are doing the manipulating; we'll let the "perverted money-makers" term stand. Gleason should have seen that, because in his very next paragraph, alluding once more to the quaint willingness of those supposed capitalists of the record companies to support the Revolution, he says: ". . . in order to make money, corporate American enterprise will, in a kind of autolysis, allow its own destruction to be preached via a product that is profitable."

Lenin said it more pithily. Something about "the capitalists will sell us the rope to hang them with," if memory serves. But "autolysis" *is,* by definition, degenerate.

And, the record companies not only "make money" by spreading the doctrines of Communist revolution in America directly, through their records, they also *spend* money supporting the so-called "underground" newspapers which flaunt their pornopolitical messages to the same audience. They do this mainly through full-page ads designed to convince the gullible that the record companies are beautifully anti-"Establishment," when in fact they are as Establishment as *Time* and *Life.* All the youthful "marks" would have to do would be to visit the home offices of said record companies. They simply drip Establishmentarianism—big glass building, "corporate image" all over their reception areas, and filled with offices containing "perverted money-makers" with those famous button-down minds—the kind of minds who think visitors would rather pick up the latest copy of, so help me, *Cash Box* magazine than anything else, if they actually want to read.

It's not at all hard to believe that regular devourers of *Cash Box* are elbowing for first grabs at the young people's fat allowances or skinny paychecks. The thing these young people had better learn in a hurry is that regular devourers of other kinds of publications are in just as advantageous a position. They'll let the *Cash Box* types keep most of the loot; what they're grabbing for are minds. They want to con these kids into enslaving themselves to drugs, sex, and revolution. They want to talk them into destroying their own society and heritage, in the perfectly asinine expectation that some Utopia will spring full-blown from an alliance of old perverts and spoiled brats.

14

THE DEGRADATION OF WOMEN

Marion Meade

Last spring I sat through three hours of the film "Woodstock" alternating between feelings of enchantment and repulsion. Sure, there was all that magnificent music, along with the generous helpings of peace and love and grass. And yet I found something persistently disturbing about the idyllic spectacle on the screen.

For one thing, with the exception of a pregnant Joan Baez who couldn't seem to stop talking about her husband, all the musicians were men. Sweaty, bearded men were busy building the stage, directing traffic, shooting the film, and running the festival. *Brother*hood was repeatedly proclaimed, both on stage and off. Woodstock Nation was beginning to look ominously like a fantasyland which only welcomed men. How about the women? Barefooted and sometimes barebreasted, they sprawled erotically in the grass, looked after their babies, or dished up hot meals. If this was supposed to be the Aquarian Utopia, it reminded me more of a Shriners' picnic at which the wife and kiddies are invited to participate once a year.

Looking back, I think the movie confirmed an uneasiness I'd felt for some time but had refused to admit: Rock music, in fact the entire rock "culture," is tremendously degrading to women. I reached this conclusion reluctantly and with a good deal of sadness because rock has been important to me. And while I still dig the vitality of the sound, I find myself increasingly turned off in nearly every other respect.

Stokely Carmichael recalls that as a child he loved Westerns and always cheered wildly for the cowboys to triumph over the Indians until one day he realized *he* was an Indian. All along he'd been rooting for the wrong side. More and more, women rock fans are discovering themselves in the same curiously surprised position. For those who have taken the trouble to listen carefully, rock's message couldn't be clearer. It's a man's world, baby, and women have only one place in it. Between the sheets or, if they're talented like Arlo Guthrie's Alice, in the kitchen.

The paradox is that rock would appear to be an unlikely supporter of such old-fashioned sex-role stereotypes. In fact, its rebellion against middle-class values, its championing of the unisex fashions and long hair styles for men seem to suggest a blurring of the distinctions between male and female. But for all the hip camouflage sexism flourishes.

The clearest indication of how rock music views womankind is in its lyrics. Women certainly can't complain that the image presented there is one-dimensional. On the contrary, the put-downs are remarkably multifaceted, ranging from open contempt to sugar-coated condescension. Above all, however, women are always-available sexual objects whose chief function is to happily accommodate any man who comes along. This wasn't always the case. Elvis's pelvis notwithstanding, the popular songs of the 'fifties and early 'sixties explored such innocuous adolescent pastimes as dancing around the clock, the beach, going steady, and blue suede shoes. In those days before the so-called sexual revolution, the typical woman portrayed in rock was the nice girl next door with whom the Beatles only wanted to hold hands. Then suddenly came the nice girl's metamorphosis into "groovy chick," the difference being that a groovy chick is expected to perform sexually. In rock songs, she never fails.

The worst picture of women appears in the music of the Rolling Stones, where sexual exploitation reaches unique heights. A woman is a "Stupid Girl" who should be kept "Under My Thumb," a "Honky Tonk Woman" who gives a man "Satisfaction." In "Yesterday's Papers," where women are equated with newspapers, the dehumanization is carried to an extreme. Who wants yesterday's papers, the song arrogantly demands, who wants yesterday's girl? The answer: Nobody. Once used, a woman is as valuable as an old newspaper, presumably good only for wrapping garbage.

But the Stone's album *Let It Bleed* is surely unrivaled when it comes to contempt for women, as well as lewdness in general. One cut in particular, "Live With Me," is explicit about woman's proper place:

Doncha' think there's a place for you in-between the sheets?

And only an extraordinarily masochistic woman could listen to the album's title song with any sense of pleasure whatsoever. There a woman is represented as a drive-in bordello, a one-stop sexual shopping center offering all the standard services plus a few extras casually thrown in as a kind of shopper's Special of the Day.

The Stone's next album has been tentatively titled "Bitch." It figures.

Misogyny is only slightly more disguised in the music of Bob Dylan who, in his early work at least, tended to regard nearly every female as a bitch. For example, in "Like a Rolling Stone," Dylan apparently feels so threatened by Miss Lonely (whose only sin as far as I can tell is that she has a rather shallow life style) that he feels compelled to destroy her. First he takes away her identity, then he puts her out on the street without shelter or food, and in the end—obliteration, as he makes her invisible. "How does it feel?" he asks.

There's no more complete catalogue of sexist slurs than Dylan's "Just Like a Woman," in which he defines woman's natural traits as greed, hypocrisy, whining, and hysteria. But isn't that cute, he concludes, because it's "just like a woman." For a finale, he throws in the patronizing observation that adult women have a way of breaking "just like a little girl."

These days a seemingly mellowed Dylan has been writing about women with less hatred, but the results still aren't especially flattering. Now he calls his females ladies and invites them to lay across his big brass bed. In short, he has more or less caught up with Jim Morrison's request to "Light my fire" and with John Lennon's suggestion, "Why don't we do it in the road?"

Again and again throughout rock lyrics women emerge either as insatiable, sex-crazed animals or all-American emasculators. Although one might think these images indicate a certain degree of aggressiveness in women, oddly enough they still wind up in a servile position where they exist only to enhance the lives of men.

As for romance, rock hasn't rejected it entirely. Rock love songs exhibit a regular gallery of passive, spiritless women, sad-eyed ladies propped on velvet thrones as the private property of a Sunshine Superman. From the Beatles we get motherly madonnas whispering words of wisdom ("Let it be, let it be") or pathetic spinsters like Eleanor Rigby who hang around churches after weddings to collect the rice. Leonard Cohen's romantic ideal is the mystical Suzanne who wears rags from the Salvation Army and acts, the composer asserts, "half crazy." Seldom does one run across a mature, intelligent woman or, for that matter, a woman who is capable enough to hold a job (one exception is the Beatles' meter maid, Rita). Only the Stones' Ruby Tuesday insists on an independent life of her own.

Since rock is written almost entirely by men, it's hardly surprising to find this frenzied celebration of masculine supremacy. But it's also understandable in terms of the roots from which rock evolved. In both blues and country music, attitudes toward women reflected a rabid machismo: men always dominated and women were fickle bitches who ran off with other men. Often they were seen in relationship to the wandering superstud who recounts his conquests in every town along the road, a fantasy which remains fashionable in rock today.

Apart from the myths of female inferiority proclaimed by rock lyricists, the exploitation and dehumanization of women also extends into the off-stage rock scene. How else can one account for a phenomenon like the groupies? That these aggressive teenage camp followers could possibly be regarded as healthy examples of sexual liberation is certainly a cruel joke. In fact, groupies service the needs of the male musicians and further symbolize rock's impersonal view of women as cheap commodities which can be conveniently disposed of after use. The Stones said it: nobody in the world wants yesterday's papers.

Finally, rock is a field from which women have been virtually excluded as musicians. Not only is it rare to find an integrated band, but the few all-female groups have been notably unsuccessful. The very idea of a women's rock band is looked upon as weird, in the same category as Phil Spitalny's all-girl orchestra, a freak show good for a few giggles.

The problem is that women have been intimidated from even attempting a career in rock. Women, the myth says, aren't smart enough to understand the complexities of electronics or tough enough to compose music of sufficient intensity or physically strong enough to play drums. The guitar is acceptable but the electric guitar is unfeminine.

As for female rock singers, you can count them on a few fingers. We did have Janis Joplin, a blueswoman in the finest tradition of Bessie Smith and Billie Holiday. When Janis wailed about love as a ball and chain and women being losers, now there were ideas with which women could identify. At least we knew what she meant. The soul sounds of Tina Turner and Laura Nyro also radiate the feeling that they know what it's like to be a woman. Otherwise, just about the only rock queen left is Grace Slick. Although some may regard her private life as liberated in that she decided to have an illegitimate child and generally appears to care little for society's conventions, even her work with the Jefferson Airplane is hardly oriented toward women.

Which leaves us with Joan Baez, Judy Collins and Joni Mitchell, who specialize in the bland folk-rock deemed appropriate for a delicate sex.

At this point, what does rock offer women? Mighty little.

Recently, however, rock bands have reported strange happenings at concerts. Instead of the usual adoring screams from the women, every so often they've been hearing boos and unladylike shouts of "male chauvinist pigs." Because the bands tend to regard these disturbances as a puzzling but passing phenomenon, they've made little effort so far to understand the changes taking place in their audience. What they fail to recognize is that the condescending swaggering which worked for Elvis in the 'fifties and the sadistic, anti-woman sneers of Mick Jagger in the 'sixties are no longer going to make it in the 'seventies.

There's no question that rock is already in trouble. The current spiritual and economic malaise has been variously attributed to the Hendrix-Joplin deaths, the general tightness of money, as well as lackluster albums and tired performances from the popular stars. Whatever the reasons, rock listeners today are plainly bored. Does anyone really care if John, Paul, Ringo, and George ever get together again? Not me.

On the other hand, isn't it about time for women to band together and invade the chauvinistic rock scene? Only then will the vicious stereotypes be eliminated and, one hopes, some fresh energy generated as well. For too long we've sat wistfully on the sidelines, acting out our expected roles as worshipful groupies.

Women have always constituted an important segment of the rock audience. Unless the industry is willing to alienate us completely, they'd better remember what Bob Dylan said about not needing a weatherman to know which way the wind blows. For the times they are a-changin', eh, fellas?

Chapter IV

CHANGING MUSICAL TASTES

Chapter III included a number of divergent interpretations of the meaning of rock music for society. Each author selected illustrations and noted examples which fit his prior conclusions. The four articles in this chapter employ scholarly methods designed to get beyond such provocative but subjective speculation. The first two papers (Articles 15 and 16) examine the changing lyrics which are *put into* popular and rock music, while Articles 17 and 18 examine the interpretations which are *taken from* the lyrics of particular popular but controversial protest songs.

Articles 15 and 16 use content analysis, a method which has been the subject of much criticism, as was noted in the Introduction. At the one extreme, an analyst may range widely over the available material to find pithy examples. In doing this, he may make a persuasive *interpretation,* but he runs the danger of selecting only those songs which fit his theories. Alternatively, he may draw a sample of songs from a well-defined universe and code their lyrics in terms of a predetermined set of categories which fit his particular theoretical interest. This *quantitative* technique has the advantage of precision but runs the risk of missing important observations which do not fit into his *a priori* categories. "Popular Music Since the 1920's," by H. F. Mooney, a scholar in the field of American Studies, is nearer the interpretative pole; while "Changing Courtship Patterns in the Popular Song" by James T. Carey, a sociologist, as well as the earlier study by Horton which Carey cites extensively, are nearer the quantitative pole. The two papers on country music lyrics can also be placed along this dimension. The DiMaggio *et al.* study in Chapter I is more quantitative, while the Lund article in Chapter II is more interpretative.

The distinction between interpretation and quantification is useful, as well, for understanding differences among the studies that attempt to assay the influence of music. The articles in Chapter III exemplify the interpretative,while the final two papers in this chapter exemplify the quantitative tendency. It is interesting that while the former sort of studies conjectures that rock has a great influence in shaping the views of its audience, Articles 17 and 18, the two studies by sociologists reprinted here, do not find any tangible effects in the particular cases they examine. Denisoff and Levine found that 400 of 490 San Francisco college students polled had heard of "The Eve of Destruction" at the time it was on top of the hit parade but, of these, only 14 percent fully understood the protest manifest in its lyrics even when the respondents could read them. Robinson and Hirsch, using a larger and more heterogeneous sample, came to very similar conclusions. Only a small minority of their high-school-age respondents could identify the drug, sex, and middle-class hypocrisy themes in several popular songs of the day.

Since the target audience of pop-rock songs cannot correctly identify or interpret the lyrics, it might be inferred that lyrics must have no tangible influence. Only the writers of the Old Left ever believed that words were the essential component of a protest song. As noted in the Introduction, many other elements go into defining the meaning of a song or style of music. Despite the long-standing public concern with the function of music, and the many studies which provide suggestive leads, this remains an underdeveloped area of research. There have been no careful studies of the meaning which music has in the lives of any segment of the popular music audience.

15

POPULAR MUSIC SINCE THE 1920's: THE SIGNIFICANCE OF SHIFTING TASTE

H. F. Mooney

In the Fall 1954 *American Quarterly,* this writer discussed the significance of shifting tastes in American popular music since 1890. In retrospect it appears that the major trends established over or during the previous seventy years continued into the 1960's. First, the long-range trend away from the blandness, urbanity or introspection of the 1920's and 1930's persisted. Second, the Negroid tone of popular music as well as of jazz was increasingly prominent in "roots" jazz and in rock and roll dance music. Third, related to the Negroid tendency, a further plebeianization—to the point of crudeness—undermined older middle-class decorum. Fourth, along with this was a diminution of romantic love, amatory frustration and sentimental brooding or nostalgia. Fifth, the folk-protest vogue paralleled the aggressive "roots" movement in jazz and the general attack on what was called the "middle-class Establishment." Sixth, orchestration of popular songs rejected older standards almost as much as did jazz technique. Seventh, there was a reaction from the sort of music once produced copiously by the nostalgic or melancholy—and often quite sophisticated—urban Jew or Irishman so prominent for several decades among songwriters in New York. Into the vacuum created by what David Ewen calls the "death of Tin Pan Alley" after the 1930's exploded the rock-folk and soul shouts from a score of urban slums throughout the country. The public was predisposed to accept this vulgarization, the latest expression of eight decades of rebellious sensationalism in American popular music beginning with ragtime "coon songs." Thus, popular

From "Popular Music Since the 1920's: The Significance of Shifting Taste," by H. F. Mooney, *American Quarterly,* 20 (1968), pp. 67–85. Copyright © 1968, Trustees of the University of Pennsylvania. Reprinted with permission of publisher and author.

music after 1930 continued to express long-range tendencies evident by the 1920's or even before. Even so, however, the tastes of the mid-1960's were sufficiently different from those of the 1920's and 1930's to necessitate retrospection.

People in the 1920's and 1930's, as before then, were rebellious in certain ways—rebellious sexually and artistically; and economically as well in the 1930's. Their rebellion was evidenced in a greater infusion of jazz into popular music, and in the growing popularity of colored vocalists and instrumentalists; but it was limited by compromises with middle-class conventions. Most Negroes were little short of outcastes, too poor and too segregated from the mainstream of life to maximally influence taste. Colored musicians were discriminated against in commercial dance orchestras, in radio and, at least until the 1930's, in recording sessions.[1] The prevailing taste in popular music was shaped by a white middle class, self-consciously hedonistic, relatively prosperous at a time when—particularly during the depression of the 1930's—income was so narrowly distributed as to prevent many people from acquiring even necessities. By 1932, the sale of phonograph records had dropped to 6 percent of the volume of 1927, a year which was itself somewhat below the sales of the postwar months of 1919–20. Small record companies which had catered to the Negro market in the 1920's were wiped out, and the larger companies curtailed or eliminated their "race" (i.e., Negro performers') catalogues as the marginal Negro market was, as usual, the first to dip in any recession.[2] Consequently, the influence of Negro jazz was further minimized. Middle-class Negroes who desired to "come up," as they put it, during the 1930's and the 1940's responded to the smoothly harmonized arrangements of a white Jimmy Dorsey's watered-down jazz. Duke Ellington himself was influenced by Guy Lombardo's "sweetest music this side of heaven," and brought something of the sound of the Roosevelt Hotel ballroom to Harlem. Commercial orchestras of the period around 1920–50 followed more or less the "safe bet"—the aesthetic aspirations of the middle-class market —as did, indeed, most of the big Negro bands. They presented a music which, despite solo variations, emphasized precise, lush, ensemble harmony.[3].The highest compliment most of the public could pay to big-band jazz between 1928 and 1950 was "symphonic" or "advanced." Orchestrations of bands like Boyd Raeburn's, Stan Kenton's, Claude Thornhill's or Elliot Lawrence's (out of which

---

[1] Neil Leonard, *Jazz and the White Americans* (Chicago, 1962), p. 146.

[2] Roland Gelatt, *The Fabulous Phonograph* (New York, 1966), pp. 191, 208, 246, 255; Leonard, p. 91.

[3] Chadwick Hansen, "Social Influences on Jazz Style," *American Quarterly,* 12 (Winter 1960), pp. 501–3; N. Ertegun, "A Style and a Memory," *Record Changer,* 6 (July 1947), p. 7; Leonard, pp. 124 ff. For Ellington's absorption of Lombardo's style, listen to "Creole Rhapsody" (1931), reprocessed in RCA Camden Album CAL 459, *Duke Ellington at the Cotton Club.*

came some of the "cool" musicians of the 1950's) reflected the influence of Debussy, Ravel and the post-Impressionists.

Who were the middle class whose buying tastes thus helped create this trend? One hazards a reasonable guess that they were older than today's record buyers and on the whole higher on the socioeconomic scale. A sale of less than 20,000 records and a sheet music sale of 100,000 characterized a "hit" in the mid-1930's as contrasted with a record sales of at least 500,000 and perhaps a million twenty years later.[4] Buyers would have belonged largely among the fortunate minority with steady income. In days when one was lucky to have a job even at less than one hundred dollars a month, expenditure of seventy-five cents or even thirty-five cents for a record or a piece of sheet music was limited. Very few, apparently, of the people who bought records desired truly Negro jazz—since, for one thing, even during past "prosperity" they had had so little opportunity to hear it. Radio networks, apprehensive over the reactions of sponsors and public, had exercised a ruthless veto over this "immoral" music. Although the censorship was aimed more at lyrics than orchestrations, it resulted in smoothing out roughness in both. The situation changed somewhat toward the end of the 1930's, when Benny Goodman, after having used the Negro Fletcher Henderson's arrangements for several years, took advantage of increasing liberalism to hire such colored artists as Teddy Wilson. But the times had not changed radically. Henderson was a middle-class Negro with remarkably sophisticated arrangements for that time; and even at that, Goodman carefully "polished" them so as to conform to the standards of European rendition.[5] Teddy Wilson's piano was urbane, light, deftly polished, as was that of the increasingly popular Count Basie. Soon Goodman hired the white Eddie Sauter to develop a rich, very "white" symphonic sound which caught public fancy so well that Sauter developed it further into the "progressive" sound of the highly acclaimed Sauter-Finnegan band of the early 1950's. Seen in retrospect, the very popular orchestral tendencies of the entire period between 1920 and 1950, from Paul Whiteman down to the progressive and "west coast" movements which looked back at him with scorn, reflected the demand of the urban middle class for a highly refined, quasi-"classical" jazz.

Lyrics no less than orchestrations and vocal style reveal much about the music patrons of the 1930's. Songs like George and Ira Gershwin's "But Not

---

[4] Gelatt, p. 272; David Ewen, *Life and Death of Tin Pan Alley* (New York, 1964), p. 300; George Marek, "Oh, Dem Golden Records," and Jim Walsh, "Crosby's . . . Disk Sales," *Variety* 205 (Jan. 9, 1957), pp. 237, 239. Frank Sinatra recalls that Bing Crosby's popularity in the 1930's was centered among post-adolescents and even older adults; "My Life and My Music," *Life,* 58 (Apr. 23, 1965), p. 99.

[5] Marshall Stearns, *The Story of Jazz* (New York, 1956), p. 144; Leonard, pp. 98–100, 122. Leonard's second chapter brilliantly analyzes the tastes of the older middle class and the reasons for its opposition to jazz.

for Me" were subtle and understated, aimed at an audience of some maturity and education—of at least a smattering of and respect for art history and Maxim Gorky. They were very popular before the lifting of the Depression by 1941, and the deepening of the market in the war and postwar years modified the prevailing taste.

The intense, lovelorn ballad, while it lasted, reflected taste and life in the 1920's and especially the 1930's, when the purchasers of records were older and more middle-class—or middle-class-aspiring—than those of the 1960's. As such they wanted more adult themes and an often timidly "respectable" jazz infused by a "sweet," "harmonious" (or sometimes even "advanced," dissonant), but always *European* tone. Teenagers made up a relatively smaller segment of the population, and were not as affluent as later. Naturally, bestselling music dealt more fully with the problems of the post-adolescent consumer, as in "Mad About the Boy" [concerning the plight of a worldly woman in search of a stable relationship]. Thoroughly middle-class sentiments! Also in deference to middle-class ideas of "taste," the bestselling records of the 1930's were frequently orchestrated like symphonic tone poems. Duke Ellington, and even a highly successful middle-of-the-road white band like Hal Kemp's, attempted to infuse Delius into ballad fox-trots.[6] The popular tastemakers of the 1930's appear as somewhat cautious, compromising, middle-class young adults experimenting gingerly with jazz but tempering it with "highbrow" innovations or just sweetly pretty styling.

This ambivalent generation of 1920–50, which supported ambivalent orchestras like that of Glenn Miller, would have its cake and eat it too. A generation of transition, facing both ways, it compromised between the gentility of the Victorian parlor and the libidinism of the beatnik's pad. If the popular music of its time appealed strongly to young women, then the personality of the girl who bought the music is well expressed therein. The middle-class young woman of the 1920's and the 1930's who had broken her home ties to take a job and an apartment in the city lived in the hothouse of a pseudo-Freudian romanticism. The theme song of the day was, "Love, Your Magic Spell is Every-

---

[6] See liner notes on RCA Camden Album 811, *Great Bands of Our Times.* The 1930's emerge as the most "intellectual" period in American popular music. The sales appeal of such songs as "Tender is the Night" and "Moon and Sixpence" was evidently to be enhanced by the titles of Fitzgerald's and Maugham's then-new novels. In the late 1930's and early 1940's were concentrated many such adaptations of highbrow music as "Reverie," from Debussy; "Pavanne," from Ravel; "June on the Isle of May," from Tschaikowsky's *Andante Cantabile;* and Victor Herbert's "Yesterthoughts" and "Indian Summer." Tschaikowsky's *Piano Concerto No. 1 in B Flat* furnished "Tonite We Love," and his waltz theme from the *Pathetique* emerged as "The Night is Filled With Music," recorded like the others, as a slow, dreamy fox-trot ballad with only the slightest pulsation of the bass fiddle and a light tapping of the cymbal or wire brushing of the drum to accent the rhythm.

where." And, said the pseudo-Freudian (perhaps sincerely, perhaps just to give the girl the latest "line"), "Love is not love, is not truly, healthily, wholly a giving and receiving, without Sexual Expression." So the girls in their little apartments, with their radios and record players, pulsed with desire unrecognized, unacknowledgeable or unfelt by the sheltered girls of the 1880's. Susceptible and vulnerable, increasingly without real religious convictions, they awaited the Great Experience and Fulfillment of Love (or Sex), listened in glaze-eyed anticipation to songs like "I Surrender, Dear." Singers, catering to the mood, moaned with frustration, "Blue Evening (after a lonely day)." There was the frustration of balked expectations; there was also the painful anxiety, the fear of losing love—("How Long Will It Last?" "Why Can't This Night Go On Forever, why must morning find you gone?") ;[7] and finally, the denouement, the last bitter dregs of what had turned out to be mere sex without love—the brushoff, the awakening, the sobbing; but still so often the assertion that love had redeemed the whole sordid affair, as in Libby Holman's number, "I'm Doing What I'm Doing for Love,"[8] and in Grace Hayes's 1930 recording of "My Lover."

> All I could give I gave him gladly;
> And I'm not sorry I did it.[9]

Such ballads reveal the interwar mood. In the 1920's and 1930's middle-class girls were not prone to "play around" for the fleshly joy of it. Despite an increasingly rebellious promiscuity, the code was still tinged with the ideals of monogamous love—that is, sex could be truly good and beautiful, truly redeemed, only if part of a romantic love affair. If not chastity, if not marriage, there must be Love. And this love must be, as in a marriage, monogamous, exclusive, rather than "cheap," promiscuous. In the words of the song from Sigmund Romberg's operetta *Desert Song* (1926)—"One Alone." In short, something of Victorian sentiments remained. Love was not to be treated casually. One might defy the Victorian double standard, but must uphold Victorian courtly fidelity. Such songs compromised in lyrics, orchestration and vocal rendition between the sacred and the profane, the "high class" and the low-down, the refined and the sensual. They approached Sex obliquely—"Tonight is Mine," "One Night of Love." The raw blues feeling underlying a ballad like Ruth Etting's "What Wouldn't I Do For that Man?" was refined by a soft

---

[7] An elegant 1932 recording of the latter is reprocessed on RCA Vintage LPV 504, *The Great Isham Jones.*

[8] Recorded on Brunswick 4459. An original pressing is in the Archives, Stanford University Music Library.

[9] Copyright 1930 by Advanced Music Corp. Recorded on Victor 22381.

vocal, a limp saxophone, violin and piano accompaniment.[10] Apparently girls who wanted love, both sacred and profane, were attracted toward a music appropriately ambivalent.

By 1960 the climate had changed. One reason for the shifting taste was a change in the music business. By 1941, the virtual monopoly of the ASCAP (American Society of Composers, Authors, and Publishers, organized in 1914), which had practically protected New York's ascendancy in the music market, was broken by legal judgment. The consequent opening of broadcasting and recording channels to non-ASCAP composers and publishers, many of them unknowns outside the conventional music establishment of Tin Pan Alley and catering to a wider public of newly-affluent people—Negroes, workers who had migrated from rural areas, especially in the Southeast and Midwest to urban war jobs—marked the end of an era of increasingly urbane New York composers. These had been heavily Jewish. For example, out of the forty-one hits listed in Sigmund Spaeth's *History of Popular Music in America* (1948) for 1930, seventeen were written by composers and/or lyricists with names *recognizably* Jewish.[11] Especially after 1945, however, the dispersal of composing and publishing throughout the nation tended to diminish their influence at a time when middle-class values had ben weakened by war. Such New York Jews as Harold Arlen, George and Ira Gershwin, Jerome Kern, Vernon Duke (né Dukelsky), Herman Hupfeld and Vincent Youmans had produced a pensive music of finesse and polish, often using minor strains in the cantorial tradition. Their melodic concepts influenced "white" jazz instrumentalists—themselves frequently Jewish—flowing with increasing facility through plaintive but delicately restrained saxophones from Benny Kreuger in the early 1920's through Frank Trumbauer to Stan Getz; and through the arabesque clarinets of Benny Goodman and Artie Shaw. Until mid-century, immigrant and other minority groups, particularly in New York City, who as they rose became so influential in popular music, embraced standards still admired by many of the American middle class and by a more middle-class-aspiring lower class. The years 1920–50 were still much closer than our own to traditional WASP values. This is one reason why it was so difficult for Negro jazz to make greater headway. Aspiring Negro artists, jazz as well as non-jazz—Marian Anderson, Paul Robeson, Ellington, Henderson—themselves rejected much of the raw, gutty blues of an embarrassing past in favor of a concert style. The New York Jew and Negro, raised in the early years of the century—especially before Harlem became so largely a slum for ex-field hands from the South—were still awfully respectful of what some of

[10] The original recording, along with others of the period and genre, is reprocessed in Columbia Album C3 L35, *The Original Sound of the Twenties.*
[11] Pp. 641–42.

their grandchildren would later call the "square" or "ofay" world of the symphony, of refinement and gentility. Indeed, there is evidence that even the more contemptuous Negroes of the 1920's adopted the "sweet" tones of pseudo-"classical" middle-class music because they were determined to beat the white man on his own grounds as a performer.[12] Regardless of their motives and outlooks, songwriters and orchestrators, white and colored, adapted the Negro idiom to the gentility of their aspirations and/or to the tastes of the white middle class, who after all purchased so many leisure-time products, including music. It may have been true that both Negro and Jew had a certain common sense of alienation, a common bitterness or sadness, and a mutual empathy; but since they also both admired the culture of the Establishment whose doors they were forcing, their music, however sad, alienated or bitter, had nevertheless passed through a "refining" process. Excellent examples of this are, again, Benny Goodman's music; and such performances as Duke Ellington's 1940 recording of Harold Arlen's "Stormy Weather," with Ivy Anderson's subdued (by 1960 standards) vocal.[13] But, encouraged by the breakdown of ASCAP's hegemony and by prosperous new markets among formerly depressed and minority groups, rival publishing and recording companies had arisen by 1950 in many other, frequently less sophisticated localities—the Negro slums of Chicago, Los Angeles, Philadelphia and Oakland and the rural-music center at Nashville, Tennessee, where Negroid and country music fused into Roy Orbison's "rocka-billy" or "folk-rock." Many of the typical million-plus sellers in the 1950's and early 1960's were written, published and/or recorded in such new centers. From Louisville, Kentucky, came "Slow Poke." From Nashville, Patti Page and "Tennessee Waltz"; Jimmy Dean's "Big Bad John"; Hank Williams' "Cold Cold Heart" and "Jambalaya"; "Your Cheatin' Heart"; "Half as Much"; and the Everly Brothers' "Bird Dog." "Rose and a Baby Ruth" came from Chapel Hill, North Carolina; "This Old House" from Arcadia, California. Such early rock numbers as "Rock Around the Clock" and "A Whole Lot of Shakin' Goin' On," originated in Philadelphia;[14] later from the Portland, Oregon, area came "Looie, Looie, Looie, Ya, Ya, Ya."

These titles amply suggest a trend. There were no references to the Russian drama, to Penthouse Serenades, to Park Avenue Fantasies, Stairways to the Stars or to the Parthenon. The nation was apparently too prosperous to glamorize wealth and highlife, and too juvenile, too aggressively lowbrow or pseudo-lowbrow to admire "polished" or high-flown songs: many lower-class and minority group high school students now *hated* the middle-class culture which they felt was being forced on them. Then too, cold war nationalism may have

[12] Hansen, *op. cit.,* pp. 496, 500.
[13] Columbia 35556.
[14] Ewen, *op. cit.,* pp. 328–29.

stimulated a marked taste for tunes with a folksy, grass-roots flavor. True, middlebrow holdouts for the old "culture" might in the early 1950's cling to Mantovani's "Shimmering Strings," but a decade later, even the worst "squares" had shifted to the Tijuana Brass, which in its own banal way leaned more to the Big Beat of the 1960's than toward the pseudo-"classic" modulations of the early 1940's. If any doubt remains about a change in mood between 1941 and 1966, the contrast between Herb Alpert's and Gene Krupa's recordings of "Flamingo" tells the story.[15] During the period [of] 1940–60, not only had many of the urban middle class become anti-bourgeois themselves, but also many buyers now came from newly-prosperous segments of the population less influenced by WASP standards to begin with. Minority groups who shared in rising affluence and leisure were able in larger numbers to demand *their* kind of music. Negroes in particular, thronging from the rural South into Northern cities, intensified a demand for gospel shouts and rough-edged blues which helped change the tone of urban popular music. Even the poorer among them, filled with a new sense of pride, were aware of grievances, bitter against whites, anxious to support Negro artists and Negro music. By 1960 they were at least prosperous enough, and sufficiently concentrated in cities, to nourish a demand for a self-consciously "black" music performed by black entertainers. Negroes had become purveyors of and consumers of a musical product which aggressively emphasized their "roots." An active and even violent black protest supported within and outside the Negro minority was reflected in the scorching heat, the volume, the drive, the guttiness, the slurred tones of "soul" or "roots" or "funky" jazz, as well as in rock and roll in gospel shouts.[16]

Such music, which blacks in particular created, appealed to youth generally by 1960. Protest, rebellion, the muscular-visceral approach to music, the dance, to life itself, is of course typical of the adolescent and the very young adult at any time. By the later 1950's, youngsters were a relatively larger segment of the population than ever before in the twentieth century. They were also more prosperous than before as their parents' earnings and their own job opportunities increased. They were now catered to as customers. Although relatively prosperous, they appeared to lack a sense of identification with the adult world. They were restlessly seeking status, pleasure, self-expression, sometimes an answer to the problems of the world. Such seeking brought them into conflict with the adult world. They were almost a minority group of their own. In 1959, Arnold Shaw found the major market for popular music to lie between the ages of nine

[15] Krupa's 1941 record is Okeh 6120. An original pressing is in the Rodgers and Hammerstein Archives of Recorded Sound of the New York City Public Library.

[16] Archie Shepp, tenor saxophonist with the late John Coltrane's 1963–66 group, tended to identify his music with the struggles of his black people, in particular with Black Nationalism, according to Martin Williams, "The Problematic Mr. Shepp," *Saturday Review,* 49 (Nov. 12, 1966), p. 90.

or ten and seventeen or eighteen, among youngsters who were much less demanding of intricacy, restraint, nuance or polish than were a previous generation of older buyers.[17] These were the youth who "bopped" to the Big Beat of rock and roll, and who sang "Yakety Yak," a flippant take-off on parental discipline. Such lyrics as could be heard in the gregarious din of vocal groups of the late 1950's and early 1960's were often mindlessly extroverted expressions of the gang—"Yeah, yeah, yeah"—the lyrical equivalent of the teenagers' private street corner or drive-in banter. Nobody who bought "Rose and a Baby Ruth," one of the most tender and romantic songs of 1957, seemed to laugh at its bathos, so appropriate was it to a pre-adolescent taste—the same taste which brought out the little sensation-seekers to gape at *Teen Agers From Outer Space*. The somber, heavily orchestrated, introspective ballads of the young adults of the 1930's were passing out of the major trend.

So much for the obvious. The trend was away from suavity, however, not only in this music for children, but also to an extent in the jazz which had become a cult of many intellectuals. To a certain degree, jazz is always visceral; and to a certain degree, the popularity of visceral music among both adolescents and rebellious intellectuals is nothing new in the twentieth century—it has been, in fact, a long-range trend since the ragtime of the 1890's. But modifications in jazz as well as popular music after around 1954 appear significant, coming as they did at the height of the extremely irrationalist "white Negro" or "beatnik" movement among young writers. The anti-intellectual intellectuals followed Norman Mailer and Jack Kerouac, and then Norman Brown and Timothy Leary, into the outer reaches of thrill or even violence. By 1960, a searingly intense "hard bop" or "soul music" was crowding the chamber-music sound of the post-progressive cool or west coast jazz. To be truly arty in the early 1960's, one had to be glandular.[18] Taste ran to a big, honking, stomping, earsplitting saxophone, heavier beat, shrieking revival shouts, recordings bursting with the din of screaming teenage togetherness. The unobtrusive Maxine Sullivan and Connie Boswell of the 1930's; the Modernaires, Pied Pipers, Jo Stafford, Margaret Whiting, Mel Torme and June Christy of the "slick" 1940's; the husky-dreamy Julie London and Johnny Mathis, the HiLos and the Honey Dreamers and the Four Freshmen and other richly-chorded precision groups who held their popularity well into the 1950's despite a reversal in taste—all

---

[17] Arnold Shaw, "Mr. Harper's After Hours," *Harper's* 218 (May 1959), p. 82.

[18] Thus, tenor saxophonist Stan Getz, once acclaimed in 1955 as "subtle" (liner notes of NorGran Album NGN 1032, *West Coast Jazz*) was acclaimed in liner notes of 1963 as "having a more mature emotionalism . . . a gutsy maleness" (Verve Album V/V6-8545, *Getz-Gilberto*). In the early 1960s it was indeed impossible to be *subtly* male—one must wear horsehide boots—or *subtly* feminine—one must wear barbaric globs of eye makeup and great varnished swirls and swatches of hair.

these were by 1960 paled by the church revival mood of the Clara Ward Singers, Mahalia Jackson, Timi Yuro; or by the often inarticulate shouts of the transistor-set favorites—the Supremes, the Orlons. Popular music, often used as a psychedelic experience, became a "happening," a numbing bombardment of the auditory nerves. On whatever cultural level one might look, to Rojack of *An American Dream* or to James Bond, there must be rawness, constant stimulation. A primitive emotionalism (non-sentimental) must make no compromises with WASPishness in life, literature, music. The "well-adjusted," modal personality, the middle-class "average guy," was Out. Bing Crosby's or Perry Como's accommodating, casual pleasantness was anathema: sweat and suffering made an artist popular in the early 1960's. He must, it would appear from the record jackets and liner notes, bear the stigma—or the stigmata, really, in the new religion of the Holy Barbarians—of Alienation from a crucificial Society —a Society composed of Crosbys and Comos with their casual tweeds and pipes and not-so-casual homes in Bel Air, their golf matches and stables of horses. Crosby and Como were passe in a period which sang, "Here's to the Losers." Perhaps the first indication of the change had been Johnny Ray's "Cry" in 1951. At any rate, music of the sort young people felt WASPS over thirty would sing, compose or listen to, went into a decline. The liner blurbs, intended to sell records at first sight, spoke less of the home and family of the performer than of his "searchings," his bitterness, his inability or refusal to accommodate to the Establishment, his mental and/or physical handicaps or deviations, his daemonic immersion in environment-obliterating alcohol, sex or drugs. Such a recitation might in whole or in part apply to many of the folk heroes, or anti-heroes (musical and non-musical) of the 1960's—Ray Charles, Billie Holiday, Parker, Mailer and his Rojack, Brendan Behan, Bob Dylan, Dylan Thomas (did the identification of the folksinger's family name with the given name of the early-deceased alcoholic poet stimulate his popularity?). The stale remnants of the placid "boy-and-girl-next-door" singers of the 1930's could hardly compete with the lacerated, gorgeously uninhibited wailing of Ray Charles —blind, drug-addicted, low-class, black, and—needless to say, to the old middle class, thoroughly disreputable—with his "Get your Buddy, and Go Get Stoned." A period in which the three leading playwrights were said to be militantly if obliquely homosexual in their work and, partly because of this, were extremely popular; a period, in short, of rising nonconformity, deviation and some sympathy for minorities, would find in Charles a welcome personification of the Outcast. The years of James Baldwin and LeRoi (*The Toilet*) Jones heard the violently surging saxophonic "sheets of sound" of John Coltrane, the explosive reed of Ornette Coleman. The suave colored singers of the 1940's and earlier 1950's who had accommodated to the white hotel and club world—Billy Eckstine, Sarah Vaughan, Lena Horne, Ella Fitzgerald (now much too poised and benignly self-possessed) were not much imitated among younger singers—

a sure sign of obsolescence. Instead, Dinah Washington, Della Reese, Roy Hamilton, Brook Benton and Hank Ballard set the trend for the Chubby Checkers, Don Covays, Dee Dee Sharps and Sugar Pie Depintos who sang ever more intensely "black." All were Negro. In quantity as well as in vocal quality, singers were now substantially—and proudly—black. Into the 1950's most singers had been white, and on the whole, rather tepid crooners. By the mid-1960's Petula Clark, one of the few top white singers, sang "soul" like blacks, which meant a full-throated openly emotional delivery such as few white or black singers had demonstrated in the past. Indeed, it had not been as greatly demanded in the past. But by 1960 the old stiff-upper-lip Calvinist distrust of emotional expression had softened more than ever before. The grim lips relaxed and opened. Songs were shouted. The older ideal of the clean-cut crew-cut Nordic hero, silently self-controlled, was shrinking, along with the phase of conformity expressed in 1954's "Counting My Blessings." Music, like the film, documents a resurgent rebellion in the mid-1950's. James Dean, Elvis Presley, Sal Mineo— all were white, to be sure, but, like Mailer's "white Negro," dropouts from the WASP world who foreshadowed the popularity of Ray Charles' "Crying Time." Here was a *man* sobbing, and he was a glamorous youth hero on account of it. And unlike his less evocative predecessor, Johnny Ray, he was black.

By the 1960's, then, the bland "white" vocal was passe. And so was the polished "white" orchestration. The typical rock group of the late 1950's and early 1960's—amplified guitars, percussion, saxophone—was designed for rhythm and individual variations rather than for tone color. It dispensed with *fortissimo-pianissimo* modulations and played one way—loud. Never had such primitive jazz been exploited with such wide success among whites as well as Negroes. Even the more advanced jazz of the 1960's, which utilized the intricate techniques and rhythmic complexities of the bop revolution, also emphasized beat, solo variations and rhythmic experiment more than harmonics and modulation. Such a trend reflected the Negro's pride in his own roots, his "funky" contempt for white aesthetic standards; and also appeared to indicate that many whites as well, ashamed of or resentful of WASPishness, were seeking in music what some of them sought in LSD, a piling up of new sensation upon sensation to smash their Square prison.[19]

It would of course be naive to call all this "new." Change, rebellion, the

[19] From liner notes by LeRoi Jones for Impulse Album A50, *Coltrane Live at Birdland* (1963): "The long tag of "Afro-Blue," with Elvin [Jones, drummer] thrashing and cursing beneath Trane's line, is unbelievable. Beautiful has nothing to do with it, but it is (I got up and danced while writing these notes, screaming at Elvin to cool it).... The crashing cymbals, bombarded tom-toms ... [are] like the wild pulse of all living." Regarding another selection in the album, called "Alabama," he wrote: "If that real Alabama was the catalyst, more power to it, and may it be this beautiful, even in its destruction." Sorel had Arrived.

distortion or smashing of old forms, has long been a part of American culture. Change is the rule. Much of the change of 1960 was really a continuation of trends begun at least by the 1890's—the elevation of the once-degraded, the degradation of the once-elevated, the rebellion against older values. *Plus ça change, plus la même chose.* The intellectual and plebeian revolt against the middle class had by 1960 turned full blast against the generation of 1920–50, themselves once rebels of a sort now passe. The rejection of the big, white-stylized, highly arranged "swing" orchestra (once thought to be so untrammeled!) in favor of smaller, cruder groups; indeed, in favor of one singer and his guitar—the epitome of individualism—came when youth was attracted by the anarchism of Paul Goodman. Joan Baez's folksinging could be seen as a rebellion against the kind of society which had produced the Big Bands of the previous generation, where musicians had been straightjacketed into an Organization formula aimed at profits more than freedom, improvization, "soul."[20] If youth in the 1960's often tended to reject large organizations, the depersonalized, self-effacing vocalists who in the 1930's and 1940's had been merely components of the big orchestras, were now scarcely heard among the folk and church-revival singers.

The immense popularity of the church-revival mood also suggested a return to or reformulation of "religion." Youth, never more millenarian than in the early 1960's, had rediscovered mysticism, the shared but intensely individual purification of the psyche through hallucinogenic "trips," which somehow suggested the transports of the old tent meeting. To those who, like Dr. Timothy Leary, searched for a transcendental "spiritual discovery," the soul singing of Sister Odetta could fill a need unsatisfied by delicate secular love ballads. Young people bored by what one critic called the "dessicated" cool jazz of the 1950's bought John Coltrane's best selling album, *A Love Supreme* (Impulse A/AS 77), whose liner notes consisted of Coltrane's devotional poetry.[21]

The love music of the 1960's, sacred or profane, was not much like that of a previous generation. Of course, in all ages men sing of love, and so they did in the 1960's, sometimes with a lachrymose sentimentality which in itself catered to a different level of taste than did many of the brittle ballads of the 1930's. Nevertheless, sentimental love songs, lachrymose or otherwise, declined

---

[20] According to Miss Baez, her simple vocal-with-guitar rejected the "commercial." "The Folk Girls," *Time,* 79 (June 1, 1962), p. 40.

[21] A college student editor, Peter B. Riley, notes that the "tough" sound of such groups as the Butterfield Blues Band (called the "Marat/Sade of Blues") "seems to act on some people in the manner of an aural LSD." *Recorder* (Central Connecticut State College), Feb. 28, 1967, 3:2. Similarly, a review of another John Coltrane devotional album, *Meditations,* says "I *feel* this. . . . It opens up a part of myself that is tightly closed. Seldom recognized emotions well up and sear my consciousness." Don DeMichael in *Downbeat,* 33 (Dec. 1, 1966), p. 28.

in popularity. Love lyrics were often so hopelessly submerged in and mangled by arrangements aimed primarily at rhythmic effect that observers could easily conclude that the love song as they remembered it had all but disappeared.[22] Certainly boys didn't worship girls in such 1942-style effusions as "You are a Poem Set to Music." Nor did girls much attempt to promote this sort of veneration. If one heard fewer "pretty songs" one saw fewer girls in "pretty dresses," even on Sundays. A sexually more casual generation appeared to reject the tradition of chivalric amour. They might be aggressively sensuous and sensual, but casually so, and not with the great daintiness or delicacy which had once characterized days of a stronger double standard and sense of sin. They were more direct and companionate in the minidress, car-coat-and-levis era. God's death, or at least the weakening of Pauline concepts of deity, evidently meant you could junk much of your Platonism and let yourself go.

The noticeable dip in the popularity of the exclusive type of love song among many younger buyers cannot be traced to any one simple cause. A decline in traditional religion probably played a part. If God were not dead, He was, at least to the "hip" culture, a God created in man's image, a "swinger" to be found in "gay" bars and in jazz happening services. As such, He did not demand chaste refinement in music. His demands of human nature were few, but He did demand of his flower children a communal love rather than middle-class monogamy. At any rate, many youths, whether "hip" or not, and particularly among the middle class, caught the spirit. They desired greater sexual freedom. They rejected the (to them) hypocritical compromises, the puritanical indirection, and often the exclusiveness as well, of many of the older ballads. For them, the egocentric, monogamous lyrics, the bourgeois-plushy orchestrations of even the passionate "Body and Soul" sort of thing was, as they would put it, "beside the point." The older love song, even the more sensual, no longer caught on. After all, among many students, particularly in the first half of the 1960's, sexual revolt was but part of a much wider rejection of middle-class mores and prejudices. It was part of a fervent attempt to regenerate man. Youthful energies flowed out toward social reconstruction—"We Shall Overcome"— or into the purification of or expansion of the individual psyche through hallucinogens—"Puff, the Magic Dragon," "The Trip." Such youth stressed the one-ness of mankind, the overcoming of the crippling guilt feelings imposed by an artificial Establishment. They opposed the middle-class mores of their parents, often attributing these to the egocentricity of western civilization; and some turned to their version of a pantheistic Buddhism as a cure for the ills of the West. (Thus the "acid rock" emanating from San Francisco's Hashbury was infused with the *raga* of an oriental culture considered beatific by the hippies.)

---

[22] See for example, Tom Prideaux, "Whatever Happened to Love Songs?" *Life,* 61 (Sept. 16, 1966), pp. 61–62.

The more activist youth in the 1960's, puritanical hedonists or hedonistic puritans, who equated sensual pleasure (widely diffused) and self-expression with cosmic betterment, saw in love not a misty-eyed, pallid, etherealized retreat from the world but a means of social regeneration. (At least so went the gospel of Lawrence Lipton's *Erotic Revolution*.) These outlooks hardly promoted the popularity of such old musical standards as "When Your Lover Has Gone." All compromise with artificial bourgeois social and sexual barriers must go—among these compromises, the romantic ballad of the past. If the middle-class record purchasers of the previous generation had stressed monogamy within or without marriage, the new, young communalists rejected songs which sentimentally glorified one girl. A new world could not be built upon middle-class hypocrisy, possessiveness, exclusiveness. This dislike of the middle class by the self-styled "neo-Marxists" contributed to the decline of the old-style love song.[23]

The youth culture we have been describing, though it did help shape a trend away from the old ballads, was only a minority of the market. However noisily influential, it is doubtful that its outlook totally determined popular trends. It just so happened that other, larger, segments of the market were also not enthusiastic middle-class devotees of the old monogamous love ballad. Perhaps one of the most potent changers of taste was the horde of highly permissive and hedonistic lower-class [buyers] entering the record market. These buyers, along with the less numerous upper-middle-class young rebels, weakened the hold of the romantic, oblique, sublimated "If I Loved You" approach toward love, taking it out of the sphere of the angels and pulling it down toward earth. (1955's "Earth Angel" was a step along the way.) Trends in music since around 1955 especially have appeared to bear out the assumptions of sociologists and of Professor Hayakawa's invaluable work on jazz,[24] that the working class generally, and especially the colored lower class, lacked the WASPish inhibitions which are apt to generate genteelly romantic, melancholy, frustrated songs. In short, they gratify themselves without making a cosmic issue out of it. By 1955

---

[23] Richard Goldstein's article on the "Flower Children" among the middle class, in the *Denver Post* Contemporary section (June 18, 1967, pp. 12, 21), points up the generalized ideal of love. Such youth of course could have plenty of fun shocking the oldsters with their Four Letter Word Movement, all for a good cause. Two of the "frank" folksongs popular in the early 1960's were at least straightforward enough to ruffle the remaining hairs on a middle-class pate—especially if sung by girls of the rising generation: i. e., "Keep her Good and Drunk and Goozy" and "Sally Let Your Bangs Hang Down," sung respectively by Gibson and Camp and by Dian and the Greenbrier Boys:
     Now we know what Sally's got.
     Makes a man think she's so hot
(from Crestview Album CRS 7807, *The Original Hootenanny*). This was hardly William Burroughs, but neither was it Irving Berlin or Cole Porter.
[24] For example, "Popular Songs versus the Facts of Life," *ETC: A General Review of Semantics*, 24 (Winter 1955), pp. 83–95.

a best-selling rock number, "Honey Love," reduced the description of desire to three little words—not "I Love You," but "I Want It." In contrast, fifteen years previously, Ray Eberle had softly vocalized, over Glenn Miller's Debussy-esque background, this Lawrence-Shapiro ballad:

> When I reached up to heaven . . .
> And gathered you a handful of stars.[25]

Boys and girls who take sexual freedom for granted would hardly be as capti-vated by such songs as would be the more frustrated. They would be just as interested in motorcycling and, the boys at least, in hot-rodding; finding in these activities something of the same muscular enthusiasm and visceral excite-ment involved in their sexual relations. Indeed, an infusion of prosperous, rather unsentimental lower-class leather boys into the record market—the kind who like to be out with their buddies Sunday afternoons—may have helped create the hot-rod music craze of the early 1960's.

Thus, lower-class youth unassimilated by middle-class culture joined with middle-class rebels against middle-class culture to alter the tone of American popular music. To the lower class, sex was nothing to moan over or sing pretty little sad poems about. To the crusading middle-class student rebels it was something which must be handled robustly, erotically, "honestly," rather than euphemized or sublimated out of all recognition as their parents had frequently done. Middle-class rebel and lower-class "swinger"; hippy and minority groups had a common distaste for pretty songs. The folk music of youth in the 1960's could hardly follow schoolmarmish rules of rhyme or the meter of Victorian poetry. Rejecting the formulae of the classroom, more and more lyrics were sung—or spoken—free style, like streetcorner or coffee house conversation.

If monogamous romantic love was out in the music of the young and many of the would-be-young, *Agape* was in. By 1964, the tone of Erich Fromm, Martin Buber and Paul Goodman pervaded even a Broadway hit musical, *Funny Girl*. Barbra Streisand (first name unconventionally spelled, last name obviously minority-group; exotic-ugly non-Anglo face; muscular voice throbbing with all the subtlety of a sledgehammer; personality problems[26]—how could she have failed?) sang "People who Need People are the Luckiest People in the World." Two years later, in similar Tennessee Williams spirit, Simon and Garfunkel (names which would have been anglicized by any sane public relations man in 1930, but only by an insane one in 1966) popularized their ironic, "I am a Rock, I am an Island":

---

[25] Copyright 1939, 1940 by Leo Feist, Inc. Recorded on Bluebird 10893.
[26] See Shana Alexander, "Barbra," *Life*, 56 (May 22, 1964), p. 52.

and a rock can feel no pain
and an island never cries.[27]

The neo-proletarian Togetherness, like the rough-edged songs and singers, was appropriate to the jeans and horsehide boots of the young "neo-Marxists." This was still romanticism, of course, but it was not "bourgeois" prettiness. The point is that the "tastefully" orchestrated romantic love ballad had such severe competition that it was much less in evidence.[28] As middle-class youth conceived of the one-ness of mankind and refurbished the vision of the noble savage, they gravitated toward the music of people considered inferior by their parents, by all who still aspired to older middle-class standards. Thus, the tastes of the young did not run heavily to "pretty" love ballads. With their fondness for the old films of James Dean and Marlon Brando and Humphrey ("gentle-tough guy") Bogart, they liked Roger Miller's "King of the Road."

This brings us back to a basic generalization. Despite eddies and cross-currents always present in the streams of taste, the outstanding trend in American popular music in the 1950's and the earlier 1960's was a rejection of prettiness, overrefinement, academic orchestration and lyrics, smoothness, even subtlety. Although by 1965 a few of the lyrics written for the recently expanded college market, like "I Am a Rock," sensitively articulated the preoccupations of young adults, many lyrics, as well as most orchestrations, of the late 1950's and early 1960's were crude. Classicism, polish, formal discipline, carefully contrived arrangements, adherence to accepted rules in music, as in literature and art— these were likely to be anathematized even by many intellectuals for coldness, lack of spontaneity or "hypocrisy." In short, there was an attack on middle-class standards, on that residue of puritanism which distrusted the "natural." It would be a mistake, however, to assert that since music contained much protest against all aspects of the Establishment, from war to "Ticky Tacky Houses" and conformity, a thoroughgoing iconoclasm was the order of the day. Even though the folk song might so often protest, it could also reaffirm for large audiences a traditional patriotism—"This Land Is Our Land," "Ballad of the Green Beret." Musical trends can hardly be made any more coherent or consistent than the society which produces them. Two hundred million Americans living in the same years could among them find room for Barry Sadler's "Green Beret" and Bob Dylan's "World War III Blues." And yet, there was a similarity between the performers. Both were leather-booted, wild-animal-type young men (one a

---

[27] Copyright 1965, Charing Cross Music.
[28] But not dead. Songs by Andy Williams, Jerry Vale, Al Martino and Tony Bennett (albeit more exuberantly and "cornily" rendered than songs in the 1930's and 1940's) were still heard on TV and especially on jukeboxes in restaurants and bars catering to people around thirty or older.

disheveled gazelle, the other a wild boar). Both were typical of years in which some of the most popular vocal and instrumental groups were called "The Animals," "The Monkees," "The Critters." Both these men were as far removed as could be from the Regional Accounting Office, the classroom, or "Cocktails for Two" in the sleek white-on-whiteness of an *art moderne* penthouse in Gotham.[29] They would, both of them, be classified at any employment agency as non-U. To this extent they perhaps validate the one generalization we can make about the musical temper of the later 1950's and the earlier 1960's: it was one of those times when the perennial reaction of youth against the norms of older people is accelerated, heightened, intensified. Youth boldly threw in the faces of its elders its own musical description of love: "Gimme Gravy for My Mashed Potatoes." The very appearance of Cass of the Mamas and the Papas—lazy-fat, slovenly, serenely sensual—affronted the middle-class ideal of refined womanhood as a trimly neat, highly disciplined, meticulous housewife, teacher or stenographer.

Again, lest we interpret such a generalization to mean that all middle-class restraints, social and musical, were on the junk heap, Jeremy Larner reminds us that the popular songs of the early 1960's, if less than those of the 1930's, still paid some lip service to older values. Some sentimental lyrics continued to be written and sung even in rock and roll numbers, if only, as Mr. Larner explains, to sublimate the orgasm of the music. True, these lyrics were often not clearly articulated; engulfed in a pounding, shrieking sound, they were rarely audible. But they were there. The new generation of rebels still hedged a bit.[30] The Critters occasionally would sing soft, subtly-blended arrangements of lovelorn ballads like "Mr. Die-ingly Sad"; and if you listened carefully enough to the young black voices of the Orlons shouting "The Rules of Love," you could hear the old plea for bourgeois fidelity.

[29] "Cocktails for Two" was introduced by Duke Ellington in a 1934 musical film. He played in full dress, and on a white piano. The song mentioned two hands slyly meeting beneath a serviette while an orchestra played "an exquisite chansonette."

[30] Jeremy Larner, "What Do They Get from Rock 'N' Roll?" *Atlantic*, 214 (Aug. 1964), p. 48.

16

CHANGING COURTSHIP PATTERNS IN THE POPULAR SONG

James T. Carey

Radio disc jockeys and rock and roll fans date the emergence of rock and roll as a distinct musical style with Bill Haley and the Comets' 1955 recording of "Rock Around the Clock." This musical style was a blend of blues and country western and for the first time introduced mass white audiences to a Negro folk musical form. More recently folk rock and psychedelic rock have appeared as variations within the same basic musical style.[1] The emergence of rock and roll music has provided a vehicle for the development of a new perspective on boy-girl relationships. A look at the changes in song content over the past eleven

From the *American Journal of Sociology* 74 (May, 1969), pp. 720–731. Copyright © 1969 by the University of Chicago Press. Reprinted with permission of publisher and author. [Footnotes have been renumbered.]

[1] The rock and roll songs of the late 1950's characterized today as *old-style rock,* emphasized standard band or orchestra instruments like the trumpet or violin. There were no background group effects. Tommy James's "Hanky Panky" and Nancy Sinatra's "These Boots are Made for Walking" are more recent examples of old-style rock. *Rock and roll, popular style,* is a direct descendant from old-style rock. There is a noticeable or emphasized use of electronic instruments, especially guitars and organs. There is also an interplay between backup groups and the lead singer in vocal pieces and between the lead instruments and backup instruments in instrumentals. The Lovin' Spoonful's "Summer in the City" and the Standell's "Dirty Water" are examples of popular style. *Folk rock* also uses electric sound, but without heavy effects and without the backup vocal groups and interplay that occur in popular-style rock and roll. The Mamas and the Papas' "I Saw Her Again" and Simon and Garfunkel's "I Am a Rock" are examples of folk rock. *Psychedelic rock* emphasizes electric, amplified instruments. Speaker effects may be used, especially the organ. There is no vocal interplay between the backup and lead. There is interplay between electronic effects and vocal. "Over Under Sideways and Down" by the Yardbirds and "You're Gonna Miss Me" by the 13th Floor Elevator are examples of psychedelic rock. For the purposes of this analysis, rock and roll includes all four styles.

years reveals marked changes in orientation, not only in the relationship between the sexes but also in the relationship of young people to the larger social
order.

Any analysis of lyrics must take into account that only the verbal content,
a secondary aspect of the music, lends itself to social examination. A superficial
comparison of the mood of popular music in the 'fifties to that of the 'sixties
suggests that the earlier music was languid, searching, "sweet"; the music of the
late 'sixties is more sensual, direct, sexual, and "gutsy."[2] Lyrics may reveal
general values, but this is not necessarily the stated reason for listening to them.
It seems to be the nature of the music itself, and not the vocal or lyrical aspects
alone, which accounts for its popularity. The words are only part of the total
sound and are responded to as such.

The first serious social-scientific inquiry into popular music was conducted
by Adorno in 1941.[3] He analyzed the fundamental character of popular songs
and the role of musical agencies in standardizing certain musical forms. Peatman[4]
differentiated themes in popular song lyrics through the use of content analysis.
He found that all dealt with "love" and could be classified into three major types
of lyrics: the "happy in love" ballad, the "frustrated in love" song, and the
"novelty song with sex interest." Several years later, Riesman[5] explored the way
in which music and musical opinions are used as a form of communication. Horton[6] analyzed the themes of popular songs as they related to the relationship
between boys and girls. Johnstone and Katz[7] concluded that preferences in popular music among teen-age girls varied according to popularity among peers and
neighborhood norms. They pointed to the role and explored the influence of
adolescent peer groups on tastes in popular music. They concluded that the peer
group may influence and restrict preference in disc jockeys and, consequently,
in the music to which its members will listen.

Content analyses of lyrics conducted by Peatman in 1944, by Horton in 1957,
and the one discussed in this paper reveal that the overwhelming majority of
songs are concerned with courtship and the boy-girl relationship. The courtship

[2] See C. Keil, "Motion and Feeling through Music," *Journal of Aesthetics and Art Criticism* 24 No. 3 (Spring, 1966), pp. 337–50, for a suggested classification of musical styles based on the combination of techniques used.

[3] T. W. Adorno, "On Radio Music," in *Studies in Philosophy and Social Science* (New York: Institute of Social Research, 1941), 9, pp. 17–48.

[4] J. Peatman, "Radio and Popular Music," in *Radio Research: 1942–43*, eds. P. Lazars-feld and F. Stanton (New York: Duell, Sloan & Pearce, 1944), pp. 335–93.

[5] D. Riesman, "Listening to Popular Music," in *Mass Culture: The Popular Arts in America*, eds. B. Rosenberg and D. M. White (Glencoe, Ill.: Free Press, 1957), pp. 408–17.

[6] D. Horton, "The Dialogue of Courtship in Popular Songs," *American Journal of Sociology*, 62 (May, 1957), pp. 569–78.

[7] J. Johnstone and E. Katz, "Youth and Popular Music: A Study in the Sociology of Taste," *American Journal of Sociology*, 62 (May, 1957), pp. 563–68.

situation is viewed differently, however. This becomes clear by noting the difference in perspective between the lyrics analyzed by Horton and the present study.

We will rely on Horton's analysis of popular song lyrics for the verbal content of 1955 songs. His data were drawn from the June, 1955, issue of four magazines: *Hit Parader, Song Hits Magazine, Country Song Roundup,* and *Rhythm and Blues.* We have tried to repeat Horton's analysis by looking at the same magazines during a two-month period in the summer of 1966.[8] This was not completely possible, since *Rhythm and Blues* had discontinued publication several years earlier.[9] In addition, we have used *Billboard* for the national top thirty listings in the same period and the top thirty listings of one radio station in San Francisco for the Bay Area. Both the national listing and the Bay Area listing rate songs in terms of popularity. Our analysis should provide us with a comparsion of courtship patterns at two different time periods based on a content analysis of song magazine listings. Further, it should indicate, through the use of two more popularity listings in addition to the song magazines, the dramatic shift in value preferences of young people.[10] These value preferences relate not only to idealized boy-girl relationships but also to a wider range of concerns.

[8] The songs included in these magazines are drawn partly from a national popularity listing and partly from staff view of what songs are likely to gross well in retail sales. Hence, in any given issue, at least 30 percent are not drawn from any popularity chart.

[9] *Billboard* does include a separate rhythm and blues rating which lists songs popular among Negroes, based on radio air-play from Negro radio stations and retail sales in Negro neighborhoods. A preliminary check of the content of the songs, despite the distinctively different musical style, indicates that the themes do not differ substantially from the three song magazines, with one important qualification. There are few lyrics which suggest that women are on a pedestal or that sexual interests are anything less than normal. Horton, *op cit.,* noted that there was nothing distinctive about the stages of the courtship relationship in his analysis of rhythm and blues lyrics. However, a more careful examination might reveal that the double standard characteristic of white popular music in the 'fifties was absent in the rhythm and blues lyrics of the same period. In short, a case could probably be made that the "new" notions about boy-girl relationships in today's lyrics represent a general acceptance of Negro notions by a white audience.

[10] The inclusion of the national popularity ratings is an attempt to overcome the limitations of the song magazines as an indicator of youth preferences. The ratings are based on radio air-play and retail sales. The inclusion of the San Francisco ratings is an attempt to suggest that the new values being celebrated are related to particular groups, particular musical styles, and particular centers of popular culture. C. Hall, in "Detroit and L.A. Sales 'Happening Places,' " *Billboard,* 78 (July 2, 1966), p. 1, reports that San Francisco had 15 original record breakouts, i.e., records that first hit the top-thirty chart there, during the first six months of 1966, of which two went on to reach *Billboard's* "Hot 100" chart. This was in contrast to New York, with 16, of which six went on to reach the chart, and Los Angeles, with 16 original record breakouts of which eight went on to reach the hit chart. Hall goes on to say: "In a similar survey last year, New York took all the honors, not only having the most original breakouts—17—but having the most that reached the charts—19. San Francisco had been second with 18 breakouts that reached the chart" (*ibid.*). *Billboard* classifies the country into twenty-two major markets, which include all the major cities in five major regions: East, South, Midwest, Southwest, and West.

A total of 227 different songs were analyzed, of which 52 percent were classified as rock and roll.

Table 1 describes the sample. It shows the distribution of songs by musical style in the 1966 song magazines and popularity listings. The distribution is somewhat skewed by including *Country Song Roundup,* since this magazine focuses overwhelmingly on one musical style—country western. If we excluded that, the proportion of rock and roll lyrics from the other four sources would increase from 52 to 62 percent.

Table 1

LYRIC MUSICAL STYLE, 1966

Style	Song Magazines and Popularity Listings					
	Country Song Roundup	Hit Parader	Song Hits	Billboard	KYA	Total (Excluding Duplication)
Rhythm and blues		20%(19)	22%(14)	23%(13)	22%(12)	17%(38)
Rock and roll.....		60%(56)	64%(41)	62%(35)	62%(34)	52%(119)
Country western..	90%(55)	7%(7)	7%(4)	3%(2)	4%(2)	24%(54)
Other............	10%(6)	13%(12)	7%(4)	12%(7)	12%(6)	7%(16)
Total............	100%(61)	100%(94)	100%(63)	100%(57)	100%(54)	100%(227)

Lyrics were classified in a general way in terms of whether they reflected "older" or "newer" values. Older values were found in lyrics which enjoined, implicitly or explicitly, the acceptance of conventional values, for example, romantic notions about boy-girl relationships or fatalistic acceptance of the demands placed on one by the larger community. Lyrics that expressed anxiety over social change were also classified as representing older values. Newer values were found in lyrics which seemed to advocate or imply a more autonomous relationship between the sexes and/or criticized conventional society because of its misplaced preferences.[11] If we look at all the lyrics in our 1966 sample, we note that the new values are being communicated primarily through rock lyrics.

Table 2 dichotomizes lyrics into two general categories for illustrative pur-

[11] Three judges sorted the lyrics into three categories: old values, new values, and other. Those classified as "other" included lyrics whose value content was neutral, *e.g.,* Barry McGuire's "On A Cloudy Summer Afternoon," or songs which did not have enough verbal content to permit classification as old or new, *e.g.,* Robert Parker's "Barefootin'." Disagreement among the judges occurred on those lyrics which were mixed, partly expressing old values, partly new. The final decision on whether the lyrics expressed old or new values was made on the basis of which value was *most* represented in counting the lines.

poses. It shows that the emphasis on autonomy in personal relations and in relation to the larger community is distinctively related to one musical style. The largest proportion of rock and roll lyrics representing older values is part of the subclassification "old style rock." If we separated them from the general rock and

Table 2

COMPARISON OF VALUES REPRESENTED IN MUSICAL STYLES

	Country Western	Rhythm and Blues	Rock and Roll	Other*
Old values	100% (54)	65.8% (25)	29.9% (35)	75% (12)
New values		29.0% (11)	68.1% (80)	19% (3)
Other		5.2% (2)	2.0% (2)	6% (1)
Total	100% (54)	100% (38)	100% (117)	100% (16)

* Includes "easy listening, popular music" sound; songs in jazz or swing style of the early fifties, chorales, and straight folk songs.

roll category, the point of Table 2 would be made even more dramatically: the proportion of lyrics representing newer values increases from 68 percent to 83 percent.[12] Our illustrations of the shift in perspective on boy-girl relationships will be primarily drawn from rock and roll lyrics, since it is here that the new outlook is most clearly stated.

Horton found that 83.4 percent of the popular songs in 1955 were conversational songs about love.[13] The proportion of conversational songs about love in three of the same magazines dropped in 1966 to 64.7 percent, as shown in Table 3.

The decline in conversational songs about love is more strikingly portrayed in looking at the national popularity rating reported by *Billboard* for the same period and at San Francisco's KYA listing.

Radio air-play combined with retail sales forms the basis for the *Billboard* and KYA listings. Therefore, Table 4 highlights not only the declining interest in love lyrics from 1955 to 1966 but also the preferences of the youth audience.

---

[12] A further indication that a specific message is being communicated through rock and roll lyrics is the fact that slightly over 65 percent of the songs were written by members of the group that recorded them. Lyrics which are not rock and roll, those celebrating older, more conventional values, were characteristically not written by the groups which recorded them. Only 13.3 percent of this type of lyrics were written by members of the group that sang them.

[13] Horton, *op. cit.,* distinguishes between lyrics in the conversational mode and those not. By the former he refers to songs written in the mode of direct address. The content can be an appeal, request, demand, complaint, or reproach, soliciting some kind of response as though the songs were fragments of dialogue. Love songs not in the conversational mode are primarily narrative and descriptive ballads on love.

Table 3

PROPORTION OF LOVE SONGS IN 1955 AND 1966*

	1955	1966
Love songs in the conversational mode..........	83.4% (196)	64.7% (108)
Love songs not in the conversational mode.........	3.8% (9)	4.8% (8)
Themes other than love and courtship................	12.8% (30)	30.5% (51)
Total........................	100.0% (235)	100.0% (167)

* x^2 = 20.02, significant beyond .001 level.

Table 4

PROPORTION OF LOVE SONGS BY POPULARITY RATING IN 1966

	Billboard*	KYA*
Love songs in the conversational mode..........	62.9% (36)	52.0% (28)
Love songs not in the conversational mode......................	....	....
Themes other than love and courtship.............	37.1% (21)	48.0% (26)
Total........................	100.0% (57)	100.0% (54)

* *Billboard* and KYA were combined and compared with the 1955 data in computing x^2 = 40.50, significant beyond the .001 level.

As we get closer to the center of popular culture, the proportion of love lyrics shows a marked decline to little more than half of the songs represented.[14]

Horton arranged his themes in terms of various stages of the love relationship. He called these stages the "drama of courtship." Basically, there were five:

1. The prologue to the courtship expresses the anticipations and longings of those who seek love affairs.

2. The initiation of courtship (Act I) describes the explosive beginning of the affair.

3. The honeymoon (Act II) portrays the euphoric phase of the courtship.

[14] J. Simmons and B. Winograd, in *It's Happening: A Portrait of the Youth Scene Today* (Santa Barbara, Calif.: Marc Laird Publications, 1966), p. 163, note the importance of San Francisco (and the West Coast generally) as an innovator in popular music: "A survey of the record buying public's tastes indicates that except for a few distinct styles ... the music of today goes from West to East, no longer traveling from New York's Tin Pan Alley to the ... hills of San Francisco."

4. The downward course of love (Act III) depicts the appearance of forces hostile to love's happiness.

5. The all-alone stage (Act IV) laments over lost love and the ensuing loneliness.

How adequately can these phases characterize the 1966 songs? If we compare the two periods, we note that most of the lyrics about love can, with some difficulty, be classified using Horton's categories, that is, there are discernible stages in the relationship from the prologue through the lover's final isolation.[15] However, the characteristics of each stage or their content are different. The main difference is in terms of activity-passivity. The actors in the newer lyrics control their own destinies and are not fatalistic about the affair. To make a comparison between 1955 and 1966 lyrics requires a slight reinterpretation of the earlier scheme to include a more active outlook on the love affair at each phase. Even with some modification, however, it was not possible to include 24 percent of the lyrics drawn from the 1966 song magazines (see Table 5).

If we look at the top thirty songs in the national listing included in *Billboard*'s popularity rating and San Francisco's KYA ranking, we note that an even larger proportion of lyrics do not fit into Horton's categories (see Table 6).

The shift in preoccupation is more dramatically noted in looking at San Francisco's KYA popularity rating for the same period. It is in the national popularity listings and rankings selected from key centers of popular culture that we would expect the new orientation toward boy-girl relationships to be most sharply drawn.

---

[15] See Horton, *op cit.;* to eliminate the possibility that the difference between the 1955 and 1966 data was simply a matter of reliability between two judges, a lengthy interview was conducted with one of Horton's judges. The author was instructed in the code originally used by Horton, and a sample of 1966 lyrics **was** sorted using the 1955 scheme. This constituted a reliability check of the author's assignment to specific categories. With the assistance of one of Horton's researchers, a further check was made in reclassifying the 1955 data into the new code. Almost 50 percent of Horton's lyrics could not be classified. A count of the 1955 and 1966 lyrics revealed the following breakdown using the revised code:

	1955	1966
Active search...............	19.7% (38)	32.9% (57)
Happy stage...............	9.7% (19)	17.1% (29)
Breakup..................	8.6% (17)	33.5% (58)
Isolation.................	14.7% (29)	16.4% (28)
Other....................	47.4% (93)	....
Total..................	100.0% (196)	100.0% (172)

Courtship in 1966

The large proportion of song lyrics not included in Horton's categories suggests a reformulation of the phases of the love relationship to take into account a 1966 view of it.

Our sequence starts not with the longing for a relationship or the reveries associated with love but with looking for an affair. The lover is not wishing and dreaming for something to happen to him; he is actively seeking it. The sequence begins with Act I, the *active search,* which includes finding a partner.

Act II portrays the *happy stage* and seems somewhat related to Horton's honeymoon phase. It is different in that there is no implication that the state is a permanent one, nor is it expected to be. The lover is less sentimental and romantic during this happy stage than previously. He is celebrating his enthusiasm over the physical relationship that has been established.

Table 5

**COMPARISON OF COURTSHIP STAGES IN
1955 AND 1966 SONG MAGAZINES**

	1955		1966	
Prologue*......................	5%	(9)	1%	(1)
Act I: courtship.................	39%	(76)	25%	(27)
Act II: honeymoon..............	9%	(19)	14%	(15)
Act III: downward				
course of love.................	17%	(34)	19%	(21)
Act IV: all alone................	30%	(58)	17%	(18)
Other.......................................			24%	(26)
Total.........................	100%	(196)	100%	(108)

* Prologue and Act I were combined in computing $x^2 = 58.52$, significant beyond .001 level.

Act III describes the *breakup,* which occurs when something contaminates the relationship between two people. The breakup occurs because the relationship is not a healthy one and the lovers decide to end it.

Act IV depicts the *isolation* phase, which is viewed as an opportunity to discover one's real self.

Since most of the lyrics which could not be classified under Horton's stages were rock and roll lyrics, it is to these songs we must turn to describe in more detail the new orientation toward boy-girl relationships.

In Act I people actively seek out lovers. They meet semicasually, but with the intention of being lovers. The looking is preceded by a recognition that one needs some release, presumably through a physical relationship. The Mamas and the Papas describe this condition in "Somebody Groovy."

Table 6

**ADEQUACY OF HORTON'S CATEGORIES
TO 1966 POPULARITY LISTINGS**

	Billboard	KYA*
Songs that fit..................	67.7% (24)	66.6% (19)
Songs that do not fit...........	32.3% (12)	33.4% (9)
Total........................	100.0% (36)	100.0% (28)

* *Billboard* and KYA were combined and compared with the 1955 data in computing $x^2 = 70.96$, significant beyond .001 level.

When love is discussed in rock and roll poetry, it refers to a different phenomenon from romantic involvement. Love seems to be reduced simply to physical desire. This is not viewed as a bad thing—it is a reality that everyone must face. The description of love by the Supremes in "Love Is Like an Itching in My Heart" finds one in the same kind of search . . . .

The protagonist at first glance seems to be telling someone that she has been bitten by the love bug, that she is in love with him; but she is speaking only about her state of desire, which is not focused on anyone at this point.

The ideology of freedom is spelled out in the song, "Go Where You Wanna Go," and enjoins one to seek out relationships with "whoever you wanna do it with." One enters a relationship with someone who moves him. The Troggs's "Wild Thing" suggests the character of the relationship:

> Wild thing, you make my heart sing,
> You make everything groovy.

The girl in these lyrics is viewed instrumentally. Love is depicted as basically physical. People are animals, but happy animals. Romantic involvement is not a necessary ingredient in the relationship. Indeed, it can actually be a hindrance to open, free enjoyment. Dusty Springfield expresses this sentiment in "You Don't Have to Say You Love Me." Sam the Sham and the Pharaohs, in their "Lil' Red Riding Hood," also emphasize that physical attraction is the main reason for getting involved with someone. They describe her as very desirable, with big eyes and full lips, and they end by saying: "You're everything that a big bad wolf could want."

The next stage of the relationship, Act II, discusses what occurs after two people have found each other. The affair at this point is very happy. The lovers spend a great deal of time with each other, as Petula Clark states in "I Couldn't Live Without Your Love": "Gotta have you all the time."

The ecstatic happiness that characterizes the early stages of the new relationship is celebrated by the Shades of Blue in their "Oh, How Happy":". . . more times than I can count I have called you mine."

The *happy stage* is soon followed by disturbing elements which enter the relationship. Alan Price, in "I Put a Spell on You," describes the lover's reaction to the beloved's behavior:

> I just can't stand it
> The way you always put me down.

When unhappiness enters a relationship, then one must try to recover the original happiness which it offered. In this case, the lover tries to recreate the earlier ecstasy by "putting a spell" on the girl. But, the relationship continues to deteriorate, almost to the point of desperation. The Animals describe this stage in their song "Don't Bring Me Down": "I feel I'm nothing in your eyes." The fundamental danger . . . is being "brought down." In love affairs, as in mental excursions with drugs, the idea of bringing someone down who is high is disparaged. In this case, the idea that the girl could bring the man down indicates that he is somehow "high" in terms of the relationship. The positive things he sees about the relationship are illusory. The necessity for the plea— "don't bring me down"—indicates that there is grave danger that the feared event will occur. [In the song the] lover needs the girl's response and is not getting it. In this vicious circle he cannot come to terms with the present state of things, and she holds the power. He is unable to make the choice for detachment and independence. This is why there is danger of being brought down. The deteriorating relationship leads to the conclusion that certain kinds of involvement can be very bad.

The Outsiders philosophize on this point in "Time Won't Let Me." The key line is: "Even though you want me to." The implication is that a person has only one life and that involvement with someone else complicates it. At this point in the relationship the protagonist is urged to disengage. The girl in this song is insisting on continuing the relationship, even though the conditions are unfavorable to the man. The girl is informed that time won't let him wait that long.

The deterioration of the relationship is followed by the *breakup* in Act III. The breakup occurs because the protagonist comes to the realization that the relationship was bad in the first place. Since one cannot know this in advance, the injunction is to terminate the affair once this becomes known. The decision to break up is difficult but must be made. The initiative seems to rest with the male to begin the relationship and terminate it. The Grass Roots, in "Where Were You When I Needed You," describe some of the difficulties involved:

Don't bother cryin', don't bother crawlin',
It's all over now, no use stallin'.

What is revealed here is that it is undesirable to lose one's dignity. The boy is putting the girl down, but he doesn't want to see her cry or crawl, not for her sake but because he doesn't like watching such things.

When the affair is over, one realizes that the involvement was unhealthy. The Cyrkle describe this realization in "Red Rubber Ball." The lesson is: "Don't get involved." The choice for detachment ends the bad experience. The love affair was a big thing, but now it's a little thing. Happiness is equated with contentment and evenness, that is, keeping whole, rather than with risky involvements. If one is going to take chances they should not be taken in interpersonal relationships.

The final stage in the sequence is Act IV, *isolation*. This is the inevitable result of the vicissitudes of human relationships. Isolation is an acceptable way out. In "Solitary Man," by Neil Diamond, a young man's bad experience with promiscuous women leads him to accept isolation as a way of life. He says: "Don't know that I will." Presumably he is prepared to accept isolation for the rest of his life rather than be hurt in love again.

In Simon and Garfunkel's "I Am a Rock," the young man seems to be certain that total withdrawal is the answer to his problem. It is ironic. Throughout the song runs an undertone indicating that he knows his position to be impossible. He is describing the result of a bad experience. There is no cry that he wants his love back. There is no wish to see her. There is no specification of how he has been hurt. There is no relationship with anyone else at all. The isolation can be interpreted in a more general sense than that due to having been hurt. There is the process of deliberately cutting oneself off, which is experienced as a way of establishing one's own identity.

So ends the stylized love affair—from active searching through various stages of involvement to isolation.

The new perspective of the love affair which is depicted in the 1966 rock lyrics seems to support a new view of the courtship sequence. The change has not involved a shift in interest away from the boy-girl relationship but rather a shift in orientation toward the relationship. In the ensuing discussion we will examine more thoroughly the nature of this change.

A New Pattern

A comparison of the "drama of courtship" in 1955 and 1966 suggests a number of significant changes in the boy-girl relationship in the lyrics of songs over the last eleven years. One of the most conspicuous changes is in the conception of love.

The popular song lyrics of 1955 portrayed love as a deep, romantic involvement. The rock and roll lyrics of 1966 usually refer to a different phenomenon when they discuss love. Love often seems to have been reduced to physical attraction. Romantic love has been rejected as the exclusive requirement for engaging in a sexual relationship. While permissiveness with affection was acceptable eleven years ago, though entailing certain risks, today's songs legitimize permissiveness without affection in relations. The Mamas and Papas endorse this position in "Go Where You Wanna Go":

> Do what you wanna do
> With whoever you wanna do it with.

The new pattern, then, is that you can sleep with someone whether you have affection for him or not—*either* is acceptable.

One of the tragedies voiced in the 1955 lyrics was that everyone wants love but that the prerequisites make it difficult to find. The rock lyrics of today indicate that these prerequisites and preconditions to love have been reduced. Songs no longer dwell on approaches to courtship but focus more on an active search and involvement with a partner.

Similarly, on the downward course of love, rock and roll lyrics do not dwell for any length of time on the deteriorated relationship but rather value a quick break when the involvement is viewed as unhealthy and pervaded with guilt. This kind of involvement impedes one's freedom of action, and a choice for detachment and independence ends the bad experience. The questions posed in the lyrics no longer focus on "Are you still mine?" or "I'm afraid that you'll get careless, and someone will steal a kiss," but center closer to the theme the Grass Roots express in "Where Were You When I Needed You " [see p. 208].

The new outlook on the love affair does not include the expectation of permanence. Freedom is celebrated for both partners. This highlights one of the dilemmas in the relationships portrayed in rock and roll lyrics. One is free not to become involved, but others have that freedom also. The relationship where each partner tries to maximize the other's freedom is a fragile arrangement which can be quickly terminated. Emphasis is on a rapid culmination of the affair as well as a quick ending when the involvement is an unhealthy one. The temporary quality of a relationship is expressed in Dusty Springfield's "You Don't Have To Say You Love Me."

These sentiments seem far removed from those of 1955 where a relationship was expected to be permanent. It would be unusual to encounter lyrics today similar to those voiced in the 1955 song "As Long As I Live," in which the singer states that he will remember and love his partner forever.

The popular songs of the middle 'fifties seem to have placed love in the hands of fate. Love is not something actively controlled by the lovers but something which happens to them. One "falls in love," and later the downward course of love is initiated by hostile forces external to one's control. Because of the lack of control in the relationship, falling in love involves taking considerable risks; the outcome is not predictable. Since love in the 1955 song lyrics is experienced as externally controlled, it is often perceived as an object or a commodity rather than something the lovers mutually create. Love frequently appears in popular song lyrics as something to be "won" or something which is subject to theft.

The rock lyrics of 1966 reject this passive orientation toward the boy-girl relationship. Love is mutually created by the partners and is not perceived as external to their relationship. The affair is actively sought by the lovers rather than passively longed for.

Two other changes have occurred in the courtship patterns. The girls portrayed in the 1966 rock lyrics have been removed from their pedestal in boy-girl relations. "Wild Thing" by the Troggs reduces the girl to an object for sexual gratification. Furthermore, the boy is no longer at the mercy of the girl in the love affair. The 1955 lyrics often show the boy powerless and helpless in the face of the girl, who appears to hold the key to the relationship. The rock lyrics of today seem to have reversed this power situation. The initiative rests with the male to initiate the relationship and terminate it. The Syndicate of Sounds, in "Little Girl," capture this new pattern:

> If you come knockin'
> You won't get past my door.

The major thrust of the 1966 rock and roll lyrics is toward an expansion of the boy-girl relationship to include a wider range of behavior and not just the limited "romantic love affair" which characterizes the 1955 lyrics. The possibility that the relationship between young people might be so quickly terminated today seems to suggest that different levels of involvement between two persons, in addition to the traditional romantic love affair, are now called for.

This whole development seems to reject the older double standard and opt for a more honest and open boy-girl relationship and has the effect of widening the range of choices for a satisfactory relationship. The net impact is to emphasize personal autonomy and eschew the kind of dependency revealed in earlier lyrics.

Wider Range of Themes in 1966

Horton found that 83 percent of the song magazine lyrics he analyzed dealt with boy-girl relationships. This proportion dropped to 65 percent in the

1966 song magazines and even less in the popular listings. The content of the rock and roll lyrics in 1966 deals with a wider range of themes than the popular songs of the preceding decade. Of the rock lyrics, 30 percent are concerned with themes other than love and courtship, in contrast to almost 13 percent of the 1955 lyrics.

The concerns expressed in the 1955 lyrics, apart from those of love and courtship, range widely and show no clearcut focus. They include song dances, general narrative ballads on love themes, religious songs, comic songs, and others which could not be classified.

The 1966 lyrics reveal more specific concerns. The major preoccupation of rock and roll lyrics seems to be with *choice*. Choice permeates the themes, relating to many areas of interest beside those of boy-girl relationships. Choice is exercised in terms of freeing one's self from external constraints. The exercise of choice is enjoined in two crucial areas: (1) personal relations, and (2) the kind of society in which one will become involved. Choice in both relates to the individual's autonomy.

We have already seen how the impact of the choice theme operates in the the relationship between boy and girl. It functions to maximize the personal freedom of the persons in the relationship by widening the range of alternatives available to those involved.

The second crucial area in which choice operates is the individual's autonomy in relation to the conventional world. Will he become part of the conventional world, or will he choose to drop out and create his own scene? The decision to do something about one's life, to think for one's self, no matter what the consequences, is generally enjoined.

Summary

The major difference in orientation toward courtship in 1955 and 1966 is the active character of the boy-girl relationship. The affair is created by the partners, and they can determine its outcome. If a position can be inferred from an analysis of the 1966 lyrics, it is that one makes his own choices. The value of existential choice is celebrated. It gives one the freedom to change, to become what he wants to be, to make of an affair what two people want it to be.

In the idealized sequence revealed by rock and roll lyrics today, one actively searches out and becomes involved with someone else rather than passively waiting for an affair. Relationships are initiated on the basis of mutual attraction, which includes both physical and "spiritual" elements. When these elements disappear, the expectation is that the relationship will be terminated. Relationships can also be ended if one or both of the parties diagnose it as "unhealthy." Usually this means that it is tainted with dishonesty. Love is not placed in the hands of fate but is actively controlled by the lovers. Consequently, rock and roll lyrics are not likely to talk about "falling in love," since that phrase refers to a romantic conception of boy-girl relationships which is rejected.

Another striking difference between the 1955 and 1966 lyrics is in the attitude toward being alone—the isolation at the end of the affair. It is viewed negatively in 1955, more positively in 1966. There is pain and suffering associated with the dissolution of an affair in 1966, but it can also be the first step in exploring those facets of the self which can only be explored when one is alone. The description of the isolation phase of the courtship cycle suggests the Zen influence operative among the more recent songwriters.

The fact that there is a distinctive set of beliefs associated with a large proportion of 1966 lyrics may reflect the growing disaffection among younger people who constitute the audience for the new lyrics, or it may simply reflect a change in those who write them.

The significance of the changing orientation depicted here can be established more clearly by a further inquiry into two related areas: the emergence of more democratic controls over songs written since 1955, and the extent to which the new belief system is incorporated ideologically into the social movements of young people today.

17

BRAINWASHING OR BACKGROUND NOISE: THE POPULAR PROTEST SONG

R. Serge Denisoff and Mark H. Levine

During the past several years the function and social effect of popular music has drawn considerable attention. A cursory examination of these discussions finds much disagreement upon the sociopolitical effect of popular music. One interpretation sees popular songs as a form of "background noise" which has little meaning when examined as a total entity. David Riesman has conceptualized popular music as a manifestation of "social atomization," with individual hit songs being sandwiched in between commercial and diffuse musical genre.[1] Given this "disconnectedness" of radio programming, listeners were not believed to be comprehending the sentiments of Top Forty songs. Jacques Barzun expanded on this argument, adding that the pervasiveness of music in American society reduces it to little more than a narcotizing "threshold of sound" against which individuals perform their daily tasks. This role of music, he continues, leads to "an increasing resistance to words . . . which is . . . reinforced by the desire to move into a world of sensations remote from those of workday life."[2]

An increasing number of writers have come to see popular music as an opinion formation device. The Beatles, particularly, have been described as "hypnotizing" and "brainwashing" American teenagers. A handful of social

A revised and expanded version of "The Popular Protest Song: The Case of 'Eve of Destruction.'" Reprinted from *Public Opinion Quarterly* 35 (Spring, 1971), pp. 117–122 with permission of publisher. We would like to thank Robert Dannehold and Marjorie Elovich for their assistance in the preparation of this paper.
[1] David Riesman, *Individualism Reconsidered* (New York, Free Press, 1954).
[2] Jacques Barzun, *Music in American Life* (New York, Doubleday, 1958), pp. 23–24.

scientists have portrayed popular music as evocative of a new "social ethic" while at the same time rejecting the "old order."

Bernhard has viewed popular music as rejecting the "old order" and as describing "a new order, one which is seen as incompatible with that already existent."[3] Simmons and Winograd perceived popular music as evocative of the "hang-loose" ethic of the "youth scene."[4] Robinson and Hirsch have defined as "protest" songs those condemning war, concerning drugs, or attacking the "status quo."[5] This latter position is that popular songs can be protest songs, a view that is in opposition to that presented by Riesman, Barzun, *et al.*, as well as to those espousing the traditional view of protest songs.

Riesman, in treating popular songs, polarizes listeners into a *majority* and a *minority*. The latter unit is one "in which certain socially rebellious themes are encapsulated."[6] Other studies also have linked songs of protest with deviant and revolutionary groups.[7] These endeavors suggest that some type of group interaction or cohesion must be present for the transfer of sociopolitical sentiments. Lazarsfeld and Merton, in their classic study of radio propaganda, indicate that propaganda by itself is not sufficient, but also must involve what they termed "supplementation." One evidence of this process is a Billy Graham crusade, where converts are urged to come forth and make their "stand for Christ," following prayers and singing. Lazarsfeld and Merton conclude that for any form of mass media propaganda to be *effective*, (1) the material must be significant to the listener; (2) it must be intelligible; and (3) it must be supplemented by personal acts of involvement.[8] If this is the case, then, according to the theories of Riesman and Barzun, popular music heard over the radio cannot be very effective in conveying sociopolitical messages because (1) the lyrics are not important to Top Forty station listeners; (2) they do not understand them, and (3) no form of supplementation regularly takes place. In order to test these ideas, the *effectiveness* of the most popular sociopolitical

[3] Anthony Bernhard, "For What It's Worth: Today's Rock Scene," paper read at American Sociological Association meetings (San Francisco, 1967), p. 4.

[4] J. I. Simmons and Barry Winograd, *It's Happening: A Portrait of the Youth Scene Today* (Santa Barbara: Marc Laird Publications, 1966), pp. 155–165.

[5] John P. Robinson and Paul Hirsch, "Teenage Response to Rock and Roll Protest Songs," paper read at American Sociological Association meetings (San Francisco, 1969), p. 4. [See Article 18 in this volume.] Robert A. Rosenstone, "The Times They Are A-Changin'," *Annals,* Vol. 381 (March, 1969), pp. 131–144.

[6] Riesman, *op. cit.,* p. 411.

[7] Cf. R. Serge Denisoff, "American Protest Songs of War and Peace: A Selected Bibliography and Discography," (Los Angeles: Center for the Study of Armament and Disarmament, California State College, 1970).

[8] Paul Lazarsfeld and Robert K. Merton, "Mass Communication, Popular Taste, and Organized Social Action," in Lyman Bryson, ed., *Communication of Ideas* (New York: Harper, 1948), pp. 78–115.

propaganda song to reach the Top Forty radio stations during the 1960's, "The Eve of Destruction," was examined.

In August of 1965, Barry McGuire, a commercial folksinger, recorded "Eve of Destruction," which was written by a 19-year-old composer, P. F. Sloane. Despite several organized campaigns by the Radical Right and others to ban the record, it reached the *Billboard* Hot 100 on August 21st and remained there until the last week of October. Rohde in *The Gold of Rock and Roll* indicates that it remained on the Top Ten for a period of ten weeks maintaining the cherished Number One position two weeks in the month of September.[9] Unlike other popular songs, "Eve of Destruction" was a political dissent song stressing the point that man was on the brink of nuclear annihilation. The significance of the piece was that it was the first protest song dealing with specific issues to reach this height of popularity.

Using a narrative style, the song documented, in emotionally charged terminology, many of the areas of discord in the world and stressed the notion that unless man became aware and involved, nuclear disaster would befall mankind:

> Take a look around you boy, bound to scare you boy,
> Ah, you don't believe we're on the eve of destruction . . .[10]

The last line served as a chorus and was repeated four times, followed by a harmonica riff further emphasizing the chorus. Each new verse chronicles various dysfunctions in American society. This structure is customary for political protest songs, e.g. labor and civil rights songs such as "Join the CIO" or "We Shall Overcome." The major difference, here, was that the music was rhythmical dance music in a mass medium, rather than the more standardized "folk" or "hymnal" structure which stresses the lyrics rather than the music. At the time "Eve" was receiving maximum exposure, music critics and a number of topical song writers in the folk idiom objected to and questioned the use of a commercial dance genre to communicate social protest.[11] "Eve of Destruction" seemed an ideal opportunity to analyze the question of the effectiveness of popular songs with sociopolitical messages.

In September of 1965 when "Eve of Destruction" was at the top of the national charts, a questionnaire was administered to a stratified sample of

[9] H. Kandy Rohde, *The Gold of Rock and Roll 1955–1967* (New York: Arbor House, 1970), pp. 280–282.

[10] "Eve of Destruction," Copyright 1965 Trousdale Music Publishers, Inc., words and music by P. F. Sloane, Steve Barri.

[11] Tom Paxton, "Folk Rot," *Sing Out!* Vol. 15 (January 1966), pp. 103–104.

sociology students at San Francisco State College ranging from incoming freshmen to graduate students. This choice of sample was predicated upon two considerations: (1) sociology students are generally regarded as more "liberal" in their political views; and (2) the capricious nature of the Top Forty and a local campaign to ban "Eve" from the airwaves prompted the use of the most readily accessible sample. Using a sample of liberally oriented students, it was felt, would maximize the effectiveness of the song. This was in keeping with several content analyses of protest songs in social movements, which generally were designed to appeal to believers.[12] Therefore, maximum effectiveness, it appeared, would be achieved by selecting a sample believed to be favorable to the message in "Eve of Destruction."

The first series of questions were addressed to the topic of exposure and the medium of transmission. As Table 1 indicates, most collegiates generally do listen to Top Forty stations.

Table 1

EXPOSURE TO "EVE OF DESTRUCTION" AND "UNIVERSAL SOLDIER" BY MEDIUM

	Eve of Destruction		Universal Soldier	
Heard song		400		323
Radio	340		284	
Television	5		5	
Records	8		26	
Two or more	46		4	
Other	1		—	
Did not hear		85		159
No response		5		8
		490		490

Nearly 89 percent of the respondents had heard "Eve of Destruction." A less popular and well-publicized anti-war song "The Universal Soldier," had been heard by 66 percent.

The respondents were then asked a number of open-ended opinion questions involving the material. The first aspect was whether the Top Forty listeners comprehend the intended message of "Eve of Destruction." Its composer P. F. Sloane defined the meaning of the song as the nuclear weapon being a "cloud hanging over me all the time." For Sloane, "this is" the reality. Further, the song states that "if the world is full of hate, we have to change it

[12] R. Serge Denisoff, "Protest Movements: Class Consciousness and the Propaganda Song," *Sociological Quarterly,* Vol. 9 (1968), pp. 228–247.

to love." The respondents were supplied with the lyrics and were asked to interpret lines from "Eve" which stressed the dominant theme: "Take a look around you boy, bound to scare you boy . . ." as opposed to "Universal Soldier." The answers to this open-ended question were then rated by three judges into the categories: "understood theme," "incorrect description," and "partially correct." The findings are presented in Table 2.

Table 2

**CORRECTNESS OF INTERPRETATION OF "EVE OF DESTRUCTION"
AND "UNIVERSAL SOLDIER"**

	Eve of Destruction		Universal Soldier	
	Total Sample	Heard	Total Sample	Heard
Understood theme	56 (11.4)	56 (14.0)	57 (11.6)	57 (17.6)
Partially understood theme	179 (36.5)	179 (44.8)	51 (10.4)	51 (15.8)
Did not understand theme	93 (19.0)	93 (23.3)	151 (30.8)	151 (46.8)
No response	162 (33.0)	72 (18.0)	231 (47.2)	64 (19.8)
	490 (100.0)	400 (100.0)	490 (100.0)	323 (100.0)

The most interesting inference here is that 41.3 percent of respondents who heard the song, either would not or could not interpret the meaning of the song correctly, apparently lending some support to Riesman's and Barzun's view of popular music. Of those students who had heard the protest song 14 percent did interpret the song correctly and 44 percent partially correctly. Twenty-three percent gave totally incorrect answers with 18 percent not responding. The non-respondents who had heard "Eve" were considered as not being affected by the song. This judgment was based upon the fact that all the available studies dealing with "protest songs" report an above-average rate of non-response, which seems to support the Barzun position of background noise.[13]

The respondents were also asked to interpret "Universal Soldier" with the answers being coded and sorted in the same manner as "Eve." This song lacked both the exposure and notoriety of the Sloane composition and was predominantly played on the local folk music program. As Table 2 evidences, only 66 percent of the students had heard the piece. The anti-war song, which had as its primary message that war was the responsibility of all men, was interpreted

---

[13] Robinson and Hirsch, *op. cit.*, p. 12. [Ed. note: See Article 18 in this volume.] A report on a sample of "conservative" junior college students and their reactions to "Eve of Destruction" exhibited a similar finding. See R. Serge Denisoff, "Protest Songs: Those on the Top Forty and Those of the Streets," *American Quarterly* 22 (Winter, 1970), pp. 807–823.

correctly by 33.5 percent. The exposure factor may, in this instance, be of importance.[14]

To further examine the ideological effectiveness of popular songs, a question was included to see if the respondents would dance to a "protest song" even if it had a "rock" background or beat.

Table 3

DANCEABILITY OF PROTEST SONGS IN THE ROCK GENRE

Would Dance	74	(15.1)
Would Not Dance	327	(66.7)
No Response	89	(18.2)
		(100.0)

This question was specifically designed to test the notion of the "social" aspect of radio music, *e.g.*, popular music was fundamentally a form of disjointed and disconnective background noise used for a myriad of purposes as Riesman suggests. As Table 3 illustrates, only 15.1 percent of those sampled would dance to a "protest song." This figure indicates some lyrical consciousness. One possible hypothesis is that while propaganda songs are not particularly intelligible on the Top Forty, they do interfere with the social aspects of the music.

To attempt to measure the degree of interest in "protest songs" beyond the Top Forty idiom, or what Lazarsfeld and Merton labeled "supplementation," the questionnaire concluded with a request to respondents to expand on the subject of protest songs if they so wished. The purpose of this type of question was to determine if the respondents had strong feelings on the subject, and also to gauge the type of response they would have if they did reply. Comments on the songs, as in other open-ended questions, were evaluated by three judges on the basis of "intellectual" response which stressed individual non-involvement, such as approval of songs for saying more than other pop songs, or disapproval of the song on the grounds it was one-sided, etc. The other category of replies was coded "emotional," stressing a statement not based on reason, such as disapproval of songs on the basis of labeling them pejoratively ("Communistic, idiotic," etc.).

Of the 400 students who had heard "Eve of Destruction," 67.5 percent expressed some kind of an opinion on this song or other sociopolitical songs.

---

[14] The exposure factor is doubly important in this case, since the respondents were provided with two lines of "Eve" and no information about Buffy Sainte-Marie's "Universal Soldier."

Of those expressing an opinion, 57.8 percent were favorable to sociopolitical songs.

Table 4

INTELLECTUAL-EMOTIONAL RESPONSE TO SOCIOPOLITICAL SONGS AS CORRELATED TO POSITIVE-NEGATIVE RESPONSES

	Intellectual	Emotional	N
Positive	128	26	154
Negative	43	73	116
N	171	99	270

$x^2 = 15.494$

As Table 4 suggests, we can expect a greater-than-chance association of intellectual responses to sociopolitical protest songs by those favoring the sentiments involved than by those opposed. At the .001 level of significance $x^2 = 15.494$, thereby indicating a greater-than-chance association. This association appears to suggest that emotional commitment is not generated by Top Forty protest songs. If anything, the opposite appears more plausible.

Findings

In the sample under consideration the writers were principally concerned with effectiveness of "protest songs" on the Top Forty. This concept, we noted, involved the listeners' reaction in relation to medium significance, intelligibility of lyric, and emotional response. The descriptive data suggests that a very small percentage of respondents correctly described the theme of "Eve" (14 percent) or "Universal Soldier" (17 percent). However, of those hearing both songs, a greater number at least partially understood the message of "Eve" (58.8) than "Soldier" (33.4).

The Riesman–Barzun hypothesis is further challenged by the 80.1 percent figure of those having heard "Eve" and other protest songs in the rock genre who would not dance to the music. Respondents either could not or would not dance to this type of song in total. This would appear to refute the notions presented by Paxton and others that popular protest songs are little more than dance tunes. Using the figures derived from Tables 3 and 5, a chi-square test was done in order to distinguish the differences between a positive response to "protest songs" and dancing to these songs. It was argued that students who approved of protest songs would not dance to this type of music. At the .01 level of significance there is a less-than-chance association in $x^2 = 7.124$. However, at the .001 level of significance this figure could have been expected on the basis of chance alone.[15]

Table 5

**APPROVAL-DISAPPROVAL AND THE DANCEABILITY OF
ROCK AND ROLL SOCIOPOLITICAL SONGS**

	Positive	Negative	No Response	Undecided	N
Would Dance	50	15	1	8	74
Would Not Dance	181	112	19	15	327
No Response	10	18	58	3	89
	241	145	78	26	490

$x^2 = 7.124$

This indicates that propaganda songs on the Top Forty appear to get across to listeners, but not to the degree of intensity and impact suggested by both critics and proponents of this idiom.

Discussion

Totally correct interpretations of the themes of popular songs, even with a segment of the lyric provided is rather small (14 percent–17 percent). However, the partially correct category is significantly larger in this study than in the Michigan survey.[16] This discrepancy is undoubtedly colored by the differentiations in the two works. The sample reported here was designed to comprise college students believed in favor of the songs in question, while Robinson and Hirsch randomly sampled high school students in two Michigan cities.

Our paper also supports Robinson and Hirsch, and Riesman in suggesting that protest songs appeal to only a small segment of the so-called "Big Sound" audience. Note the small percentages of deviant responses on correct interpretation of theme and emotion, implying that propaganda songs may still be geared only to converting the faithful and evoking negative responses from non-believers. This subject requires further research.

One inference that can be made here from studies of the political use of television is that while listeners do tend to tune in candidates and commentaries of their own ideological set, the use of a disconnective idiom such as the Top

[15] A 2x2 table was used in the figuring of this chi-square. The row and columns labeled "No response" and "Undecided" were eliminated.

[16] Robinson and Hirsch, *op. cit.*

Forty will create a negative reaction. The reason for this appears to be that the listener has control—at least to turn the set on and off—of network programming. The listener to the Top Forty does not have any control over content if he desires to hear music. In this latter context, negative responses may be intensified. This impact is more in keeping with Coser's notion of group solidarity vis-a-vis negative inputs than with Durkheim's notion of moral reaffirmation and commitment.[17]

In sum, the impact of sociopolitical songs on the Top Forty at this writing appears somewhere between the Barzun position and the position of the Brechtian school that music must be "a cry for justice." Given the novelty of this area of research there are still many unresolved problems, both qualitative and quantitative.

---

[17] Lewis Coser, *The Functions of Social Conflict* (New York: Free Press, 1956), pp. 36–38; and Harry Alpert, "Durkheim's Functional Theory of Ritual," *Sociology and Social Research* 23 (Spring, 1930), pp. 102–108.

18

TEENAGE RESPONSE TO ROCK AND ROLL PROTEST SONGS

John P. Robinson and Paul M. Hirsch

> We've had all we can stand of the record industry's glorifying mari-
> juana, LSD, and sexual activity. The newest Beatles record has a line
> of 40,000 purple hearts in one arm. Is that what you want your
> children to listen to? . . . (I call for) a rather updated version of the
> Boston Tea Party. I suppose you might call it the Wax Party—one in
> which all the distasteful records which deal with sex, sin, and drugs
> (would be purged from radio air-play).
>
> Gordon McClendon, President of the McClendon chain
of radio and television stations[1]

The above commentary on the output of the record industry in the last
several years reflects the concern of many media critics about the content of
recent popular song "hits" and their possible effect on teenage listeners. The
size of the youth market and the advent of radio programming aimed at this
audience have encouraged the production and air-play of records with increasingly "deviant" message content. While popular music has flirted with controversial issues in the past, such content has recently mushroomed to the extent

Included by permission of the authors.
This article is based on a paper presented at the 1969 Annual Meetings of the
American Sociological Association. The authors have subsequently conducted further
empirical studies, and a more theoretical discussion may be found in Paul Hirsch,
"Sociological Approaches to the Pop Music Phenomenon." *American Behavioral Scientist*
14, 3 (January/February 1971), pp. 371–388. We wish to thank John Magney for
critical comments on an earlier version of this paper.

[1] "Anti-Smut McClendon to Set Up Fringe Panel," *Billboard,* August 5, 1967, p. 1.
[Ed. note: See Articles 12, 13 and 24 for an elaboration of this stance.]

that numerous citizens' groups have taken positions either praising or denouncing this trend.[2] However, these events have gone largely unnoticed by social scientists and have been subjected to little empirical study.

Beyond the number of copies a record sells and the age groups to which it appeals, there is very little published information about record consumers. Which song styles appeal to particular groups, and whether records are preferred for their sound or their meaning, for example, are two questions which are often discussed but seldom researched.[3] Although our primary interest is in the mass consumption of hit songs of social protest,[4] we shall try to cast some light in this paper on the above two questions and on several others as well, mainly: (1) Among which teenagers is rock 'n' roll most popular? (2) How closely can musical taste preferences be predicted from a knowledge of background variables?, and (3) How strong a role do geographical and rural-urban differences play in influencing musical taste preferences?

To learn something about the extent to which the deviant subject matters of protest songs are perceived by teenagers, and to which groups they appeal the most, we surveyed two groups of Michigan high school students—one in Detroit and one in Grand Rapids, an upstate community of about 400,000 residents. Seven schools were selected in each city in an attempt to maximize differences in the social class, race, and religion of the students sampled. At each school one classroom of eighth-graders and one classroom of eleventh-graders filled out a confidential questionnaire. Four hundred and thirty students in Detroit were sampled in November 1967, and 340 in Grand Rapids were sampled in March 1968.[5] The backgrounds of some students in Grand Rapids

[2] Concerning the decision-making process among record company and radio station executives on whether to market and "expose" rock and roll protest songs, see: Paul Hirsch, *The Structure of the Popular Music Industry* (Ann Arbor: Survey Research Center, University of Michigan, 1969, and "The Economics of Rock," *The Nation* (March 9, 1970), pp. 275–276; also Paul Hirsch, with John Robinson, Elizabeth K. Taylor and Stephen B. Withey, *Progress Report on an Exploratory Study of Youth Culture and the Popular Music Industry: A Project Looking at Changes in the Music Industry, Audiences and Popular Preferences, and the Possibilities of Using Music as a Social Indicator* (Ann Arbor: Survey Research Center, University of Michigan, 1970).

[3] See Articles 16 and 22 in this volume. Also J. Johnstone and E. Katz, "Youth and Popular Music: A Study in the Sociology of Taste," and D. Horton, "The Dialogue of Courtship in Popular Songs," both in *The American Journal of Sociology* 62 (1957), pp. 563–579.

[4] What we are calling "protest" music is known under several different names in the music industry. Before it received radio air-play on a large scale, it was called "underground" music, and is now increasingly referred to as "progressive rock." "Protest" is its best description for our purposes because of its frequently political content and/or its generally positive evaluation of the effects of drug usage. Our coding procedures will be elaborated upon in the text. [Ed. note: See Articles 1 and 9 and Hirsch *et. al.*, 1970 on differing definitions of a protest song.]

[5] Items concerning song style preference and media usage have since been replicated nationally. See Hirsch *et. al.*, 1970, *op. cit.*

differ from those in Detroit in that several rural schools were included, fewer black students were sampled, and parental status tends to be slightly higher than in Detroit. These differences in our samples reflect demographic patterns reported for each city in the 1960 census.

Popularity of Different Types of Music

The popularity of "current popular hits" among teenagers is nearly total. When asked to rank their preferences for all types of music on a three-point scale, our respondents gave "current popular hits" an average rating of 1.2, where a score of 1.0 would be the highest possible rating. Modern jazz and folk music received the next highest scores (about 2.0 each), and were followed by show tunes, classical, and country-and-western music—in that order of preference, as shown on the "scale" below.

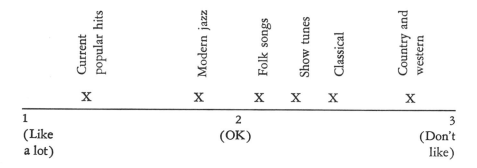

Less than 1 percent of all the students said they "don't like" current popular hits. These came predominantly from upper-middle-class white households in Detroit. Teenagers holding fundamentalist religious beliefs in the Grand Rapids area also constitute a portion of this group. In each case, these students are a small minority among their peers. The small number of respondents stating a preference for country-and-western music were either almost exclusively from the rural areas surrounding Grand Rapids or had migrated from the South.

Most of the variance, then, occurs *within* the musical category, "current popular hits." It will soon become apparent that it is explained, to a surprisingly large extent, by differences in the race and social class of the respondents.

Types of Hit Songs Listed as Favorites

We asked the students to list their three favorite songs, their favorite singer, and the names of three records they had recently purchased. The choices listed were coded into one of four categories: "rhythm-and-blues," "social protest," "other hits," and "square." Most rhythm-and-blues songs are characterized by a lyric about personal relations and a very hard-driving beat. They are generally recorded by black artists. With few exceptions, they are unconcerned with messages about drugs or politics.

Songs were coded as social protest if they contained lyrics which condemn war, concern drug usage, or attack the "status quo." One of the best known hit protest songs in recent years (a trenchant condemnation of American society) is "The Eve of Destruction."[6] Four recent examples of the type of song we code as "social protest" are: Ray Stevens' "Mr. Businessman"; Bob Seger's "2 + 2"; Hensen Cargill's "Skip a Rope"; and the Amboy Dukes' "Journey to the Center of the Mind."[7] "Mr. Businessman" is an accusatory song, in which the businessman is pictured as a product-oriented individual, concerned only with self-gratification, at the expense of his wife, children, and virtually all social responsibility. After each verse the singer concludes, "You better take care of business, . . . while you can." In a similar vein, "Skip a Rope" chronicles the contradictions of American life as seen by adolescents, *e.g.:*

> Cheat on your taxes, don't be a fool
> Now what was that you said about a Golden Rule?

In "2 + 2," the singer bitterly attacks a military system in which he must kill or be killed, concluding:

> It's the rules, not the soldiers
> That are my real enemy, 2 + 2 is on my mind.

Finally, in "Journey to the Center of the Mind," the pleasures (and possible dangers) of a "trip" are described, and the listener is invited to:

> . . . come with us and find
> The pleasure of a journey to the center of the mind.

Virtually all other records on the hit parade not coded as rhythm-and-blues or as social protest were coded as "other hits." This category is not as broad as it might appear to be. Almost all songs in this category concern courtship or sex, or are novelty items (such as "Git Tarzan" or "Simon Says") and are sung by white singers. They are distinguished from rhythm-and-blues records mainly by accent and beat.

Any record not falling into one of these three categories was coded as "square." Only 7 percent of *all* records named were so coded at the time

---

[6] [Ed. note: See Article 17, this volume.]
[7] These songs are discussed further in Hirsch, 1971, *op. cit.*

of each survey. "Songs" named here ranged from Brahms's Piano Concertos to "The Old Rugged Cross."

In comparing each student's named favorites with his race and social class, it soon became apparent that the song style categories into which preferences fall were consistently predictable. The vast majority of students preferring protest songs came from homes where the father was a professional or in a white-collar occupation. (In both cities, the children of white-collar workers scored slightly higher in their preference for protest music than the children of professionals.) The probability that a teenager would list protest songs among his favorites was over twice as great for the children of white-collar or professional fathers as it was for the children of blue-collar workers.

Conversely, songs categorized as "other hits" were likely to be listed among a (white) respondent's favorites if his father worked in a blue-collar rather than a white-collar or professional occupation.

The largest differences occurred in the listing of rhythm-and-blues records, which were cited by black students in a ratio of 8 to 1 over white students (a point to which we shall return shortly).

Comprehension of Song Meanings

At the time of each survey we selected four songs which were high up on the "charts" and asked each student whether he had heard the song and, if so, to describe what it was about. Each of the songs selected was either described by national news media as a "message" song with a meaningful lyric (*e.g.,* "Lucy in the Sky with Diamonds" and "Ode to Billy Joe"), or appeared to us as falling in this category (*e.g.,* "Skip a Rope"; "Incense and Peppermints"). Seven songs concerned with "deviant" topics were selected for analysis. Except for "Ode to Billy Joe," records were chosen that were popular at the time of each survey. These songs and their general themes are given below:

	Detroit	Grand Rapids
Indifference	Ode to Billy Joe	Ode to Billy Joe
Drugs	Incense and Peppermints	The Condition my Condition
	Lucy in the Sky with	Was In
	Diamonds	
Sex	Heavy Music	Gimme the Green Light
Hypocrisy	. . . .	Skip a Rope

We found only 10 to 30 percent of the teenagers were able to write out "correct" interpretations of the meanings of these songs (as defined by either the news media or as appeared obvious to us). Each student was asked whether he (she) had or had not heard of the song and, if he had, he was asked what the song was about. We coded the interpretations that the students gave into one of four categories. The obtained distributions are shown in Table 1 below.

Table 1

HOW MANY TEENAGERS UNDERSTOOD HIT SONG LYRICS WITH "MESSAGES"?*

DETROIT	Ode to Billy Joe		Incense and Peppermints		Heavy Music		Lucy in Sky	
Didn't hear	7%		33%		31%		61%	
Heard—no meaning given	14	(15)	32	(48)	28	(41)	18	(46)
Heard—inadequate description	60	(64)	21	(32)	27	(39)	11	(27)
Heard—understood theme	19	(21)	14	(20)	14	(20)	10	(27)
	100%	(100%)	100%	(100%)	100%	(100%)	100%	(100%)

GRAND RAPIDS	Ode to Billy Joe		My Condition		Green Light		Skip a Rope	
Didn't hear	11		17		27		33	
Heard—no meaning given	14	(16)	28	(34)	19	(26)	21	(32)
Heard—inadequate description	60	(67)	29	(35)	23	(32)	17	(25)
Heard—understood theme	15	(17)	26	(31)	31	(42)	29	(43)
	100%	(100%)	100%	(100%)	100%	(100%)	100%	(100%)

* Two percentages are given: one for all students and, in parentheses, the percentage of only those who reported having heard the song. A large number of students who had heard the songs did not attempt to describe what the songs meant; many of these students probably were aware of the songs but were afraid to guess in a classroom setting, or didn't reply for some other reason. This non-response leads to conservative estimates and should be kept in mind in interpreting the percentages.

In examining specific responses to the songs shown in Table 1, it was found that "Ode to Billy Joe," the most widely recognized of the songs, provided the most diffuse responses. More of the Detroit than the Grand Rapids students were able to identify the song's basic theme of indifference to personal tragedy.[8] Fewer students in Detroit got the sexual message of "Heavy Music"—the most blatant and straightforward song on this topic we have encountered—than correctly interpreted the meaning of "Gimme the Green Light" as sexual. We noticed some

[8] Many responses coded as inadequate here, however, expressed an awareness of the essential "plot" related in this song's lyrics, *i.e.*, that a couple threw something of consequence from a bridge.

tendency for middle-class students to say that the singer wanted a date with the girl, while children of working-class families more accurately said he wanted the girl "to go all the way" in the song "Green Light."

Few Detroit students heard or could remember the meaning of "Lucy in the Sky with Diamonds," the alleged "LSD" song which aroused so much press controversy. Knowledge of the song's existence was all but nil among black and white working-class students. (This underscores the importance of radio air-play of pop songs as a prerequisite to their wider dissemination, as "Lucy" was never played on Top Forty radio.) Many Grand Rapids teenagers were tuned in to "Skip a Rope," the sardonic blast at parental moral inconsistency.

There were some patterns common to students who comprehended these song messages. Not surprisingly, older teenagers, those who listened for meaning rather than sound (see "Other Findings," below), heavier listeners to pop music radio programs, and steadier record buyers were more knowledgeable, as were students who got better grades in school (although students with better grades were also more likely to report not having heard the songs at all). Teenagers who knew the meaning of one song were more likely to know the meaning of others.

Analysis of these items provides further evidence that teenage listeners to "Top Forty" radio do not constitute a single audience with a homogeneous preference for the "lowest common denominator." The composite audience, rather, breaks down into separate social groupings, each of which selectively listens for the air-play of the song style with which it is associated. The stratified pattern of song style preferences found when students listed their own favorites was repeated when we chose the songs for them to comment upon. In other words, although records by Frank Sinatra and James Brown may be aired over the same radio station, the audience segments which appreciate one or the other of the song styles represented by these singers tend to be mutually exclusive. In Grand Rapids particularly (where there are fewer radio stations to choose among), each audience segment was found to selectively listen (only) to particular songs while, at the same time, it tended to "tune out" other selections played over the same radio station. For example, white working-class students expressed familiarity with a number of "other hits," but wrote that they "had not heard" selections of a "protest" nature which were broadcast by the same radio station that featured their favorites.

Black students in Grand Rapids were almost unanimously aware of the latest rhythm-and-blues records played over the local Top Forty station, but claimed to have "not heard" songs by a number of white singers which were aired by the same stations.

The correlation between race of respondent and musical style preference is strikingly high—$r = .87$. It strongly suggests that far fewer white students are attracted to rhythm-and-blues records than might have been expected; and that few black students are consuming records by white artists. The popularity of "soul" celebrities (such as Ray Charles, Aretha Franklin, and The Supremes) with white audiences should not be taken to signal the "integration" of the musical preferences of black and white audiences. In Detroit, where there are separate "black" and "white"-oriented Top Forty radio stations, race of respondent was nearly perfectly correlated with the station to which he listened.

Other Findings

Liking a particular song and understanding the meaning of its lyrics were found to be two distinct phenomena. The data suggest, in fact, that one need have little to do with the other. Over 70 percent of all students sampled wrote that they are attracted more by the "sound" of a song than by its "meaning." And only 30 percent of those who reported having "heard" a song were able to write out an adequate interpretation of its lyrics.

The general preference for sound over meaning in hit songs may help to explain the following rather curious finding. The last item on our questionnaire proposed seven possible song themes and asked whether the respondent would like to see "more," "fewer," or "the same number" of songs dealing with this topic. (A "don't care" choice was also provided.) One of the proposed themes was "the advantages of taking drugs." A number of students who had purchased records with lyrics concerning drug usage expressed a desire for "fewer" songs of this kind, while others who had not mentioned them as favorites on any other part of the questionnaire expressed a desire for "more" songs about drugs. Some who had purchased *and* correctly interpreted the meanings of these records said they desired "fewer." The proposed song themes are scaled for the entire sample as follows:

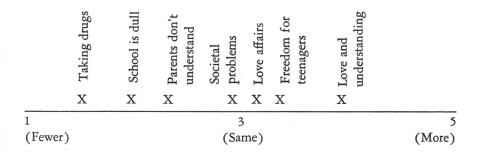

Differences in Orientation to Pop Music by Student Background

A number of background variables tell a good deal about what a teenager's media habits and record preferences are likely to be. As they move into high school, eighth-graders are entering into adolescence. Eleventh-graders are in the midst of it. Some distinct differences are observable between students in the two grades. The younger students watch television more, listen to the radio less, prefer fewer protest songs and "square" musical selections, and are less knowledgeable about what the songs mean than are the eleventh-graders. All students in both samples listen to the radio for an average of an hour-and-a-half daily. Television commands under two hours a day of their time. Radio listening and television viewing tend to go together, in that if a student is indifferent to one, he is more likely to ignore the other as well.

Girls in both grades buy more records and listen more to the radio than boys do. They also exhibit a stronger preference for folk music and show tunes and would like to see more songs concerned with love affairs and the "need for love and understanding among all people." However, they are no more interested than boys in songs concerning specific social problems such as war. In each sample, blacks (of both sexes) purchased 25 percent more records than their white counterparts. While the majority of white students said they would prefer fewer songs concerned with drugs, and were more aware of protest songs than were black students, many more blacks expressed greater tolerance or indifference to these songs. Many of them checked "don't care" or "same as now" when asked whether more or fewer drug songs should be on the market.

Teenagers in middle-class homes spend less time with both radio and television than kids in working-class homes. They, and students with higher grades (who are more likely to be from the middle class), also like other types of music than current pop hits better than those from working-class homes or/and with lower grades. Students with better grades are more likely to know the meanings of the songs they hear.

Finally, and not surprisingly, teenagers with fundamentalist religious views are less likely to have heard songs with deviant lyrics, to claim protest music as a favorite, to say that they like pop music, and to spend much time listening to the radio. They are also less likely to want more songs in favor of more freedom for teenagers.

One remaining question for discussion is the extent of rural-urban differences between the two samples from Detroit and Grand Rapids. We were surprised to discover that the percentage of students expressing a preference for social protest songs is about the same in both cities. Here we had suspected that the less urban environment of Grand Rapids (which is one-tenth the size of Detroit) might result in less awareness of and preference for protest songs on the part of its teenage population. The Grand Rapids students (14 percent) were as likely to name a protest song as one of their favorite records as were their counterparts in Detroit (13 percent), and also seem to have a better comprehension of the songs' "messages." (This finding still holds after differences in the composition of the two samples are taken into account, *e.g.,* the presence of far fewer black students in the Grand Rapids sample.)

Conclusion

This receptivity of high school students in both cities to social protest songs argues strongly that what was formerly "underground" music will be increasingly sponsored by the mass media and will increase in popularity. At the same time, it should be remembered that (1) the market for this music is class-based, and (2) that the vast majority of teenage listeners are unaware of what the lyrics of hit protest songs are about.[9]

[9] Events since the writing of this paper have borne out our prediction: (1) the number of FM radio stations employing the progressive rock format rose to 4 percent; (2) the audience for these stations tends to be upper- and middle-class white students; and (3) record sales for progressive rock records increased. The extent of radio air-play for "protest" rock may well decline, however, as a result of recent statements issued by the Federal Communications Commission concerning a possible conflict between the public interest and radio air-play of songs whose lyrics concern drug usage.

Chapter V

MUSICIANS AND THE MUSIC INDUSTRY

Wherever they reach, the mass media of communication which have been developed in this century provide the opportunity for quickly disseminating ideas charged with strong oral and visual impact to millions of scattered and heterogeneous individuals. During the 1930's, the political leaders of Fascist and Communist states began to use the new media of radio and the movies as prime tools of state propaganda. As noted in the Introduction, this led early scholars to speculate that the mass media necessarily had the effect of weakening democracy.

In the capitalist countries, particularly the United States, the media were not systematically used by the state to disseminate new ideas, although Franklin Roosevelt did institute the "fireside chats" to convince the public of the necessity of his New Deal policies. Rather, government control and censorship was avoided so long as media remained ideologically innocuous or produced "morality plays" reinforcing middle-class standards and expectations. Self-appointed industry, political and religious groups outside government arose to censor material considered offensive to their parochial interests in the name of morality, patriotism, and free enterprise. Thus, the Tin Pan Alley formula pop tune of the 1930's (described in Chapter IV), like the Hollywood formula movie of the same era, did not represent what the audience had selected from among a wide range of alternatives. Rather, they were tailored by the industry to be inoffensive to all influential groups in society. Such forms of influence on the radio, movie, TV and record industries are still crucially important in shaping the nature and content of popular culture as the readings in this chapter demonstrate.

Each of the selections deals in one way or another with the ways in which the operation of the record, radio, and/or live entertainment industries has shaped the message communicated in music. The first article, by Peterson, shows how the development of jazz was influenced by forces within the music industry in combination with outside pressures from moralistic critics. He points out a close parallel between the changing white attitude toward jazz and toward blacks—at least through the middle 1960's when the article was written.

Focusing less on moralistic critics and more on the relationship between record industry structure, marketing practices, and audience tastes, Article 22 by Gillett shows how a number of small independent record companies managed to circumvent the tight control that a few large corporations had on the industry. Their success ushered in the rock era of popular music with its new sound and more controversial lyrics discussed in the previous chapter.

The Becker and Coffman articles focus on the job lives of jazz and rock musicians respectively. Together they show that many of their "deviant" and "radical" ways are generated by the exigencies of the milieu in which they work. Becker focuses on the conflict between the would-be jazz musician and his audience. While the nightclub audience wants simple, melodic, danceable music, the musician wants to create sounds of complexity and beauty which will be applauded by his musician peers. As Becker describes it, this conflict is crystallized by a set of subcultural norms which intensify the conflict as much as they help the musician escape the expectations of the audience.

While Becker deals with anonymous musicians barely able to make a living from their calling, Coffman focuses on rock musicians caught up in a world in which they may, overnight, become rich celebrities adored by thousands of teenagers. For these performers, as Coffman notes, being "radical and deviant" is part of the image demanded by the audience, but this life style is at the same time a source of much conflict when dealing with music industry businessmen. Coffman suggests that much of the radicalism of rock musicians comes from their experiences in the industry. Much credence is given to this assertion both from interviews with rock musicians and from an analysis of song lyrics. A good deal of the most pointed criticism of contemporary society to be found in rock lyrics, deals directly with the economic exploitation of rock musicians by the music industry. In a like vein, Kofsky, in his *Black Nationalism and the Revolution in Music,* has noted that their own personal experiences with the "cock-

roach capitalism" of nightclub owners, promoters, record company executives, and critics has done much to radicalize black jazz musicians since
World War II.

Based on all of the elements discussed in the other articles in the
chapter, as well as much from earlier parts of the anthology, Peterson and
Berger's concluding paper offers an explanation for the change in popular
music during the rock era. In surveying the popular music industry since.
the American Revolution, they suggest that changes in music occur when
there is a change in music industry technology, music industry structure,
and marketing practices. Only during such times of restructuring, they
argue, are the forces weakened which ordinarily inhibit innovations in
musical and ideological style.

19

MARKET AND MORALIST CENSORS OF
A BLACK ART FORM: JAZZ

Richard A. Peterson

Like other aspiring artists, the jazz musician seeks freedom to follow his individual creative genius (Peterson, 1965); at the same time it remains a fact of life
for him as for all artists of any age that "he who pays the piper calls the tune."
In a free mass society such as our own, the artist need not please a royal patron
or official Academy. Rather, he must compete successfully in an open market to
make a living from his work. Researchers studying painting (Pelles, 1963; Peterson and Peterson, 1964), theatre (Lowenthal, 1961b), and literature (Lowenthal, 1961a; Watt, 1964) have documented the impact of this changing support
of artists on the nature of the art produced. They suggest that in our sort of society the most potent censor of art works is not police, patron, or Pope, but profit.

Marketers and Moralists

The demise of noble patronage and the advent of a market of art produced
for sale has given rise to several distinct sorts of middlemen such as promoters,
merchants, and dealers who "sell" art to the mass consumer. At the same time, in
a free society there are no authoritative criteria to differentiate art from non-art.
Thus, what will "sell" is importantly shaped by a welter of critics, reviewers,
moralists and "taste-makers" of diverse kinds. Each art form has its technical
critics, those who evaluate the excellence of particular men, productions or performances. Although numerous in jazz, such technical critics have had little
impact on the shape and direction of jazz. What is more, critical acclaim or con-

From "Market and Moralist Censors of a Rising Art Form, Jazz," *Arts in Society,
Censorship and the Arts*, Vol. 4, No. 2 (1967). Reprinted with permission of the editors.

demnation has no clear relationship to popular acceptance or financial success for jazz musicians (Balliett, 1959; Goldberg, 1965; Jones, 1963). Yet, as Edward Shils (1958) asserts, the creative artist is always "at war" with society. If this be the case, the writings of institutional critics are of central importance in interpreting the "meaning" of an art form. They may play up the "war," de-emphasize it, or as we shall see, turn the "war" against acceptable enemies by defining its meaning for society.

The influence of such moralizers, while always present, is most clearly evident when the art form is in the process of formation or radical change. One classic example was the burst of creativity in painting during the early Renaissance. In that period, institutional critics of the plastic arts were able to elevate the lowly medieval craft of painting to a high art on a par with the ancient arts of poetry and music (Holt, 1959; Peterson and Peterson, 1964). In like manner, moralizers of jazz have influenced its development profoundly by defining and redefining its meaning for society. Early in this century these critics saw jazz as a bad influence and did much to push it out of the mainstream of American life. Quite recently they have come to see it as a positive influence. It is instructive to trace this change of definition because it suggests just how the meaning ascribed to an artistic activity can directly affect the direction and pace of artistic development.

In the early days of jazz in the latter third of the nineteenth century there was no need for professional critics to convey its meaning and evaluate its performers, for jazz was purely a folk music. There was then little separation between performer and audience; both were primarily black. As the late Leadbelly was fond of saying, "All Negroes know the blues." While certain sorts of jazz may still be classified as folk music, after the turn of the twentieth century it has been played for an ever broader audience by ever more professionalized performers.

After the First World War, jazz rapidly gained an audience beyond the confines of the black community. Very quickly, a "commercialized" form of jazz became a big industry. For example, in 1922 Paul Whiteman alone controlled twenty-eight bands playing commercial jazz; the Original Dixieland Jazz Band's records sold millions of copies, breaking the sales records of Caruso and the Sousa Band; jazz was demonstrated on the concert stage; groups toured the United States, Europe, and Asia as well; and the various dance forms associated with jazz became the standard fare in most popular entertainment centers of the day according to Neil Leonard (1962) whose book is the single best review of the specific facts cited.

Thus, early in the 1920's jazz was well on its way to becoming a popular and widely disseminated art form. A mass audience was responsive to it and diverse promoters were quick to take advantage of the potential market. Its distinctive elements might have been rapidly infused into the mainstream of "classical" music. Yet this brief effervescence was stunted almost as quickly as it grew. Two major groups joined hands to put jazz "in its place." One group comprised those in the traditional music industry such as orchestra directors, bandmasters, and music instructors. Their comments that jazz is not music or is at best a degenerate form were picked up and used by a much more influential group which we might call institutional moralists or moralizers.

The Moralist Attack

These late Victorian spiritual descendants of the "know-nothing" party espoused the values of the vanishing agrarian America in the face of rapid industrialization and urbanization. Just as these institutional moralists found in the cause of prohibition a means of attacking the growing power of the new urban Catholic and eastern European immigrants (Gusfield, 1963), they found in the campaign against jazz a means of denigrating the blacks who had migrated north in massive numbers during World War I. A full treatment of the political and economic issues involved would take us well beyond the scope of this discussion. It is sufficient to say that the appeals of such moralizers against jazz struck a resonant chord in the bread-and-butter interests of a large segment of the population.

In the early part of the 1920's institutional moralists polemicized against jazz in tones of alarm. In articles and speeches they asked "Does Jazz Put the Sin in Syncopation?" "Is Jazz the Pilot of Disaster?" and pointed out, "Jazz is a signboard on the road that was travelled by Greece and Rome." A popular play of 1922, *The National Anthem,* depicted a jazz band as the Pied Piper of twentieth-century sin. Jazz was identified as the direct cause of heart attacks, drunkenness, and neural deterioration, but its effect on morals was most often stressed. A report of the Illinois Vigilance Association, directed by Reverend Phillip Yarrow, found that in 1921–1922 jazz had "caused the downfall" of one thousand girls in Chicago alone. Dr. Florence Richards, medical director of a Philadelphia high school for girls, warned that jazz "may tear to pieces our whole social fabric." These institutional critics of jazz in the 1920's pressed to outlaw jazz performances, and a number of communities did pass statutes to prohibit the playing of jazz in public places. Such statutes were enacted in Cleveland, Detroit, Kansas City, Omaha, Philadelphia, and some fifty other cities (Leonard, 1962).

The Attack Refined

By the latter part of the decade, however, there had been a shift in strategy. Jazz was still defined as a negative influence, but complete prohibition was not so often stressed. A dual strategy was developed. The first was a policy of containment: jazz was to be kept out of the home, school, concert stage, social function, and relegated to the "den of iniquity," the nightclub. From the perspective of 1966, the nightclub might seem the "natural" home of jazz, but it certainly was not restricted to this context in the Negro community in which jazz emerged. Jazz was played on all festive occasions from weddings to wakes. Jazz might have been presented to the new, wider audience from the concert stage, but this form of presentation which began in the cities of the North before World War I was eliminated by the institutional critics crying for containment of jazz (Charters and Kunstadt, 1962; Leonard, 1962). Jazz, like the Negro, was all right, in its place. This strategy of containment satisfied the moralists because it meant that jazz could be isolated from "proper" society. It satisfied the traditional music professionals because it placed the aesthetic and cultural value of jazz conspicuously below that of classical music.

The second compromising strategy was to modify the "excess" of jazz. This strategy involved the elimination of the more "objectionable" elements of jazz presentations. The lyrics were censored, the melody and phrasing brought closer to the Tin Pan Alley model of the popular song, and the syncopated beat de-emphasized. In a word, jazz was increasingly "commercialized." Various jazz promoters took the lead in cleaning up jazz in the late 1920's.

An excellent example of the "purification" strategy is found in the record industry. A "commercialized" jazz was recorded for the mass pop music market, and what came to be called "race records" were produced and sold to a primarily black market (Ewen, 1961). Technically crude as the "race records" were, they provided an avenue by which creative jazz could be heard outside the nightclub context. However, about 1928 several of the large commercial recording companies took control of the "race record" industry and they systematically eliminated the "objectionable" and "wild" sounds in order to "protect the American home" from such influences (Leonard, 1962). In part this drive to clean up records was prompted by the rather vague Federal Communications Commission's standard of "decency" for all records to be played on the radio. This led to a severe "self-censorship" (Leonard, 1962). From that time on, jazz records were few and far between. Through the 1930's and 1940's jazz fans made a fetish of listening carefully for each snatch of creative jazz work backing up popular singers.

Retreat to the Bars

In consequence of the attacks of the institutional moralists and their allies in the traditional music industry, the ordinary channels for the dissemination of musical ideas were effectively closed to jazz. It was relegated to the nightclub and thus became *de facto* an adjunct of "sin." This was and remains a forced marriage; neither musician nor club owner, for the most part, likes the place of jazz in clubs. Musicians dream of the club where they can play over extended periods of time the kinds of music they want to play to an audience which is quiet, attentive, appreciative, but undemanding (Berton, 1959; Nelson, 1963; Peterson, 1965). Yet, the conditions under which jazz was brought into clubs in the 1920's were almost the opposite of this ideal. The club was a place devoted to drinking and dancing; jazz was introduced not as a worthwhile thing in itself—to be listened to and appreciated—but as a loud and boisterous symbol of "roaring twenties" high life.

The number of clubs featuring jazz has varied widely over the following decades, but the conditions in the clubs militating against the development of creative ideas in jazz have changed very little over the years. First of all, playing in clubs has ramifying consequences for the musician. A shocking number have their lives cut short by violent death in auto accidents or medical ills complicated by sleeplessness, alcohol, drugs, and narcotics, all of which are concomitants of the nightclub milieu. Bix Beiderbecke, Charlie Parker, and recently Eric Dolphe, are but the most famous cases among many. Not a few of those who survive do so with their artistic capabilities severely blunted. Still others leave the music world to escape these conditions.

Less dramatic but probably as important in militating against the development of jazz are several economic "facts" of the club field. Clubs depend not on how many patrons they attract but on how much alcohol they are able to sell. Bands which by their reputation can attract a big following attract people to "listen," but the more that people listen, the less they are likely to drink. So the more expensive groups may attract a greater number of people but actually bring in less revenue (Berton, 1959; Roach, 1964).

The way out of this dilemma adopted by most club owners, other than a few in the large cities, is to hire inexpensive groups without great talent who will play music the customers find most entertaining. The music which results, whether it be in the style of Dixieland, cool jazz, or some fad such as bossa nova, tends to be an artless rendering of once vital and creative music. This trivialized rendering of "classical" jazz music, like its parallel in art reproductions, popular magazines, movies and television, has been termed "kitsch" culture as distinct from "high" culture (Greenberg, 1957).

Over the years various groups have tried to do something about this situation in the clubs, to set up jazz key clubs, coffee houses, lofts, workshops, and the like where jazz as art can be the focus. There is a high rate of failure among such ventures. They may go under for financial reasons; they may become successful and tend toward the type of club described above; or they may be harassed out of existence by police, boards of health, and other authorities. Such "harassment" may derive from feelings against "racial mixture," or because a successful club threatens the business of burlesque bars and similar establishments which are closely linked with a city's political underworld. Where such jazz-oriented clubs continue to operate, they usually do so in all but the largest cities only on the edge of the Negro section of town, isolated from the larger potential audience.

If the commercially oriented clubs have fostered a form of music best described as kitsch, the "fugitive" clubs just described have fostered a series of jazz cults. Certain of these cult movements have attracted attention and eventually become part of the mainstream of jazz. Perhaps the most prominent example is the cult of "be-bop" created in New York during World War II, which evolved into "cool" jazz that became the mainstream of jazz in the 1950's.

There is a dialectical relationship between cult and kitsch. The styles which have been bred and nurtured as cults have often been adapted, trivialized, and commercialized into kitsch. New cults develop to escape the now-trivialized, old style. Bop, for example, arose out of a rebellion against trash Dixieland as the "New Thing" style is now developing to get beyond the trivialized cool jazz of today. Yet this dialectical development does not argue in favor of the club as a beneficial environment for artistic development, because the major advances have arisen outside the nightclub field—in jam sessions, lofts, and ghetto bars.

The Moralizers Withdraw

The retreat of jazz into the nightclub comprises only one phase of the continuing impact of moralists on the nascent art form of jazz. During the Great Depression the entertainment business suffered a considerable decline, and jazz suffered as much as any other sector. Those looking for "causes" of social decay turned their attention away from the arts and alcohol to poverty and then to Fascism and war. Jazz was the focus of little popular critical concern during the Second World War and through the 1950's except as it was associated with dance and dress fads such as "jitterbugging" and "zoot suits." Academically oriented moralists of this extended period focused on the alienation of the jazz musician from the broader culture and his withdrawal to a special "deviant" community within Bohemia (Merriam and Mack, 1960). While much of this material is presented as if jazzmen voluntarily retreated from the larger society for psychological reasons (Becker, 1963), the analysis presented above suggests that it was a strategic retreat in the face of the attacks of institutional moralizers and their twin policies of containment and commercialization.

New Technologies and New Morality

While the moralizers of art ignored jazz, several innovations in the presentation of jazz have taken place which have greatly broadened its scope beyond the confines of the nightclub. The first of these is the advent of the long-playing record. From an artistic point of view, the LP and the associated technology of microphones and tape recorders have meant the player is no longer constrained to fit the mold of the three-minute "side" or otherwise inhibited by the once macabre technology of recording. Likewise the fidelity is so improved that subtleties of rhythm, color, and tone are clearly recognizable (McLuhan, 1965).

From an economic point of view, LPs have been sold at such a high markup that it is possible to make money on a record which has only limited sales. This has made it possible for numerous, small, independent recording companies to produce jazz records successfully. In consequence, since 1950 the number of jazz recordings available has rapidly expanded, and these are being featured on the ever-increasing number of jazz-oriented radio stations. Now for the first time creative jazz is available to a genuinely national audience. Thus the LP has had the effect of bringing jazz out of its nightclub refuge. Not only has the LP increased the size of the jazz audience; it has probably also affected its composition. I have no accurate figures, but I would suggest that it is less centered in the largest cities, less black, less centered in the age range of eighteen to twenty-five, less cultish about jazz, and more musically sophisticated than even fifteen years ago (Bessom, 1965; Ewen, 1961).

There has been at least as great a change in the music as well. There is now an extremely fast rate of diffusion of innovative instrumental techniques, an equally rapid succession of musical styles, "fads," and "schools," and increasingly professionalized musicians, who keep pace with the rapidly developing art. While it once was considered outstanding to be able to read music proficiently, now a fair number of musicians have had formal, conservatory training.

The impact of the LP has not been entirely benign. The wider exposure and rapid diffusion provided by the LP recording have led to pressure to find something unique to get attention. Where ideas are wanting, gimmicks prevail. Record companies have contributed to this tendency by pushing particular artists as madcap geniuses. In 1959, for example, much was made of Ornette Coleman's personal life and plastic saxophone. A decade earlier they advertised Thelonious Monk as akin to the Abominable Snowman. Record promotion has moved in the opposite direction, kitsch, as well. Jazz musicians are featured playing "jazzed" show tunes, such as *West Side Story* and *The Threepenny Opera*. While the impact of the LP record has not been entirely positive, it clearly has had the great effect of bringing jazz out of the narrow artistic and audience confines of the nightclub.

If advances in recording technology have had a great impact on jazz, so has another technology: transportation. For forty years "road" bands have toured the country playing for dances. The major early innovation was the "swing" arrangement. This format left room for jazz solos to be played over a steady dance rhythm. Although it was an ingenious way of allowing some melodic improvisation while satisfying dancers, it left little room for rhythmic improvisation which has always been basic to jazz innovation.

Not only was such "road work" musically confining, it had most of the same negative job attributes as the nightclub described above plus the element of constant travel with weeks and even months away from home. Many excellent musicians left the music field in order to "settle down" to a more usual family life.

For better or worse, the large, touring, jazz-oriented dance band has practically gone out of existence. The reasons are various, but perhaps most importantly large formal dances have gone out of style, being replaced by informal affairs featuring rock 'n' roll combos and records. While many in the industry understandably lament the demise of the touring dance band (Tynan, 1962; Ulanov, 1946; Walker, 1965), its niche in the social calendar of universities and community centers has been filled by quite another sort of music, and one more conducive to the artistic development of jazz; the jazz concert or festival. Here at last jazz is presented live in a context *sans* dancing or drinking. The first important, genuine jazz concert was performed by Benny Goodman at Carnegie Hall in New York in 1938. But only for the past ten years has concertizing become an important element in broadening the audience for jazz and allowing a platform for the expression of new ideas. While the "road tour" was once a long and arduous trip by bus or rail, a concert gig anywhere in the world is only a day or two away by plane, and thus concertizing does not have the same impact on the musician's life that touring once did.

Looking back, it may seem inevitable that the concert-festival field would develop as it has, but I don't think this is the case. Here is where the jazz promoter has had the biggest creative impact in building the demand for jazz and advancing the capital to put on such ventures. While all sorts of interests from local Catholic groups to the State Department, from the Ford Motor Company to Chambers of Commerce now back shows, a very few men such as John Hammond, Norman Granz and Abe Turchen pioneered the field (Lees, 1963).

The New Moralizers of Jazz

Beginning earlier, but gathering momentum rapidly in the 1960's, institutional critics have begun to make quite a different assessment of the meaning of jazz. While between the world wars jazz was seen as the call to sin, and at mid-century jazz was seen as the cry of an alienated cult, it now has come to be viewed as a weapon in the two-front war against communism and racial inequality. Thus for the first time in its history, jazz is being interpreted in the popular press and even within the halls of the United States Congress as a positive cultural force.

The *Time* cover story on jazz pianist Thelonious Monk (February 28, 1964) points the way of this new evaluation of jazz. It accepts Monk with all his eccentricities of dress, speech, and habit, viewing these as means he employs to maintain his artistic self-integrity—his "essential humanity." Significantly, ten years earlier these same characteristics were seen as evidence that jazz musicians were rather *less* than human. To further signal the acceptance of jazz, *Time* notes the critical acclaim given Monk by classical music scholars, the sellout crowds he draws at concerts, and his fat income.

The *Time* article, like a similar one appearing a month and a half later in the *Saturday Evening Post,* only hints at the set of themes which has become so important in the new evaluation of recent years. The two main assertions of the new moralists of jazz are: (1) *jazz is the one distinctly American art form;* and (2) *the Negro is the prime creative force in the development of jazz.* Combining these two statements they are able to assert that blacks have made a significant contribution to American culture, and the integration of blacks is closely associated with the acceptance of jazz into the mainstream of American culture. Each of these themes is suggested in the July 29, 1966 feature article in *Life* on the blind black pianist-singer-arranger, Ray Charles.

In addition, jazz is seen as a potent and fitting ambassador of American culture to the rest of the world. Not only does it exhibit America's acceptance of blacks and their contributions, but the elements of spontaneity and improvisation demonstrate the impact of American values of freedom on our culture. In this connection, the success of jazz behind the Iron Curtain is prominently featured by these new moralizers of jazz (Jones, 1963; Williams, 1964).

This new elevation of jazz is not restricted to the popular press. In May 1965, jazz and one of its prime contributors, Louis Armstrong, were roundly praised on the floor of the United States Senate when Jacob Javits nominated the black jazz trumpet player to receive the Presidential Medal of Freedom. Not only did Javits express the new themes outlined above, but he saw in Armstrong's career the success-through-hard-work-from-humble-beginnings theme that has been an important element in the "American Dream" for at least one hundred and fifty years.

The new high level of popular respectability of jazz is evidenced in the numerous State Department-sponsored tours by jazz groups, the increasing numbers of radio and FM stations that feature jazz, and the growing number of jazz concert and touring groups. At another level, the new respectability is shown by the introduction of jazz instruction, demonstrations, and competitions at all levels of the educational system. In still another sphere, its acceptance can be seen in the ubiquitous presence of jazz backgrounds in contemporary TV advertising.

At the same time, jazz has gained a considerable degree of legitimacy in traditional circles. Evidence of this new stature can be seen in the fact that *The New York Times* regularly reviews jazz records and performances (Balliett, 1959); the Museum of Modern Art annually holds a jazz concert series which this year drew over 28,000 patrons (*Down Beat,* 1966a); Rutgers University has established an Institute of Jazz Studies (*Down Beat,* 1966b); and the leading conservatories teach the fundamentals of jazz.

Some Implications

It is difficult to foretell the long-term impact that the new approval will have on the development of jazz into a high art form. It does seem certain, however, that the rate of innovation will be greatly accelerated as compared with the "dark ages" when jazz was relegated to the nightclub. Such innovations will come from many sources. Among them are likely to be the following: (1) conservatory training affords a whole range of new perspectives on composition, on improvisation, and on instrumental technique; (2) the constant introduction of new or modified instruments makes possible the expression of an impressive array of new ideas; and (3) the greater economic security which goes with acceptance means fewer years of a man's creative life need be spent in jobs outside of music. *Whatever* the specific direction of these innovations, it seems safe to assert that jazz has penetrated close enough to the center of American cultural life, that like the Black Revolution, it cannot be stunted in its development as it was between the world wars by the cultural equivalent to the "white backlash."

REFERENCES

Adderly, Julian.
    1960   "Paying dues; the education of a combo leader." The Jazz Review
             3:12–15.
Balliett, Whitney.
    1959   The Sound of Surprises. New York: Dutton.
Becker, Howard S.
    1963   Outsiders: Studies in the Sociology of Deviance. New York: Free
             Press. Chapters 5 and 6.
Berton, Ralph.
    1959   "The half note." The Jazz Review 2:39–41.
Bessom, Malcolm E.
    1965   "The academician looks at the jazz musician." Down Beat Music
             '65 Yearbook. Chicago: Maher. 96–100.
Charters, Samuel B. and Leonard Kunstadt.
    1962   Jazz: A History of the New York Scene. New York: Doubleday.
Down Beat
    1964   "Jazz internationalism." (September 10): Entire issue.
    1966   "Jazz goes to high school." (September 8): 14.
             "Museum jazz series sets attendance mark." (October 20): 9.
             "Rutgers and Carnegie plan jazz concerts." (October 20): 9.
Ewen, David.
    1961   The History of Popular Music. New York: Barnes and Noble.

Goldberg, Joe.
   1965   "The personal basis of jazz criticism." Down Beat (February 21):
           22–24.
Greenberg, Clement.
   1957   "Avant-garde and kitsch," in B. Rosenberg and D. M. White (eds.),
           Mass Culture. New York: Free Press. 98–100.
Gusfield, Joseph R.
   1963   Symbolic Crusade: Status Politics and the American Temperance
           Movement. Urbana, Illinois: University of Illinois Press.
Holt, E. G. (ed.)
   1959   A Documentary History of the Arts. Volume 2. Garden City, New
           York: Doubleday. 310–311.
Horton, Donald.
   1957   "The dialogue of courtship in popular songs." American Journal of
           Sociology 62:569–578.
Jones, LeRoi.
   1963   "Jazz and the white critic." Down Beat (August 15): 16.
Lees, Gene.
   1963   "Herman's swinging new herd." Down Beat (April 25): 22–23.
Leonard, Neil.
   1962   Jazz and the White Americans. Chicago: University of Chicago
           Press.
Lowenthal, Leo.
   1961a   Literature, Popular Culture and Society. Englewood Cliffs, New
           Jersey: Prentice-Hall. 19.
   1961b   "An historical preface to the popular culture debate," in N. Jacobs
           (ed.), Culture for the Millions. Boston: Beacon. 28–42.
McLuhan, Marshall.
   1965   "New media and the arts." Arts in Society 3:239–242.
Merriam, Alan P. and Raymond W. Mack.
   1960   "The jazz community." Social Forces 38:211–222.
Nelson, Don.
   1963   "Inside the half note." Down Beat (September 12).
Pelles, Geraldine.
   1963   Art, Artists and Society: Origins of a Modern Dilemma. Englewood
           Cliffs, New Jersey: Prentice-Hall.
Peterson, Richard A.
   1965   "Artistic creativity and alienation: the jazz musician versus his
           audience." Arts in Society 3:244–248.
Peterson, Richard A. and Claire L. Peterson.
   1964   "Occupational differentiation and the elaboration of the 'art' ideol-
           ogy." Paper presented to the Society for Social Research. Chicago
           (May).

Pevsner, Nikolaus.
    1940   Academies of Art Past and Present. Cambridge: Cambridge University Press.
Roach, Mark.
    1964   "The business." Variety (February 12): 13.
Russell, William and Stephan W. Smith.
    1939   "New Orleans music," in F. Ramsey, Jr., and C. E. Smith (eds.), Jazzmen. New York: Harcourt, Brace. 22.
Shils, Edward.
    1958   "Ideology and civility." Sewanee Review 66:467–468.
Tynan, John.
    1962   "Vamp till ready: Terry Gibbs' big band." Down Beat (November): 18.
Ulanov, Barry.
    1946   Duke Ellington. New York: Creative Age.
Walker, Leo.
    1965   The Wonderful Era of the Great Dance Bands. New York: Howell-North.
Watt, Ian.
    1964   "Literature and society," in R. N. Wilson (ed.), The Arts in Society. Englewood Cliffs, New Jersey: Prentice-Hall. 300–314.
White, Harrison C. and Cynthia A. White.
    1965   Canvases and Careers: Institutional Change in the French Painting World. New York: Wiley.
Williams, Martin.
    1964   "Ambassador jazz." Down Beat (January 2): 21–23.

20

THE PROFESSIONAL JAZZ MUSICIAN
AND HIS AUDIENCE

Howard S. Becker

The service occupations are, in general, distinguished by the fact that the worker in them comes into more or less direct and personal contact with the ultimate consumer of the product of his work, the client for whom he performs the service. Consequently, the client is able to direct or attempt to direct the worker at his task and to apply sanctions of various kinds, ranging from informal pressure to the withdrawal of his patronage and the conferring of it on some others of the many people who perform the service.

This contact brings together a person whose full-time activity is centered around the occupation and whose self is to some degree deeply involved in it, and another person whose relation to it is much more casual. It may be inevitable that the two should have widely varying pictures of the way the occupational service should be performed. Members of service occupations characteristically consider the client unable to judge the proper worth of the service and bitterly resent attempts on his part to exercise control over the work. Conflict and hostility arise as a result, methods of defense against outside interference become a preoccupation of the members.

The present paper outlines the dimensions of such an occupational dilemma as observed among professional dance musicians in a large American city. This occupation presents an extremely favorable situation for studying such phenomena, since in it the problem is to a greater degree than in many occupations, frankly faced and openly discussed. Musicians feel that the only music worth

From "The Professional Dance Musician and his Audience," *American Journal of Sociology* (Sept., 1951), pp. 136–144. Copyright © 1951 University of Chicago Press. Reprinted with permission of publisher and author.

playing is what they call "jazz," a term which can be partially defined as that music which is produced without reference to the demands of outsiders. Yet they must endure unceasing interference with their playing by employers and audience. The most distressing problem in the career of the average musician, as we shall see later, is the necessity of choosing between conventional success and his artistic standards. In order to achieve success he finds it necessary to "go commercial," that is, to play in accord with the wishes of the nonmusicians for whom he works; in doing so he sacrifices the respect of other musicians and thus, in most cases, his self-respect. If he remains true to his standards, he is usually doomed to failure in the larger society. Musicians classify themselves according to the degree to which they give in to outsiders; the continuum ranges from the extreme "jazz" musician to the "commercial" musician.

The discussion will focus on the following points: (1) the conceptions that musicians have of themselves and of the nonmusicians for whom they work and the conflict they feel to be inherent in this relation; (2) the basic consensus underlying the reactions of both commercial and jazz musicians to this conflict; and (3) the feelings of isolation musicians have from the larger society and the way they segregate themselves from audience and community. The analysis is based on materials gathered during eighteen months of interviewing and participant observation. My research was disclosed to few people. In general, I was accepted as just another young piano player by most of the men from whom this material was gathered. The bulk of the material comes from younger men, but enough contact was made with other musicians to permit the analysis of basic occupational problems.

Musician and "Square"

The system of beliefs about what musicians are and what audiences are is summed up in a word used by musicians to refer to outsiders—"square." It is used as a noun and as an adjective, denoting both a kind of person and a quality of behavior and objects. The term refers to the kind of person who is the opposite of all the musician is, or should be, and a way of thinking, feeling, and behaving (with its expression in material objects) which is the opposite of that valued by musicians.

The musician is conceived of as an artist who possesses a mysterious artistic gift setting him apart from all other people. Possessing this gift, he should be free from control by outsiders who lack it. The gift is something which cannot be acquired through education; the outsider, therefore, can never become a member of the group. A trombone player said, "You can't teach a guy to have a beat. Either he's got one or he hasn't. If he hasn't got it, you can't teach it to him."

The musician feels that under no circumstances should any outsider be allowed to tell him what to play or how to play it. In fact, the strongest element in the colleague code is the prohibition against criticizing or in any other way trying to put pressure on another musician in the actual playing situation "on the job." Where not even a colleague is permitted to influence the work, it is unthinkable that an outsider should be allowed to do so.

This attitude is generalized into a feeling that musicians are different from and better than other kinds of people and accordingly ought not to be subject to the control of outsiders in any branch of life, particularly in their artistic activity. The feeling of being a different kind of person who leads a different kind of life is deep-seated, as the following remarks indicate:

> I'm telling you, musicians are different than other people. They talk different, they act different, they look different. They're just not like other people, that's all. . . . You know it's hard to get out of the music business because you feel so different from others.

> Musicians live an exotic life, like in a jungle or something. They start out, they're just ordinary kids from small towns—but once they get into that life they change. It's like a jungle, except that their jungle is a hot, crowded bus. You live that kind of life long enough, you just get to be completely different.

> Being a musician was great, I'll never regret it. I'll understand things that squares never will.

An extreme of this view is the belief that only musicians are sensitive and unconventional enough to be able to give real sexual satisfaction to a woman.

Feeling their difference strongly, musicians likewise believe they are under no obligation to imitate the conventional behavior of squares. From the idea that no one can tell a musician how to play it follows logically that no one can tell a musician how to do anything. Accordingly, behavior which flouts conventional social norms is greatly admired. Stories reveal this admiration for highly individual, spontaneous, devil-may-care activities; many of the most noted jazzmen are renowned as "characters," and their exploits are widely recounted. For example, one well-known jazzman is noted for having jumped on a policeman's horse standing in front of the night club in which he worked and ridden it away. The ordinary musician likes to tell stories of unconventional things he has done:

> We played the dance and after the job was over we packed up to get back in this old bus and make it back to Detroit. A little way out of town the car just refused to go. There was plenty of gas; it just wouldn't run. These guys all climbed out and stood around griping. All of a sudden, somebody said, "Let's set it on fire!" So someone got

some gas out of the tanks and sprinkled it around, touching a match
to it and whoosh, it just went up in smoke. What an experience! The
car burning up and all these guys standing around hollering and clapping their hands. It was really something.

This is more than idiosyncrasy; it is a primary occupational value, as indicated
by the following observation of a young musician: "You know, the biggest
heroes in the music business are the biggest characters. The crazier a guy acts,
the greater he is, the more everyone likes him."

As they do not wish to be forced to live in terms of social conventions, so
musicians do not attempt to force these conventions on others. For example, a
musician declared that ethnic discrimination is wrong, since every person is
entitled to act and believe as he wants to:

> Shit, I don't believe in any discrimination like that. People are
> people, whether they're Dagos or Jews or Irishmen or Polacks or what.
> Only big squares care what religion they are. It don't mean a fucking
> thing to me. Every person's entitled to believe his own way, that's the
> way I feel about it. Of course, I never go to church myself, but I don't
> hold it against anybody who does. It's all right if you like that sort of
> thing.

The same musician classified a friend's sex behavior as wrong, yet defended
the individual's right to decide what is right and wrong for himself:

> Eddie fucks around too much; he's gonna kill himself or else get
> killed by some broad. And he's got a nice wife too. He shouldn't treat
> her like that. But what the fuck, that's his business. If that's the way
> he wants to live, if he's happy that way, then that's the way he oughta
> do.

Musicians will tolerate extraordinary behavior in a fellow-musician without
making any attempt to punish or restrain him. In the following incident the
uncontrolled behavior of a drummer loses a job for an orchestra; yet, angry as
they are, they lend him money and refrain from punishing him in any way. It
would be a breach of custom were anyone to reprimand him.

> JERRY: When we got up there, the first thing that happened was
> that all his drums didn't show up. So the owner drives all around try-
> ing to find some drums for him and then the owner smashes a fender
> while he was doing it. So I knew right away that we were off to a
> good start. And Jack! Man, the boss is an old Dago, you know, no

bullshit about him, he runs a gambling joint; he don't take any shit from anyone. So he says to Jack, "What are you gonna do without drums?" Jack says, "Be cool, daddio, everything'll be real gone, you know." I thought the old guy would blow his top. What a way to talk to the boss. Boy, he turned around, there was fire in his eye. I knew we wouldn't last after that. He says to me, "Is that drummer all there?" I said, "I don't know, I never saw him before today." And we just got finished telling him we'd been playing together six months. So that helped, too. Of course, when Jack started playing, that was the end. So loud! And he don't play a beat at all. All he uses the bass drum for is accents. What kind of drumming is that? Otherwise, it was a good little outfit.... It was a good job. We could have been there forever.... Well, after we played a couple of sets, the boss told us we were through.

BECKER: What happened after you got fired?

JERRY: The boss gave us twenty apiece and told us to go home. So it cost us seventeen dollars for transportation up and back, we made three bucks on the job. Of course, we saw plenty of trees. Three bucks, hell, we didn't even make that. We loaned Jack seven or eight.

The musician thus views himself and his colleagues as people with a special gift which makes them different from nonmusicians and not subject to their control, either in musical performance or in ordinary social behavior.

The square, on the other hand, lacks this special gift and any understanding of the music or way of life of those who possess it. The square is thought of as an ignorant, intolerant person who is to be feared, since he produces the pressures forcing the musician to play inartistically. The musician's difficulty lies in the fact that the square is in a position to get his way: if he does not like the kind of music played, he does not pay to hear it a second time.

Not understanding music, the square judges music by standards foreign to musicians and not respected by them. A commercial saxophonist observed sarcastically:

It doesn't make any difference what we play, the way we do it. It's so simple that anyone who's been playing longer than a month could handle it. Jack plays a chorus on piano or something, then saxes or something, all unison. It's very easy. But the people don't care. As long as they can hear the drum they're all right. They hear the drum, then they know to put their right foot in front of their left foot and their left foot in front of their right foot. Then if they can hear the melody to whistle to, they're happy. What more could they want?

The following conversation illustrates the same attitude:

> JOE: You'd get off the stand and walk down the aisle, some-body'd say, "Young man, I like your orchestra very much." Just because you played soft and the tenorman doubled fiddle or something like that, the squares liked it. . . .
>
> DICK: It was like that when I worked at the M_____ Club. All the kids that I went to high school with used to come out and dig the band. . . . That was one of the worst bands I ever worked on and they all thought it was wonderful.
>
> JOE: Oh, well, they're just a bunch of squares anyhow.

"Squareness" is felt to penetrate every aspect of the square's behavior just as its opposite, "hipness," is evident in everything the musician does. The square seems to do everything wrong and is laughable and ludicrous. Musicians derive a good deal of amusement from sitting and watching squares. Everyone has stories to tell about the laughable antics of squares. One man went so far as to suggest that the musicians should change places with the people sitting at the bar of the tavern he worked in; he claimed they were funnier and more entertaining than he could possibly be. Every item of dress, speech, and behavior which differs from that of the musician is taken as new evidence of the inherent insensitivity and ignorance of the square. Since musicians have an esoteric culture these evidences are many and serve only to fortify their conviction that musicians and squares are two different kinds of people.

But the square is feared as well, since he is thought of as the ultimate source of commercial pressure. It is the square's ignorance of music that compels the musician to play what he considers bad music in order to be successful.

> BECKER: How do you feel about the people you play for, the audience?
>
> DAVE: They're a drag.
>
> BECKER: Why do you say that?
>
> DAVE: Well, if you're working on a commercial band, they like it and so you have to play more corn. If you're working on a good band, then they don't like it, and that's a drag. If you're working on a good band and they like it, then that's a drag, too. You hate them anyway, because you know that they don't know what it's all about. They're just a big drag.

This last statement reveals that even those who attempt to avoid being square are still considered so, because they still lack the proper understanding, which only a musician can have—"they don't know what it's all about." The jazz fan is thus respected no more than other squares. His liking for jazz is without understanding and he acts just like the other squares; he will request songs and try to influence the musician's playing, just as other squares do.

The musician thus sees himself as a creative artist who should be free from outside control, a person different from and better than those outsiders he calls squares who understand neither his music nor his way of life and yet because of whom he must perform in a manner contrary to his professional ideals.

Reactions to the Conflict

We will now consider the attitudes of "commercial" and "jazz" musicians toward the audience, noting both the variation in attitude and the basic consensus underlying the two sets of feelings. Two themes run through this conflict; (1) the desire of the musician to live in terms of the creative principle, and (2) the recognition of many forces influencing him to abandon that principle. The jazzman tends to emphasize the first, the commercial musician the second; but both recognize and feel the force of each of these guiding influences. Common to the attitudes of both kinds of musician is an intense contempt for and dislike of the square audience whose fault it is that musicians must "go commercial" in order to succeed.

The commercial musician, though he conceives of the audience as square, chooses to sacrifice self-respect and the respect of other musicians (the rewards of artistic behavior) for the more substantial rewards of steady work, higher income, and the prestige enjoyed by the man who goes commercial. One commercial musician commented:

> They've got a nice class of people out here, too. Of course, they're squares, I'm not trying to deny that. Sure, they're a bunch of fucking squares, but who the fuck pays the bills? They pay 'em, so you gotta play what they want. I mean, what the shit, you can't make a living if you don't play for the squares. How many fucking people you think aren't squares? Out of a hundred people you'd be lucky if 15 percent weren't squares. I mean, maybe professional people—doctors, lawyers, like that—they might not be square, but the average person is just a big fucking square. Of course, show people aren't like that. But outside of show people and professional people, everybody's a fucking square.[1] They don't know anything.
>
> I'll tell you. This is something I learned about three years ago. If

---

[1] Most musicians would not admit these exceptions.

you want to make any money you gotta please the squares. They're the ones that pay the bills, and you gotta play for them. A good musician can't get a fucking job. You gotta play a bunch of shit. But what the fuck, let's face it. I want to live good. I want to make some money; I want a car, you know. How long can you fight it? . . .

Don't get me wrong. If you can make money playing jazz, great. But how many guys can do it? . . . If you can play jazz, great, like I said. But if you're on a bad fucking job, there's no sense fighting it, you gotta be commercial. I mean, the squares are paying your salary, so you might as well get used to it, they're the ones you gotta please.

Note that the speaker admits it is more "respectable" to be independent of the squares, and expresses contempt for the audience, whose squareness is made responsible for the whole situation.

These men phrase the problem primarily in economic terms: "I mean, shit, if you're playing for a bunch of squares you're playing for a bunch of squares. What the fuck are you gonna do? You can't push it down their throats. Well, I suppose you can make 'em eat it, but after all, they *are* paying you."

The jazzman feels the need to satisfy the audience just as strongly, although maintaining that one should not give in to it. Jazzmen, like others, appreciate steady jobs and good jobs and know they must satisfy the audience to get them, as the following conversation between two young jazzmen illustrates:

CHARLIE: There aren't any jobs where you can blow jazz. You have to play rumbas and pops (popular songs) and everything. You can't get anywhere blowing jazz. Man, I don't want to scuffle all my life.

EDDIE: Well, you want to enjoy yourself, don't you? You won't be happy playing commercial. You know that.

CHARLIE: I guess there's just no way for a cat to be happy. 'Cause it sure is a drag blowing commercial, but it's an awful drag not ever doing anything and playing jazz.

EDDIE: Jesus, why can't you be successful playing jazz? . . . I mean, you could have a great little outfit and still play arrangements, but good ones, you know.

CHARLIE: You could never get a job for a band like that.

EDDIE: Well, you could have a sexy little bitch to stand up in front and sing and shake her ass at the bears (squares). Then you could get a job. And you could still play great when she wasn't singing.

CHARLIE: Well, wasn't that what Q_____'s band was like? Did you enjoy that? Did you like the way she sang?

EDDIE: No, man, but we played jazz, you know.

CHARLIE: Did you like the kind of jazz you were playing? It was kind of commercial, wasn't it?

EDDIE: Yeah, but it could have been great.

CHARLIE: Yeah, if it had been great, you wouldn't have kept on working. I guess we'll always just be unhappy. It's just the way things are. You'll always be drug (unhappy) with yourself. . . . There'll never be any kind of a really great job for a musician.

In addition to the pressure to please the audience which emanates from the musician's desire to maximize salary and income, there are more immediate pressures. It is often difficult to maintain an independent attitude. For example:

I worked an Italian wedding on the Southwest Side last night with Johnny Ponzi. We played about half an hour, doing the special arrangements they use, which are pretty uncommercial. Then an old Italian fellow (the father-in-law of the groom, as we later found out) began hollering, "Play some polkas, play some Italian music. Ah, you stink, you're lousy." Johnny always tries to avoid the inevitable on these wedding jobs, putting off playing the folk music as long as he can. I said, "Man, why don't we play some of that stuff now and get it over with?" Tom said, "I'm afraid if we start doing that we'll be doing it all night." Johnny said, "Look, Howard, the groom is a real great guy. He told us to play anything we want and not to pay any attention to what the people say, so don't worry about it. . . ."

The old fellow kept hollering and pretty soon the groom came up and said, "Listen, fellows. I know you don't want to play any of that shit and I don't want you to, but that's my father-in-law, see. The only thing is, I don't want to embarrass my wife for him, so play some Dago music to keep him quiet, will yuh?" Johnny looked around at us and made a gesture of resignation.

He said, "All right, let's play the *Beer Barrel Polka.*" Tom said, "Oh shit! Here we go." We played it and then we played an Italian dance, the *Tarentelle.*

Sometimes the employer applies pressure which makes even an uncompromising jazzman give in, at least for the duration of the job:

I was playing solo for one night over at the Y____ on ____rd St. What a drag! The second set, I was playing *Sunny Side,* I played the melody for one chorus, then I played a little jazz. All of a sudden the boss leaned over the side of the bar and hollered, "I'll kiss your ass if anybody in this place knows what tune you're playing!" And everybody in the place heard him, too. What a big square! What could I do? I didn't say anything, just kept playing. Sure was a drag.

Somewhat inconsistently, the musician wants to feel that he is reaching the audience and that they are getting some enjoyment from his work, and this also leads him to give in to audience demands. One man said:

> I enjoy playing more when there's someone to play for. You kind of feel like there isn't much purpose in playing if there's nobody there to hear you. I mean, after all, that's what music's for—for people to hear and get enjoyment from. That's why I don't mind playing corny too much. If anyone enjoys it, then I kind of get a kick out of it. I guess I'm kind of a ham. But I like to make people happy that way.

This statement is somewhat extreme; but most musicians feel it strongly enough to want to avoid the active dislike of the audience: "That's why I like to work with Tommy. At least when you get off the stand, everybody in the place doesn't hate you. It's a drag to work under conditions like that, where everybody in the place just hates the whole band."

Isolation and Self-Segregation

Musicians are hostile to their audiences, afraid that they must sacrifice their artistic standards to the squares. They exhibit certain patterns of behavior and belief which may be viewed as adjustments to this situation. These patterns of isolation and self-segregation are expressed in the actual playing situation and in participation in the social intercourse of the larger community. The primary function of this behavior is to protect the musician from the interference of the square audience and, by extension, of the conventional society.

As a rule, the musician is spatially isolated from the audience. He works on a platform, which provides a physical barrier that prevents direct interaction. This isolation is welcomed because the audience, being made up of squares, is felt to be potentially dangerous. The musicians fear that direct contact with the audience can lead only to interference with the musical performance. Therefore, it is safer to be isolated and have nothing to do with it. Once, where such physical isolation was not provided, a player commented:

> Another thing about weddings, man. You're right down on the floor, right in the middle of the people. You can't get away from them. It's different if you're playing a dance or in a bar. In a dancehall you're up on a stage where they can't get at you. The same thing in a cocktail lounge, you're up behind the bar. But a wedding—man, you're right in the middle of them.

Musicians, lacking the usually provided physical barriers, often improvise their own and effectively segregate themselves from their audience.

> I had a Jewish wedding job for Sunday night. . . . When I arrived, the rest of the boys were already there. The wedding had taken place late, so that the people were just beginning to eat. We decided, after I had conferred with the groom, to play during dinner. We set up in a far corner of the hall. Jerry pulled the piano around so that it blocked off a small space, which was thus separated from the rest of the people. Tony set up his drums in this space, and Jerry and Johnny stood there while we played. I wanted to move the piano so that the boys could stand out in front of it and be next to the audience, but Jerry said, half-jokingly, "No, man. I have to have some protection from the squares." So we left things as they were. . . .
>
> Jerry had moved around in front of the piano but, again half-humorously, had put two chairs in front of him, which separated him from the audience. When a couple took the chairs to sit on, Jerry set two more in their place. Johnny said, "Man, why don't we sit on those chairs?" Jerry said, "No, man. Just leave them there. That's my barricade to protect me from the squares."

Many musicians almost reflexively avoid establishing contact with members of the audience. When walking among them, they habitually avoid meeting the eyes of squares for fear this will establish some relationship on the basis of which the square will then request songs or in some other way attempt to influence the musical performance. Some extend the behavior to their ordinary social activity, outside of professional situations. A certain amount of this is inevitable, since the conditions of work—late hours, great geographic mobility, and so on—make social participation outside of the professional group difficult. If one works while others sleep, it is difficult to have ordinary social intercourse with them. This was cited by a musician who had left the profession, in partial explanation of his action: "And it's great to work regular hours, too, where you can see people instead of having to go to work every night." Some younger musicians complain that the hours of work make it hard for them to establish contacts with "nice" girls, since they preclude the conventional date.

But much self-segregation develops out of the hostility toward squares. The attitude is seen in its extreme among the "X____Avenue Boys," a clique of extreme jazzmen who reject the American culture *in toto*. The quality of their feeling toward the outside world is indicated by one man's private title for his theme song: "If You Don't Like My Queer Ways You Can Kiss My Fucking Ass." The ethnic makeup of the group indicated further that their adoption of extreme artistic and social attitudes was part of a total rejection of conventional American society. With few exceptions the men came from older, more fully assimilated national groups: Irish, Scandinavian, German, and English. Further, many of them were reputed to come from wealthy families and the higher social classes. In short, their rejection of commercialism in music and squares in social life was part of the casting aside of the total American culture by men who enjoyed a privileged position, but were unable to achieve a satisfactory personal adjustment within it.

Every interest of this group emphasized their isolation from the standards and interests of conventional society. They associated almost exclusively with other musicians and girls who sang or danced in nightclubs in the North Clark Street area of Chicago and had little or no contact with the conventional world. They were described politically thus: "They hate this form of government anyway and think it's real bad." They were unremittingly critical of both business and labor, disillusioned with the economic structure, and cynical about the political process and contemporary political parties. Religion and marriage were rejected completely, as were American popular and serious culture, and their reading was confined solely to the more esoteric *avant garde* writers and philosophers. In art and symphonic music they were interested in only the most esoteric developments. In every case they were quick to point out that their interests were not those of the conventional society and that they were thereby differentiated from it. It is reasonable to assume that the primary function of these interests was to make this differentiation unmistakably clear.

Although isolation and self-segregation found their most extreme development among the "X_____ Avenue Boys," they were manifested by less deviant musicians as well. The feeling of being isolated from the rest of the society was often quite strong; the following conversation, which took place between two young jazzmen, illustrates two reactions to the sense of isolation.

> EDDIE: You know, man, I hate people. I can't stand to be around squares. They drag me so much I just can't stand them.
>
> CHARLIE: You shouldn't be like that, man. Don't let them drag you. Just laugh at them. That's what I do. Just laugh at everything they do. That's the only way you'll be able to stand it.

A young Jewish musician, who definitely identified himself with the Jewish community, nevertheless felt this professional isolation strongly enough to make the following statements.

> You know, a little knowledge is a dangerous thing. That's what happened to me when I first started playing. I just felt like I knew too much. I sort of saw, or felt, that all my friends from the neighborhood were real square and stupid. . . .

You know, it's funny. When you sit on that stand up there, you feel so different from others. Like I can even understand how Gentiles feel toward Jews. You see these people come up and they look Jewish, or they have a little bit of an accent or something, and they ask for a rumba or some damn thing like that, and I just feel, "What damn squares, these Jews," just like I was a *goy* myself. That's what I mean when I say you learn too much being a musician. I mean, you see so many things and get such a broad outlook on life that the average person just doesn't have.

On another occasion the same man remarked:

You know, since I've been out of work I've actually gotten so that I can talk to some of these guys in the neighborhood.
(You mean you had trouble talking to them before?)
Well, I'd just stand around and not know what to say. It still sobers me up to talk to those guys. Everything they say seems real silly and uninteresting.

The process of self-segregation is evident in certain symbolic expressions, particularly in the use of an occupational slang which readily identifies the man who can use it properly as someone who is not square and as quickly reveals as an outsider the person who uses it incorrectly or not at all. Some words have grown up to refer to unique professional problems and attitudes of musicians, typical of them being the term "square." Such words enable musicians to discuss problems and activities for which ordinary language provides no adequate terminology. There are, however, many words which are merely substitutes for the more common expressions without adding any new meaning. For example, the following are synonyms for money: "loot," "gold," "geetz," and "bread." Jobs are referred to as "gigs." There are innumerable synonyms for marijuana, the most common being "gage," "pot," "charge," "tea," and "shit."

The function of such behavior is pointed out by a young musician who was quitting the business:

I'm glad I'm getting out of the business, though. I'm getting sick of being around musicians. There's so much ritual and ceremony junk. They have to talk a special language, dress different, and wear a different kind of glasses. And it just doesn't mean a damn thing except "we're different."

*   *   *

21

"SO YOU WANT TO BE A ROCK 'N' ROLL STAR!"
ROLE CONFLICT AND THE ROCK MUSICIAN

James T. Coffman

The modern rock musician has been characterized as both a social deviant leading the nation's youth to a corrupt future and a capitalist exploiter; a spokesman for an emerging counterculture and a tool of the corporate state; or simply a mass entertainer and an artist of the new technological age. Although rock music has captured the attention of many journalists and a few social scientists,[1] the role of the producer has seldom been the topic of serious inquiry. The role of the rock star is complex and demanding since once the status of stardom has been achieved, diverse and conflicting role expectations converge upon the performer.

Empirical studies of jazz musicians during the 1950's and 1960's suggest that conflicting expectations may have serious consequences for the role incumbents and their products. Becker documented the expectations of the audience and the employer as well as the expectations of the performer.[2] The audience generally directed the performer to play commercially popular tunes in an orthodox manner. The employer applied financial sanctions in an attempt to coerce the performer to fulfill the expectations of the audience. The musicians,

An expanded version of "Everybody Knows This is Nowhere: Role Conflict and the Rock Musician," *Popular Music and Society* 1 (Fall, 1971). Reprinted by permission of *Popular Music and Society* and the author.

[1] R. Serge Denisoff and Mark H. Levine, "The Popular Protest Song: The Case of 'The Eve of Destruction,'" *The Public Opinion Quarterly,* 35 (Spring, 1971), pp. 117–122. [Ed. note: See Article 17 in this volume.]

[2] Howard S. Becker, "The Professional Dance Musician and His Audience," *The American Journal of Sociology,* 62 (Sept., 1951), pp. 136–144. [Ed. note: Reprinted as Article 20 in this volume.]

conversely, preferred to play jazz, a noncommercial and esoteric type of music. Becker, Stebbins, Peterson and others suggested that the role conflict experienced by the musicians gave rise to the development of "deviant groups,"[3] "jazz communities,"[4] and special forms of social adaptation employed by the performer to minimize the conflict.[5] Later work investigated the structural sources of conflict within the larger context of American society.[6]

It would appear, from recent articles in the fanzine and so-called "underground press," that conflicting role expectations may also impinge upon the contemporary rock star. This role conflict is manifested in the relationship of the performer to his audience and the entertainment industry. The nature of these dissonant demands, while somewhat similar to those described vis-a-vis the jazz musician, are considerably larger in scope and fraught with new and more complex contingencies upon the role of the performer.

Rock stars are international celebrities. They have successfully and repeatedly recorded for a world audience. They make concert tours. The performance of their music, as well as related testimonials, provides a lion's share of their income.

The groups chosen for this study meet the above criteria. Some are of British origin, in which case they have occupied the position of rock star since the early to middle 1960's. Most American groups selected for investigation originated from or attained stardom during the San Francisco "summer of love" in 1967. One American group was selected which met all but the final criterion. In this case, the Byrds have been associated with the development of folk-rock since the mid-1960's and still exist as a recording band today.

The audience for these musicians has been characterized in recent literature as a post-adolescent youth counterculture and bearers of a distinguishing "consciousness."[7] While this group may be an ambiguous analytical entity, Roszak points out that it contains "a cultural constellation that radically diverges from

[3] Howard S. Becker, *The Outsiders: Studies in the Sociology of Deviance* (New York, 1963), pp. 79–120.

[4] Robert A. Stebbins, "A Theory of the Jazz Community," *The Sociological Quarterly,* 9 (Summer, 1968), pp. 318–331.

[5] Richard A. Peterson, "Artistic Creativity and Alienation: The Jazz Musician Versus His Audience," *Arts In Society,* 3 (Spring, 1965), pp. 253–264.

[6] Richard A. Peterson, "Market and Moralist Censors of a Rising Art Form, Jazz," *Arts In Society,* 4 (Spring, 1967), pp. 253–264. [Ed. note: Reprinted as Article 19 in this volume.]

[7] Theodore Roszak, *The Making of a Counter Culture* (Garden City, N.Y.: Doubleday, 1967); also see Charles A. Reich, *The Greening of America* (New York: Random House, 1970).

values and assumptions that have been in the mainstream of our society at least since the Scientific Revolution . . . "[8] Because this group is composed of youth, and because it is not fully developed, it occupies a subordinate position in modern society. The counterculture alone does not comprise the entire audience for the musicians selected. And the counterculture may contain other, more traditional and less sophisticated elements of the youth group. No precise figures exist, but evidence indicates that the audience for the rock groups selected are older, more critical of society, experimenting with new values and ideas, and more demanding of the performer and his product.[9]

The entertainment industry is another major group that places expectations and sanctions on the rock performer. It is an integral part of the superordinate social structure of America.[10] This group controls access to the means of production of the musician's art—instruments, equipment, financing, recording and manufacturing of records, both singles and LP's. It controls the musician's access to national markets as well, both in terms of promotion and distribution of the recorded product, and also through the arrangement, financing and promotional functions of touring and personal appearances.[11]

The relationship between the counterculture and the industry is characterized by conflict. These two groups promote competing definitions of social reality as well as ideological and generational conflict.[12] As a member of both groups, the rock musician is subject to these conflicting expectations and evaluative standards.

The music industry has expectations to which the performer as an employee must respond. As is characteristic of all business enterprises in the U.S., all products are evaluated on the basis of commercial success. In the case of rock music, sales of 75,000 copies of an LP are necessary before profits are earned.[13] If this performance level is not achieved after several attempts, the artist's contract is usually terminated.

Within the structure of the recording industry, at least until the late 1960's, the musician was usually subjected to the direction of other corporate

---

[8] Theodore Roszak, *op. cit.*, xii.

[9] Jann Wenner, "The Recording Company Executive Thing: *Rolling Stone* interviews Joe Smith," *Rolling Stone,* 86 (July 8, 1971), p. 34.

[10] T. Proctor Lippincott, "The Culture Vultures," in Jonathan Eisen, ed., *The Age of Rock 2* (New York: Random House, 1970), pp. 124–132.

[11] Paul N. Hirsch, *The Structure of the Popular Music Industry,* Institute for Social Research, University of Michigan (mimeograph). Also see Richard A. Peterson and David G. Berger, "Entrepreneurship in Organizations: Evidence from the Popular Music Industry," *Administrative Science Quarterly,* 16 (March, 1971), pp. 97–106.

[12] R. Serge Denisoff and Mark H. Levine, "Generations and Counter Culture: A Study in the Ideology of Music," *Youth and Society,* 2 (Sept., 1970), pp. 33–58.

[13] Jann Wenner, *op. cit.*, p. 32.

employees during the rehearsal, recording and "mixing" of the product.[14] To an even greater extent the packaging, promotion and exposure of the final product, the LP, is still controlled by the industry. Formal and informal controls are often exercised in the course of these activities if the rock musician does not conform to the expectations of the industry.[15]

The position of the music industry in the superordinate strata of American society makes it vulnerable to the demands of other major interest groups. The rules of the FCC and the "good taste" of the mass media proprietors and the "gatekeepers" may influence the entertainment business to censor, restrict or edit the product of the musicians. The actions are usually taken in the interest of "corporate image" or, more often, for the sake of increased sales and profits. The increasing frequency of references to political dissent, drug usage and frank sexuality in song lyrics has mobilized public and political forces to suggest greater industry control over popular music. As a contracted employee of the industry, the musician is expected to submit to the needs of his employer. However, too much adjustment on the part of the musician, either for commercial reasons or for the public morality, may violate the aesthetic and cultural values of either the musician himself or those of his audience.

Empirical evidence suggests that rock music reflects the values, attitudes and concerns of its audience. Horton, Carey, Rosenstone, and others have demonstrated that popular songs contain elements of and references to the social situation of the audience.[16] In the case of the counterculture, the reviews and criticisms of rock music found in such specialty papers as *Rolling Stone, Creem* and *Crawdaddy,* as well as in the music columns in the "underground" press, seem to support this contention. The popularity of such protest songs as "The Universal Soldier," "Ohio," "Revolution" and others may be interpreted as audience support for those themes that reflect the attitudes, values and ideas found within the youthful audience.[17] This being the case, the audience may influence the performer to incorporate such themes, values and ideas in his product. Several means exist by which these expectations may be expressed.

[14] Paul N. Hirsch, *op. cit.,* pp. 7 and 20 especially.

[15] Paul N. Hirsch, *ibid.;* examples of these procedures may include the setting up and budgeting of promotional priorities and programs and the amounts of money allocated for the recording and engineering of the singles and albums.

[16] Donald Horton, "The Dialogue of Courtship in Popular Songs," *American Journal of Sociology,* 62 (May, 1957), pp. 569–578; James T. Carey, "Changing Courtship Patterns in the Popular Song," *American Journal of Sociology,* 74 (May, 1969), pp. 720–731 [Ed. note: Reprinted as Article 16 in this volume], and "The Ideology of Autonomy in Popular Lyrics: A Content Analysis," *Psychiatry,* 32 (May, 1969), pp. 150–164; Richard R. Cole, "Top Songs in the Sixties," *American Behavioral Scientist,* 14 (Jan./Feb., 1971), pp. 398–400; and Robert A. Rosenstone, " 'The Times They Are A-Changin' ": The Music of Protest," *Annals,* 381 (March, 1969), pp. 131–144.

[17] Denisoff and Levine, 1970, *op. cit.,* pp. 121–122.

The rock stars are chronologically all members of the youth culture. Informal mechanisms may be employed, such as primary group relationships, which may influence the performer. In the cases of the Jefferson Airplane and the Grateful Dead, their residency in the Haight-Ashbury district and their involvement in community "happenings" certainly influenced their music and their lyrics. More often the performer, as a member of the youth group, shares many identifying characteristics with his audience, including styles of dress, hair length and consumption preferences. In this case, the performer will be subjected to the same types of prejudice, discrimination and harassment from the dominant society as the other members of the youth culture. As mentioned earlier, the "underground media" and cult press may influence the performer. And finally, the economic variable may be viewed as a sanction. The rock performer depends upon the audience for his income. If the audience does not consume his product or attend his concerts, the performer cannot maintain his status of stardom for long.

In addition to the conflicting expectations of both the audience and the industry, the musicians have their own role expectations. Similar to the jazz musicians, the rock musician is also "a person whose full-time activity is centered around the occupation and whose self is deeply involved in it.[18] The performer desires to control his music and its content, and struggles to extend this control to the recording and performance sectors of his role. It is nearly a cliche with rock musicians that a producer or promotion department is responsible for any misfortune that befalls their careers. Elektra and MGM Records in the latter half of the 1960's received considerable disapprobation from their acts, many of whom switched labels. Few companies have been exempted. Capitol experienced the disaffection of the Beach Boys, and Columbia lost Aretha Franklin. The role of musician also transcends the performer's involvement with the counterculture, and his general audience. However, the economic security and life style which permit such fulltime attention to music and innovation requires the performer to persist in his relationships with both the audience and the industry, while maintaining his quest for artistic freedom and autonomy.

Horton and Wohl's conceptualization of parasocial interaction provides a vehicle whereby the expectations of the audience may be satisfied without excessively compromising the expectations of the performer.[19] According to this conceptualization, the rock star must be perceived by the audience as a member of their group. Shared primary and counterculture group membership may be implied by the performer or perceived by the audience.[20] But this image must

---

[18] Howard S. Becker, *The American Journal of Sociology, op. cit.,* p. 136.

[19] Donald Horton and R. R. Wohl, "Mass Communication and Para-Social Interaction," *Psychiatry,* 19 (August, 1956), pp. 215–229.

[20] *Ibid.,* p. 216.

be preserved if the status of stardom is to be maintained. The content of the product and its significance, as stated above, is important, but shared social group membership and common values are also necessary. These can be either stated by the performer or assigned by the audience. These shared characteristics should be among those which are the subject of conflict between the normative order and the youth culture.

The mode of expression employed by the performer in his song may be one vehicle to promote intimacy with his audience. Rock songs often express the relationship of the performer, as a member of the youth culture, with the dominant social order. Direct address by the performer to his audience is sometimes used. According to Horton and Wohl, "The more the performer seems to adjust his performance to the audience, the more the audience tends to make the response anticipated."[21] Because the relationship between the performer and his audience is of a mass nature and not at the primary level of interaction, certain means may be employed to promote a two-sided illusion of intimacy and shared experience. While articles have appeared which accuse the performer of cynical manipulation of his image for economic purposes, the audience may be guilty of self-deception through the imputation of shared characteristics and values.

The audience is also ambiguously aware of their role in making a rock star. They too feel they are in an economic relationship of ownership and control of the musical product. As stated earlier, one vehicle of control has been the development of a medium of communication, the journals of the rock cult. These papers also provide information whereby the audience can keep track of the latest experiences and activities of the performers. They may also function to create the characteristics of primary group interaction with the rock stars. These media function to create and maintain an illusion of intimacy and contact with the performers and provide a source of data and details that may be used by the audience in the creation and maintenance of a compendium of characteristics which they and their primary group share with the distant performer. While a certain degree of image management is carried on by the performer, more often it is the manipulations of the industry and its marketing sector, and the selective consumption of the audience which accounts for much of the rock star's "image" as a youth culture member.

In the extreme case of parasocial interaction we find the example of the "groupie" and Abbie Hoffman crashing the stage at Woodstock. More often, however, the life styles, attitudes, values and norms of the rock star, necessary for the role and occupation, are interpreted by the audience as an implicit or explicit justification for their own emerging subculture.

[21] *Ibid.,* p. 215.

Modern rock music has been characterized as "honest," "topical" and "personal" statements by the performer. This characterization would suggest that if the expectations of the performer, the audience and the industry are in conflict, references to the situation should be found in the lyrics of rock and the statements of rock stars. Furthermore, if parasocial interaction is to be a useful concept in the investigation of the rock musician, examples should be evident in the lyrics and performance of the music.

A non-comprehensive and incomplete investigation of the recordings of selected rock stars supports the contention that references to the relationship between the performer and the industry have found their way into the lyrics of the music. The Rolling Stones, in "Underassistant West Coast Promo Man," cynically assume the role of a member of the distributive sector of the business of rock. The mocking vocal inflections and sneers of Mick Jagger have the obvious intention of promoting distance between the artist and the industry. This removes the artist from the Establishment and absolves him of any responsibility for the excessive "hype" and unacceptable practices of the industry. It may also be interpreted as an application of youth culture standards in evaluating the marketing and promotion of his product. Thus, the song may promote both the image of the performer as a member of the youth culture, and his desire to control his product. Several years ago, a disagreement between the Rolling Stones and their record company over the packaging of an album postponed the product's release for nine months. In this particular case, the album cover designed and selected by the performers was ruled objectionable by the company. The record jacket design was eventually changed and the album released. The Rolling Stones have since founded their own record label, so they record, produce, mix and manufacture their own LP's. But, in the words of Keith Richard, their guitarist, "Nearly all the Rolling Stones' records—you know this is the first album that hasn't [their recent release, *Sticky Fingers*]—have gone through this very straight English private f—— company, man. They're the people that are really giving it to you. It's not us that are giving it, we're giving it to them."[22]

Another song in this genre is "Drug Store Truck Drivin' Man" by the Byrds. Here the rock star attacks an all-night deejay for his intolerance toward political action, the counterculture, and rock music. While directed to Ralph Emory of WSM in Nashville, the song acknowledges the power and bias of a disk jockey over what the audience hears. Further implied in the lyric is that the "pop" star is "of the people," a member of the anti-Establishment forces, and in struggle with the dominant economic group. It should be noted, that

---

[22] Robert Greenfield, "The *Rolling Stone* Interview: Keith Richard," *Rolling Stone,* 89 (August 19, 1971), p. 36.

alienating an all-night country and western radio personality whose main appeal is to truck drivers did little to harm the career plans of the Byrds. This song did, however, promote the group with the youth culture and underground radio stations. Here, the rock star is defining the in-group and out-group membership, separating himself from the business of rock. He bases his appeal upon the political and ideological standards of the audience.

Another song by the Byrds, "So You Want To Be a Rock 'n' Roll Star" is one of the most complete statements of the conflicting expectations of the audience, the industry, and the performer. The Byrds, by the time this song was recorded, had attained a degree of pop star status. But in the beginning of their recording careers they were not even allowed to play their own instrumentals on their records, these being provided by the company's own musicians under the direction of the company's producer.[23] But with the attainment of status and popularity, they began to record their own compositions with greater control of the production process. In the context of this song they make specific reference to the performer's relationship to the industry—he must "sell his soul" to gain access to the means of production and distribution. The lyrics also make reference to the industry's attitude toward rock music, equating it with "plasticware," simply another product to be manufactured and marketed for a profit. This theme reinforces the standards of the audience which are obviously superior to corporate profits as an index of the value of rock music.

The lyrics also contain references to the audience. The rock 'n' roll star begins as just another kid with a desire for musical success. He is a member of the audience and the youth culture and not solely a creation of the dominant group imposed on the audience by the industry. But "All the money that came/ And the public acclaim" have separated the performers from the audience. They cannot come into direct contact with the audience because the girls may "tear them apart." This is obviously a reference to the commercial nature of the expectations of the audience and the role of the rock star.

Another example of the rock star's relationship with his audience is found in a song documenting the experiences of being a rock star. "A Song for All Seasons," recorded by the Jefferson Airplane, concerns conversation between a member of.a renowned rock band and a "friend" he meets on the street. The friend proceeds to recount all the rumors "on the street" concerning the recent personal and personnel problems of the band members: the guitarist just wrecked his new car—a usual symbol of status—while another band member has just had his car repossessed. The drummer is said to be "flipped out," probably on drugs, while their manager is rumored to have "skipped town" with all the pay. This seems to verify the suggestion that the fans seek infor-

[23] Ben Fong-Torres, "The *Rolling Stone* Interview: David Crosby," *Rolling Stone*, 63 (July 23, 1970), pp. 20–27.

mation (true and false) about the personal and professional life of the pop star. They even go so far as to impute motives into the situation—"all you ever really wanted was just to play." Finally the "friend" turns out to be a member of a local band which hopes to soon achieve "success," to be "heard on Top Forty radio." By recounting these real or imagined occurrences in a song, the pop star demonstrates that his audience attributes certain shared characteristics to him and parasocially interacts with him, imputing shared values and motives, possibly even to the extent that the fan hopes to achieve a similar status and role himself.

"A Song for All Seasons" was written by Spencer Dryden, the second drummer to join the group since 1966. Following the recording and release of the album on which the song appeared, Dryden, too, left the group.

It is appropriate that the Airplane include such lyrics in their albums. They were the first San Francisco band to attain national fame. Their recording of "White Rabbit," with its obvious references to drugs, became a million seller. Their album, *Volunteers*, documents and praises the emerging anti-Establishment counterculture—its life styles, politics and infatuation with drugs. Their recordings have been the object of attack by Spiro Agnew and the FCC, as well as by right-wing organizations [Ed. note: see Epilogue].

Conflict between the group and their recording company, RCA, has accompanied the recording and release of nearly all their albums. Their lyrics have been censored, usually to delete language which might restrict air-play or which could offend the listener (or more likely, his parents). The design of their album covers has also been restricted.[24] There was also a conflict concerning the price of their third album, which the group felt was too expensive. The album has since been re-released at a significant reduction in price.[25]

References to the role of the rock star and the expectations of the audience and the industry can also be found in the lyrics of songs by Doug Sahm and the Sir Douglas Quintet. The group had their first million selling single in 1965. At that time they lived in San Antonio, Texas, where most of them were born and raised. They are often credited with being one of the first American rock groups to successfully incorporate the British "sound" into their recordings. After their initial national Top Forty success they moved to San Francisco, where the "flower power and love" youth movement was beginning to evolve. Although they played a part in the movement—played the Family Dog and familiar ballrooms—they were never fully accepted by the youthful counterculture because of their initial Top Forty success.

In the song, "Stoned Faces Don't Lie / Baby, When You're High," Doug

[24] Ben Fong-Torres, "The *Rolling Stone* Interview: Grace Slick with Paul Kantner," *Rolling Stone,* 70 (November 12, 1970), pp. 24–30.

[25] Fong-Torres, *ibid.,* p. 24.

Sahm recalls the group's involvement in the emerging culture: the concerts at Golden Gate Park and the smiling faces of the intoxicated participants. The lyrics ask, rhetorically, what has happened to those days and the joy and optimism as well as the innocence which accompanied them. Another song, "Me and My Destiny," found on the same album, is a biographical account of the performer's infatuation with music, his initial success and rise to stardom, his move to San Francisco to "find himself" and his retreat to the Big Sur to avoid the pressures and expectations of both the audience and the industry, and finally his move back to San Antonio, again to "find himself."

Both these songs detail the conflicts of stardom. The first can be interpreted as an appeal to the audience to accept the changes which have occurred in the music and artist. This appeal is based on the values and experiences the performer shares with the audience and the current changes in the youth culture. In the second song, the performer recounts his personal experiences. He documents his own expectations as a performer for autonomy, privacy and the right to apply his own standards when judging his performance. While he acknowledges the contingent and conflicting expectations—presumably those of the audience and the industry—which accompany "stardom," the song reaffirms the primacy of the artist's expectations of himself and his dedication to his music.

Another illustration of the performer's expectations appearing in lyrics can be found in the recent recording by The Who entitled "We Won't Get Fooled Again." The song concerns the "revolution" of the counterculture and the rock musician's role within it. As the title indicates, the performer is disaffiliating himself from the political-cultural context of the audience. In doing so, he screams, ". . . the new boss / is the same as the old boss," implying that the current youth scene is corrupt and that the expectations and demands of the audience are no more valid than those of the corporate state against which their actions are directed. The performers return to their original interests, their music and their occupations by "picking up my guitar . . . just like yesterday." Thus, through sarcasm and satire, the musician separates himself from his audience, defines his own expectations as most important, and through the promotion of social distance attempts to minimize the conflict between himself and the audience. The Who is the same group that attained stardom in the youth culture by recording such songs as "My Generation," Eddie Cochran's "Summertime Blues," as well as the rock opera *Tommy*. But, as Peter Townshend, the leader of the group has said, "Pop audiences and pop musicians are geared to different time structures, they lead different lives entirely."[26]

Songs by rock stars about rock stars seem to reveal that the original conflict between the marginal performer and the dominant economic institution, the

[26] Jann Wenner, "The *Rolling Stone* Interview: Peter Townshend," *Rolling Stone,* 18 (September 28, 1968), p. 16.

recording industry, is often more easily resolved in favor of the star—with the star gaining control of his product—than the conflict between the performer's expectations and those of his audience. If the star is to retain his status and control his product in the industry, he must fulfill the expectations of the audience. If he resorts to standardized techniques to satisfy his audience, he may violate his own expectations of himself as an innovator and an artist. Thus, our schema would lead us to investigate the process whereby the performer may appeal to the audience to accept an innovation. Parasocial interaction suggests that such appeals are based upon values and characteristics possessed by the audience. These types of appeals are directed at the audience and delivered in the mode of direct address. They should be found in recordings which vary in style and content, both musically and lyrically, from the previous products of the stars.

The Beatles, who were enjoying unprecedented success in 1967, had gained virtually unlimited control over the production and distribution of their work with Capitol Records. In recording the album *Sgt. Pepper's Lonely Hearts Club Band,* the Beatles spent some 900 hours in the studio and nearly $100,000. They had hired the full London Philharmonic Orchestra and introduced instruments, lyrics and arrangements into a single product, the complexity of which was unprecedented in the period. They were also faced with the problem that their audience was changing, growing up. They had already attracted the attention of serious music critics as well as the various social critics of both the left and right political orientations. Given this situation—the status of the performers and the innovations in the product—it is not surprising to find direct address appeals to the audience in the introductory title song of the album, supporting the illusion of intimacy and interest. These appeals were based on values found in the emerging youth culture; the beginning of extensive drug use and widespread experimentation with mysticism and Eastern religious forms. It may not even be stretching the point too much to suggest that the appeal to "sit back and let the evening go" was an appeal based on the shared experience of drug and mystically induced intoxication. However, whether because of the illusions of intimacy, the direct appeal, or whatever, the album enjoyed a huge success.

The same technique has been employed more recently by one of the San Francisco bands, the Grateful Dead. Their two most recent albums show a marked departure from the sound, lyrically and musically, that was at least partially responsible for their original success. This case, however, varies from those previously discussed, because while they enjoyed much success in terms of demands for personal appearances and concert dates, they never experienced phenomenal success as a recording band. (They earned Warner Bros. Records only a modest profit.) However, they had achieved virtually autonomous control of the production process through rigorous contract negotiations with the industry. They, like the Jefferson Airplane, have been known as a group from the Haight-Ashbury scene and psychedelia. They continued to provide free entertainment for "community functions" of the youth culture, were involved with Ken Kesey, a leader of the psychedelic movement, and, until recently, they resided in the Haight district. The opening song (of a two album set)[27] contains an appeal to the audience to accept their product. This appeal is delivered in the first person and is based upon values they share with their audience. More specifically, they base their appeal on a characterization of the dominant culture:

> Their walls are built of cannonballs,
> Their motto is "Don't trek on me."
> — © Ice Nine Publishing Co.

This passage is followed by another which implies recognition of the audience's control of the performer's future and contains the appeal "won't you come with me."

The second album of this two album set ends with a similar type of song, "Truckin'." This selection is a complex piece, containing autobiographical vignettes of the band's experiences over the past five years, including getting "busted" for drugs while on tour and reminiscences of an old friend, presumably from the Merry Pranksters period, who is "living on reds, Vitamin C and cocaine." They respond, "All a friend can say is / Ain't it a shame." The implication here is that while the rock star shares many important characteristics and experiences with his audience, he has, over a period of time, come to interpret these experiences differently. It is an appeal by the artist to the audience to accept the performer's interpretation and his product. It may also be an appeal to the audience to re-examine its values and situation, based upon the performer's similar experiences. The song is an appeal by the performer for freedom from the rigid, ideological expectations of both the audience and the dominant social order.

The above material appears to indicate that the role of the rock star entails complex and conflicting expectations. The lyrics of selected songs suggest that the expectations directed toward the role incumbent from both the audience and 'the industry of rock may be in conflict and pull the performer in different directions. The expectations of both these groups, while antagonistic, may also conflict with the performer's expectations of himself and his work. Thus, unlike the local jazz musician studied earlier, the rock star must meet new and larger contingencies which result from the size, nature and values of the audience, as well as the values and rules of the dominant corporate order of American society.

The hypothesis that parasocial interaction, as conceptualized by Horton

---

[27] From an advertisement in the trade and underground papers. See "American Beauty: The Grateful Dead," *Rolling Stone,* 72 (Dec. 2, 1970), p. 2.

and Wohl, may be one means by which the performer and the audience act to reduce this conflict does appear to be supported by the data. Finally, the schema and the evidence suggests that the audience may take an active part, along with the industry and the performer, in maintaining the myth of the rock star as a counterculture leader and hero.

22

THE BLACK MARKET ROOTS OF ROCK

Charles Gillett

Practitioners and students of education well know that formal schooling is only one, and perhaps the least significant, aspect of what it means to grow up and learn in the American city. The mass media also teach; and while it is important to know what they teach, and how, it is equally important to discover how they learn—how, that is, they respond to demands from their audiences. This essay on the development of "rock 'n' roll" examines one instance of such "learning" and suggests that the dominance of this type of music in the popular culture of adolescents may have a social significance far beyond the probably ephemeral agitations that nightly transpire in the nation's dance halls.

Among the best-selling records in Negro communities in 1953 was "Hound Dog," recorded by Willie Mae Thornton for the Peacock Record Company, an independent Houston firm that specialized in gospel music. Three years later the same song reappeared in record stores, but this time it was sung by Elvis Presley, a former country-and-western singer who was now acclaimed as the foremost exponent of rock 'n' roll.

Willie Mae Thornton's version had never reached the white communities, owing to the lack of adequate distribution facilities available to a small company like Peacock. However, soon after Presley's "Hound Dog" was released, a Negro group's rendition of "Crying in the Chapel" joined three other versions of the song on the list of twenty best-selling records in white retail districts. This

From "Just Let Me Hear Some of That Rock and Roll Music," *Urban Review* 1 (Dec. 1966), pp. 11–14. Reprinted with permission of publisher.

group called themselves the Orioles and, like Willie Mae Thornton, they had recorded for an independent company, Jubilee, of New York.

The appearance of the Orioles among the nation's top singers signaled a new era in popular music, in which the tastes of white and Negro consumers would become increasingly similar and consequently bring about an unprecedented degree of mutual imitation in the singing styles of the two cultures.

Willie Mae Thornton's singing style had elements of blues and gospel music which could be traced back to the date of the first recorded blues—1920. Historians have mapped out the development of Negro vocal music from its origins in the country blues of street singers and the classic blues of female band vocalists, through the shouting blues of male band singers and the rhythm-and-blues of Delta-born, Chicago-based nightclub singers to the various dance-oriented styles of T-bone Walker, B. B. King, Fats Domino, and Chuck Berry.[1] The many different styles of gospel singing have been less carefully studied, but they evidently have origins far back in the past of the Negro musical tradition, and were constantly changed as new techniques of amplification and accompaniment were introduced. But, before 1953, the innumerable blues-based or gospel-based styles shared a common feature in being almost totally ignored by the white audience of popular music. At various times aspects of the musical accompaniment—jazz—had been found attractive by this audience, usually in a bowdlerized form produced by white musicians; but the singers had rarely appealed to white persons outside the very small audience which has treated Negro popular music as part of its own "elite" culture.

The Orioles began recording in 1948; but their "sound" had very little apparent connection to Negro tradition. Sonny Til, the lead singer, affected an accentless, almost effeminate style, and sang in a high wavering tenor, against which the rest of the group pitched a series of unbroken wails, occasionally setting up a different rhythm to Til's. The result was a very distinctive musical effect, which owed something to the intense commitment characteristic of religious singers, and something to the popular "barbershop," close harmony style of the Ink Spots.

A number of factors combined to produce the Orioles' unusually rapid availability to and acceptance by their mixed audience. This essay is an examination of the changes in taste and cultural outlook that enabled it to happen.

Before 1955 Negro singers had to make a deliberate choice between white and Negro markets because the divergent tastes of the two audiences prohibited

---

[1] Samuel Charters, *The Country Blues* (New York: Rinehart, 1959); Charles Keil, *Urban Blues* (Chicago: University of Chicago Press, 1966); Charles Gillett, *The Evolution of Rock and Roll* (unpublished M. A. thesis, Teachers College, Columbia University, New York, 1966).

all but the most versatile singers from appealing to both. The difference in tastes was reinforced by an "institutional discontinuity" between the two markets—different companies supplied records to each of them. The white market was dominated by six recording companies before 1955 (Columbia, Decca, Victor, Capitol, MGM, and Mercury) to such an extent that they shared seventeen or eighteen of the twenty best-selling records throughout the ten-year period following the end of the war. In the Negro market these companies played a minor but predatory role. Because they so little understood the tastes of the Negro audience, they allowed the independent companies to field performers in the [black] community and then offered large contracts to the singers, or sometimes bought an entire firm to obtain a particular performer.

Negroes formed a relatively small part of the total popular music market—5.7 percent in 1953—but because it was the only segment open to real competition, the Negro market attracted many enterprising businessmen who employed various legitimate and illegitimate methods to establish a viable hold on it. These men constantly sought out new talent because all the established singers were already under contract to the major recording companies.

Independent companies existed in most of the large cities across the nation, including Chicago (Chess), Cincinnati (King), Houston (Peacock), Los Angeles (Modern, Specialty), Newark (Savoy), and New York (Atlantic and Jubilee). In contrast to the major companies in the white market, these smaller companies tended to specialize in particular aspects of Negro music: Chess and Modern concentrated on the rhythm-and-blues of the Delta-born singers; King stressed a dance rhythm on most of their records, and recorded many dance bands.

The discontinuity between the white and Negro market-cultures, dividing the audiences, musical styles, singers, and institutions responsible for communicating the music, exemplifies a condition that Talcott Parsons has called the *exclusion* of a minority group from the mainstream of society. Parsons has suggested that there is a necessary order of social adjustments that must be made before a minority group is fully integrated in a society.[2] Drawing from an essay by T. H. Marshall that discussed how the British working class gained full citizenship in the nineteenth century,[3] Parsons used the term *inclusion* to express his concept of social integration. But, whereas Marshall had stressed the importance of educational qualifications in rendering the British working class *eligible* for what he called full citizenship, Parsons emphasized the changes required in the attitudes of the majority group to produce an *acceptance* of the

[2] Talcott Parsons, "Full Citizenship for the Negro?" *Daedalus* "The Negro American—1" (Fall, 1965).
[3] T. H. Marshall, *Sociology at the Crossroads* (London: Heineman, 1966).

minority group. Inclusion means that the larger society accepts the minority group as an entity and does not require each member of the minority to sever connections with his group and its culture in order to be accepted by the larger society. This latter kind of integration Parsons called *assimilation*, and he considered this to be an intermediate stage between total exclusion, when no members of the minority group were accepted, and total inclusion, when the entire group was accepted.

Using this vocabulary, one could say that in popular music before the mid-'fifties there was a generally exclusive situation, with some instances of assimilation. When Negro singers achieved unusually great popularity within the Negro market-culture, the major companies contracted them and recorded them for distribution to the white audience. Because of the differences in audience tastes, however, this procedure required considerable adjustments in the singer's style and mode of expression. Thus Billy Eckstine, Nat "King" Cole, Sarah Vaughn and Ella Fitzgerald made their reputations in the Negro market-culture singing jazz and blues songs; but then for the white market all switched to the kind of ballad-singing developed by such white singers as Bing Crosby, Frank Sinatra, and Jo Stafford. Traces of the original Negro jazz style remained, but the change was sufficient to deter most Negro record buyers, and these singers were never again as popular with Negroes as with whites. Thus these singers, to be assimilated into the white music culture, were required to change their styles and to sever their connections with their former audience. The Mills Brothers and the Ink Spots went through a similar process, though they were able to maintain their popularity with Negro audiences for some time after they became popular with whites.

To reach the white audience, a singer had to have a contract with a major company that had access to the national record distribution system; such a contract was granted only to those who had already established their reputations after years with a famous dance band. Therefore most young Negro singers modeled their styles on those of the less successful vocalists who were popular in the Negro market and whose careers were thought to be more within their reach, singers like Muddy Waters, Charles Brown, and Joe Turner.

Another model was the group structure of the Ink Spots whose style was more flexible than that of a Billy Eckstine, particularly for young singers who lacked the control to achieve Eckstine's smooth delivery. Because it was not directly connected to the Southern musical heritage, but grew out of white-Negro interaction, the harmony style proved to be a base from which Negro adolescents could evolve a specifically Northern urban sound. Standing on street corners, in school yards, and in tenement halls where they bounced echoes off the walls, Negro youths produced what they called "the ghetto sound," a new group sound. After the Orioles became the first to make a successful recording in this new style, with "It's Too Soon To Know" in 1948, the independent record companies quickly began to look for more groups, and welcomed applications for auditions. These companies assumed a new role in the popular music industry by taking on unknown singers and presenting them to the public through their records, and thereby creating an audience for public performances instead of capitalizing on the demand from an existing audience.

This group sound developed into a major genre in Negro popular music by 1954, but apart from the success of "Crying in the Chapel," Negro singers before that time had not been popular in the white market. Then, during 1954, several groups employing variations of "the ghetto sound" made records which reached the top twenty lists, revealing both a change in audience tastes and a breakdown in the dominance of the white market by the major record companies.

The change in taste seems to have resulted from the new adolescent self-consciousness that developed throughout the country during the early 'fifties. Partly as a result of the increased affluence which came with more generous allowances from parents, and partly because prolonged education kept adolescents together longer, an adolescent subculture developed. This expressed itself sometimes violently in various kinds of anti-adult rebellion, and more often in stylized selections from mass-produced consumer goods and mass-communicated entertainment.

Peg pants, motor-bikes, expressions like "dig"—each person has his own memory of those times, as a participant adolescent, or as an incredulous adult. But perhaps the best mnemonic to the mood of the early 'fifties is Nicholas Ray's film *Rebel Without a Cause,* with James Dean, whose role epitomized the ambivalent emotions of loyalty and independence being felt with a new strength by his audience. Dean and Marlon Brando became cultural models, whose behavior on and off the screen drew from the attitudes of their adolescent audience and contributed to them.[4]

In the same year that *Rebel Without a Cause* played to restless but enthusiastic audiences throughout the United States and many other parts of the world, Richard Brooks completed production of *Blackboard Jungle.* The film was released in early 1956, and often caused a violent response by its younger audiences. The initial excitement arose from the song "Rock Around the Clock," which was played over the titles of the film. Youngsters who had previously listened to the music only in places where they could dance proceeded to tear out the seats of the movie houses and to dance in the aisles. The excitement caused by the song was reinforced by the content of the film, which included several scenes in which school students defied or beat up their teachers. And in one scene which symbolized the mood of the film and its audience, a class of students destroyed the record collection of a teacher who had brought in jazz and swing records, by Stan Kenton, Harry James and others, to play to his class.

[4] Edgar Morin, *The Stars* (New York: Evergreen Profile Book, 1960).

The plot of *Blackboard Jungle* was more involved than this characterization indicates, being concerned with the rationale of vocational high schools, the problems of punishing a Negro student without implying prejudice, and with the mandatory sexual relationships of American fiction. But the association of the film's violent content with "rock 'n' roll" music was part of the adult perception of the music as an expression of youth's violent attitude towards authority.

But while the film industry responded to (and helped shape) the new adolescent consciousness relatively quickly, the popular music industry gave little sign of recognizing any change in its audience's structure of feeling. The singers during the early 'fifties were the same singers who had made their reputations as dance-band vocalists in the previous decade or more—Doris Day, Jo Stafford, Perry Como. Some others had become well-known as singers on live radio shows. The record companies did not expect to promote an unknown singer and were geared to the prewar industrial structure in which publishers had been the dominant element. Songs were submitted to record companies, each of which then produced a version by one of their singers who did not happen to have a popular record on recent release. Often several versions of the same song were simultaneously on the hit parade. The style of the singer does not seem to have been a significant consideration in determining his suitability for a song—only his or her availability.

Meanwhile, the audience began looking elsewhere to satisfy its changing tastes and new mood. White listeners began to tune into Negro radio stations. By 1954 there were 700 radio stations across the country providing Negro popular music for Negro communities. The insistent rhythm of the blues-influenced songs, and the intense emotions of the group sound contrasted sharply with the bland "sing-along" records played over the white-oriented radio stations. The most celebrated of these was Cleveland's WJW-Radio, which broadcast Alan Freed's "Moondog's Rock and Roll Party" from 1952. Freed, playing only Negro records, developed a large white audience and had an important part in popularizing Negro music among white Americans, particularly after he moved to New York's WINS-Radio in 1954.

The white audiences of these stations grew steadily throughout the early 'fifties and in 1956, of the four available versions of "Crying in the Chapel," the one preferred by the largest group of record buyers was the Orioles', heard initially over the broadcasts intended for the Negro community. Having pressured their local retailers in vain to supply the records they heard on Negro radio stations, the white listeners had to buy the records in Negro districts. The white retailers, seeing the lost trade, began to deal with the independent distributors supplying the Negro records. The major companies, feeling the competition, tried to forestall it by a second stage of assimilation. Having previously recorded Negro singers using white styles, they now recorded the popular Negro songs using white singers imitating the Negro styles, a procedure known as "covering." Thus the McGuire Sisters covered Negro versions of "Goodnight, Sweetheart, Goodnight" and "Sincerely" for Decca's subsidiary, Coral; and the Crew Cuts covered "Earth Angel" and "Sh-Boom" for Mercury. The two most important major companies, Columbia and RCA-Victor, did not join this trend until 1955, when both companies recorded versions of "Ko-Ko-Mo," with Tony Bennett and Perry Como. Neither singer's style was appropriate to the song's simple beat, but until the major companies discovered singers better suited to the idiom, they persisted in using their older performers.

This method of assimilation delayed the inclusion of Negro singers using original material in their own styles throughout 1954 and much of 1955. But by 1956 several Negroes had defeated the competition from white versions of their songs, and reached high positions in the bestselling lists for white retailers. White singers who could offer nothing beyond their copies of Negro songs lost popularity, or, like Pat Boone, adopted a more conventional white singing style which had no connection with rock 'n' roll.

The first relatively original white style was that of Bill Haley and the Comets, a former country-and-western group that adopted the instrumental line-up and emphatic off-beat of rhythm-and-blues groups as early as 1953. Unlike his contemporaries, Haley used original material, with the exception of "Shake, Rattle and Roll." Joe Turner's version of the song, written by Charles Calhoun, was recorded for the Negro market and contained several allusions to sexuality of a maturity that Haley felt unable to retain in a song recorded for the white market. . . .

From the beginning rock 'n' roll had been identified with a youthful rebellion against conventional morality. In the South, churchmen regarded the commercial dissemination of the music as part of an NAACP plot to corrupt the nation's (and particularly Southern) youth.[5] Further criticism came from the American Society of Composers, Authors and Publishers (ASCAP), the long-established defender of royalty rights. Billy Rose of ASCAP was vehement in his opposition to the less formal Broadcast Music Inc. (BMI), with which most songwriters for the Negro market were affiliated and whose importance in the white market was growing rapidly with the popularity of rock and roll. "Not only are most of the BMI songs junk," said Rose, "but in many cases they are obscene junk, pretty much on a level with dirty comic magazines."[6] And Bill Haley insisted in an interview: "We steer completely clear of anything suggestive; we take a lot of care because we don't want to offend anybody. The music is the main thing, and it's just as easy to write acceptable words."[7]

[5] *The New York Times*, March-April, 1956.
[6] Vic Fredericks (ed.), *Who's Who in Rock 'n' Roll* (New York: Fall, 1958).
[7] "Rock 'n' Roll Personality Parade," *Weekly Film News* (London: 1957).

Haley and the Comets were the first white rock 'n' roll singers to achieve national and then international popularity but the group was weak both musically and vocally and lacked the ability to adjust to the more sophisticated tastes of the audience after it had become familiar with the authentic Negro exponents of rock 'n' roll. As Haley's weaknesses became apparent, a more creative singer replaced him as the most popular white rock 'n' roll singer. Elvis Presley shared Haley's country-and-western background, but had the advantages of being younger and better-looking, and having excellent vocal control.

Presley drew from several stylistic sources, religious and secular, white and Negro, and succeeded in expressing the peculiar quality of the emergent rebelliousness of his generation more effectively than any other singer. His records sold well in Negro markets until he lost spontaneity and had to try to contrive excitement or else fall back on the conventional ballad mode of expression.

By 1956, then, the popular music culture included Negro music—the styles, singers, and record companies—and affected (and was affected by) the industrial structure which linked composers, singers, record company personnel, radio stations, and audiences in a much more intimate and responsive relationship than had previously existed in the white market. After the breakdown of the domination of the industry by the major companies, record companies were much more accessible to new composers and singers, and began to commission songs for particular singers.

*   *   *

In the past ten years popular music has strengthened its role as the chief medium of expression for adolescents; the age-level of singers, composers, and record company personnel has dropped steadily to a relatively stable twenty years for singers and twenty-five for composers. Throughout this time most of the musical changes have resulted from white interpretations of Negro styles, interpretations which have brought the original Negro exponents into prominence. Contemporary adolescents have become accustomed to seeing Negro singers on television and on stage shows. The Negro has always been acclaimed as an exceptional entertainer, though without any significant resultant change in white social attitudes towards Negroes in general. Moreover, Negroes had previously had to adjust their style to accommodate white taste. Now, he entertains in his own style. Does this fact indicate a more general tolerance of the Negro as he is? I would not press the question; this essay has attempted to show only that the one instance of inclusion in American society matches the model described by Talcott Parsons. If the Negro is to be more generally included within the society, there must be structural upheavals comparable to those which took place in the music industry between 1954 and 1956. And for such upheavals there must first be pressure from the including group—white Americans.

23

THREE ERAS IN THE MANUFACTURE OF POPULAR MUSIC LYRICS

Richard A. Peterson and David G. Berger

There has been a radical change in popular music over the period from 1948 to 1968. While all its aspects have changed, the difference in lyrical content has received the most widespread academic as well as popular attention. Sex, drugs, social commentary, war, and race pride, all taboo subjects in 1948, were widely voiced two decades later. Even the travail of romantic love, that continuing staple of popular songs, was often being phrased in entirely new terms. "I want to be yours forever somewhere beyond the stars" had given way to "Let's spend the night together" and "Let's do it in the road."

Most explanations of this difference are rooted in the assumption that there has been a rapid change in public consciousness, but this is, at best, a partial explanation. It does not take into the account either the long-term trends in popular music or the ways it has been influenced by changes in the technology of disseminating popular culture, the music industry structure, and the market of popular songs. The interplay between consciousness and these latter elements will be shown by tracing their interaction in three eras of American popular music from 1750 to the present. The popular songs of each era will be described first. Then the structure of the industry producing the music will be analyzed.

In each of the three eras, as well as in a fourth which seems to be emerging,

We are most grateful for the helpful suggestions of Howard S. Becker, R. Serge Denisoff, Norman K. Denzin, Alvin W. Gouldner, Paul M. Hirsch, Jerry Hopkins, Proctor Lippincott, Claire L. Peterson, and Eugene Weinstein given over the six years since the first draft of this paper was delivered at the 1967 meetings of the Southern Sociological Society.

there is a close association between the nature of the industry and the messages contained in the lyrics. What is more, changes in the former precede changes in the latter in each case. This leads us to conclude that the outspoken rock lyric of the 1960's (and the counterculture it animated) were largely unintended byproducts of earlier mundane changes in technology, industry structure, and marketing.

I. BROADSIDES AND BALLADS (1750–1890)

Until the middle of the eighteenth century, popular music was transmitted almost entirely as an oral tradition nurtured by troubadours and street singers and absorbed into the general folklore by amateur musicians (Ashton, 1888). The turmoil of the American Revolutionary War era, however, saw the development of a regular topical song market. "Broadsides," consisting of newly written lyrics set to a familiar tune, were struck off and sold on street corners like penny newspapers. They chronicled the various events leading to the war, depicted each major battle, and hymned the praises of revolutionary leaders. (Dichter and Shapiro, 1941; Ewen, 1961:5–10). Our national anthem, "The Star-Spangled Banner," was penned during the British bombardment of the Baltimore harbor defenses during the War of 1812 and published as a broadside the next day as "The Defense of Fort McHenry."

After the war the fledgling industry turned to bawdy love songs, political commentary and current events. Prosperity, depression, the Whiskey Rebellion, international events, canal and railroad construction, Indian massacres, major crimes, campaign slogans, political corruption, immigration policy, land acquisition and many more themes were chronicled in popular songs (Greenway, 1953; Ewen, 1961:10–14; Mattfeld, 1962).

These topical broadsides were produced at little expense in composition, production, or distribution in many small print shops in each of the major cities of the United States (Dichter and Shapiro, 1941; Howe, 1917). Because the market was fiercely competitive and as much oriented to disseminating news as providing entertainment, the wide-ranging topical subject matter and polemical style were quite appropriate. As a means of disseminating news, the broadside could not compete with the newspaper as literacy became more nearly universal; but it represented the first commercialization of the traditional topical folk-tune medium.[1]

---

[1] In sharp contrast with the popular music of this century, a higher proportion of the printed broadsides dealt with topical matters than did the popular music carried through the oral tradition of the time. This latter music more often dealt with love, religious, and moral problems (Greenway, 1953).

Nineteenth-Century Secular Sermons

For most of the nineteenth century, new tunes were disseminated by touring troupes such as the Hutchinson family. Their repertoires contained numerous sentimental ballads and novelty tunes which parodied the ways of new immigrants (particularly Irish and German), and blacks. Many of the numerous "sentimental ballads" of the nineteenth century were painfully realistic in chronicling the travails of particular lovers, the deceits of salesmen, the fruits of alcoholism, the pains of industrial accidents, and the tragedy of natural catastrophes.[2]

Songs of Henry Russell, the most commercially successful composer of sentimental ballads before the Civil War, are typical of the realism inherent in this genre. Many of his 800 songs attack slavery and alcoholism, lament the demise of preindustrial Americana, and chronicle the shocking conditions prevalent in insane asylums. His popular ballad "The Maniac," for example, describes in clinical detail the successive stages of insanity produced by institutionalization. Not simply pandering to popular taste, Russell clearly saw song-writing as a means of working for social reform (Ewen, 1961:18–19). Whereas the eighteenth-century broadside had been a form of news, these nineteenth-century sentimental ballads were secular sermons.

The small broadside-printing industry did not grow during most of the nineteenth century for reasons of market and law. The market for sheet music was usually small and when a song did excite great interest the copyright laws of the time did not effectively prevent the production of multiple issues of the same song for which the author and publisher received no royalty. To make a living, song writers sold the performance rights to their material (often for no more than $25) to touring performers or traveled as singers themselves (Ewen, 1961, 1962). Not until the end of the century with the enactment and policing of firmer copyright laws enacted in 1870, 1897 and 1909 (Shemel and Krasilovsky, 1965) and the consolidation of the Tin Pan Alley music business in New York, did sheet music publishing become the center of the popular music industry.

II. THE TIN PAN ALLEY ERA (1890–1950)

The diverse topical music of the era just discussed contrasts sharply with the popular music of the more recent past. A vast majority of all popular songs of the first half of the twentieth century deal with the stages of courtship in

[2] This amalgam of sentiments which provided the text for nineteenth-century popular ballads is still central in "country" music (Malone, 1968), whose fans are a decade older than those of what is now defined as "popular" music. The changing ethos of popular music during the past century may reflect the lower age of the consumers of popular music as much as any great change in American values.

rather abstract and romantic terms. Neither depression, economic boom, ethnic conflict, prohibition, the New Deal, nor World War II brought forth any number of topical hit-parade tunes.[3]

Berger (1966) clearly shows a nearly universal focus on love themes in popular music over the first half of this century in his study based on songs taken at five year intervals between 1910 and 1950 from the hit tunes listed by the American Society of Composers, Authors and Publishers (ASCAP), which was the prime music royalty collection agency of the period. In each of the nine years sampled, no fewer than seven of the ten tunes selected were on a love theme while over the entire period, 82 of the 90 songs were on love themes. Almost without exception, these do not place love in any larger institutional or social framework. They praise the hedonistic powers of love and the hurt felt in its loss. The few songs which do not deal with love, create a mood of nostalgia for a place or a time, such as "Lullaby of Broadway" or are novelty tunes such as "Rag Mop." Berger's data extend only through 1950, but Horton (1957) finds strikingly similar results in a study of the popular songs of 1954. Fully 83.4 percent of the 235 songs he analyzed are on love themes in the conventional mode. These studies, as well as those by Adorno (1941), Riesman (1950), Hayakawa (1955) and Mooney (1954) highlight the dream-filled idealized escapist tone of pop tune lyrics during the first half of the century.

Thus, seen in historical perspective, the pallid pop song of the early twentieth century stands out in clear contrast to the older tradition of topical popular songs. In large part the Tin Pan Alley formula-tune was a product of the oligopolistic concentration of the music industry in a few firms.

The Tune Factory

Physically, Tin Pan Alley was located in a number of publishing firms on and near Union Square in New York City but as Ewen (1961:49–50) notes:

Tin Pan Alley refers to a way of life in American popular music—
a way of life in which the American popular song became a big busi-

---

[3] Only the great debate over our entry into the First World War is a partial exception to this generalization. And even here the songs which became popular in successive years reflect changing popular opinion on the war issue. For example, "Don't Take My Darling Boy Away" and "I Didn't Raise My Boy To Be A Soldier,"—hits of 1914— gave way by 1917 to "America Needs You Like A Mother—Would You Turn A Mother Down?" "Over There," and "Hello, Central, Give Me No Man's Land," and were followed a year later by the bitter-sweet "Oh! How I Wish I Could Sleep Til Daddy Comes Home" and "She Gave Her Only Begotten Son" (Mattfield, 1962; Ewen, 1961: 86–87; ASCAP, 1964: 5–12). Throughout the Tin Pan Alley period there continued to be a lively demand for more polemical lyrics (Greenway, 1953). As we will show, this demand was partially satisfied through channels beyond the mass market.

ness, . . . a way of writing songs to established patterns and a science of marketing and popularizing them. . . . The publishers sensed that a song could be sold to the public like any other commodity—through continual and unrelenting exposure.

Tin Pan Alley procedures emerged in the 1880's on the wave of a rising popular demand for sheet music to be played on the home piano, the newly fashionable adornment of middle-class living rooms. To be acceptable for this market, tunes and rhythms had to be kept simple and rigidly uniform. What is more, lyrics could not offend Victorian sentimentalities. Several songs, including "Grandfather's Clock" and "Silver Threads Among the Gold" sold over a million copies of sheet music; and a host of publishers, their property rights to songs now clearly protected by law, tried to repeat this bonanza. Between 1900 and 1910 almost 100 songs sold over a million copies each (Ewen, 1961:79).

In a market soon flooded with products, the only way to sell a song was by vigorous "plugging." Famous singers and bandleaders were paid to play a new song—often by granting them co-authorship so that they shared in royalties. Songs were placed into musical stage reviews; children were coached to "spontaneously" sing a new song during lulls in vaudeville performances. Pluggers sang their wares in department stores, railroad stations, public parks, and anywhere else a crowd might gather. This new importance of song promotion greatly increased the costs of production and squeezed out those unable or unwilling to pay the costs necessary to gain public exposure. Thus, by the first decade of this century a small number of publishing firms had attained effective control of the mass market for popular music (Goldberg, 1930; Spaeth, 1934; Ewen, 1964).

Changing Technology

Tin Pan Alley, originally geared to producing sheet music, successfully adapted to the production and marketing of player piano rolls, cylinder records, shellac 78 rpm records, 45 rpm discs, LP's, prerecorded tape cassettes, quadrasonic sound, and TV cassettes.[4] The new media of radio, movies, and TV have replaced personal appearances as the prime means of song plugging. Through the first half of the twentieth century every successive stage in technological advance tended to reinforce the tendency to oligopolistic concentration of the industry because each increased the costs of production and promotion which had

---

[4] The adaptation, while complete, was never smooth. At almost every turn, the largest companies began research on innovations only after smaller rivals, companies in other industries, or foreign competitors were ready to market the innovation (Gelatt, 1966; Klein, 1968).

to be paid before a record or a performer who was to be promoted into "star" status could give any return on the investment (Merz, 1928; Goldberg, 1930; Green, 1962; Shemel and Krasilovsky, 1965; Ewen, 1964; Gillett, 1970).

The prime mechanism for insuring the success of the large initial investment has been the vertical concentration of the industry. Music publishing companies became closely linked to the record-making companies who retained performers under long-term exclusive contract. These record companies, in turn, were linked to Broadway theatres, movie studios, and broadcast networks. Thus, through the years the various factors of production—talent, reputation, copyright, distribution, and promotion—became concentrated into several huge combines (Goldberg, 1930; Ewen, 1961, 1964; Green, 1962; Belz, 1969; Gillett, 1970; Hopkins, 1970; Shaw, 1971). What is more, the Great Depression did much to drive independent companies out of the field so that by the end of World War II there were but four major companies in the popular music field— Capitol, Columbia, Decca, and RCA Victor. The oligopolistic concentration of the industry can be seen from the fact that, in 1949, these four companies owned all but seven of the 63 records which were *ever* listed on the weekly *Billboard* "Top Ten" charts for that year.

The industry structure and marketing tactics of the first half of the century provided little incentive for merchandising controversial tune lyrics. Rather, it was more profitable to write songs in the accepted escapist love formula in order to catch as wide a segment of the market as possible. Success came from marketing a song that was more "average" than any of the others then being offered. This strategy was codified early; by 1900 songs were literally manufactured according to a number of fixed formulas and promoted in standard ways. In 1908 a pamphlet appeared on how to write hit tunes by formula (Ewen, 1964), and a number of similar pamphlets and books were written through the Tin Pan Alley era (Silver and Bruce, 1939; Korb, 1949). The economics which insured the homogeneity of product in this mass market industry are not unlike those that produced the formula Hollywood movies of the 1930's, the Detroit automobile of 1946–1965, and the TV series of the 1960's.

The Tin Pan Alley mass media-disseminated popular music represents only the most conspicuous music of the time, however. Beneath the surface several sorts of "communal" music—that is, music not merchandised through the mass media but disseminated primarily through live performance to relatively homogeneous groups of fans—developed in the first half of this century. Each of these: blues (Johnson, 1929; Gellert, 1936; Ames, 1950; Oliver, 1960; Keil, 1966); jazz (Jones, 1963; Peterson, 1967; Miller and Skipper, 1968); country and western (Malone, 1968); gospel (Larkin, 1970); and trade union and Radical Left (Denisoff, 1971a) expressed contrasting world views and engaged in political-social commentary much as popular music had done before it was commercialized. Thus, taken as a whole, popular music consisted of an ideologically sterile mass media-disseminated mainstream and several ideologically rich but segmented communal side streams.

The continuing vitality of these communal genre strongly suggests that Tin Pan Alley popular music did not reflect the range of sentiments that the mass audience would pay to hear. Even more telling evidence is provided by the explosive popular reaction which occurred when one or another of the communal musics entered the mainstream. The two major cases are, of course, the injection of jazz in the early 1920's (Leonard, 1962; Peterson, 1972) and the far greater incursion of blues and country music as rock 'n' roll after 1954. In that year, the industry sold $213 million worth of records, but by 1957 sales had more than doubled, reaching $460 million (*Billboard,* 1968: 12).

But a communal music has never entered the mainstream unchanged. For the most part, the rawer elements of rhythm, melody, and lyric have been altered or kept entirely out of the mainstream pop renditions.[5] The reasons for this censorship show much of the nature of social control in a liberal democracy, for it was performed in the pursuit of profit rather than in the interest of the state or church by police or priests.

The form that the censorship of recorded music has taken is primarily a result of the close link between the radio and recording industries. In 1927 the Radio Act was passed and its provisions were incorporated in the Federal Communications Act of 1934. These laws disavowed government censorship but asserted that licensed radio stations must "maintain a level of decency" to keep their right to broadcast over public air waves. Over the years, organized religious groups and those with a financial stake in the standard forms of popular music mounted numerous campaigns to have the Federal Communications Commission ban certain songs or song styles. For example, as late as 1938 the Bach Society of New Jersey petitioned the Commission to ban the playing of all "jazz" on the radio because it was deemed a corrupting form of music (Leonard, 1962: 100). The radio industry, like the movie industry of the same era, responded by establishing a self-censorship far more restrictive than that which the government would enforce. Radio networks developed internal censorship under the euphemistic titles of "Continuity Acceptance" and "Continuity Editing." Those topical songs which were recorded, such as Billie Holiday's "Strange Fruit," a bitter commentary on the institution of lynching, were not broadcast over the air. By 1942 the National Broadcasting Company had officially "blacklisted" the lyrics of 290 songs (Leonard, 1962:100–101) and many more were banned in the early days of rock 'n' roll (Belz, 1969: 57–59).

Since mainstream popular music is merchandised by receiving repeated ex-

---

[5] Case studies of industry-based censorship are provided for the 1920's and 1930's by Leonard (1962: 109–119); the 1940's by Brand (1962), Russell (1970) and Denisoff (1971a); and the 1950's and 1960's by Keil (1966), Belz (1969), Gabree (1968), Gillett (1970), and Hopkins (1970).

posure on radio and TV, the industry became oriented to producing only those songs that could meet the current standards for air-play. And, at the same time, the close oligopolistic control of the industry which characterized the Tin Pan Alley era meant that there was no competitive pressure to *test* the boundaries of permissible lyrics.

III. THE ROCK ERA (1950–1970)

The mass media-merchandised popular music has changed over the past two decades, taking on many of the rhythmic, melodic, and lyrical characteristics of the various underground musics. The physical and social *image* of the performing groups as well as the rock beat and electronic guitar sound of popular music of the late 1960's stands in sharp contrast to the popular music of 1948 purveyed by Bing Crosby, Dinah Shore and Vaughn Monroe; yet have the lyrics changed to a comparable degree?

Numerous recent articles and books have noted a marked change in the lyrics of mainstream popular music beginning with the advent of rock 'n' roll in the mid-1950's.[6] Comparing Tin Pan Alley with rock lyrics, they find the latter to be less sentimental, not as abstract or conformist, and less myopically focused on the travails of love. Instead, they are addressed to the problems of teenagers, to sexual suggestion, and are increasingly critical of middle-class American beliefs and behavior generally. All these commentators, however, select particular songs or song writers, and these may not fairly represent the total range of songs which have been popular during this time.

The Changing Message

In order to get a more representative sample of hit tunes, the authors have content-analyzed the lyrics of ten tunes from each of the even years between 1948 and 1958 and in each of the years from 1960 to 1970.[7] Songs were selected at random from the *Billboard* Magazine's listing of all songs ever to reach the weekly Top Ten (in recordings and records sold, jukebox and radio aired) in each year sampled. Recognizing the pitfalls in the method of content analysis (Denzin, 1970; Holsti, 1969; Denisoff and Levine, 1971; DiMaggio, 1971), our results are compared with the similar studies made by Horton (1957) and

[6] Published works that focus on the change in lyrics by choosing particular songs include (Scodel, 1961; Mooney, 1968; Gabree, 1968; Robinson and Hirsch, 1969; Rosenstone, 1969; Belz, 1969; Allen, 1969; Hopkins, 1970; Gillett, 1970; Laing, 1970; Melly, 1971).

[7] The authors would like to thank Steven Cobb, Diane Levy and Claire L. Peterson for assisting in the coding process.

Carey (1969a; 1969b) of song lyrics published in 1955 and 1966 in *Hit Parader* magazine, and, in the Carey study, of a sample drawn from *Billboard* magazine hit tunes as well.

Both authors classify their songs into five stages of a "courtship cycle," plus seven other categories: narrative ballads, religious songs, other ballads, comic songs, dance songs, tune songs, and miscellaneous. We have used the same scheme but for presentation here have compressed their five stages of love into three: (1 and 2) courtship, which includes wanting a partner and trying to get one; (3) honeymoon, the enjoyment of love; and (4 and 5) the dissolution and end of the relationship. We will discuss the other six categories when they are a substantial part of the subsample under consideration.

Our data show clear shifts over time which can be described in terms of three distinct internally stable periods (1948–1952, 1954–1958, 1960–1965), and a final five-year period (1966–1970) which has two distinct phases. Fully 90 percent of the tunes of the pre-rock 1948–1952 era are in the conventional love cycle. Of the latter, 33 percent deal with courtship, 15 percent with honeymoon, and 52 percent with dissolution of love. These figures clearly parallel those of Berger (1966) for the entire Tin Pan Alley era.

The songs of 1954–1958 show the influx of teen-oriented rock 'n' roll. Comic and dance tunes such as "Short Shorts" comprised 20 percent of the sample but 73 percent of the songs are still in the conventional love mode. Among these, however, 59 percent deal with the teenage problems of finding love while only 27 percent deal with love's dissolution. Horton's (1957) data for this period show the same shift, although not in the same degree.

The 1960–1965 period saw the increasing commercialization of rock 'n' roll into several cliche formulae (Belz, 1969:88–108; Gillett, 1970:51–58; Hopkins, 1970:38–52) and Beatle-mania (Taylor, 1966). Our data show a stable 77 percent of songs in the conventional love mode but 8 percent of the others are folk genre social ballads on non-love themes such as "If I Had a Hammer," and 8 percent are songs extolling the Twist, Watusi, and similar dance styles. Within the domain of love lyrics the accent is no longer predominantly on the courtship stage. It occupies only 39 percent of the love songs, 13 percent celebrate the honeymoon, while fully 48 percent deal with love's dissolution.

The 1966–1970 period saw the flowering of electronic rock and self-conscious artistry (Belz, 1969:168–177, 209–219). A new complexity of lyrical themes as exemplified by "Sounds of Silence," "Yellow Submarine," "Judy in Disguise," and "Let it Be," is indexed by the fact that during the 1950's our sample songs had a medium length of 82 words in unrepeated lyrical lines, while the songs of the 1960's have an average of 137 unrepeated lines. Fully 15 percent of the lyrics of the 1966–1970 period could not be fit into any of our 12 categories, and our coders reported difficulty in coding other songs of this period. Carey (1969a) reports the same problem; nevertheless, his results are quite comparable with ours. He finds 64 percent of his *Hit Parader* and 63 percent of his *Billboard* samples are in the conventional love mode, while a comparable 64 percent of our songs for the period are in this mode.

Within the five-year period, however, our data show a radical shift of focus. In the first three years, 1966–1968, 73 percent deal with the dissolution of love while only 21 percent deal with courtship and 5 percent with honeymoon. In the latter years, 1969–1970, there is a resurgence of courtship (38 percent) and honeymoon (23 percent), and a drop in songs dealing with love's dissolution (38 percent), almost to the level of the early rock period of 1954–1958. In this period, however, religious songs, never before a notable genre, represented 10 percent of the sample. Thus, love still spins more than half of the top hit songs but it is significantly less predominant than during the late Tin Pan Alley era.

An even more complete change has taken place in the mood of hit songs. Several authors have noted that the saccharine-romantic mood of Tin Pan Alley tunes stands in stark contrast to the more frank and realistic tunes of folk, soul, or country (Hayakawa, 1954; Malone, 1968; Larkin, 1970). Our 170 songs were coded as romantic versus realistic. Our three coders disagreed on 18 percent of the lyrics, but the trend over time is quite clear. In the 1948–1952 period all three agreed that 80 percent were romantic. Between 1954 and 1963 the romantic songs dropped gradually from 50 percent to 10 percent of the sample. For 1964 through 1967 *none* were romantic, while for 1968 through 1970, 20 percent were classed as romantic by all three coders.

Next, we analyzed the message in the lyric. Again the classification of a given song is not always clear but the general trend is quite consistent.[8] In the early 1948–1952 period, 81 percent of the songs have nonsense lyrics, express personal states, or describe interpersonal relations. The other four songs of this period describe a moral dilemma and three of these find a conformist resolution. The 1954–1958 period shows much the same pattern except that three songs including "Transfusion" exalt deviant ways of life. In the 1960–1965 period, we find the first three songs, including "Busted," pointing to a general social problem. One of these, "If I Had a Hammer," points to a collective solution. In the most recent period, 1966–1970, there are 50 songs, four of which express

---

[8] Lyrics were evaluated on the basis of written words. No account was taken of the musical "packaging" they were given in the hit rendition. Such performance and sound effects clearly affect the impact of the lyric but it is not easy to quantify the obvious difference in the musical packaging between a hit tune of 1950 and 1970. Where the former is sentimental, the latter tends to be both rhythmic and tonally arresting. While records of the later period sometimes more clearly accent the lyrics, others have almost unintelligible lyrics. The difference between "manifest" message and total effect is particularly striking in some of the tunes popular on black-oriented radio stations. For example, "Born Free," an innocuous theme tune from a movie about a tamed lion in Africa, when sung by a black group in the "pop-gospel" idiom with a chorus singing, "Born Free, Hallelujah!" becomes a stirring anthem of black pride.

an unresolved moral conflict, five point to a general social problem, and seven exalt a way of life deviant from middle-class standards. Carey (1969a:722) reports comparable results for his 1966 sample. Fully 68 percent of his rock 'n' roll songs had "lyrics which seemed to advocate or imply a more autonomous relationship between the sexes and/or criticized conventional society because of its misplaced preferences."

The Problem Restated

Thus far, we have made several points: (1) historically, popular folk music was rich with lyrics of social commentary; (2) the Tin Pan Alley formula tune was a product of a consolidation of a music industry which was dependent on mass market techniques of merchandising; (3) there was a continuing consumer demand for lyrics outside of the Tin Pan Alley mode; and (4) since 1948, and particularly in the 1960's, there has been a marked incursion of underground music into the mainstream of mass market-disseminated popular music. The history of the first two eras suggests that an explanation of these more recent shifts in popular music themes might be found by examining changes in industry structure, technology, and marketing practices. It is to this analysis that we now turn.

The Demise of Oligopoly

As noted earlier, a small number of companies enjoyed oligopolistic control of the popular music industry through the first half of this century. By the end of World War II, four companies, Capitol, Columbia, Decca, and RCA Victor, were preeminent in the industry. For the years 1948 through 1955 they averaged over 75 percent of all records which were ever on *Billboard's* weekly top ten Hit Parade. Their hegemony withered rapidly so that by 1958 the four companies had only 36 percent of the hits, and the average of the period from 1958–1968 is well below 33 percent.

The number of record companies having hits has expanded rapidly as well. For the 1948–1955 period only 8 to 11 companies had even one hit tune in a given year, but by 1958, 31 companies had hits, and over the 1959–1970 period an average of 37 companies had at least one hit per year. Many of these new independent companies including Atlantic, Motown, Cameo, Reprise, Epic, and Liberty, had become major corporations by the mid-1960's.[9] Thus, a large num-

---

[9] These figures were compiled by the authors from information provided by *Billboard* magazine. It was not always easy to classify companies because many company *labels* continue to be used on records long after the firm has been absorbed by another company. But we could not always learn the date upon which companies were absorbed. The analysis is further complicated by the fact that major companies, particularly in recent years, often distribute the product of more-or-less independent concerns.

ber of new companies have successfully entered the market and the greatest part of this influx took place in the short period between 1956 and 1959 with the entry of rock 'n' roll into the mass market.

A break in the oligopolistic control can be seen at yet another point in the industry structure. Before World War II, ASCAP, the only royalty collection agency then in existence, was a virtual closed shop of less than a thousand writers and 140 publishers. In 1941 a rival agency, Broadcast Music Incorporated (BMI), was formed by a number of independent radio stations. BMI began primarily with country and western songs but developed rapidly into the rhythm and blues area, the Detroit, Liverpool, and Nashville "sounds." ASCAP and BMI began to compete actively in recruiting new writers, and by 1960 there were ten thousand active professional songwriters and five thousands publishers. The growing importance of BMI can be seen from the following figures of the top song on the weekly Hit Parade over the years. In 1948 all tunes were controlled by ASCAP, and in the years through 1955 at least 50 percent of the tunes were ASCAP-controlled. From 1956 on, however, only two years have seen more than one-third of the tunes being ASCAP-controlled. (ASCAP, 1964; BMI, 1960, 1966).

Each of the other elements in the industry structure underwent a parallel shift from a closed shop to open competition between 1954 and 1960 (Hirsch, 1969; Peterson, and Berger, 1971). Thus, for the first time in seventy years the Tin Pan Alley masters lost control of the music industry. What broke the control of the big four record producers over popular music taste? We do not have the definite answer but we can point to a number of factors which together have been important.

Changing Radio Technology and Marketing Techniques

The first factor is the changed nature of radio which remains the key to selling records. In 1950, there were still only ten million TV sets in use, and radio continued as the prime form of family entertainment with 99 million sets in use. Radio then was oriented to the single large American audience, but by 1958 three television networks had captured this function with fifty million sets in use (*Billboard*, 1968:13). There were widespread predictions that radio would die out as soon as television technology improved so that it could reach virtually every American home. The radio networks dissolved and valuable radio franchises were sold at a loss.

Yet, the dismal predictions were not to come true, for the cheap, truly portable *transistor* radio was introduced in 1957 and sold by the millions two years later. Total radios in use, which had increased at a stable four million a year in the prior decade, rose 12 million in 1959 and have increased at least as rapidly each year since, so that by 1964 there were more radios than people in the United States (*Billboard*, 1968: 13). Now each family member could have a radio and it could follow wherever he went, whether at home, on the job, at school, in the car, or at play. That the announced death of radio was premature can be gauged from the fact that between 1950 and 1967 the number of AM stations doubled while the number of FM stations tripled, with most of this increase being due to the development of independent stations (*Billboard,* 1968: 13).

The revitalization of radio was due to a radical change in programming which began in the large cities in the mid-1950's and is still continuing. Rather than a few networks each changing the style of program over the course of the day to fit the interest of those family members most likely to be listening, the ten to 25 stations in a market now program music, information, and advertisements for one particular sort of listener, teen, black, country fan, housewife, etc., throughout the day. A Federal Communications Commission regulation promulgated in 1966 did much to press FM stations to single-format programming. In that year, the Commission required FM stations in cities with populations over 100,000 to broadcast a different program from their AM affiliate for at least 50 percent of their air time. After brief experiments with "public service programming," many FM stations found a lucrative market for topically oriented "underground" rock. Thus, most radio stations now have, in effect, only one program aimed at a single segment of the audience as long as they are on the air (Honan, 1967; Hirsch, 1969, 1972; Hopkins, 1970; Deni, 1971). This new marketing technique of single-format programming created a tremendous new demand for records specifically oriented to one or another of these special audiences.

Changing Music Industry Technology and Structure

Oriented to the large, middle-of-the-road market, the major record companies were ill-prepared in the mid-1950's to satisfy the newly apparent demand fostered by changes in radio formats (Gillett, 1970:59–134; Hirsch, 1971:65), and by the purchasing power inherent in the new wealth of teenagers, blacks, country-and-western fans, and other minorities. As we have already seen, the large corporations lost their predominance in the market after 1954 to a large number of newly formed independent companies.[10]

Several factors aided the entry of the new companies into the record market. The first is the way in which the introduction of high-fidelity plastic 45 and 33⅓ rpm records was managed. In 1948 when they were introduced, Columbia and RCA corporations intended them primarily for classical music which could not

---

[10] The large companies continued to earn profits throughout the period because they retained dominance in the older markets of popular and classical music while keeping control of the rapidly expanding country music market (McIntire, 1969). The new independent companies thrived in the exploding teen and soul music markets which accounted for most of the rapidly rising total industry sale figures (*Billboard,* 1968).

be recorded well on the short-play, fragile, low-fidelity, shellac 78 discs (Gellat, 1966). Banking on snob appeal, prices on the new format records were set well above cost to enhance the probability of profit. As a consequence, independent producers, sometimes literally working out of a garage, were able to turn a profit on sales of only a few thousand copies per record. Thus, for the first time in seventy years it was possible for an enterprising individual with little capital to enter the popular music field. What is more, one hit recording and rights to its performer could put the independent on the road to building a new corporate giant. Many failed, but notable among the early successes were the Chess Family of Chicago (Chess and Checker Records), Berry Gordy of Detroit (Motown), Ahmet Ertegun of New York (Atlantic), Sam Phillips of Memphis (Sun), and Phil Spector who made his first million dollars soon after turning twenty (Gillett, 1970:79–134). Each of these established his position by backing a different "sound" with a distinctive "message" for an element of the burgeoning potential market.

A second factor which helped the independents was a new form of "plugging" records. The "payola scandal" of 1959–1960 did much to open the radio and TV air-play to all producers. Payola was then a new word but the practice of bribing artists to feature a particular new tune is at least as old as the commercialization of popular music. For example, Sullivan, who with Gilbert produced the classic English operettas, almost a century ago got his early songs played by sharing royalties with the leading baritone of the time (Hopkins, 1970:50), and such bribed "plugging" was common practice during the Tin Pan Alley era.

The singular importance of radio in record promotion by 1940 focused attention on a few influential disc jockeys in the major cities. The major companies of the era regularly gave them inducements for playing particular songs which they wanted to be featured. As one promoter told Paul Hirsch (1969:62), "In those days you paid your money and got your hit. Today, nobody can predict what will be played on the air."

In the early 1950's rock 'n' roll was exposed to the mass public by a few venturesome deejays such as Alan Freed, operating out of independent stations and, later in the decade, by the television program Bandstand, hosted by Dick Clark. These men did much to expose the new music and its concomitant life styles (Hopkins, 1970:38–52; Belz, 1969:49–52, 101–108; Passman, 1971).[11] In an effort to curb the influence of the new independents, and protect their in-

---

[11] The role of the disc jockey as "gate keeper" in deciding what should be played on the air should be more carefully studied. On the one hand there is pressure from sponsors, the FCC, and citizen groups to avoid the controversial; on the other hand, there is the urge to hold an audience and to make a name through the "discovery" of new material. Presumably, the greater the competition between stations, the greater will be the latter pressures. For a picture of the linked careers of a deejay and a rock group, see "The Fifth Beatle" (Wolfe, 1965: Ch. 3).

vestment in the crooners they had promoted into stardom, the older established Tin Pan Alley-oriented companies "exposed" the payola practices of these new entrepreneurs in 1958. The ensuing Congressional investigation of 1959–1960, however, resulted in new federal laws which curbed the gross forms of payola by all companies (Green, 1962; Shemel and Krasilovsky, 1965). In the long run the new regulations did not eliminate payola, but they did open the product of *all* independents to wider mass media exposure.

Even when the large established companies began to sign contracts with any and all rock groups after the phenomenal success of the Beatles in the mid-1960's, the companies could not exercise the "artistic control" they had over the "first generation" of rock performers such as Elvis Presley (Hopkins, 1971). The rush to sign groups made for a "seller's market," in which the groups could demand the right to sing the songs they themselves were writing (Gleason, 1969; Hirsch, 1971:66–67; Melly, 1971:88–117).

The Developing Youth Class

We have traced the technological, organizational, and marketing changes in the radio and record industries which allowed the underground music of blacks and southern whites to rapidly infuse the popular music market. But to say that rock 'n' roll began as a sort of managerial mistake of Tin Pan Alley executives is not to deny the importance of the audience in its later development. In fact, this remains one of the most intriguing and least studied aspects of the whole process.

The proliferation of companies competing for audience attention together with the broadening range of radio programming formats of the 1950's reversed the process which had created the Tin Pan Alley formula tune in the previous era of oligopoly. With competition, there was a search for lyrics that would be ever more daring in exposing the old taboo topics of sex, race, drugs, social class, political commentary, and alternatives to middle-class standards generally.

But rock *changed* the audience as well by gradually creating a self-conscious teen generation. Remember that before 1955 there was no music which spoke clearly to the interests and needs of teenagers. Rock changed that. It defined the correct behavior of a "teen queen," outlined the "fast stud" and "bad-good" male ideal, reveled in the joys and agonies of puppy love, noted the irrelevance of school routines as compared with the reality of fast cars, surfing, and the exhilaration of dancing. Throughout rock lyrics there were pointed contrasts between the teen way of life and the behavioral norms imposed by adults (Peterson, 1971). The genre of "death songs" noted by Denisoff (1971b), built on a Romeo and Juliet motif, express most of these ideas: a middle-class girl goes out with a tough but tender lower-class biker; the girl's father says they must break up; on hearing this he speeds off to a violent death. Finally, she gets revenge on her parents by suicide and reunion with Mr. Tough but Tender.

By the early 1960's, popular rock music had done much to galvanize the millions of scattered youth into a self-conscious generation having many of the characteristics of a class *for itself* as defined by Karl Marx. Young people became increasingly critical not only of their own parents but of the larger political and social institutions they seemed to represent. Rock was pivotal in the collective youth activities of the late 1960's, the "love generation" emulation of California hippies, the anti-Vietnam war rallies, involvement with hallucinogenic drugs, and the great rock festivals which embodied all of these elements.

Music had at least once before been important in an American youth movement. In the years following World War I, jazz, symbolizing a break with Victorian mores, had been at the core of the "flaming youth" generation. But that movement was confined to the large cities and the affluent classes. Rock, carried by the mass media and supported by the vastly greater financial resources of today's youth, has reached every sector of society.

IV. OLIGOPOLY WILL RISE AGAIN
(1970 AND BEYOND)

Since 1968, however, three movements have done much to dampen the radicalizing potential of mass media-disseminated popular music. These are the same factors which "tamed" jazz (Peterson, 1967). They are the "re-enoligopolization" of the industry, the emergence of moralistic critics of the rock ethos, and the co-optation of rock's critical thrust (Karshner, 1971). The importance of these three trends may be seen in the softening of the ideological thrust of popular music since 1969 which was previously noted.

Since the mid-1960's there has been a rapid re-concentration of the radio and recording industry. Most of the independent radio stations have been grouped into corporate chains and they increasingly buy music programming services that set out which types of music and even which particular records should be played. At the same time, large recording companies have bought up most of the independents of the early rock era (Gottschalk, 1970). In the first half of 1971, for example, the Kinney Corporation, a combine formed out of Warner Brothers, Reprise, Electra, Flying Dutchman, the Atlantic family of companies, and numerous smaller labels, had the greatest sales in the industry, and the five leading companies had 46.3 percent of the singles and 57.2 percent of the LPs on the charts of the period (*Billboard*, 1971:14).

This re-concentration of the decision structure in the radio and recording industries has facilitated the efforts of moralistic critics such as Spiro Agnew [Ed. note: see pp. 307–310 in this volume], who decry popular music for its corruption of youth (Noebel, 1966; Allen, 1969; Peterson, 1970). In a number of recent rulings the Federal Communications Commission has aided the efforts of moralistic critics. Among other things they have required radio stations to censor drug lyrics and a diffuse set of other sorts of "objectionable" material (M. Hall, 1971a; C. Hall, 1971; Sobel, 1971) and have forbidden "free form" programming in the rock field (M. Hall, 1971b). Critics have resorted to direct action in a number of cases, the most extreme example being the repeated dynamiting of a "revolutionary" underground Texas FM transmitter.

While the puritanical critic has tried to eliminate the ideological thrust of pop-rock music, many major corporation advertisements have co-opted their rhetoric and associated life styles to sell their products (Lydon, 1969). As early as 1968 a full-page ad in the *Wall Street Journal* suggested in inch-high block letters, "Let's put the power suckers up against the wall." Repeated use of such strong symbols to sell automobiles and body shirts renders the symbols impotent and makes those who use them with their original intent seem to be passe sloganeers. As Melly (1971) and Fong-Torres (1971) note, what began as a genuine *revolt* against bourgeois society has become for most mere *style*.

*   *   *

Put in its most condensed form, the relationships between popular music lyrics and the music industry structure can be put into three statements: (1) The amount of diversity of sentiments in popular music lyrics has varied widely over time, at least since the mid-eighteenth century; (2) The diversity of sentiments contained in popular music lyrics correlates directly with the number of independent units producing songs; (3) Change in technology, industry structure, and marketing precede changes in the diversity of sentiments in music lyrics.

REFERENCES

Adorno, T. W.
   1941   "On popular music." Studies in Philosophy and Social Science 9: 17–48.
Allen, Gary
   1969   "That music: There's more to it than meets the ear," American Opinion 12:49–62. [Reprinted as Article 12 in this volume.]
Ames, Russell
   1950   "Protest and irony in negro folksong," Science and Society 14: 193–213.
ASCAP
   1964   ASCAP 50th Anniversary Hit Tunes. New York: American Society of Composers, Authors, and Publishers.

Ashton, John
    1968   Modern Street Ballads. London: Chatto and Windus, 1888. (Re-
              published by Singing Tree Press, Detroit with a new introduction
              and bibliography by Leslie Shepard.)
Belz, Carl
    1969   The Study of Rock. New York: Oxford University Press.
Berger, David
    1966   "The unchanging popular tune lyric, 1910–1955." Unpublished
              manuscript. New York: Columbia University.
Billboard
    1968   1968–69 International Buyers Guide of the Music-Record Industry.
              New York: Billboard.
    1971   "Midyear industry performance report." July 31:14.
BMI
    1960   BMI 1940–1960: Twenty Years of Service to the Industry. New
              York: Broadcast Music Inc.
    1966   BMI Pop Hits: 1940–1966. New York: Broadcast Music Inc.
Brand, Oscar
    1962   The Ballad Mongers. New York: Funk and Wagnalls.
Carey, James T.
    1969a   "Changing courtship patterns in the popular song." American Jour-
              nal of Sociology 74:720–731. [Reprinted as Article 16 in this
              volume.]
    1969b   "The ideology of autonomy in popular lyrics: A content analysis."
              Psychiatry 32:150–164.
Deni, Laura
    1971   "Nevada's KVOV switch to soul, gains listeners." Billboard (Au-
              gust 14): 34.
Denisoff, R. Serge
    1971a   Folk Consciousness, The People's Music, and American Communism.
              Urbana: University of Illinois Press.
    1971b   "Teen angel: Resistance, rebellion, and death in popular music."
              Paper presented at the Popular Studies Association meetings, East
              Lansing, Mich. April.
Denisoff, R. Serge and Mark Levine
    1971   "The Popular Protest Song: The Case of 'The Eve of Destruction'."
              Public Opinion Quarterly 35:117–122. [See Article 17.]
Denzin, Norman K.
    1970   "Problems in analyzing elements of mass culture: Notes on the
              popular songs and other artistic productions." American Journal of
              Sociology 75:1035–1038.
Dichter, Harry and Elliott Shapiro
    1941   Early American Sheet Music: 1768–1889. New York: Bowker.
DiMaggio, Paul
    1971   "Theoretical issues in media study: Be not content." Unpublished
              manuscript, Nashville, Tennessee.

Ewen, David
 1961   The History of Popular Music. New York: Barnes and Noble.
 1962   Popular American Composers from Revolutionary Times to the
           Present. New York: H. W. Wilson.
 1964   The Rise and Fall of Tin Pan Alley. New York: Funk and Wag-
           nalls.
Ferris, William R., Jr.
 1970   "Racial repertories among blues performers." Ethnomusicology 14:
           439–449.
Fong-Torres, Ben
 1971   "Jefferson airplane grunts: 'Gotta evolution'." Rolling Stone (Sep-
           tember 30): 1, 28–30.
Gabree, John
 1968   The World of Rock. Greenwich, Conn.: Gold Medal.
Gelatt, Roland
 1966   The Fabulous Phonograph. New York: Appleton Century.
Gellert, Lawrence
 1936   Negro Songs of Protest. New York: American Music League.
Gillett, Charlie
 1970   The Sound of the City. New York: Outerbridge and Dienstfrey.
Gleason, Ralph J.
 1969   The Jefferson Airplane and the San Francisco Sound. New York:
           Ballantine Books.
Goldberg, Isaac
 1930   Tin Pan Alley: The American Popular Music Racket. New York:
           John Day.
Gottschalk, Earl C., Jr.
 1970   "The sound of money: Rock records spawn fortunes and attract
           growth-minded firms." Wall Street Journal (January 13): 1, 16.
Green, Abel
 1962   "Introduction: The music biz," in Julius Mattfield (ed.), Variety
           Music Cavalcade, 1620–1961; A Chronology of Music Popular in
           the U.S. New York: Prentice-Hall.
Hall, Claude
 1971   "Storz follows FCC rule—demands lyric with disc." Billboard
           (April 3): 1, 41.
Hall, Mildred
 1971a   "FCC 'clarification' notice on drug lyrics draws challenge." Bill-
           board (June 5): 1, 58.
 1971b   "FCC opposes 'free form' radio format." Billboard (August 21):
           1, 50.
Hayakawa, S. I.
 1955   "Popular songs vs. the facts of life." A General Review of Seman-
           tics 12:83–95.
Hirsch, Paul
 1969   "The structure of the popular music industry: An examination of

the filtering process by which records are preselected for public consumption." Ann Arbor: Survey Research Center, Institute for Social Research, The University of Michigan.

1971   "A progress report on an exploratory study of youth culture and the popular music industry." Ann Arbor: Survey Research Center, Institute for Social Research, The University of Michigan.

1972   Processing fads and fashions by cultural industries: An organization set analysis. American Journal of Sociology, in press.

Holsti, Ole R.
1969   Content Analysis for the Social Sciences and Humanities. Reading, Mass.: Addison-Wesley.

Honan, William H.
1967   "The new sound of radio." New York Times Magazine (December 3): 56–76.

Hopkins, Jerry
1970   The Rock Story. New York: New American Library.
1971   Elvis. New York: Simon and Schuster.

Horton, Donald
1957   "The dialogue of courtship in popular songs." American Journal of Sociology 62:569–578.

Howe, Mabel Almy
1917   Music Publishers of America Before 1850. New York: New York Public Library.

Johnson, Guy B.
1929   "Double meanings in the popular negro blues." Journal of Abnormal and Social Psychology 22:9–28.

Jones, LeRoi
1963   "Jazz and the white critic." Down Beat (August 15): 16–19.

Karshner, Roger
1971   The Music Machine. Los Angeles: Nash

Keil, Charles
1966   Urban Blues. Chicago: University of Chicago Press.

Klein, Frederick C.
1968   "The inventors: Inventions by Goldmark of CBS have sweeping social, economic force." Wall Street Journal (May 17): 1, 8.

Korb, Arthur
1949   How To Write Songs that Sell. New York: Greenberg.

Laing, Dave
1970   The Sound of Our Time. Chicago: Quadrangle.

Larkin, Rochelle
1970   Soul Music. New York: Lancer.

Leonard, Neil
1962   Jazz and the White Americans. Chicago: University of Chicago Press.

Lydon, Michael
1969   "Rock for sale." Ramparts (June): 19–24.

McIntire, Ronald
    1969   "Structure of the country music industry." Unpublished manuscript,
             Nashville, Tennessee.
Malone, Bill C.
    1968   Country Music U.S.A. Austin, Texas: University of Texas Press.
Mattfeld, Julius
    1962   Variety Music Cavalcade, 1620–1961: A Chronology of Music
             Popular in the U.S. New York: Prentice-Hall.
Melly, George
    1971   Revolt into Style. New York: Doubleday.
Merz, Charles
    1928   The Great American Bandwagon. New York: Macmillan.
Miller, Lloyd and James K. Skipper, Jr.
    1968   "Sounds of protest: Jazz and the militant avant-garde," in Lefton,
             Skipper, and McCaghy (eds.), Approaches to Deviance: Theories,
             Concepts, and Research Findings. Des Moines: Meredith Press.
             [Reprinted as Article 2 in this volume.]
Mooney, Hughston F.
    1954   "Songs, singers, and society." American Quarterly 6:221–232.
    1968   "Popular music since the 1920's: The significance of shifting taste."
             American Quarterly 20:67–85. [Reprinted as Article 15 in this
             volume.]
Noebel, David A.
    1966   Rhythm, Riots and Revolution. Tulsa, Oklahoma: Christian Crusade
             Publications.
Oliver, Paul
    1960   The Meaning of the Blues. New York: Collier.
Passman, Arnold
    1971   The Deejays. New York: Macmillan.
Peterson, Richard A.
    1967   "Market and moralist censors of a rising art form: Jazz." Arts in
             Society 4:253–264. [Reprinted as Article 19 in this volume.]
    1970   "Rock as fad, revolution, moral solvent, opiate, and bread." Paper
             delivered at the Ohio Valley Sociological Meetings. Akron, Ohio.
    1971   "The changing behavioral norms taught by rock lyrics." Illustrated
             lecture delivered at the University of Minnesota. Minneapolis, Min-
             nesota.
    1972   "A process model of the folk, pop, and fine art phases of jazz." In
             Charles Nanry (ed.), American Music: From Storyville to Wood-
             stock. New Brunswick, New Jersey: Rutgers University Press.
Peterson, Richard A. and David G. Berger
    1971   "Entrepreneurship in organizations: Evidence from the popular
             music industry." Administrative Science Quarterly 16:97–107.
Riesman, David
    1950   "Listening to popular music." American Quarterly 2:359–371.

Robinson, John P. and Paul M. Hirsch
  1969   "It's the sound that does it." Psychology Today 3:42–45.
Rosenstone, Robert A.
  1969   "The times they are a-changin': The music of protest." The Annals
          of the American Academy of Political and Social Science 382:131–
          144.
Russell, Tony
  1970   Blacks, Whites and Blues. New York: Stein and Day.
Scodel, Alvin
  1961   "Changes in song lyrics and some speculations on national char-
          acter." Merrill-Palmer Quarterly 7:39–47.
Shaw, Arnold
  1971   The Rock Revolution. New York: Macmillan.
Shemel, Sidney and M. William Krasilovsky
  1965   This Business of Music. New York: Billboard.
  1967   More About This Business of Music. New York: Billboard.
Silver, Abner and Robert Bruce
  1939   How to Write and Sell a Song Hit. New York: Simon and Schuster.
Sobel, Robert
  1971   "RIAA acts versus FCC, ACLU: Delay edict." Billboard (April
          10): 1, 10.
Spaeth, Sigmund G.
  1934   The Facts of Life in Popular Music. New York: McGraw-Hill.
Taylor, A. J. W.
  1966   "Beatlemania—A study of adolescent enthusiasm." British Journal
          of Social and Clinical Psychology 5:81–88.
Wolfe, Tom
  1965   The Kandy Kolored Tangerine Flake Streamline Baby. New York:
          Simon and Schuster.

EPILOGUE

Reprinted here are excerpts from speeches (1) by Vice President Agnew to a gathering of Republican party campaign contributors in Las Vegas and (2) by Nicholas Johnson, Commissioner of the Federal Communications Commission, which regulates the licensing of radio and television stations. These two papers illustrate the age-old debate over the role of music in disseminating ideas. Agnew argues that rock songs have helped to glamorize the use of illegal consciousness-altering drugs. Johnson answers that, on balance, popular rock music has done as much to caution against the misuse of such drugs. He goes on to note that mass media advertising has done much more to glamorize legal but harmful drugs such as alcohol, tobacco, pep pills, sleeping pills, and tranquilizers.

Johnson's speech was intended as a critique of Agnew's position but their ideas are much alike in one vitally important way. Both advocate greater government control of the media. Agnew would censor drug-related song lyrics; Johnson would allow these, but censor a much broader range of media content. Thus, both advocate the elimination of material they personally find objectionable, and both ignore the problem of how this can be done without greatly increasing the level of government censorship of the media generally. These problems of censorship are as complex as they are vital.

REFERENCES

Clark, David G. and Earl R. Hutchison (eds.).
   1970   Mass Media and the Law. New York: Wiley.
Gross, Gerald (ed.).
   1966   The Responsibility of the Press. New York: Simon and Schuster.
Randall, Richard S.
   1968   Censorship of the Movies. Madison: University of Wisconsin Press.
Schiller, Herbert L.
   1969   Mass Communications and the American Empire. New York: Augustus M. Kelly, Publisher.
Vizzard, Jack.
   1970   See No Evil. New York: Simon and Schuster.

24

TALKING BRAINWASHING BLUES

Spiro Agnew

Our America is made up of many cultures. They reflect our diversity as a people and make us unique as a nation. But there is one rapidly growing culture that contributes nothing to our well-being and, indeed, threatens to sap our national strength unless we move hard and fast to bring it under control.

I am talking about the *drug culture* that pervades our adult population and is spreading like cancer through our youth.

When I speak of the "drug culture," I refer to a much wider circle than those who are actually hooked on drugs. I refer to those who are adopting "escape" as a way of life, who seek a release from human responsibility by pretending there is a world other than the real world.

There are millions of Americans, young and old, who believe that if the music is loud enough, the distractions strong enough, the sedatives or stimulants active enough, they will drown out their frustrations and loneliness. By yielding to pressure to conform from their friends, they are creating a rigid establishment of their own, building an altar to alienation.

Tonight, I would like to identify this culture, show some of the unlikely ways it disseminates its propaganda, and finally, point out some of the action you can take to reverse the trend and help its victims cope with the world we all live in.

There are two reasons why the growth of the drug culture concerns us especially today:

Press release: Las Vegas, September 14, 1970.

Number One: Although the drug problem is by no means only a youth problem, our youth is involved to a degree never known before. The abuse of drugs extends to children, eight, ten and twelve years old.

Number Two: America's present drug culture poses the danger of mind-eroding chemicals previously unknown to man, and relatively easy to produce.

We have arrived at this culture partly because society's natural resistance has been broken down by the "pill popping" of adults who fancy they need a pill to get to sleep and a pill to wake up. This, coupled with growing adult alcoholism, was all that some of our younger citizens have needed to do some experimenting on their own.

It should not be surprising, then, that in recent years so many young people have been drawn into the drug culture. It is, after all, the "in" thing to do among their friends. And it has been urged on them by some of their pop heroes.

Consider, as one example, the influence of the drug culture in the field of music.

A generation that shocked its parents by doing the Charleston has no right to mock the development of progressive jazz, and the people who were hep to swing are wrong to look down their noses at those who are now hip to folk-rock. Much of today's popular music is complex and exciting, and some lyrics use the images of poetry far more skillfully than the old moon-and-June routines of Tin Pan Alley.

But in too many of the lyrics, the message of the drug culture is purveyed. We should listen more carefully to popular music, because at its best it is worthy of more serious appreciation, and at its worst it is blatant drug-culture propaganda.

I do not suggest that there is a conspiracy among some song writers, entertainers, and movie producers to subvert the unsuspecting listener. In my opinion, there isn't any. But the cumulative impact of some of their work advances the wrong cause. I may be accused of advocating "song censorship" for pointing this out, but have you really heard the words of some of these songs?

One of the hits of the 1960's, registering more than one million dollars in sales, was a record entitled, "With a Little Help From My Friends." The key lines are:

> I get *by* with a little help from my friends,
> I get *high* with a little help from my friends...

It's a catchy tune, but until it was pointed out to me, I never realized that the "friends" were assorted drugs with such nicknames as "Mary Jane,"

"Speed" and "Benny." But the double meaning of the message was clear to members of the drug culture—and many of those who are tempted to join.

Or this one, called "White Rabbit":

> One pill makes you larger and one pill makes
> you small
> and the ones that mother gives you don't do
> anything at all.
> Go ask Alice when she's ten feet tall . . .

There are scores of such songs: the titles themselves often whisper or shout the message. Listen to these: "The Acid Queen," "Eight Miles High," "Couldn't Get High," "Don't Step on the Grass, Sam," and "Stoned Woman." These songs present the use of drugs in such an attractive light that for the impressionable, "turning on" becomes the natural and even the approved thing to do.

And all the while that this brainwashing has been going on, most of us have regarded it as good, clean, noisy fun.

I am sure that very few, if any, station managers in America would deliberately allow the use of their radio facilities to encourage the use of drugs. Few parents would knowingly tolerate the blaring of a drug-approving message from phonographs in their homes. And few musicians intend their "in-jokes" and double meanings to reach past the periphery of pot users. But the fact is that the stations do, the parents do, and the musicians do.

Music is only one medium used by the drug culture. Strong approval, or at least an indulgent attitude, also comes across in certain movies, books, and the underground press of more than two million circulation.

A popular recent movie—I will not name it here because I don't want to promote it—has as its heroes two men who are able to live a carefree life off the proceeds of illegal sales of drugs. When they come to a violent end, the villain, it turns out, is an allegedly repressive society. No sympathy is wasted on the wrecked lives of the people who bought their drugs and financed our heroes' easy ride.

I feel as a reviewer did in the *New York Times,* who writes about the trend toward movies that exalt violence, flirt with pornography, promote pot and glorify the seamy side of life: ". . . the filmmakers' sensibilities are so jaded, their senses so atrophied, that I doubt they would even feel the swift kick they so richly deserve."

We can expect more of this for one good reason: there's money in it. Look at the exploitation of music festivals, run by men who use young people

as props in pot-smoking, acid-dropping events. These parasites of the drug culture care nothing about human rights; they're interested only in movie rights.

Fortunately, some of the networks, motion picture companies, magazines
and newspapers are beginning to counter drug abuse with excellent documen-
taries, dramatic productions and articles. These can help to educate the nation
to the dangers involved. But far too many producers and editors are still
succumbing to the temptation of the sensational, and playing right into the
hands of the drug culture.

Recently, I had a letter from a Philadelphia physician who described, and
I quote: "the apparent irresponsibility of the press in glamorizing, or at least
rewarding with sensational publicity, diverse psychopathic behavior."

His letter continued:

> The point which needs stressing is that both addicts and persons
> with addiction-prone personality, are immensely gratified by any pub-
> licity, and especially by dramatic and sensational publicity. They are,
> and they feel that they are, shallow and inadequate and unimportant,
> but now that suddenly everybody is looking at them, discussing them,
> considering their imagined grievances, they are important . . . One can
> see how publicity given to drug "festivals" will attract vulnerable per-
> sonalities, perhaps not yet addicted.

It is time that we wake up—that we listen to and understand what's going
on in the drug culture. It's time that we counter this propaganda with the truth.

What, you may rightly ask, is our Nixon administration doing to counter
the drug culture? As the "happy warrior" Al Smith used to say: let's look at
the record.

*   *   *

25

TURNING ON THE VICE PRESIDENT

Nicholas Johnson

This is an appropriate time for you and I to be giving a listen to America's newest musical idiom, "rock." Earlier this week Vice President Agnew revealed that even he has been listening to rock music. I don't think this should be cause for panic—even though he does. I think it holds out some promise. The Administration may just find out what's happening in the country.

Now it's true that the Vice President has kind of missed the point in his Las Vegas speech of September 14. But then perhaps he hasn't listened to much of the music yet, or taken enough time to think about it. I'm sure he'll come around.

Mr. Agnew now seems to think that music is the cause of (rather than the relief from) the pressures that lead people to use hard drugs. Perhaps we can understand and excuse this rather fundamental error as he came down from his first trip, but I think we can fairly hold him to a higher standard in the future.

The Vice President has asked us to "Consider . . . the influence of the drug culture in the field of music. . . . [I]n too many of the lyrics the message of the drug culture is purveyed." That's where he makes his mistake. No song writer I know of is urging as a utopia a society in which the junkie's life is a rational option. Most would agree with his suggestion that dependence on hard drugs is "a depressing life style of conformity that has neither life nor style."

. . . [Listen to the music:]

Prepared for delivery to a retraining program symposium for Foreign Service Officers of the United States Information Agency; Panel Discussion on "Rock Music: Underground Radio and Television," Thursday, September 17, 1970, United States Information Agency, Washington, D.C.

> Your mind might think it's flying on those little pills
> But you ought to know it's dying ... because ... speed kills!

That's Canned Heat in "Amphetamine Annie." Here's Steppenwolf, singing about the "Pusher":

> If I were the President of this land
> I'd declare war on the Pusher Man ... god damn the pusher.

Or listen to the Rolling Stones' "Mother's Little Helper," because they're really trying to help you understand what your generation's problem is, as well as giving the kids some good advice (that is, pills are not the answer). There is comparable advice in Love's "Signed, D.C.," in "Crystal Blues" by Country Joe & the Fish, and in The Who's *Tommy*.

No, the real issue, Mr. Vice President, is not the desirability of hard drugs. The issue is whether you, and the rest of the Administration, are—to borrow Eldridge Cleaver's (and VISTA's) phrase—part of the solution, or part of the problem. The question is whether you have done anything to alter the repressive, absurd and unjust forces in our society that drive people to drugs. ...

You see, Mr. Vice President, somebody's trying to tell you something— "And you don't know what it is ... do you, Mr. Jones?" These music people aren't really urging death through drugs; they are urging life through democracy. They believe that governments are instituted among men to promote "life, liberty and the pursuit of happiness." And many don't think yours is doing it.

As the Chairman of the Bank of America, Louis Lundborg, said recently:

> What (young people) ... say they want doesn't sound so different, you know, from what our Founding Fathers said they wanted—the men who wrote our Declaration of Independence, our Mayflower Compact, the Bill of Rights, the other early documents that laid the foundation for the American Dream. They said they wanted the freedom to be their own man, the freedom for self-realization. We have lost sight of that a bit in this century—but the young people are prodding us and saying, "Look, Dad—this is what it's all about."

But this is not all. It's not just that corporate, governmental, and other institutions have turned away from our original goals, and that they have created conditions that stimulate the desire to escape; they are actually encouraging the drug life and profiting from it.

Senator Frank Moss has observed that,

> The drug culture finds its fullest flowering in the portrait of American society which can be pieced together out of the hundreds of thousands of advertisements and commercials. It is advertising which mounts so graphically the message that pills turn rain to sunshine, gloom to joy, depression to euphoria, solve problems and dispel doubt.

And the former Chairman of this Administration's Federal Trade Commission, Caspar W. Weinberger, has noted that, "Advertisements for over-the-counter medicines may be a contributing factor in drug abuse problems in the United States." (TV ran almost $20 million worth of ads for sleeping aids alone in 1969.)

Our entire consumer-manipulating economy is based on a dishonest, destructive exploitation of human emotions and motivations. Television teaches—with continuous, air-hammer effectiveness—the dangerous and debilitative lie that the solution to all life's problems and nagging anxieties can be found in a product, preferably one that is applied to the skin or taken into the body. It has so distorted and demeaned the role of women as to make it almost impossible for either men or women to relate to each other in other than a sex-object, manipulative way. It has educated our children to go for the quick solution, to grow impatient and disinterested in developing the skills and solutions requiring discipline and training. And it has urged us all to seek "better living through chemistry."

The Vice President is going after the song writers. One cannot help but wonder how he overlooked Ford's urging [to] "blow your mind," TWA's taking us "up, up and away," the honey company that suggests we "get high on honey," the motor-bike company that advertises "a trip on this one is legal," or the Washington, D.C. television station that promotes its programming as great "turn-ons." Perhaps the critical point is that young song writers and performers don't make political campaign contributions, but that Ford, TWA, and other drug-image merchandisers do.

The Vice President might better turn his attention to the corporate campaign contributors (of both parties) who finance their fat campaign donations with the profits they make from worthless or harmful drugs, and from cigarettes and alcohol that first "addict" and then kill hundreds of thousands of Americans a year.

The Vice President has urged each of us to do our own part, to "set an example" within our families. How about the "political families" of the major political parties? To what extent is the Vice President's own party prepared to refuse to accept contributions from (or do special favors for) those politically influential corporate interests that feed, and feed upon, the artifically-induced thirst for drugs, pep pills, tranquilizers, alcohol, cigarettes, and other contemporary commercial "panaceas"?

The Vice President has pointed with pride to what the Administration has done to crack down on "drugs." But what has it done to deal with our number-one drug problem, alcoholism? It is, perhaps, symbolic of the basic hypocrisy in government today that he chose Las Vegas as the battlefield to attack drugs. For the only thing that flows faster than the gamblers' money in Las Vegas is alcohol. There are estimated to be at least five million alcoholics in this country. There are more alcoholics in San Francisco alone than there are narcotics addicts in the entire country. If you're interested in "law and order," one-third to one-half of all arrests by police in the United States are for chronic drunkenness. More Americans are killed by drunk drivers every year than are killed by murderers and the war in Southeast Asia combined. And, of course, the economic loss through absenteeism, the physical damage to the body (cirrhosis is the sixth leading cause of death; psychosis due to alcoholic brain damage is irreversible), and the impact upon family and friends, are far more severe from alcoholism than from all other hard drugs combined.

Or how about nicotine addiction? There are 300,000 deaths a year related to cigarette smoking. What is the Vice President doing to cut down on these pushers? One recent survey found that of *seventh graders* only 30 percent of the boys and 40 percent of the girls had never tried tobacco. There are a lot more kids who are being exposed to drugs because of the deliberate efforts of greedy, immoral television and tobacco company executives to hook 'em on nicotine—executives who are revered as the pillars of our society, and whose activities are sanctioned by the federal government—than there are those who get pot "with a little help from their friends."

So who's kidding whom? If we're really serious about doing something to alter the drug culture in America, let's get on with the work and stop worrying about the music. Let's not indulge [in] the hypocrisy of going after the drug users who are poor, black, and young with a vengeance, as if they were criminals, without even providing them adequate treatment centers, and ignore the far more serious problem of the hard drug pushers (of alcohol and cigarettes) who are respectable, rich and middle-aged. Let's stop accepting the campaign contributions of the "respectable" liquor manufacturers with one hand while we're imprisoning some of our finest young people with the other.

Above all, let us stop going for help to advertising executives who sit around, after their three-martini lunches, coming up with ad campaigns that preach the get-away-from-it-all qualities of caffeine, nicotine, aspirin and other pain killers, alcohol, stomach settlers, pep pills, tranquilizers and sleeping pills (plus the whole range of mouthwashes, deodorants, cosmetics, etc.). How, in the midst of the chemical life they've glamorized, can they absolve their consciences by telling our kids that a 16th or 17th chemical will bring the downfall of their lives and the republic? They can run it up your flagpole, Mr. Vice President, but nobody's going to salute it.

The forces of censorship are subtle. This administration repeats and repeats that it is not censoring—just as the Russians did when they rolled their tanks into Czechoslovakia in August, 1968. But when the Vice President starts criticizing television, pretty soon the "analysis" of the presidential speeches is watered down or disappears, and President Nixon builds up a record of (free) prime-time television usage that exceeds every prior president. The President shows up on a Bob Hope special; the Vice President opens the Red Skelton show. Now they are moving in on radio. FCC Chairman Burch says he's interested in "obscenity" in lyrics; the Vice President is concerned about mention of drugs. That's the way you do it. You don't come right out and say, "Cut the controversial stuff, guys. We don't like the people getting that social criticism set to music." Of course not. You talk about obscenity and drugs. But the radio station owners get the message: the administration's listening to them, just like it's watching their big, wealthy brothers, the TV stations.

If we really want to do something about drugs, let's do something about life. Because if we make an effort to strike at the real causes of addiction to alcohol and other less prevalent and dangerous drugs, we will find that we have also made a big dent in mental illness, divorce, suicide rates, and the other statistical indicia of social disintegration. Let's get on with the job of giving people the physical, mental and spiritual environment they need in order to grow closer to their full potential. That means more money (not vetoes of appropriations) for rebuilding our cities, education, food programs, urban transportation, welfare, job training, and health care. It means more meaningful job opportunity for all Americans—white and black; a meaningful attack on the problems of underemployment and meaningless employment, as well as unemployment. It means appropriations for the Corporation for Public Broadcasting, parks, libraries, and beautification programs.

The song writers are trying to help us understand our plight and deal with it. It's about the only leadership we're getting. They're not really urging you [to] adopt a heroin distribution program, Mr. Vice President. In fact they don't think that you can "spray it with cologne and the whole world smells sweet" either. It stinks. They want us to help them clean it up.

The song you quoted, "With a Little Help from My Friends" is not a joyful pitch for drugs. It contains the lines:

> Do you need anybody
> I need somebody to love.
> Could it be anybody
> I want somebody to love.

How many Americans seek in drugs the solace from a vicious, cruel world they did not create, but cannot escape? What are you doing to change that world?

Some song writers are hopeful. Mama Cass sings:

> Yes a new world's coming . . .
> Coming in peace, coming in joy, coming in love.

She's holding out optimism. She's giving you a little more time, Mr. Vice President. But we can't wait much longer if history is not to record your presiding over the decline and fall of the American empire—complete with words, music, and a drug culture sold to the American people by large contributors to presidential campaigns.

INDEX

PRINTED IN U.S.A.